Can Economic Growth Be Sustained?

Can Economic Growth Be Sustained?

The Collected Papers of Vernon W. Ruttan and Yujiro Hayami

EDITED BY KEIJIRO OTSUKA

and

C. FORD RUNGE

OXFORD
UNIVERSITY PRESS

OXFORD
UNIVERSITY PRESS

Oxford University Press, Inc., publishes works that further
Oxford University's objective of excellence
in research, scholarship, and education.

Oxford New York
Auckland Cape Town Dar es Salaam Hong Kong Karachi
Kuala Lumpur Madrid Melbourne Mexico City Nairobi
New Delhi Shanghai Taipei Toronto

With offices in
Argentina Austria Brazil Chile Czech Republic France Greece
Guatemala Hungary Italy Japan Poland Portugal Singapore
South Korea Switzerland Thailand Turkey Ukraine Vietnam

Published by Oxford University Press, Inc.
198 Madison Avenue, New York, New York 10016

www.oup.com

Library of Congress Cataloging-in-Publication Data
Ruttan, Vernon W.
Can economic growth be sustained? : the collected papers of Vernon W. Ruttan and Yujiro Hayami / edited by Keijiro Otsuka and C. Ford Runge.
p. cm.
Includes bibliographical references and index.
ISBN 978-0-19-975435-9 (cloth: alk. paper) 1. Economic development. 2. Sustainable development. 3. Agriculture—Economic aspects. I. Hayami, Yujiro, 1932- II. Otsuka, Keijiro. III. Runge, C. Ford (Carlisle Ford) IV. Title.
HD87.R88 2011
338.1—dc22 2010022627

2 3 4 5 6 7 8 9
Printed in the United States of America
on acid-free paper

To Marilyn Ruttan and Takako Hayami

CONTENTS

PREFACE

Yujiro Hayami and Vernon Ruttan worked well together; they did so because they had a profound respect for each other. That respect was the bridge to listening and thinking together in ways that allowed them to build an important theoretical perspective referred to as the "most widely accepted model used today both for understanding agricultural growth processes and as the basis for agricultural development policy" (Shuh and Brandão 1992: 611). Responsive to the then current challenges in the search for increases in food production, their induced innovation approach focused on the interactions of technological change and institutional, cultural, and resource environments. In terms of scholarly abilities and experiences, Ruttan and Hayami complemented each other, and this allowed them to see more. Together, they had greater success in working across contexts to integrate Western models of technological change and more holistic Asian perspectives on multifactorial interaction. For a more complete understanding of their work, their personal, educational, and academic backgrounds are relevant, which, while quite different in some ways, also had similarities that contributed not only to their ability to work well together but also to their role as influential mentors of future leaders in the field.

Ruttan, born in 1924, grew up on a 140-acre dairy farm in northern Michigan on poor-quality, sandy, glaciated soil that by the late 1960s was placed in the U.S. soil bank program and removed from production. The farm next door belonged to his great-uncle, and two farms beyond that, the best farm in the immediate area, was his grandfather's farm, diversified into dairy, grain, and small orchards. During the Depression, when Ruttan was a boy, his father's farm operated primarily at a subsistence capacity. Personal learning that Ruttan brought from this experience to his later work with Hayami included his parents' differing reactions to new technologies. His mother, a former schoolteacher who was now swamped with the unending duties of a farm wife, was thrilled when they were able to purchase one of the new labor-saving wringer-type washing machines; it made a huge difference in her life. By contrast, his father resisted the adoption of tractors as long as possible, preferring his team of prized workhorses. It was only during

World War II, when his sons were in the military and unable to help him with milking, haying, and other labor-intensive tasks, that he finally bought a tractor; yet, at the same time, he was not averse to the use of new milking machines. An additional useful observation was the value Ruttan's parents placed on the government-funded rural extension agents who came out and talked with his father about the latest in seed, tillage, and milking technology and with his mother about food preservation and preparation techniques.

In terms of education both Hayami and Ruttan benefited from quirks of fate. Ruttan attended a multigrade one-room schoolhouse, daily walking, and sometimes skiing, the couple of miles each way. In his last year of high school his mother, determined that her bright son have a chance at better opportunities, sent him to stay in the nearest market town, where he ended up being the valedictorian of his class of thirty students. Entering Michigan State University the following fall, he managed to support himself by continuing to get up early and milk cows at the university's dairy barn. The following year, now in the army but nearly blind in one eye, he was sent to New Haven, Connecticut, to work as a physical therapist in the army hospital there. At the same time, due to his intellectual aptitude, the army enrolled him in nearby Yale University to study medicine, something that would have been inconceivable for him otherwise but that also involved a steep cultural and academic learning curve. As soon as the war was over, and with postwar GI Bill educational benefits in hand, he switched from medicine to economics, the course in which he had so far gotten his highest grade. Ruttan frequently mentioned that he was very lucky that T. W. Schultz, the great University of Chicago agricultural economist, later a Nobel prize winner, and also from a farm background, had decided to try to mentor farm boys in graduate agricultural economics even if their grades weren't quite up to snuff, similar to Schultz's own background. Ruttan was accepted in this program at a vibrant stage in its evolution; work at Chicago with Schultz and Gale Johnson was to have a profound effect on his later work.

Born in 1932, Hayami grew up in Tokyo during the difficult war years, which saw food shortages. As an urban youth, after completing a degree in liberal arts at the University of Tokyo, he took the civil servants exam expecting to become a government bureaucrat. Although he didn't think so at first, Hayami considered himself lucky in his assignment to work with Professor Seiichi Tobata, the founder of modern agricultural economics in Japan, at the Research Institute of the Ministry of Agriculture, Forestry, and Fishery. Needless to say, Tobata had a big impact on him, as Shultz did on Ruttan. In a recent book chapter on food security (2000) Hayami continued to quote his mentor. Tobata, like Schultz, had come from a rural background, in this case the agricultural village of early twentieth-century Japan, and although he felt ill prepared, he succeeded. Mentoring bright young men to develop a modern approach to Japan's technical and rice production issues was seen by Tobata as key to overall postwar growth (1968). When it came time to do his doctoral work at Iowa State University, Hayami also experienced initial difficulties in adjustment to the academic and sociocultural environment. Persevering, he succeeded in becoming the first Japanese scholar to get his doctorate in agricultural economics in the United States. Hayami was influenced by Schultz as well, particularly in the area of giving sufficient credence to the role of nonconventional inputs in development, including the education of farmers and investment in agricultural research capital (Akino & Haymi 1974); these factors contribute to the accumulation of social/human capital, a matter of interest to both later on.

It probably helped their work together that both Ruttan and Hayami had experience in both U.S. and Asian contexts, where the differences in land scale produced obvious differences in labor, yields, and equipment. The size and mechanization of the farms in Iowa and later Minnesota must have impressed Hayami, just as the small but much denser farmscapes in Asia impressed Ruttan. During his tenure at IRRI in the Philippines, frequent drives in the countryside fascinated Ruttan; every family trip resulted in more pictures of farmers and water buffalo than it did of his children! And, given his own father's preference for horse teams, he understood the farmers' attachment to the water buffalo, accepted that for some the cultural traditions behind questions of whether to adopt new technologies, like mechanized power-tillers and threshers, were more complex than traditional economic principles would imply.

At the same time, like most IRRI staff members at that time, Ruttan remembered being highly motivated by then-director Robert Chandler's call for immediate solutions to hunger in Asia. With assistance from Lloyd Johnson, Ruttan began to think about how technological adaptation resulting in increased production could work overall in Asia then experiencing increasing threats of famine. Highly influenced by his ongoing fieldwork in the Philippines, begun in 1974, Hayami also believed the technological developments occurring in developing countries could be adopted and adapted. He and Ruttan agreed that local environmental, social, and political factors could not be ignored—they had to be accounted for. In their efforts at inducing innovation, they emphasized factors that had sometimes been forgotten in large-scale economic planning: farmers' choice, respect for local conditions, and the need to be aware not just of regional resource endowments but also of local institutions and cultural endowments. Institutional change occurs not just at the state level, or as strategic planning at the state level, but also needs to be understood in ways that respect local choice making and regional institutional strategies. Ruttan frequently mentioned being proud that their model was one of the first to bring culture into the equation. For Hayami this was a given. Indeed, one of the unique contributions made by Ruttan and Hayami is their emphasis on culture or cultural endowments as one of the factors that influences adoption of technological innovation. Culture as an aspect of technological change has usually been ignored; given their cross-cultural partnership and their own backgrounds, they were able to recognize culture as a key aspect of their pattern model. Considering some of the failures in development efforts where this factor was ignored or misunderstood, their model highlighted the need to be more cognizant of culturally based opportunities and constraints in planning development strategies; this remains a key contribution.

This book came about as a result of reflection by Ruttan on his own work, about whether a volume of collected works was warranted, but as he soon suggested in an email to Hayami: "When I started reviewing my publications it was obvious that four or five of our joint articles should be included in such a collection. It then occurred to me that the most appropriate thing would be a collection of papers edited by the two of us." Hayami responded modestly but with a touch of humor: "Thank you for inviting me to co-edit a collection of papers. I feel much honored, and am glad to accept your kind offer—unless I will become a free rider." In response, Ruttan wrote back that he was "delighted that you are potentially interested in joining me in editing a collection of our papers," adding that after reviewing them again he found himself "very impressed with the quality of some of the papers we collaborated on." Confirming his interest in a following email, Hayami concluded, "It will be great if I can conclude my academic life by this collaboration with you once again after so many years."

This email correspondence took place over a three-day period in June 2008. Shortly after his last email to Ruttan, Yujiro Hayami had a massive stroke. Hearing the unfortunate news, Ruttan wrote to Hayami's assistant to say he would continue to work on the book, hoping that Hayami would recover before too long. While Hayami later recovered his ability to walk and has attended gatherings in his honor held at GRIPs (National Graduate Institute for Policy Studies), where he was professor and chairman of the Foundation for Advanced Studies on International Development's graduate studies program, his ability to communicate clearly is still affected.

In mid-August, after returning from his much-loved summer home in northern Minnesota, Ruttan ended up being hospitalized; he died a few days later. He discussed the possibility of completing the book with family members in the days before he passed away. Following Ruttan's death, both Brian Buhr, chair of the Department of Applied Economics at Minnesota, where Ruttan, as a University of Minnesota Regent's Professor Emeritus, maintained an active involvement, and Keijiro Otsuka, Hayami's former student and colleague, for whom Hayami had served in the special role of sensei for so long, expressed interest in helping complete the book. In light of Hayami's stroke, Otsuka had already had some contact with Ruttan regarding the book. We all felt that completing this book would be important, not only out of respect for the academic and personal contributions of both authors, but also due to the shared belief in the continuing importance of their work together. A partnership between the two institutions was proposed: Otsuka and Ford Runge at Minnesota would serve as co-editors, while Lia Ruttan would carry out an intermediary and facilitating role.

Looking back, it is quite clear that both Hayami and Ruttan were lucky in educational experiences, in mentors, and in their early career opportunities; they both believed in once again passing on that luck. Both men were active in mentoring students, a role that in many cases lasted through whole careers; and they particularly supported students who had great potential but felt ill at ease in a new context. Their students became leaders worldwide and include many well-known contributors to their fields in academic, research, and government capacities.

Both men served on research and advisory boards, were presidents of their national professional societies, and contributed to government policy and direction. They both received numerous honorary degrees and awards. Along with awards for his work in agricultural economics, Ruttan received the Von Humboldt Award in 1984, and Hayami was designated by the government of Japan as a Person of Cultural Merit (2004) and installed in the Order of Sacred Treasure (2007). Ruttan received the American Agricultural Economics publication award for ten papers between and 1956 and 1997. Hayami also received recognition in book and article awards. Ruttan found his involvement with the U.S. National Academy of Science, where he served on several committees, very stimulating. Hayami served as an advisory committee member for the UN World Hunger Program and CGIAR, among others. Both men were lifelong learners and maintained their professional activity far beyond what one would normally expect. In 2007 Ruttan published a new book on the role of war and the military in advancing technological change, a conclusion he might not have liked personally but couldn't avoid professionally, and Hayami continued an active publishing schedule, including the third edition of a textbook on development economics in 2005 (Hayami and Godo 2005) and an important article on human and social capital in 2009 (Hayami 2009).

There are many continuing implications of their work. New researchers would benefit from taking a look at the basic model and the broader implications of using it on many levels of analysis, while looking at problems on both a regional and international scale. As with any framework, over time additions and revisions have been made; they made some themselves. Other important changes resulted from work with Hans Binswanger for Ruttan and Keijiro Otsuka for Hayami, among others. Their work's significance rests in its analysis of the factors that influence and constrain institutional change and that support the spread of technological change within given environments, and their efforts remain useful in policy and institutional design. The model of induced innovation and induced technological change has been used and tested in regions all over the world. A number of important contributions have been made, more recently, by Karagiannis and Furtan (1990), Machado (1995), Acemoglu (1998, 2003), Balcombe et al. (2002), Umetsu et al. (2003), Acemoglu and Linn (2004), and Liu and Shumway (2008); they all acknowledge the contribution made by Hayami and Ruttan.

What was most important to these two scholars, however, was not simply scholarship and theory, but usefulness in real-life applied projects that help ordinary farmers and communities to make strategic choices, and for the development of workable institutions that support this effort. The work of Ruttan and Hayami continues to draw out key questions and strategies for research design, agricultural and economic policy, and local implementation. Their work certainly contains much more than one note, something that makes their role as contributors unusually dynamic. Nevertheless, they would not expect or desire a "fixed in stone" approach to their work; they would hope that their work and their working relationships as colleagues and as mentors continue to inspire others. This edition is meant to locate their contribution and its implications, and to encourage new work in light of new challenges.

—Lia Ruttan
Edmonton, Alberta
October 2009

Vernon W. Ruttan

Yujiro Hayami

PART

I

INTRODUCTION

CHAPTER 1

The Contributions of Ruttan and Hayami

Keijiro Otsuka

1. Introduction

Nothing could be more valuable than creating a new paradigm in economics, particularly in the field of agricultural development. A notable example is T. W. Schultz's (1964) thesis regarding "efficient but poor" small-scale farmers in low-income or developing countries who remain unable to increase their yields without increases in technological and human capacity. In the 1960s Schultz's thesis completely changed the dogmatic perception of researchers, aid agencies, and policy makers regarding traditional farmers' strategies and behaviors. Ruttan and Hayami point out that Schultz's research "led to the abandonment of policies that viewed peasant households as unresponsive to economic incentives" (chapter 16); historically this view also led to an increase in research investment.

No less influential was Vernon Ruttan and Yujiro Hayami's thesis concerning the role of induced technical and institutional innovation: they argued that as the scarcity of a factor of production (e.g., labor) increases, technology that saves on the use of the factor is induced to develop, along with supportive institutions, including property rights systems, public sector research, extension systems, and marketing institutions. In chapter 2 of this volume, they note that "it became clear that the induced technical change theme could provide the structure needed to integrate a large body of theoretical and empirical research on agricultural development." In fact, their research provided a consistent and effective framework for analyzing how markets, technology development, and institutional changes interact to facilitate agricultural development. It is now widely recognized that farmers can increase agricultural production significantly when technology and institutions work effectively, as exemplified by the Asian Green Revolution, which saved land when this factor became scarce relative to other inputs. Another major contribution was to establish a greater awareness of the role that research, extension, and education hold as key nonconventional inputs that could propel agricultural development.

Ruttan and Hayami created a profound vision of the crucial role of agriculture in the process of overall economic development and of the strategies necessary to enhance agricultural growth. This vision is missing in the recent literature in development economics—for example, the World Bank's *World Development Report 2008: Agriculture for Development*, which does not provide clear-cut strategies for the development of agriculture in low-income economies. Neglect of the role of agriculture in economic development in some of the more influential literature in development economics in the past is also evident in the World Bank's (1993) *East Asian Miracle*. What would have happened to East Asia had there been no Green Revolution? It is not easy to provide an accurate answer, but it is clear that the development of East Asian economies would likely have been deterred by shortages of food or high food prices and much more widespread poverty.

How did Ruttan and Hayami develop and elaborate the idea of induced technical and institutional innovation? What are the theory's contributions and limitations? What were the critical factors affecting the success of the Asian Green Revolution? What are the main implications of studies by Ruttan and Hayami for the development of agriculture? Why has sub-Saharan Africa (SSA) failed to realize a Green Revolution more than forty years after the advent of modern high-yielding rice varieties in 1966, which triggered the revolutionary and unprecedented productivity increase in Asian farming systems? Because these two authors are now unable to respond, the task of addressing these issues is now ours. It is therefore timely to review the visions and perspectives contributed by Ruttan and Hayami.

This volume is a collection of their papers, often jointly authored, but sometimes authored alone. Most of them have already been published, but here we bring them together in one collection. The aim is not only to make these works accessible but also to show how the work of Ruttan and Hayami developed jointly and then was applied in a variety of ways.

The introduction, Part I, provides a convenient road map for understanding their contribution. Chapter 2, written by the authors themselves, offers an excellent overview of their studies. Part II identifies the sources of productivity growth in agriculture. Part III shows the results of several case studies of technical change and agricultural development in Asia. Part IV concerns induced technical and institutional change. Finally, Part V discusses the broad perspectives of the two authors.

The striking feature of Ruttan and Hayami's work is their ability to take micro-level economic behavior based on village-level studies and integrate it with macro-level behavior at the country and cross-country levels. Parts II and IV basically concern the aggregate analyses, while Part III is oriented toward micro-level case studies. These chapters provide invaluable insight into how Ruttan and Hayami developed their perspective, a term that appears in the subtitles of many of their works including *Agricultural Development: An International Perspective* (1971, 1985). Part V is aptly titled "Perspectives." It is unfortunate that Ruttan and Hayami could not prepare the concluding chapter, contrary to their original plan; careful reading of the last four chapters, however, reveals why this volume is entitled "Can Economic Growth Be Sustained?"

In what follows, a summary of the four major parts of the book is provided to facilitate understanding of the work of Ruttan and Hayami and their contributions to the literature on agricultural development, as well as implications for current issues.

2. Productivity Growth in Agriculture

The two chapters included in this section address the importance of technical change in agriculture at the country level in the United States and other countries. Chapter 4 was published in *American Economic Review* in 1970 and represents the backbone of the entire research contribution of Ruttan and Hayami. Although it pertains to agriculture, the estimation of an aggregate production function using cross-country data was a pioneering study in economics. They find that it was not conventional inputs but human capital and scientific knowledge that led to agricultural growth through technological progress. This thesis is now well established and widely accepted as a core ingredient of development. These findings are confirmed in many other studies, including their own article using more recent evidence (Kawagoe, Hayami, and Ruttan 1985).

The fundamental question in agricultural development is how technological change in agriculture has taken place. This issue is not one of understanding markets alone, because major determinants of agricultural production, including the contribution of research activities and extension services, are largely public goods. Ruttan and Hayami explored the process of technical change in terms of the incentives that induce technological and institutional changes. And they pointed to the importance of social science knowledge "required for the technical and institutional infrastructure needed for the invention, development, and extensions of a more efficient agricultural technology." They thus identified the role that economists must play in bringing about technological and institutional change in agriculture—an important but often forgotten point. Rather than lamenting past failures to initiate a Green Revolution in SSA, economists should prepare for a new takeoff by designing an optimum strategy to realize it.

3. Technical Change and Agricultural Development

Five interesting case studies make up Part III. Chapter 5, on Korean rice, Taiwan rice, and Japanese agricultural stagnation between the two World Wars, is concerned with rice technology transfer from Japan to Korea and Taiwan and its implications for Japanese agriculture. It concludes that technology transfer depended on the investment of the Japanese government in irrigation and water management and in research and extension in order to develop and diffuse rice varieties adapted to the ecology of Korea and Taiwan. Chapter 6 analyzes why rice farming productivity was so much higher in Taiwan than in the Philippines and

Thailand before the Asian Green Revolution of the late 1960s. The lesson of these country studies is that investments in research and development and in irrigation and water management, as well as improved institutions (e.g., the development of credit systems to enable farmers to purchase chemical fertilizer), are key factors that explain the performance of the three countries. Differences in agro-ecological factors do not explain much of the productivity differentials.

These conclusions were supported by the experience of the Green Revolution, which began precisely when this article was published. The rice sector in Taiwan developed successfully due to technology transfers from Japan; in the Philippines, Thailand, and other tropical Asian countries, rice developed later due to transferring useful rice genes from Taiwan. These genes were necessary to shorten the height of rice plants and make its straw stiff and avoid lodging and to accommodate larger volumes of grains (conventionally called "dwarfing"), critical for the development of fertilizer-responsive rice varieties.

The Green Revolution in Asia was criticized for its impacts on income distribution. The popular argument was that the new varieties conferred few benefits to small farmers because they required heavy applications of chemical fertilizers, which these small farmers could hardly afford to purchase. Large farmers and landlords were assumed to purchase land from small farmers and use large machines to operate the consolidated farms, thereby replacing the labor supplied by the landless and near landless; such a conjecture, however, was not widely supported by empirical evidence. Ruttan emphasized the importance of evidence-based discussion, noting that further empirical investigations were needed.

The next two chapters, on the role of peasants and the effects of ecology and history on agricultural development in Asia, are single-authored articles that demonstrate Hayami's ability to grasp variegated patterns of agricultural and rural development in Asian countries. Why does peasant farming dominate in the cash-crop sectors in Thailand, while plantations are important in the Philippines? Why did Thai agriculture grow much faster than Philippine agriculture? How much is this difference attributable to ecological differences between the two countries? Do middlemen exploit peasants in cash-crop production, and if so, are there regional differences? Can peasants be rural entrepreneurs, who develop marketing systems and initiate other nonfarm activities in rural Asia? Hayami shows ingenuity in interpreting these issues in a consistent and convincing fashion. He also shows how important it is to understand micro-level behavior as a foundation for macro-level issues in Asian agriculture.

4. Induced Technical and Institutional Change

Economists who consider Figure 10.6, which shows historical changes in fertilizer/land prices relative to the fertilizer/land ratio (on the vertical axis) in the United States and Japan, will note that the U.S. and Japanese cases are similar, even though factor endowments and technologies differ enormously in the two countries. Ruttan and Hayami conjecture that the same economic forces are at work in both U.S. and Japanese agriculture. These results were reconfirmed by Kawagoe, Otsuka, and Hayami (1986), who applied more rigorous statistical methods. They conclude that dynamic factor substitution, involving biased technological changes, is a key to understanding the success of agricultural growth in the United States and Japan.

Hayami and Ruttan then probe more deeply into the process of technical change and analyze why institutional changes undergird technological change. Chapter 11 deals with the role of the social sciences in increasing the supply of institutional changes, while chapter 12 broadens the scope of induced innovation theory by specifying how resources, technology, culture, and institutions shape, govern, and interact in this process. They emphasize that "changes in the demand for institutional innovation are induced by changes in relative resource endowment and technological change."

5. Perspectives

Chapter 13 begins with Ruttan's remark "The challenge of the twenty-first century will be to make the transition to sustainable growth in both presently developed and low-income countries." Sustainable agricultural growth may be constrained by limited resources (e.g., land and water) and also jeopardized by soil losses, all affected by climate change. Ruttan, however, does not think that agroclimatic conditions pose as fundamental a constraint to sustainable agricultural growth as the technical and institutional innovations needed to confront these changes. For these innovations to be realized, the proper incentives, including price signals, must be in place. In addition, agricultural research is essential to adaptation to climate change leading to higher temperatures and water scarcity. Based on useful empirical evidence, his arguments are indeed forceful.

In chapter 14 Ruttan asks, "What should development economists learn from the new growth economics?" His answer: "Not much." He questions why the new growth theory does not address fundamental development issues, including technical and institutional changes. This is related to chapter 2, where Ruttan and Hayami conclude that the major remaining issues are (1) construction of a theory of the behaviors of individual farmers, research scientists, and planners responding to changes in their external environments and resource and cultural endowments, (2) analysis of the societies where progressive technical and institutional change has yet not occurred, and (3) construction of a theoretical model that integrates "factor-induced" and "demand-induced" technical change. These are practical issues rendering economics a truly useful social science; it ought to be able to solve these problems.

Technical and institutional changes in agricultural systems are important not only for low-income but also for middle- and high-income economies. As per capita incomes increase rapidly, comparative advantages in agriculture tend to be lost, and an income gap between the farm and nonfarm sectors widens. In response to this development, the governments of Japan, Korea, and Taiwan introduced protectionist policies to support farmers' income. At present, other high-performing countries in Asia, including China, have followed similar paths. Such policy distortions could have serious negative consequences not only in the short run but also in the long run (e.g., the failure to develop labor-saving technologies by means of mechanization due to the persistence of small-scale farms). In chapter 15 Hayami analyzes needed investments in appropriate agricultural technology to prevent or mitigate the loss of comparative advantage in agriculture and investments in human capital to facilitate the transfer of labor from farm to nonfarm sectors. The prospect for such changes remains dim, since distorted market prices do not provide correct signals.

The central message of chapter 16 is that "the demand for social science knowledge is derived from the demand for institutional change." While advances in knowledge in the social sciences can reduce the cost of institutional change, this dynamic has received only limited attention by economists and other social scientists. According to Ruttan, this can provide a better understanding of the historical process involved and of institutional reform. Empirical assessment of the process of economic development is required in order for social scientists to contribute to economically sustainable growth.

6. Final Remarks

It seems that the major threats to sustainable economic growth are climate change and the incidence of deepening poverty in countries with extremely low incomes, particularly those in sub-Saharan Africa. What are this volume's implications for sustainable development? In other words, how can we both mitigate climate change and reduce widespread poverty?

Climate change requires major technological breakthroughs, including innovation in fossil fuel–saving technology, renewable energy, and heat-, drought-, and flood-tolerant agricultural technologies to adapt to a worsening climate. How can we realize such changes? It is clear that we need institutions to support them, as emphasized by Ruttan and Hayami. They argue that inducing such changes requires prices that reflect the changing scarcity value of resources. Hence, pricing carbon emissions through carbon trading is an important step in bringing about the necessary technological and institutional changes. If the price of carbon reflected its negative environmental value, the market for carbon emissions could contribute enormously to the development of appropriate new technologies and institutions. Specifically, new institutions would be required to monitor carbon emissions and to facilitate its trading.

How can we facilitate the development and dissemination of yield-enhancing technologies suitable for unfavorable climate conditions in SSA, where agricultural productivity has been stagnant or even declining? In order to think about a strategy to develop agriculture in SSA, we need to know whether market prices reflect the scarcity value of resources, whether effective agricultural research institutions and extension systems are in place, and whether economists have provided proper guidance in development policy. Although agricultural markets in SSA seem to work to a considerable extent, prices of inputs, such as chemical fertilizer, are often exorbitantly high, and product prices are generally low, due mainly to poor infrastructure. Indeed, fertilizer price/product price ratios in SSA are two to three times as high as those in Asia. Promoting a more efficient market system by reducing marketing costs is clearly a prerequisite for technological and institutional changes.

To date economists have played only a small role in designing strategies to develop agriculture in SSA. The Asian Green Revolution resulted from the transfer of rice technology, through research and extension, from countries in the temperate zone to Southeast and South Asian countries in the tropical zone. Why, then, are we unable to transfer rice, wheat, and maize technologies from Asia to SSA, both of which are located in the tropics? Did we invest enough in research and extension and in water management to facilitate the agricultural technology transfer from Asia to SSA? Our answer is largely no. Economists have been silent on this for long time. Ongoing projects to transfer Asian rice technology to SSA under the leadership of the Japan International Cooperation Agency and the Alliance for Green Revolution in Africa in collaboration with the International Rice Research Institute, the West African Rice Development Association, and other international organizations is an innovative attempt to achieve sustainable growth in agriculture in SSA.

In short, although technical and institutional changes are guided by market signals, further guidance is needed from economists and other social scientists to achieve major revolutionary change. Governments, international organizations, research institutions, extension workers, input suppliers, traders, and farmers must play their respective roles in synchrony. Social scientists, in general, and development economists, in particular, can develop institutional frameworks effectively to organize the economic agents and policy-making bodies to achieve major technological and institutional progress. The depth, breadth, and quality of thought of these two great economists was acclaimed in their lifetimes, and to many in development economics, it still resounds loudly in both theory and practice.

CHAPTER 2

Induced Innovation Theory and Agricultural Development

A PERSONAL ACCOUNT

Vernon W. Ruttan and Yujiro Hayami

Beginnings

We first met in Tokyo in the summer of 1966. Ruttan had been attracted by a survey article by Hayami on the role of technical change in agriculture, which he had been asked to review. Ruttan arranged to stop in Tokyo, while en route to the Philippines, to talk to Hayami about his work. Our common work on productivity growth and our emerging sensitivity to the role of factor endowments in shaping the direction of technical change resulted in a highly stimulating exchange. This exchange was continued in the summer of 1968, at a conference in Japan on the role of technical change in the history of Japanese agriculture (see Ohkawa et al. 1969, vol. 3).

The actual collaboration that led to our work on induced technical and institutional change began when Yujiro Hayami spent the 1967–68 and 1968–69 academic years as visiting professor in the Department of Agricultural and Applied Economics at the University of Minnesota.

We each brought to the joint project a substantial body of research on technical change and productivity growth in agriculture. Ruttan had published a paper in the mid-1950s challenging the pessimistic views that were prevalent at that time concerning the future of agricultural production capacity in the United States (Ruttan 1956). This was followed by a series of papers during the late 1950s and 1960s that attempted to refine and interpret measures of agricultural productivity growth in U.S. agriculture at both the regional and national levels (Ruttan 1958, 1960; Stout and Ruttan 1960). In addition, Ruttan brought to the collaboration several years of research in Southeast Asia, where he was an economist with the Rockefeller Foundation at the International Rice Research Institute (IRRI).

There he had conducted research on issues related to the design and introduction of the new seed-fertilizer technology being developed by IRRI (Ruttan and Moomow 1964; Ruttan 1966; Ruttan et al. 1966).

Hayami brought to the enterprise a substantial body of research on technical change in Japanese agriculture. His initial papers were on the development of the Japanese fertilizer industry and its role in enhancing agricultural productivity growth in Japan (Hayami 1964, 1967). The paper drew from his contribution to the monumental *Estimates of Long-Term Economic Statistics of Japan*, organized and edited by Kazashi Ohkawa et al. (1965–67). Before arriving at the University of Minnesota, he had embarked upon an exceedingly ambitious effort, in the spirit of earlier work by Colin Clark, to assemble a complete set of agricultural sector input, output, and productivity data on a global basis and to estimate cross-country "metaproduction functions," which would then serve as a basis for efforts to "account" for the sources of differences in land and labor productivity among countries (Hayami 1969a; Hayami and Inagaki 1969).

Our growing sensitivity to the significance of differences and changes in relative resource endowments and relative factor prices drew on several sources. Ruttan had been very impressed by a lecture by H. J. Habakuk (1962) at Purdue in 1963 on the history of British and American technology. We were both familiar with the articles by E. O. Heady (1954) and A. K. Sen (1959) that had employed the concept of "landesque" (land-saving) and "laboresque" (labor-saving) capital.[1]

We were, however, influenced even more directly by our own experience and research. Hayami had been impressed by the response of Japanese rice breeders to the long-term decline in the price of fertilizer relative to land in Japan: they countered by breeding "fertilizer-consuming" rice varieties. While working at IRRI, Ruttan was impressed with the tendency of the international group of scientists at IRRI to carry with them, etched in their subconscious, the relative factor endowments of their home countries.[2]

We were also familiar with John R. Hicks's (1932) pronouncement, in *The Theory of Wages*, that changes or differences in relative prices of factors of production could be expected to influence the relative labor-saving direction of technical change, and with the criticism of Hicks's assertion by W. E. G. Salter (1960).[3] Salter argued, in effect, that entrepreneurs were interested in profitability "from whatever source" and that, while changes in relative factor prices might affect the choice of technology, they could not be expected to result in a bias in the direction of inventive activity. We noted in our 1970 *Journal of Political Economy* article (Hayami and Ruttan 1970a) that Salter's results were based upon an excessively broad definition of technical change. We did not, however, become aware of the important debate in the theoretical literature beginning in the mid-1960s, centering around the issue of induced technical change, until our own formulation and initial testing of the theory was well under way.

In the mid-1960s, seminal articles by Charles Kennedy (1964) and Syed Ahmad (1966) had staked out alternative versions of the theory of induced technical change.[4] The initial drafts of the articles were written while Kennedy was teaching at the University of the West Indies (Kingston) and Ahmad was teaching at the University of Khartoum (Sudan). Ahmad submitted his article to the *Economic Journal* in 1963; the editor sent it to Kennedy for review. Kennedy's article, which was published in 1964, was originally written as a comment on the Ahmad article. The Ahmad article was initially rejected, but a revised version was resubmitted and published in 1966. The Kennedy version was cast within the context of contemporary growth theory. It was presented as a contribution to the solution of the puzzle about the seeming stability of the factor shares of labor and capital in spite of rapid substitution of capital for labor. The Ahmad version was built directly on the Hicks microeconomic foundation. When we became aware of the Kennedy and Ahmad articles, and the series of exchanges that had gone on in the literature, we very rapidly assimilated the Ahmad microeconomic version into our own work. In our judgment, the Kennedy growth theory approach could not serve as a productive foundation for empirical research.[5]

Our initial collaboration was a paper dealing with the effect of Japanese colonial policy in Korea and Taiwan on rice production in Japan (Ruttan and Hayami 1970). We then collaborated on two additional articles. One used a production function framework to account for agricultural productivity differences among countries (Hayami and Ruttan 1970b), and it was where we first introduced the term *metaproduction function* to refer to the frontier production function. In a second article, we elaborated and tested a preliminary version of the induced technical change hypothesis against historical experience in both Japan and the United States. (Hayami and Ruttan 1970a).

As we proceeded with our writing, it became clear that the induced technical change theme could provide the structure needed to integrate a large body of theoretical and empirical research on agricultural development. We then began outlining a joint research program that led to the elaboration and further testing, in our book *Agricultural Development*, of the induced technical change hypothesis (Hayami and Ruttan 1971).

One of our objectives was to develop a single model of agricultural development that would be able to incorporate historical agricultural development experience in both the presently developed and the less developed countries. This involved integrating a number of models that had been proposed to interpret the process of agricultural development during specific epochs in particular countries or regions. These earlier models were identified as the conservation, urban-industrial impact, diffusion, and high pay-off input models. We also wanted to be able to incorporate the location-specific characteristics of agricultural technology in the model. Our personal experience, and our reading of the technical literature, had convinced us that, by and large, agricultural technology must be invented in the agroclimatic and socioeconomic environment in which it is to be used. These observations, combined with the induced innovation framework, turned out to be exceedingly powerful in interpreting the alternative paths of technological change we observed, among both the presently developed and the developing countries and among developing countries characterized by different resource endowments.

Agricultural Development

Agricultural Development was published in 1971 and was generally well received. We were, however, surprised that some reviewers interpreted our findings as implying that technical change in agriculture could be left primarily to the private sector, guided by the invisible hand of the market. The inference was apparently drawn from our demonstration that the path of technical change in both Japan and the United States had been induced by relative resource endowments interpreted through changes or differences in relative factor prices (Figures 2.1 and 2.2). A careful reading of our book should have made it clear, however, that our purpose in attempting to understand the role of resource endowments and market

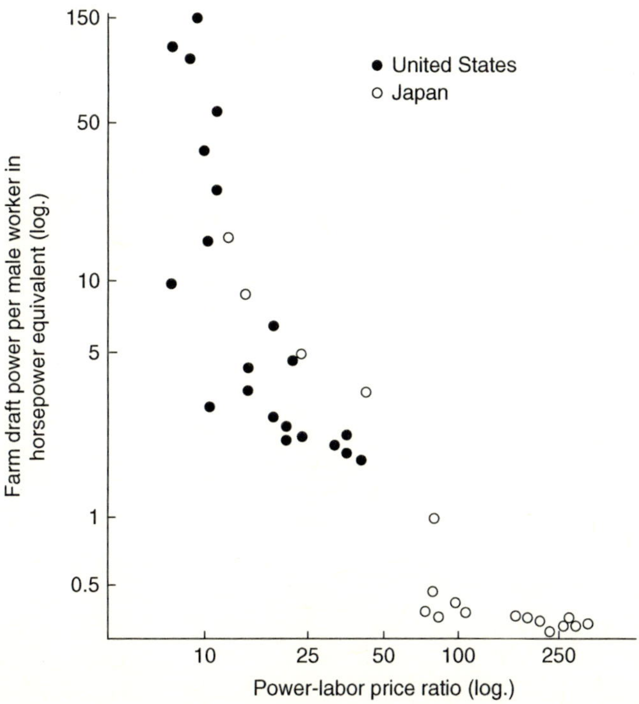

Figure 2.1 Relation between Farm Draft Power per Male Worker and Power-Labor. price ratio (= hectares of work days which can be purchased by one horsepower of tractor or draft animal), the United States and Japan, quinquennial observations for 1880–1980. Source: Hayami and Ruttan (1985: 179).

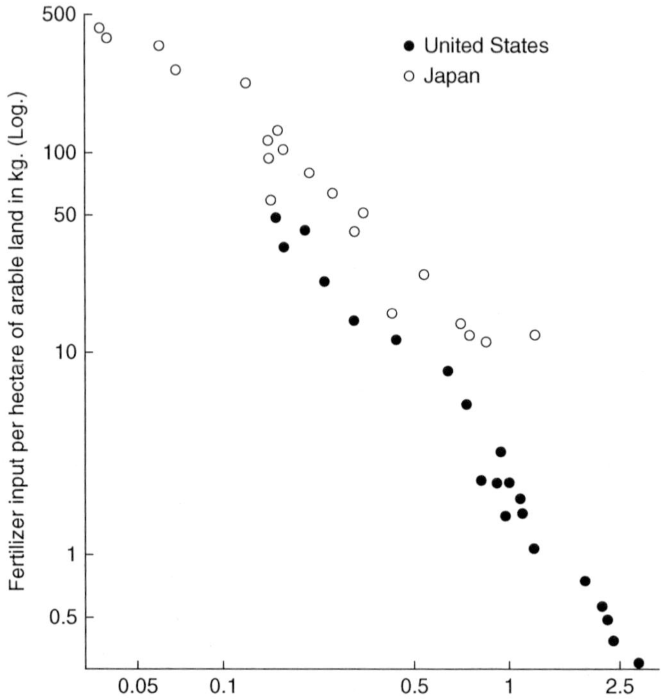

Figure 2.2 Relation between Fertilizer Input per Hectare of Arable Land and Fertilizer-Arable Land Price Ratio (= hectares of arable land which can be purchased by one ton of N + P_2O_5 + K_2O contained in commercial fertilizers), the United States and Japan: quinquennial observations for 1880–1980. Source: Hayami and Ruttan (1985: 180).

forces in directing technical change was to be able to design the policies and institutions that would lead to more efficient paths of technical change.

We were also somewhat surprised at the strong negative reaction to our research by a number of scholars writing in a neo-Marxian political economy tradition.[6] We had expected that our analysis, particularly of the relationship between resource endowments and the direction of technical change, and of the relationships between technical and institutional change, would receive a more sympathetic hearing from the political economy school.

It became clear to us fairly soon, however, that we should not remain too certain about the adequacy of the induced technical change model to interpret the process of technical change in agriculture. Much of agricultural research, particularly that leading to advances in biological technology, was produced by public sector institutions—research institutes, experiment stations, and universities. The induced technical change model represented a modest extension of the neoclassical theory of the firm, which we were using to explain the innovative behavior of public sector bureaucratic organizations. But there was no available theory of bureaucratic productivity. Indeed, the prevailing orthodoxy denied even the possibility of innovative behavior in the public sector.[7] In our book, we suggested the elements of a theory of induced institutional change; at that point, however, it represented primarily a suggestion for future research.[8]

Extensions and Refinements

In the early 1970s, Ruttan began a collaboration with Hans P. Binswanger that led to the development of more rigorous tests of the induced technical change hypothesis and to a more intensive effort to interpret institutional change within the induced innovation framework. In 1970, while a student at North Carolina State University, Binswanger attended a seminar in which Ruttan presented the Hayami-Ruttan tests of the induced technical change hypothesis. Binswanger later wrote a term paper in which he argued that while the Hayami-Ruttan results appeared plausible, their tests were not able to distinguish between price-induced factor substitution and induced technical change. While searching for a thesis topic, Binswanger discovered an article by Ryuzo Sato, written in 1970, that presented a rigorous two-factor (labor and capital) test. Binswanger hypothesized that if induced technical change could be distinguished from factor substitution for the two-factor case, it should also be possible, in principle, to design a multifactor test. He proceeded to develop a generalized multifactor test; later, using a translog function, he operationalized the procedure as a four-factor test (land, labor, fertilizer, and power). The test was first applied against U.S. and Japanese experience and reported in his 1973 Ph.D. thesis (Binswanger 1973).

In retrospect, the method employed by Hayami and Ruttan was more of a plausibility test than a fully integrated, rigorous test of the hypothesis. It relied on the consistency between microeconomic observations of experimental results and sectoral-level statistical associations. The method developed by Binswanger partitioned the historical changes in factor shares into two components. One component reflected the change due to pure substitution effects—the result of choice of technology in response to changing relative prices along a given production function. The second component represented the change in the factor share resulting from shifts in the production function itself. This enabled Binswanger to determine whether the second component of the factor share shift was consistent or inconsistent with an induced technical change explanation.

Following the completion of his thesis at North Carolina State University, Binswanger spent the 1972–73 academic year at the University of Minnesota. While at Minnesota Binswanger (1974a, 1974b, 1984) published a series of important papers drawing on his thesis research. Binswanger and Ruttan also began discussing the possibility of a book that would include tests of the induced technical change hypothesis against Western European and Latin American experiences. The book would be a thorough review and evaluation of the burgeoning theoretical literature on induced technical change, as well as an application of the more rigorous tests of the model developed by Binswanger and an attempt to extend the elements of a model of induced institutional innovation.

As their discussions were getting under way, Ruttan left the University of Minnesota to become president of a small private foundation, the Agricultural Development Council (ADC). The council's program focused on strengthening rural social science research and graduate education capacities in Asia. Binswanger accepted an appointment as ADC associate in India and was located at the International Crops Research Institute for the Semi-Arid Tropics (ICRISAT) at Hyderabad (India). At ICRISAT he initiated, in collaboration with several colleagues, a series of large village-level studies. These changes in institutional affiliations and responsibilities slowed work on the proposed book, which was finally completed and published in 1978.[9]

During the early and mid-1970s, Yujiro Hayami and several collaborators were also engaged in a series of studies designed to advance the theory of induced institutional innovation and test it against Southeast Asian experience. Hayami spent 1974–76 as economist at the International Rice Research Institute in the Philippines. While at IRRI he initiated, with Masao Kikuchi, a series of studies of village-level changes in land tenure and labor relations (Kikuchi and Hayami 1980; Hayami and Kikuchi 1982). The studies provided both a more fully elaborated hypothesis of induced institutional innovation and carefully constructed microeconomic tests of the hypothesis.[10] The Hayami and Kikuchi analysis also drew on the work of the public choice theorists for inspiration, including that of Harold Demsetz (1967) on property rights, Mancur Olson (1965) on collective action, Gary Becker (1974) on social interactions, and Ronald Coase (1937), Oliver Williamson (1975), Steven Cheung (1969), and others on the role of risk and transaction costs in shaping economic organization.

Both Hayami and Ruttan were also deeply influenced by the broad historical work of Douglass North and R. P. Thomas (1970, 1973). Our work went beyond the earlier literature, however, in explicitly distinguishing between the sources of demand and supply of institutional change. The sources of demand for institutional change included changes in resource endowments and in technology. Ruttan (1978, 1981, 1984), in the book with Binswanger, had identified advances in social science knowledge as an important source of the supply of institutional change and had elaborated this perspective in a series of articles.

As our work with other collaborators was maturing, we began in the late 1970s to discuss writing a second edition of *Agricultural Development*, which would incorporate the new research on induced technical and institutional change and the experience of agricultural development between the mid-1960s and the early 1980s.

By this time, Hayami had returned from IRRI to Tokyo Metropolitan University and Ruttan had returned to the University of Minnesota. In the early 1980s, we prepared a revised outline and started to exchange chapters of the revision.

The Rockefeller Foundation awarded us a joint fellowship that enabled us to spend a month at the foundation's Bellagio Center in Italy to argue out our differences and coordinate our revisions. In preparing the new edition, we were able to draw upon longer time-series data for Japan and the United States (1880–1980), a broader set of country studies, and the advances in methodology that had occurred since the mid-1960s.

The new edition contained a separate chapter on induced technical and institutional innovation.[11] The model of induced institutional change maps the general equilibrium relationships among resource endowments, cultural endowments, technology, and institutions (Figure 2.3). However, the empirical testing of the model remained incomplete, primarily because the recursive relationship among the several elements of the model did not lend themselves to econometric testing as readily as did the earlier induced technical change hypothesis. Consequently, historical and case studies became our primary methodological approach. The revised edition of our book was published in 1985 (Hayami and Ruttan 1985).

While preparing the second edition, Hayami was also engaged in collaboration with Kym Anderson in an effort to utilize the induced institutional change perspective to interpret the emergence of protectionist import-substitution policy in Japan and the other rapidly developing economies of East Asia (Anderson and Hayami 1986). Ruttan (1982a) was applying the induced technical and institutional change perspective in an analysis of agricultural research organization and to the reform of agricultural research policy.

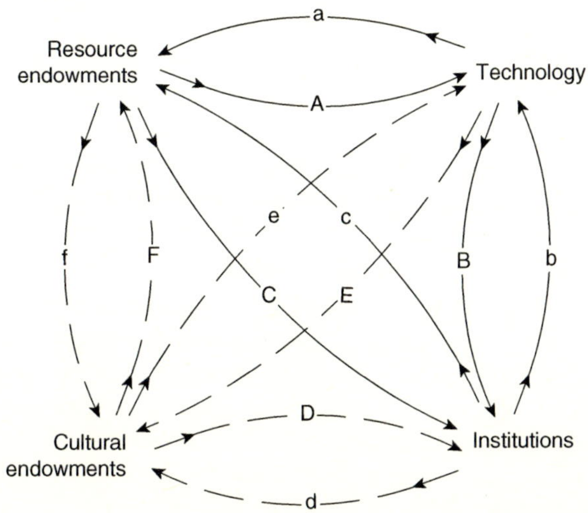

Figure 2.3 Interrelationships between Changes in Resource Endowments, Cultural Endowments, Technology, and Institutions. Source: Hayami and Ruttan (1985: 111).

By the late 1980s, the induced technical change model had been successfully tested against the experience of a large number of developed market economies,[12] and Ruttan, in cooperation with several students, had initiated a program to test the model in the centrally planned economies (Wong 1988; Fan 1991; Fan and Ruttan 1992).

Conclusion

In retrospect, several things stand out about our collaboration, which now extends back almost twenty-five years. One is how difficult it now is to identify which of us has been responsible for particular contributions. As we were working on the second edition, we found that we were frequently attributing the same contributions in the first edition to the other person.

By the time the second edition of the book was in print, our work was also coming under increased scrutiny. Examples of the more critical perspectives are included in this volume. We will return, at the end of this book, to an evaluation of the comments and criticisms. We will also outline some of our own concerns and suggest some priorities for the induced innovation research agenda. Among the issues that we will deal with are the following:

- The lack of a theory of action. The inducements that lead individual farmers, mechanics, research scientists, and planners to respond to changes in their external environments and to changes in resource and cultural endowments to bring about changes in technology and institutions remain largely a black box.
- We have been fairly successful in explaining the rate and direction of institutional change when it occurs. But we have very little to say about those societies where progressive technical and institutional change is not occurring or, in some cases, is regressing.
- We, and our colleagues, have not yet developed and tested a well-integrated model of (a) the theory of "factor-induced" technical change, which explains the direction of technical change, and (b) the theory of "demand-induced" technical change, which explains the rate of technical change. Nor have we yet effectively integrated the theory of induced innovation with the theory of trade. This is a serious incompleteness, since relative resource endowments play such a dominant role in both the trade theory and the theory of technical change.

Notes

Vernon W. Ruttan and Yujiro Hayami, in Bruce M. Koppel (ed.), *Induced Innovation Theory and International Agricultural Development: A Reassessment* (Baltimore: Johns Hopkins University

Press, 1995). The article had been commissioned by John Dillon for a survey volume on agricultural economics literature. The Dillon project was never brought to completion; however, the manuscript was later revised and published in collaboration with Willis Peterson. See Peterson and Hayami 1977.

1. Hayami had studied with Heady at Iowa State University. Ruttan had written a critique of the Heady article, which was not accepted for publication by the *Journal of Farm Economics*. See also A. K. Sen 1960.
2. It may be useful to cite a somewhat amusing example. At an IRRI semiannual internal research review in 1964, the Japanese plant physiologist Akira Tanaka and the American agronomist James Moomow reported sharply different results from the same experiment carried out in the same environment. Tanaka reported a classic S-shaped yield response to fertilizer. Moomow reported a rather flat inverted U-shaped response. After considerable discussion, the agricultural engineer Lloyd Johnson and Ruttan suggested that Tanaka and Moomow were controlling for the independent variables that interested them, in this case fertilizer, and doing "whatever else it took to make a good experiment." Tanaka came from a traditionally low-wage labor-surplus economy. He employed a very labor-intensive system of weed control. Moomaw, accustomed to working in a high-wage labor-scarce economy, waited until the weed infestation had become competitive with the rice and then applied herbicide and killed some rice plants as well as the weeds. There were also differences in views regarding the relative emphasis that should be given to green manure as a source of soil fertility that reflected the relative land resource endowments of their home countries.
3. Ruttan (1961) had reviewed the Salter book.
4. The key articles in the "growth theory" and "microeconomic" approaches were Kennedy 1964 and Ahmad 1966. The best review and evaluation of this controversy, which extended from the mid-1960s to the mid-1970s, is by Binswanger (1978). In our judgment, the Ahmad contribution received less attention than it deserved in part because of this unlikely location, the University of Khartoum, at the time his article was published.
5. The Kennedy version incorporated a fixed innovation possibility trade-off. It is of some interest that neither Ahmad (1966) nor Kennedy (1964) had thought of their work as even potentially productive of empirical research. They were both primarily concerned with the factor share stability puzzle—a puzzle that disappeared shortly after the Kennedy and Ahmad articles were published.
6. See Oasa and Jennings 1982. For a more sympathetic perspective, also written from a "political economy" perspective, see Palladino 1987.
7. Orthodox economic doctrine had held that institutional innovation was not the appropriate concern of economics. According to Samuelson (1948), "The auxiliary constraints imposed upon the variables are not themselves the proper subject of welfare economies, but must be taken as given."
8. For an initial attempt to apply the induced institutional change framework outside agriculture, see Ruttan 1971.
9. Binswanger, Ruttan, and others, *Induced Innovation* (1978). For the test of the model against Western European historical experience, see Ruttan et al. 1978; for the Latin American tests, see de Janvry 1978 and Sanders and Ruttan 1978.
10. The plausibility of the hypothesis was reinforced by study of long-run institutional change in Thai agriculture by Feeny (1976).
11. This chapter first appeared in Ruttan and Hayami 1984.
12. See the large number of studies summarized in Thirtle and Ruttan 1987.

PART

II

PRODUCTIVITY GROWTH IN AGRICULTURE

CHAPTER 3

The Contribution of Technological Progress to Farm Output, 1950–1975

Vernon W. Ruttan

Recent discussion of future farm output requirements have stressed heavily the important role which technological progress is expected to play in meeting the projected output requirements.[1] This is as true of the studies which have emphasized the "transitory nature of present food surpluses"[2] as of the studies which point to continuation of the present "pressure of food supplies on population."[3]

In spite of this emphasis on the importance of technological change, these studies have generally failed to make explicit the relationship between technological progress and changes in factor input requirements other than labor inputs. This failure seems to stem from use of an analytical scheme which fails to distinguish between technological change and change in labor productivity, thus confusing the contributions to farm output made by technological change and increased nonlabor inputs.[4]

In this paper, I shall attempt (a) to outline an analytical scheme which distinguishes between the contributions of technological change and increased nonlabor inputs, (b) to present a set of alternative technological change and factor input models for American agriculture which will illustrate the possible consequences of alternative rates of technological change on certain aggregate input categories during the next quarter century, and (c) to discuss some questions of agricultural policy stemming from the close relationship between technological change and input requirements.

Measurement of Technological Progress

Economic progress is generally conceived in terms of a rising level of consumption or real income per person (Clark 1940: 2). Defined in this manner, economic progress can occur as a result of advance in the techniques of production (in technological progress) which enables us to produce a greater output with the expenditure of a given quantity of resources, or it can occur as a result of the substitution of other factors of production for labor in such a manner that real income per person rises even though the ratio of output to total input remains unchanged.

If we accept this concept of technological progress, then use of *change in labor productivity*—output per unit of labor input—as a measure of the contribution of technological progress to output becomes at best rather imprecise and at times even misleading.[5] In any industry, such as agriculture, where the rise in labor productivity has been achieved as a result of substitution of capital and current inputs for labor as well as from changes in output per unit of total input, the change in labor productivity overstates the contribution of technological change to output.[6] Conversely, in an industry such as meatpacking, where technological progress during the last twenty years has apparently been primarily capital saving rather than labor saving, the change in labor productivity tends to understate the contribution of technological change to output (Ruttan 1954: 8–10).

As an alternative to the use of labor productivity as a measure of technological change, a number of authors have suggested an approach based on the change in total input per unit of output (e.g., Copeland and Martin 1938: 127; Stigler 1947: 43–45; Barton and Cooper 1948; Schmookler 1952; Leontief 1953). The argument is that if one selects a base year (t_0) in which a firm or industry is operating at or near equilibrium and corrects for price changes in the items entering into the input and output accounts of a second year (t_1) in which equilibrium conditions also hold, the percentage difference between the Laspeyres input index and the Laspeyres output index in the second year (t_1) measures the contribution which technological change has made to output between t_0 and t_1.

This is equivalent, in the special case of a linear production function, to stating that if one constructs a production function for the base period (t_0) and then substitutes the inputs of some given period (t_1) into the function, one can measure the contribution which technological change has made to the change in output between the two periods by the difference between the index of output actually produced in the given period and the index of output estimated from the base period production function (Leontief 1944; D. G. Johnson 1950: 559). Although the suggested procedure permits an exact measure of the contribution of technological change only under rather restrictive conditions,[7] the procedure does permit one to establish effective upper and lower limits within which the "true" measure of technological change must lie. This is accomplished by reversing the procedure and estimating the output that could have been secured in the base period (t_0) if base period inputs had been employed with the given period (t_1) production function. The "true" measure of technological change will then lie between the two estimates arrived at by the above procedures.

In the event that the production function for the firm or the industry under consideration is nonlinear, the use of an appropriate nonlinear function will of course permit the establishment of even more precise limits between which the "true" measure of technological change must fall.

Use of a nonlinear production function does imply, however, that a greater increase in inputs will be required to achieve a given increase in output for any given level of technological change than if the function is linear, except in the case where the use of all inputs changes at the same rate (or where increasing returns to scale of a sufficiently large magnitude offset the effect of a diminishing marginal rate of substitution between input factors). Alternatively, a given increase in input, coupled with a given level of technological change, will result in a smaller increase in output if the production function is nonlinear than if it is linear (again, except in the case where use of all inputs changes at the same rate or where increasing returns to scale of sufficiently large magnitude prevail).

The above results stem from the fact that with a nonlinear function the level of marginal productivity of any resource depends on the relative amounts of the various inputs used. Unless all inputs change in the same proportion through time, the marginal productivities will not bear the same relationship to each other at the beginning of the period and at the end of the period. In other words, given differential rates of change in use of the several inputs and a nonlinear production function, part of the total increase in inputs is required to compensate for the effects of changes in relative inputs on marginal productivities.[8]

In preparing the projections of alternative farm output and factor input indexes for 1960 and 1975, a nonlinear function of the Cobb-Douglas type was employed. The decision to employ a nonlinear function was based on the desirability of employing a production function which would permit the assumption of neutral technological change coupled with changing input ratios and changing marginal productivity of the several input factors.[9]

Alternative Output and Factor Input Models

In Table 3.1, eight alternative input models for 1975 are presented. The procedure employed in constructing each model was (a) to adjust recent output requirement estimates upward to take into consideration the latest population and disposable income projections; (b) to project labor and land input requirements on the basis of past trends in output per unit of labor and land input; and (c) to estimate as residuals the capital and current expenditure inputs necessary to produce the projected output requirements under alternative rates of technological change. The assumptions upon which each of the projections is based are discussed below.

THE OUTPUT PROJECTIONS

The farm output requirements presented in Table 3.1 are projected on the basis of a rise in per capita disposable income from $1,347 in 1950 to $1,630 in 1960 (21 percent)[10] and to $2,075 in 1975 (54 percent);[11] and increase in population from 152 million in 1950 to 177 million (16 percent) in 1960 and 221 million in

Table 3.1 **Projections of Alternative Farm Output and Factor Input Indexes for 1960 and 1975 (1950 = 100)**

		Zero technical progress [a]		*Slow technical progress* [b]		*Rapid technical progress* [c]		*Very rapid technical progress* [d]	
		Low land inputs (I)	*High land inputs (II)*	*Low land inputs (III)*	*High land inputs (IV)*	*Low land inputs (V)*	*High land inputs (VI)*	*Low land inputs (VII)*	*High land inputs (VIII)*
1960 Projections									
Inputs:									
Labor		88	88	88	88	78	78	78	78
Land		96	104	96	104	96	104	96	104
Capital [e]	(A)	178	172	140	136	149	143	124	121
	(B)	183	177	145	140	153	147	127	124
Current [e]	(A)	214	207	169	163	178	172	148	145
	(B)	204	198	161	155	171	164	141	138
Contribution to output from:									
Inputs		122	122	112	112	110	110	100	100
Technological change		0	0	10	10	12	12	22	22
Total output		122	122	122	122	122	122	122	122
1975 Projections									
Inputs:									
Labor		81	81	81	81	67	67	67	67
Land		90	110	90	110	90	110	90	110

Capital [e]	(A)	346	318	199	169	218	201	132	122
	(B)	378	348	218	185	238	219	144	133
Current [e]	(A)	547	505	317	240	346	318	210	193
	(B)	491	441	285	234	311	277	189	173
Contribution to output from:									
Inputs		160	160	135	135	129	129	100	100
Technological change		0	0	25	25	31	31	60	60
Total output		160	160	160	160	160	160	160	160

[a] Increased inputs are assumed to account for the entire increase in output.

[b] Technological change is assumed to occur at a sufficiently rapid rate to permit an increase in output per unit of input of 1.0 percent per year between 1950 and 1975. This is the 1910–50 rate calculated on the basis of 1945–48 prices and techniques.

[c] Technological change is assumed to occur at a sufficiently rapid rate to permit an increase in output per unit of input of 1.23 percent per year between 1950 and 1975. This is the 1910–50 rate calculated on the basis of 1910–14 prices and techniques.

[d] It is assumed that technological change occurs at a sufficiently rapid rate to account for the entire increase in output. This requires an increase in output per unit of input of 2.2 percent per year between 1950 and 1960 and 2.4 percent per year between 1950 and 1975.

[e] Estimate (A) for capital and current inputs is based on the assumption that the ratio of capital to current inputs (C_1/C_2) will continue to decline at the same percentage rate as during the period 1910–14 to 1945–48. Estimate (B) is based on the assumption that, the 1925–27 to 1949–50 rate will continue. See text for further discussion of estimates A and B.

1975 (45 percent);[12] income elasticity of demand for food of 20 and of nonfood items of –.05 at the farm level;[13] and no change in military use and net exports as a percentage of total farm output.[14]

The indexes of farm output requirements obtained in this manner—122 for 1960 and 160 for 1975 (1950 = 100)—are well above current projections chiefly because of the greater populations which seem likely to obtain.[15] Otherwise the projected situation conforms roughly to the situation which has been characterized as "chronic hot and cold wars" by Cochrane and Lampe (1953: 211).

THE LABOR INPUT PROJECTIONS

The labor input of 88 for 1960 and 81 for 1975 shown in models I to IV of Table 3.1 were projected on the basis of an average increase in output per farmworker of 3.9 percent per year. This was the rate achieved during the entire 1910–52 period. The indexes of 78 for 1960 and 67 for 1975 shown on models V to VIII are based on the much more rapid rate—5.6 percent per year—achieved between 1929 and 1952.[16]

According to the *Annual Report on the Labor Force*, an average of 7.5 million farmworkers were employed in producing the 1950 farm output. In 1975 it appears that approximately 5.0 million workers will be required under conditions of rapid technological progress and about 6.1 million workers under conditions of slow technological progress to produce a farm output 60 percent above the 1950 level. In 1960, between 5.9 and 6.6 million farmworkers will probably be required to produce a farm output 22 percent above the 1950 level.

Given the assumption of neutral technological change the continued decline in farm employment posited above depends on the assumption that labor input prices will continue to rise relative to nonlabor inputs.

THE LAND INPUT PROJECTIONS

The oft-observed difficulty of arriving at a satisfactory treatment of aggregate land inputs (e.g., Schultz 1953) led to the specification of two alternative land input models for each technological change situation.

Regardless of the direction of change in land inputs during the next quarter century, recent studies seem to agree that these changes will be rather small. If we can assume that 4.75 acres of plowable pasture are, on the average, equivalent to 1 acre of cropland and that changes in the relative contribution to total farm output of nonplowable pasture,[17] woodland pasture, and grazing lands outside of farms will be sufficiently small to be ignored, then the land use change projections by Black and Gauss in the President's Materials Policy Commission (Paley) (1952) indicate a land input of III in 1975 (1950 = 100), while the changes suggested in the President's Water Policy Commission (Cooke) Report indicate a land input of 100 in 1975. Projections based on past changes in farm output per unit of land input indicate a land input index of 116 in 1975 (1950 = 100) if the 1910–50 annual average increase in output per unit of land input (1.75 percent) continues to 1975; an index of 107 if the 1920–50 rate (2.10 percent) continues; and an index of only 87 if the 1930–50 rate (2.85 percent) continues.

In view of the possibility that changes in land input may be either positive or negative and because of the emphasis on land use changes in the recent literature cited above, we will examine the consequences both of a decline in land inputs to an index of 96 in 1960 and 90 in 1975 and of a rise to 104 in 1960 and 110 in 1975 under each technological change situation.[18] These input situations would appear to adequately reflect the range of expectations currently held.

CAPITAL AND CURRENT EXPENDITURE INPUTS

In projecting the labor and land input indexes presented in Table 3.1, the assumption is made that changes in technology and prices during the period 1950–75 will permit the continuation of certain past relationships in output per unit of labor input and per unit of land input. In estimating the inputs of nonland capital and current inputs, a somewhat different approach has been employed. An attempt has been made to answer the question, "If technological change occurs at a given rate, and if the projected changes in labor inputs and land inputs obtain, what nonland capital and current inputs will be required if an aggregate farm output index of 122 in 1960 and 160 in 1975 (1950 = 100) is to be achieved?"

The answers to this question, as shown in Table 3.1, range from extremely large increases in the case of model I (zero technical progress with low land inputs) to relatively minor increases in model VIII (very rapid technical change with high land inputs). These indexes were obtained by solving the following set of equations for C_1 (the index of nonland capital inputs) and C_2 (the index of current inputs):

$$P = (1+rt)W_t^a L_t^b C_{1t}^c C_{2t}^d$$

$$(a+b+c+d=1) \qquad (1)$$

$$\left(\frac{C_1}{C_2}\right)_t = \left(\frac{C_1}{C_2}\right)_0 (1+f)^{-t} \qquad (2)$$

where $T = 1 + rt$

$$W_t = \frac{W_0 P_t}{P_0(1+st)}$$

P = the index of farm output
W = the index of labor input
L = the index of land input

C_1 = the index of nonland capital inputs
C_2 = the index of current inputs
a = the labor productivity coefficient
b = the land productivity coefficient
c = the nonland capital productivity coefficient
d = the current input productivity coefficient
f = the rate of percentage increase in the ratio (C_1/C_2)
r = the average annual change in output per unit of total input
s = the average annual change in output per unit of labor input
t = the number of years over which the increased output is to be achieved
T = the total contribution of technological change to output during a given period.

What do these equations imply? Equation (1) is a Cobb-Douglas production function. The restriction $(a + b + c + d = 1)$ implies constant returns to scale (when all inputs are increased by the same proportion), while the exponential form of the equation permits the marginal productivity of individual inputs to vary depending on the relative amounts of the various inputs used without violating the assumption of neutral innovation.

In estimating the productivity coefficients for equation (1), the assumption is made that the productivity coefficient for each factor is equal to the percentage share of total agricultural output received by that factor in 1945–48. This assumption is permissible if the inputs actually used in agriculture during 1945–48 were reasonably close to the inputs that would have been used under conditions of competitive equilibrium. Under conditions of competitive equilibrium, the productivity coefficients for factors are proportional to their average productivities (Robinson 1948; Heady 1953).

The contribution of technological change to output is expressed as a function of time. In models I and II (Table 3.1) zero technological change is assumed—the complete change in output is achieved by increasing the quantities of inputs employed in agriculture. In models III and IV, the assumption is made that technological change will continue to occur at a sufficiently rapid rate to permit an average increase in output per unit of input of 1.0 percent per year—the 1910–50 rate calculated on the basis of 1945–48 prices and techniques. In models V and VI, technological change is assumed to occur at a sufficiently rapid rate to permit an average increase in output per unit of input of 1.23 percent per year—the 1910–50 rate of change calculated on the basis of 1911–14 prices and techniques.[19] In models VII and VIII, it is assumed that output per unit of total input increases at a sufficiently rapid rate to account for the entire increase in output between 1950 and 1975. The rate required varies from an average of 2.2 percent per year between 1950 and 1960 to an average of 2.4 percent per year between 1950 and 1975. This is well above even the higher estimates for the period 1910–50 and probably exceeds by a considerable amount the rate achieved during the period 1925–50, when most increase in output per unit of total input apparently occurred.[20] The projections of output per unit of total input presented in models III to VI were chosen merely as convenient reference points rather than in the expectation that these rates which were achieved in the past might actually hold in the future.

Equation (2) attempts to specify the relationship between nonland capital inputs (C_1) and current inputs (C_2). In effect, it states that the ratio of nonland capital inputs (C_1/C_2) can be expected to continue to decline at the same percentage rate as during the period 1910–14 to 1945–48 (estimate A) or the period 1925–27 to 1949–50 (estimate B).[21]

Two alternative projections for capital and current inputs are presented for each model in Table 3.1. It is felt that projections based on the 1910–14 to 1945–48 period (estimate A) might overstate the rise in current inputs relative to the nonland capital inputs for two reasons: (a) mechanization of motive power in American agriculture has occurred almost entirely since 1910–14. At present, it is difficult to visualize, even with continued mechanization and the rapid growth of inputs of such items as insecticides and fertilizers, any developments that will permit quite as rapid substitution of current for capital inputs as has occurred since 1910. (b) The level of capital inputs during 1945–48 was probably influenced by the lag in capital investment during 1942–46, when machinery and materials were in short supply. On the other hand, use of the period 1925–27 to 1949–50 (estimate B) as a basis for projecting the relationship between capital and current inputs (C_1/C_2) may understate the relative rise in current inputs: first, because mechanization of motive power had already made substantial progress on American farms by 1925–27, and second, because it is doubtful that capital investment will persist at the extremely high rates of 1949–50 without the stimulus of rising farm prices.[22]

In view of the above considerations, estimates A and B are both presented in Table 3.1. These estimates appear to set the limits within which increases in capital and current inputs are likely to occur.

Some Policy Implications

The projections of disposable income and population growth employed in this paper indicate substantially higher farm output requirements in both 1960 and 1975 than appeared likely even a few years ago. Regardless of the rate of technological change that is achieved, it appears that the output requirements can be met with approximately the same land inputs as at present and a continually declining agricultural labor force. The factor input-output models in this paper also illustrate the high degree of substitution that exists between technological change and inputs of capital and current expense items.[23]

HOW MUCH TECHNOLOGICAL CHANGE?

The changes in land inputs, nonland capital inputs, and the level of technology that actually take place will be strongly influenced by governmental policy.

A major share of the costs of the research and development involved in advancing the level of technology in agriculture is borne by the states and the federal government.

If, as argued in this paper, technological change and capital inputs can be viewed as substitutes, it then becomes possible to get away from the question of the quantity of resources (or income) which the nation "needs" to devote to research if output requirements are to be met. A more appropriate question is: What combination of private and governmental expenditure on (a) research and extension, (b) land reclamation and improvement, and (c) investment incentives and expenditures will minimize the cost of obtaining the required increments to farm output?

No attempt will be made in this paper to present a precise answer to this question. One would expect, however, that the situation represented by models I and II would be extremely costly. Cochrane and Lampe (1953: 208) state that they expect a situation similar to model VII or VIII to hold during the next quarter century. Although this appears to be a substantially more rapid rate of change in output per unit of input than has been achieved for any period of similar length in the past, the possibility exists that this may be the least expensive method to the nation for providing its food and fiber requirements.

LAND AND CREDIT POLICY

In the event that technological change is pushed rapidly enough to account for the entire increase in farm output (from an index of 100 to 160) during the next quarter century, problems of land reclamation and development and availability of farm credit are likely to become much less important than at present. Indeed, if the situation outlined in model VII were to obtain, it would be possible to achieve the desired farm output with a 10 percent decline in land inputs and only a 32–44 percent increase in nonland capital inputs over the twenty-five-year period. This increase in capital inputs is far below the rate of increase achieved during the 1940–50 decade, when nonland capital inputs in agriculture increased by approximately 65 percent (Schultz 1953: 108).

At the other extreme, failure to achieve substantial increases in output per unit of total input would point to continued rapid growth of capital requirements in agriculture and would increase the productivity of both private and public investment in reclamation or drainage enterprises designed to increase land inputs. At the level of technological progress posited in models III and IV, for example, an increase in land inputs of 20 points (from 90 to 110) permits a compensating decrease of 30–33 units of capital and 51–77 units of current inputs between 1950 and 1975 (valued at 1945–47 prices), while at the levels posited in models VII and VIII the same increase in land inputs will release only 10–11 units of capital and 16–17 units of current inputs.

The magnitude of the increase in capital inputs required in models I to VI is of considerable interest. Some economists have expressed concern over the high capital requirements per farm unit even at present (e.g., Cowden 1953: 87; Baughman 1952; Buck 1954). Substantial increases in total capital requirements coupled with further declines in the number of farms may make the ideal of an owner-operated family farm unencumbered by substantial long-term debt even less attainable than at present. Certainly it will require more effective arrangements for the acquisition of capital assets with long-term financing and will probably be accompanied by separation of the farm ownership and managerial control functions to a much greater extent than exists at present.[24]

PRICE POLICY

In all of the farm output–factor input models shown in Table 3.1, inputs of current expense items are indicated as expanding much more rapidly than long-run capital inputs. In the past, increased expenditures on motor fuels have accounted for a major share of the increase in current inputs. It seems likely that rapidly expanding inputs of fertilizer, insecticides, machinery repairs, processed feeds, and other input factors purchased from the nonagricultural sectors of the economy will continue this trend.

As the importance of such items continues to expand, one might expect that farm output would become somewhat more sensitive to downward shifts in the prices of farm products than in the past.[25] For any given level of technology (ratio of output per unit of total input), increased sensitivity of farm output to downward fluctuations in the movements in the prices of farm products (i.e., greater elasticity in the supply curve for farm products) would decrease the magnitude of the price decline required by a decline in demand for farm commodities not subject to price supports. The old idea that farm output does not decline during a depression may have to be revised. For supported commodities, it would increase the amount of product that would have to be taken off the market to maintain any given support level above the equilibrium level. This suggests that the recent buildup of farm surpluses in the last few years may be related to increased elasticity in the supply curve for farm products as well as to advances in farm technology and a short-run shift to the left in the demand curve for farm products.

Notes

Vernon W. Ruttan, *Review of Economics and Statistics* 38 (February 1956): 61–69. This paper was completed while the author was a member of the Government Relations and Economics Staff of the Tennessee Valley Authority. He is indebted to D. Gale Johnson of the University of Chicago; to Glenn T. Barton of the Agricultural Research Service, U.S. Department of Agriculture; and to his colleagues on the Tennessee Valley Authority's Government Relations and Economics Staff and the Agricultural Economics Branch for helpful comments and criticisms.

1. Most of the current discussions regarding future output requirements are based on five recent studies: (a) U.S. Department of Agriculture 1952a, (b) President's Materials Policy Commission 1952, (c) President's Water Resources Policy Commission (undated), (d) Cochrane and Lampe 1953, and (e) Daley 1954. For comments on the projections presented in the above studies, see (a) Heisig 1953, (b) Halvorson 1952, (c) S. E. Johnson 1952, (d) Trelogan and Johnson 1953, (e) Clark 1954, (f) Mason 1954, and (g) Black 1955. See also U.S. Department of Agriculture 1952b, Johnson and Barlowe 1954, and Koffsky 1954.
2. According to the Water Resources Policy Commission (undated: 159), "present food surpluses are transitory. The real agricultural problem is how to assure sufficient production to meet the requirements of an expanding population."
3. According to Cochrane and Lampe (1953: 209), "in peace time, technological advance can turn the old pressure of population on food supplies into the pressure of food supplies on population, at least insofar as the United States is concerned."
4. Cochrane and Lampe (1953: 208) are prevented from falling into this confusion, not by their analytical scheme, which lumps together all factors acting to shift the supply curve to the left and expresses them as a simple function of time, but by their assumption that technological progress will occur at a sufficiently rapid rate to permit aggregate inputs to remain unchanged or even decline.
5. It seems rather unlikely that many economists actually view change in labor productivity as an adequate indicator of technological change. The common tendency in current literature is to disavow reliance on labor productivity as an indicator of technological change and then to proceed to use it in the absence of any readily available alternative. See, for example, Black 1945: 180–84, 198, and Colm 1952: 19–22, as well as most of the studies referred to in footnote 1. For further comment on this point, see Siegel 1953.
6. According to Barton and Cooper (1948: 120–23), output per unit of labor input increased approximately twice as fast as output per unit of total input between 1910 and 1945. Productivity gains since 1945 have pushed this ratio to close to three.
7. Exact determination of the contribution of technological change to output is possible only if the following conditions hold: (a) the firm (or industry) must be operating under conditions of equilibrium in both t_0 and t_1; (b) the production function must be homogeneous of degree one (i.e., constant returns to scale must hold); (c) the prices of the factors of production relative to each other and the prices of the products of the firm (or industry) relative to each other must remain unchanged; (d) technological progress must be neutral. Neutrality is defined as follows: let $P(x, y, a, b) = 0$ be the production function before technological change. This technological change is neutral if, and only if, it yields the production function $P(T_x, T_y, a, b) = 0$ where T is a constant greater than one if the change is progress. In spite of the restrictive appearance of the above conditions, they do permit us to "bracket" the range within which the "true" contribution of technological change falls. In many cases, it is not possible even to set reliable one-sided limits when the labor-productivity approach is used. For demonstration of the above points, see Ruttan 1954.
8. The effects of using a nonlinear production function rather than a linear function as discussed above are essentially the same as those of using a geometric rather than an arithmetic mean. See, for example, Yule and Kendall 1946.
9. Possession of the last two characteristics has apparently been an important factor in contributing to the extensive use of the Cobb-Douglas function in examining production relationships in the field of agriculture. See, for example, G. L. Johnson 1952, Heady and Shaw 1954, and R. B. Hughes 1954.
10. This is the rate of growth employed in Colm 1952: 159. Income is expressed in 1950 dollars.
11. This is the rate of growth employed in President's Material Policy Commission 1952: 63.
12. These are the highest projections now being made by the U.S. Bureau of the Census (see *Current Population Reports*, Series P-25, No. 78). Justification for employing the highest projection rather than the more moderate figure of 213.6 million is to be found in a rather consistent pattern of underestimation of future population growth in recent projections. See, for example, the critical review of recent population projections by Davis (1953).
13. These are the levels implicit in the projections by Black and Gauss in President's Material Policy Commission 1952: 63–65. It might possibly be argued that, with the expected rise in per capita

disposable income, the income elasticity of demand for food at the farm level would fall to at least .14, the level which Fox (1951: 81) obtained for urban families in 1948. Other estimates of the income elasticity of demand for food products at the farm level run as high as .30, however. See the studies quoted in Schultz 1953: 55. The income elasticity of demand assigned to nonfood items (<min>.05), which is implicit in the estimates by Black and Gauss, is based on much less empirical evidence than the income elasticity of demand for the food items. However, even a difference of as much as 10 points would not affect total output requirements very much, since nonfood items represent a relatively small share of total farm output (about 20 percent in 1950). Thus, if the income elasticity of demand for nonfood items were .05 rather than <min>.05, the output requirement estimate would be 162 rather than 160 in 1975.

14. In the event of continuous peace and high-level price supports between the present and 1975, net exports will no doubt fall considerably below the assumed level unless some sort of export subsidy is resorted to.
15. President's Water Resources Policy Commission (undated: 156–58) projects food requirements of 132 in 1975 (1949–51 = 100). Black and Gauss project a 1975 demand for all farm products of 138 in President's Material Policy Commission 1952: 63. The Cochrane and Lampe projections (1953: 211–14) of food consumption for 1975 range from about 114 (serious business recession during late 1960s) to 135 (continuous peacetime prosperity).
16. The output series employed in estimating changes in output per farmworker is U.S. Department of Agriculture 1952c: 661. The farm employment series employed in models I to IV is the revised Bureau of Agricultural Economics farm employment estimates as presented in *Farm Labor* 1952. In models V to VIII, the BLS-Census *Annual Report on the Labor Force* estimates of farm employment were employed (see Joint Committee on the Economic Report 1953). These estimates appear to reflect "work done" more closely than even the recently revised BAE estimates, which reflect "participation" in agricultural employment. For a more adequate discussion of this point, see Fuller et al. 1953.
17. The figure 4.75 is derived from data presented in Barton and Cooper 1945: 24.
18. Between 1910–14 and 1949–51, the value of farmland (excluding buildings) declined from \$76.6 to \$53.1 million (in 1950 dollars). This historical trend has been disregarded in arriving at the two alternative indexes of land input used in this paper. The assumption is made that the investment requirements for land will be proportional to physical land inputs. For data on the cost of additional land inputs, see Ulrich 1953; and President's Water Resources Policy Commission (undated, vol. 2: 28–30).
19. The above rates of increase in output per unit of total input were estimated from the following production functions:

$$1910-14: P=(1+rt)W^{.400}L^{.194}C_1^{.273}C_2^{.073}$$

$$1945-48: P=(1+rt)W^{.426}L^{.169}C_1^{.209}C_2^{.136}$$

and the following input and output indexes:

	1910–14 Prices		*1945–48 Prices*	
	1910	1950	1910	1950
Output (P)	100	175	57	100
Inputs:				
Labor (*W*)	100	72	139	100
Land (*L*)	100	107	93	100
Capital (C_1)	100	175	55	100
Current (C_2)	100	596	26	100

Both the production functions and the input and output indexes are adapted from data presented in T. W. Schultz 1953: 101–9, 120–22, and 137–39.

20. By using the capital input estimates developed in Tostlebe 1954, and the current input estimates developed by Kendrick and Jones (1951), rather than the Department of Agriculture estimates employed by Schultz, it is possible to obtain a somewhat higher estimate of the contribution of technological change. Calculations for the period 1910–50, based on 1910–14 techniques and prices with the Tostlebe capital input index (C_1) of 160 and the Kendrick-Jones current input index (C_2) of 362, indicate an estimated average increase in output per unit of input of 1.53 percent per year. Calculations using BAE data for the period 1925–50 based on 1935–39 techniques and prices indicate an average increase in output per unit of input of about 1.6 percent per year. Even if the data necessary to make similar calculations on the basis of, say, 1925–27 techniques and prices were available, it seems unlikely that the estimate of average increase in output per unit of total input would rise above 2.0 percent per year.
21. The rate of nonland capital inputs to current inputs (C_1/C_2) declined from 3.74 in 1910–14 to 2.65 in 1925–27, to 1.98 in 1946–48, and rose to 2.05 in 1949–50. The 1910–14 and 1946–48 ratios are from Schultz 1953: 137. The 1925–27 and 1949–50 ratios were calculated from unpublished data made available to the writer by the Agricultural Research Service. Current plans by the Agricultural Research Service to revise the series from which these ratios were computed may result in some changes in the ratios. Because of the extreme difficulty of arriving at an appropriate measure of capital inputs, it would be well to consider the indexes presented in Table 3.1 as indicative of the relative rather than the absolute level of inputs required.
22. See Kendrick and Jones 1953 for a discussion of recent fluctuations in farm capital outlays. See also U.S. Department of Agriculture 1953: 36, Table 18, "Farm Capital Expenditures, Depreciation, and Net Investment, 1910–52."
23. This is not to argue that a certain amount of complementarity does not exist between innovation and capital inputs. In many cases both capital investment and purchase of current inputs are necessary if the advances in technology are actually to be introduced. This may be true even though the innovation results in a reduction in total capital inputs required to produce a given output. For further discussion of this point, see Hendrix 1951.
24. This point has been made by Ellickson and Brewster (1947). While arguing rather strongly that technological advance in agriculture does not tend to reduce the efficiency of family-scale relative to larger-than-family-scale farms, they do point out that the association between owner-operatorship and managerial control is not a necessary condition of family-scale farming.
25. D. G. Johnson (1950) indicates that the relatively fixed prices of current input items have not, in the past, been important enough to bring about a downward shift in farm output during periods of declining farm prices. If inputs of current items should expand as indicated in the projections shown in Table 3.1, however, one might expect a somewhat greater impact on farm output if prices of current inputs fail to decline as rapidly as the prices of farm product.

CHAPTER 4

Agricultural Productivity Differences among Countries

Yujiro Hayami and Vernon W. Ruttan

The sources of productivity growth over time and of productivity differences among countries and regions have emerged as a central unifying theme of growth theory and development economics.[1] In recent years a consensus seems to have emerged to the effect that productivity growth in the agricultural sector is essential if agricultural output is to grow at a sufficiently rapid rate to meet the demands for food and raw materials that typically accompany urbanization and industrialization (Adelman and Morris 1968; Jorgenson 1961; Ranis and Fei 1961; Ruttan 1968). Failure to achieve rapid growth in agricultural productivity can result either in the drain of foreign exchange or in shifts in the internal terms of trade against industry and thus seriously impede the growth of industrial production. Failure to achieve rapid growth in labor productivity in agriculture can also raise the cost of transferring labor, and other resources, from the agricultural to the nonagricultural sector as development proceeds.

Extremely wide differences in agricultural productivity exist among countries. Agricultural output per worker in India is approximately one-fiftieth of that in the United States. Relatively few underdeveloped countries have achieved levels of output per worker one-fifth as high as in the United States. Furthermore, these differences have widened during the last decade (Hayami et al. 1970). This lag in the rate of productivity growth in agriculture represents a serious constraint on economic growth in many developing economies. Recent empirical research supports a classification of the sources of productivity differences, or of productivity growth, into three broad categories: (a) resource endowments, (b) technology, as embodied in fixed or working capital, and (c) human capital, broadly conceived to include the education, skill, knowledge, and capacity embodied in a country's population. Although this is clearly an oversimplification, it does represent a substantial advance over the earlier emphasis on a single key or strategic factor (Griliches 1964; Krueger 1968; Nelson 1968; Schultz 1964a).

Our analysis indicates that the three broad categories outlined above account for approximately 95 percent of the differences in labor productivity in agriculture between a representative group of Less Developed Countries (LDCs) and of Developed Countries (DCs). In this comparison the three factors are of roughly equal importance. When compared to the DCs of recent settlement (Australia, Canada, New Zealand, and the United States), favorable resource endowments account for somewhat more than one-third of the differences. Resource endowment is the major factor accounting for differences in labor productivity between the DCs of recent settlement and the older DCs. Nevertheless, it seems apparent that the LDCs could, over time, achieve labor productivity levels in agriculture well over half as high as in the more recently settled DCs, roughly comparable to the levels achieved in the older DCs, through increased use of technical inputs supplied from the industrial sector and improvements in the quality of the labor force, even in the absence of substantial changes in man-land ratios.

1. The Method and the Data

The approach used in this study involves the estimation of a cross-country production function of the Cobb-Douglas type for thirty-eight developed and underdeveloped countries.[2] Differences in agricultural output per worker are accounted for by differences in the level of conventional and nonconventional inputs per worker, classified as (a) internal resource accumulation, (b) technical inputs supplied by the nonagriculture sector, and (c) human capital.[3] All of the data used in this study are taken from a recent compilation of international agricultural production statistics by Yujiro Hayami and associates (1970).[4]

Production functions were estimated for three different periods: 1955 (1952–56 averages), 1960 (1957–62 averages), and 1965 (1962–66 averages).[5] The analysis was conducted in gross output (net of seeds and feed) terms in order to include the effects of current intermediate inputs such as fertilizer. Individual agricultural commodities were aggregated by the farm gate (or import) prices of the United States, Japan, and India, to produce three different output series. The series were then averaged geometrically into a single composite output series which was used as the dependent variable.[6]

The independent variables used in the study include labor, land, livestock, fertilizer, machinery, education, and technical manpower. In summing up the effects of resource endowments, technology, and human capital on productivity per worker, land and livestock serve as proxy variables for internal resource accumulation; machinery and fertilizer for technical inputs; and general and technical education in agriculture for human capital.

Land (measured by hectares of agricultural land) used for agricultural production cannot be regarded as a mere gift of nature. It represents the result of previous investment in land clearing, reclamation, drainage, fencing, and other development measures. Similarly, livestock (as measured by livestock units) represents a form of internal capital accumulation. Thus, in our perspective, land and livestock represent a form of long-term capital formation embodying inputs supplied primarily by the agricultural sector.[7] Both high inputs of land and of livestock per worker tend to be associated with low levels of labor and high levels of land per unit of output. In contrast, fertilizer (as measured by the $N + P_2O_5 + K_2O$ in commercial fertilizers) and machinery (as measured by tractor horsepower) represent inputs supplied by the industrial sector. Technical advances stemming from both public and private sector research and development are embodied in or complementary to these modern industrial inputs. Mechanical innovations are usually associated with larger inputs of power and machinery. Biological improvements, such as the innovations embodied in high-yielding varieties, are typically associated with higher levels of fertilizer use. In this analysis these two industrial inputs represent proxies for the whole range of inputs which carry modern mechanical and biological technologies.

The proxies for human capital include measures of both the general educational level of the rural population and specialized education in the agricultural sciences and technology. Two alternative measures of the level of general education were attempted: (a) the literacy ratio and (b) the school enrollment ratio for the primary and secondary levels. Both sets of data are deficient in that they apply to the entire population and are not sensitive to differences in the quality of rural and urban education. Education in the agricultural sciences and technology was measured by the number of graduates per ten thousand farmworkers from agricultural faculties at above the secondary level. These graduates represent the major source of technological and scientific personnel for public sector agricultural research and extension and for research development and marketing in the private agribusiness sector.[8]

A critical assumption in this approach is that the technical possibilities available to agricultural producers in the different countries can be described by the same production function. Cross-section production functions, using individual countries or regions as observations, have been widely used. Cross-country aggregate production functions for the agricultural sector were first estimated by Jyoti Bhattacherjee in 1955. An aggregate agricultural production function similar to that used in this study, using states in the United States as observations, was employed by Zvi Griliches (1964) in an attempt to account for the impact of research and education on agricultural output. Anne Krueger's (1968) recent effort to estimate the contribution of factor endowment differentials to variations in per capita income employs the assumption that all countries are subject to a uniform production function.

In a recent paper Richard Nelson (1968: 1229) has argued that the assumptions of a common production function "get in the way of understanding international differences in productivity—particularly differences between advanced and underdeveloped countries.'" Nelson's objections appear directed primarily to the empirical results obtained from use of relatively primitive two-factor production functions, where intercountry differences in value-added per worker are related to the capital-labor ratio. He insists, as a result of differential diffusion of new technology, that "at any given time one would expect to find considerable variation among firms with respect to the vintage of their technology, certainly between countries, but even within a country" (ibid.: 1230).

We share the Nelson perspective. Agricultural producers in different countries, in different regions of the same country, and on different farms in the same region are not all on the same microproduction function. This reflects differences among producers in their ability to adopt new technology. More importantly, it is also the result of differential diffusion of agricultural technology, and, to an even greater degree, of differential diffusion of the scientific and technical capacity to invent and develop new mechanical, biological, and chemical technology specifically adapted to the factor endowments and prices in a particular country or region.

We may call the envelope of all known and potentially discoverable activities a secular or "metaproduction function." The full range of technological alternatives described by the metaproduction function is only partially available to individual producers in a particular country or agricultural region during any particular historical "epoch."[9] It is, however, potentially available to agricultural scientists and technicians.

We view the common or cross-country production function which we have estimated as a metaproduction function. It is assumed that the invention and diffusion of a new "location-specific" agricultural technology through the application of the concepts of physical, biological, and chemical science and of engineering, craft, and husbandry skills is capable of making the factor productivities implicit in the cross-country production function available to producers in less developed countries. It is also assumed that the capacity of a country to engage in the necessary research, development, and extension is measured by the two proxy variables for human capital, namely general education and technical education in agriculture. It appears to us that this effort, and that of Griliches (1964) and Krueger (1968), are not inconsistent with the perspective presented by Nelson (1968) in his criticism of the empirical results obtained from two-factor cross-country production functions.

The production function employed in this study was of the Cobb-Douglas type. It was used mainly because of its ease in manipulation and interpretation. A test presented in the Appendix indicates that the unitary elasticity of substitution implicit in the Cobb-Douglas production function is an acceptable assumption. The ordinary least squares estimation procedure was used. The possibility of simultaneous equation bias seems small because all inputs, except fertilizer, are measured in stock terms and can be treated as predetermined. In a few cases, however, the method of instrumental variables was tried to see if any different inferences might be drawn. The assumption of a common production function among countries is a testable hypothesis. However, it appears that the data used in this study are too crude to be employed for such a test.[10]

2. Estimation of the Production Function

We conducted an especially detailed analysis for 1960 because of (a) better comparability of output data and (b) availability of data for the number of farms in that year.[11] Table 4.1 presents the estimates of the unrestricted Cobb-Douglas production function on the cross-country data; each column reports the results of a regression of agricultural output on a different set of inputs in the log linear form, including estimates of the production elasticities and their standard errors (in parentheses), the standard errors of estimate, and the coefficients of determination adjusted for the degrees of freedom.[12] The estimation was made both on per farm data (output and conventional inputs deflated by the number of farms) and on national aggregate data. The results from these two sets of data are not sufficiently different to lead to different inferences regarding the agricultural production structures among countries.

Considering the crudeness of data, the levels of statistical significance of the estimated coefficients seem satisfactory in most cases. The coefficients stay fairly stable when nonconventional variables are added or subtracted, though the coefficients for labor and livestock tend to move opposite to the coefficient for machinery. The results of estimation by the method of instrumental variables (denoted as IV) compared with the least squares estimates provide no *prima facie* evidence against the use of least squares.

Attempts to include other variables, for example, the ratio of irrigation land to total land area and the ratio of cropland to pasture land, were tried in an attempt to adjust for differences in the quality of land input; but it turned out that the coefficients for such variables are either negative or nonsignificant.[13]

Plausibility of the estimates may be checked by a comparison with the results of earlier attempts to estimate aggregate production functions in various countries. Bhattacharjee (1955) obtained aggregate production elasticities for his cross-country production function (including only conventional variables) centered on 1950 of around 0.3 for labor; 0.3 to 0.4 for land; and 0.3 for fertilizer. The coefficients for livestock and tractors were not significant at commonly accepted levels. The Bhattacharjee (1955) results indicate higher production elasticities for land and fertilizer than the results obtained in our study. It would appear that our model is somewhat better specified in that we obtained statistically meaningful coefficients for livestock and machinery as well as for the two proxy variables for human capital.

The aggregate production elasticities of U.S. agriculture were estimated by Griliches (1964) as 0.4 to 0.5 for labor; 0.1 to 0.2 for land, fertilizer, and machinery; 0.3 to 0.5 for education; 0.04 to 0.1 for research and extension. It is rather surprising that the Griliches estimates, despite the completely different nature of the data used, coincide so well with the ones in this study.

The production elasticities estimated for Japanese agriculture by Yasuhiko Yuize (1964) in value-added terms are in the ranges of 0.4 to 0.6 for labor and 0.2 to 0.4 for land. Such figures are consistent with the estimates in this study

Table 4.1 **Estimates of Agricultural Production Function on Cross-Country Data, 1960 (1957–62 Averages)**

	Per farm Basis						
Regression number	*(1)*	*(2)*	*(3)*	*(4)*	*(5)*	*(2-IV)*	*(3-IV)*
Sample size	*38*	*37*	*37*	*37*	*37*	*37*	*37*
Labor (L)	0.336 (0.121)	0.432 (0.114)	0.393 (0.117)			0.490 (0.110)	0.454 (0.113)
Land	0.071 (0.074)	0.108 (0.065)	0.097 (0.067)	0.117 (0.062)	0.104 (0.066)	0.108 (0.069)	0.097 (0.072)
Livestock	0.166 (0.099)	0.241 (0.089)	0.136 (0.062)	0.249 (0.086)	0.232 (0.091)	0.210 (0.094)	0.192 (0.097)
Fertilizer	0.174 (0.055)	0.124 (0.058)	0.136 (0.062)	0.121 (0.053)	0.126 (0.059)	0.096 (0.058)	0.108 (0.067)
Machinery	0.205 (0.061)	0.057 (0.067)	0.104 (0.064)	0.038 (0.053)	0.092 (0.059)	0.074 (0.068)	0.124 (0.064)
General education Literacy ratio (E1)		0.348 (0.186)				0.366 (0.196)	
School enrollment ratio (E2)			0.360 (0.247)				0.263 (0.274)
Technical education		0.190 (0.057)	0.148 (0.055)	0.197 (0.055)	0.146 (0.054)	0.197 (0.060)	0.153 (0.056)
LxE1				0.418 (0.109)			
LxE2					0.383 (0.114)		
Coef. of det. (adj)	0.908	0.932	0.926	0.934	0.928	0.928	0.921
S.E. of est.	0.138	0.119	0.124	0.118	0.123	0.123	0.128
Sum of conventional coefficients	0.952 (0.098)	0.962 (0.085)	0.957 (0.088)	0.943 (0.074)	0.937 (0.080)	0.978 (0.088)	0.975 (0.094)
Sum of Conventional coefficients	0.952 (0.098)	0.962 (0.085)	0.957 (0.088)	0.943 (0.074)	0.937 (0.080)	0.978 (0.088)	0.975 (0.094)

			National Aggregate basis				
Regression number	*(6)*	*(7)*	*(8)*	*(9)*	*(10)*	*(7-IV)*	*(8-IV)*
Sample size	*38*	*37*	*37*	*37*	*37*	*37*	*37*
Labor (L)	0.335 (0.064)	0.451 (0.074)	0.413 (0.075)			0.474 (0.072)	0.434 (0.074)
Land	0.056 (0.065)	0.088 (0.062)	0.076 (0.063)	0.097 (0.061)	0.080 (0.063)	0.092 (0.065)	0.080 (0.067)
Livestock	0.091 (0.096)	0.247 (0.089)	0.235 (0.092)	0.263 (0.086)	0.243 (0.091)	0.219 (0.093)	0.205 (0.095)
Fertilizer	0.161 (0.053)	0.112 (0.059)	0.123 (0.063)	0.105 (0.058)	0.108 (0.061)	0.090 (0.057)	0.104 (0.064)
Machinery	0.192 (0.056)	0.071 (0.065)	0.116 (0.060)	0.040 (0.053)	0.102 (0.058)	0.082 (0.065)	0.127 (0.061)
General education Literacy ratio (E1)		0.326 (0.187)				0.321 (0.196)	
School enrollment ratio (E2)			0.324 (0.248)				0.290 (0.271)
Technical education		0.182 (0.057)	0.142 (0.055)	0.195 (0.055)	0.139 (0.054)	0.182 (0.060)	0.142 (0.056)
LxE1				0.464 (0.072)			
LxE2					0.432 (0.072)		
Coef. of det. (adj)	0.955	0.953	0.950	0.954	0.950	0.951	0.948
S.E. of est.	0.131	0.118	0.123	0.118	0.122	0.120	0.125

(continued)

Table 4.1 **(*continued*)**

	National Aggregate basis						
Regression number	*(6)*	*(7)*	*(8)*	*(9)*	*(10)*	*(7-IV)*	*(8-IV)*
Sample size	38	37	37	37	37	37	37
Sum of conventional coefficients	0.935 (0.035)	0.969 (0.039)	0.963 (0.040)	0.969 (0.039)	0.965 (0.040)	0.957 (0.048)	0.950 (0.040)
Sum of Conventional coefficients	0.952 (0.098)	0.962 (0.085)	0.957 (0.088)	0.943 (0.074)	0.937 (0.080)	0.978 (0.088)	0.975 (0.094)

Notes: Equations linear in logarithms are estimated by the least squares except those denoted as *IV*, which are estimated by the instrumental variable method. The standard errors of coefficients are in parentheses.

Dependent variable: Gross agricultural output net of seeds and feed in thousand wheat units (one wheat unit is equivalent to a ton of wheat).

Labor : Number of male workers active in agriculture in thousands.

Land : Area of agricultural land in thousand hectares.

Livestock : Livestock in agriculture in thousand livestock units (conversion factors: 1.1 for camels; 1.0 for buffalo, horses and mules; 0.8 for cattle and asses; 0.2 for pigs; 0.1 for sheep and goats; 0.01 for poultry).

Fertilizer: Sum of N, P_2O_5 and K_2O in thousand metric tons contained in commercial fertilizers consumed.

Machinery: Horsepower of tractors for farm purposes in thousands horsepowers.

Literary ratio: Literacy ratio in percent.

School enrollment ratio: Ratio of school enrollments in the primary and secondary schools in percent, adjusted for differences in the school system.

Technical education: Number of graduates from agricultural schools of the third level (college level) per ten thousand male farm workers. Number of farms: Number of agricultural holdings in thousands.

Source: Hayami and associates (1970).

since according to the social account study by the Japanese Ministry of Agriculture and Forestry (1968) the ratio of value-added to gross output was around 0.7 in Japanese agriculture in the period when Yuize's study was made. In the less developed countries we do not have comparable estimates of the aggregate agricultural production function. Theodore Schultz (1964a) has, however, inferred from the impact of the 1918–19 influenza epidemic that the production elasticity of labor in Indian agriculture was 0.4. This is consistent with our estimates. Such consistency with other studies gives support to the results of estimation in this study.

Griliches (1964) has found that in U.S. agriculture, a given percentage increase in education, which improves the quality of labor, has the same output effect as an equal percentage increase in labor itself. In order to test whether the same assertion holds in the international dimension, we have estimated the production function by combining labor L and general education E in a multiplicative form LxE; this resulted in little change (compare regressions 2 with 4, 3 with 5, 7 with 9, and 8 with 10). Furthermore, the analysis of variance provides evidence in support of the equality in the coefficients of labor and general education.[14]

Judging from the sums of coefficients of conventional inputs, compared with the standard errors of those sums (shown in parentheses below the sums of coefficients), constant returns seem to prevail both on the farm firm level and on the national aggregate level. Note, however, that increasing returns prevail when both private and socially controlled inputs are allowed to vary. The constant returns at the farm level may explain the existence of farms of extremely different sizes producing the same commodities. The constant returns at the national aggregate level might be one of the distinctive characteristics of agricultural production and, if so, would have important implications for the intersectoral investment priorities for national economic development.

The stability of the agricultural production function over time is tested on the 1955, 1960, and 1965 cross-country sample. Because comparable data on the number of farms were not available for 1955 and 1965, we assumed the linear homogeneity in the Cobb-Douglas production function and regressed output per capita (per male worker) on conventional inputs per capita and on nonconventional inputs. The linear homogeneity assumption is based on the information contained in Table 4.1. In order to make the data comparable among years we restricted the countries included in the sample to thirty-six (Mauritius and Surinam were dropped from the sample for lack of labor data).

The results of our estimations are summarized in Table 4.2. Comparing the estimates of the per capita production function with those of the unrestricted form in Table 4.1, we see that the land coefficients become smaller and the livestock coefficients become larger. This appears to be caused by high intercorrelation between land area per worker and livestock per worker. Differences in the two sets of estimates do not seem to imply different conclusions. The production parameters seem largely stable over time. The null hypothesis of the equality of the production coefficients among 1955, 1960, and 1965 is accepted according to the results of analysis of variance (the *F*-statistic calculated from regressions 12, 13, 14, and 17 is only 0.95).

3. Accounting for Productivity Differences

The results obtained from estimation of the agricultural production function in the previous sections may be used to account for intercountry differences in labor productivity (output per male worker) in agriculture in 1960. Since our production function is now assumed to be linear homogeneous (with respect to conventional inputs) in the Cobb-Douglas form, the percentage difference in output per worker can be expressed as the sum of percentage differences in conventional inputs and nonconventional inputs per worker each weighted by the relevant production elasticities. Based on the results shown in Table 4.1 and Table 4.2 the following set of production elasticities was adopted: 0.40 for labor, 0.10 for land, 0.25 for livestock, 0.15 for fertilizer, 0.10 for machinery, 0.40 for education, and 0.15 for research and extension. Only the school enrollment ratio was used as the education variable in this accounting, but the results would have been essentially the same if the literacy ratio had been used.

Two alternative sets of results are presented. The first set involves group comparisons between LDCs and DCs. The second set involves individual comparisons of selected LDCs and DCs with the United States.

Group Comparisons

The sources of differences in labor productivity between the eleven LDCs and different groups of DCs are presented in Table 4.3. Each column compares for each group the percentage difference in agricultural output per worker between LDCs and DCs with the percentage differences in input variables weighted by the specified production elasticities. Inside the parentheses is shown the index with the output-per-worker difference set equal to 100. The countries classified as LDCs, for the purposes of this comparison, all had per capita income of less than US$350 and more than 35 percent of their labor force engaged in agriculture. The countries classified as DCs had per capita income higher than US$700 dollars and less than 30 percent of the labor force engaged in agriculture. Countries falling between these criteria are not included in the comparisons presented in Table 4.3.

The difference in average agricultural output per worker between the eleven LDCs and the thirteen DCs of group 1 was 88.8 percent; the difference between the eleven DCs and the nine older DCs of group 2 was 83.5 percent; and the difference between the eleven LDCs and the four DCs of recent settlement—group 3—was

Table 4.2 **Estimates of Agricultural Production Function on Cross-Country Data: 1955 (1952–56 Averages); 1960 (1957–62 Averages); and 1965 (1962–66 Averages)**

	Per-capita basis						
Regression number	*(11)*	*(12)*	*(13)*	*(14)*	*(15)*	*(16)*	*(17)*
Year	*1960*	*1960*	*1955*	*1965*	*1955–60*	*1960–65*	*1955–60–65*
Sample size	*36*	*36*	*36*	*36*	*72*	*72*	*108*
Land	0.072 (0.061)	0.056 (0.063)	0.082 (0.061)	0.043 (0.073)	0.068 (0.042)	0.047 (0.047)	0.066 (0.038)
Livestock	0.289 (0.092)	0.281 (0.094)	0.311 (0.093)	0.273 (0.101)	0.300 (0.064)	0.276 (0.066)	0.286 (0.055)
Fertilizer	0.105 (0.057)	0.107 (0.063)	0.124 (0.057)	0.142 (0.083)	0.120 (0.041)	0.125 (0.049)	0.137 (0.038)
Machinery	0.076 (0.063)	0.125 (0.059)	0.061 (0.049)	0.152 (0.063)	0.090 (0.036)	0.144 (0.041)	0.106 (0.032)
General education Literacy ratio	0.362 (0.180)						
School enrollment ratio		0.337 (0.243)	0.168 (0.182)	0.356 (0.336)	0.320 (0.141)	0.324 (0.189)	0.243 (0.134)
Technical education	0.182 (0.055)	0.137 (0.053)	0.194 (0.051)	0.099 (0.050)	0.168 (0.035)	0.113 (0.034)	0.122 (0.029)
Dummy: 1960					−0.009 (0.026)		−0.017 (0.029)
1965						−0.019 (0.029)	−0.021 (0.030)

(continued)

Table 4.2 **(continued)**

	Per-capita basis						
Regression number	*(11)*	*(12)*	*(13)*	*(14)*	*(15)*	*(16)*	*(17)*
Year	*1960*	*1960*	*1955*	*1965*	*1955–60*	*1960–65*	*1955–60–65*
Sample size	*36*	*36*	*36*	*36*	*72*	*72*	*108*
Coef. of det.(adj)	0.934	0.930	0.931	0.919	0.934	0.929	0.924
S.E. of est.	0.115	0.119	0.111	0.135	0.111	0.123	0.122
Implicit coefficient of labor	0.458	0.431	0.422	0.39	0.422	0.408	0.405
Sum of Conventional coefficients	0.952 0.098	0.962 0.085	0.957 0.088	0.943 0.074	0.937 0.080	0.978 0.088	0.975 0.094

Notes and Source: See Table 4.1.

Equations linear in logarithms are estimated by the least squares. The standard errors of coefficients are in parentheses.

Table 4.3 **Accounting for Difference in Labor Productivity in Agriculture between Less Developed and Developed Countries**

	Group 1		*Group 2*		*Group 3*	
	(13 DCs)		*(9 DCs)*		*(4 DCs)*	
Difference in output per male worker-percent	88.8	(100)*	83.5	(100)	93.6	(100)
Percent of difference explained: Total	84.2	(95)	71.1	(85)	90.0	(96)
Resource accumulation:	29.2	(33)	17.5	(21)	32.6	(35)
Land	9.2	(10)	1.8	(2)	9.7	(10)
Livestock	20.0	(23)	15.7	(19)	22.9	(25)
Technical inputs:	24.3	(27)	24.3	(29)	24.5	(26)
Fertilizer	14.5	(16)	14.5	(17)	14.6	(16)
Machinery	9.8	(11)	9.8	(12)	9.9	(10)
Human capital:	30.7	(35)	29.4	(35)	32.9	(35)
General education	18.2	(21)	17.6	(21)	19.5	(21)
Technical education	12.5	(14)	11.7	(14)	13.4	(14)

*Inside of parentheses are percentages with output per worker set equal to 100.

LDCs: Brazil, Ceylon, Colombia, India, Mexico, Peru, Philippines, Syria, Taiwan, Turkey, UAR.

DCs: Australia, Belgium, Canada, Denmark, France, Germany, Netherlands, New Zealand, Norway, Sweden, Switzerland, UK, USA.

Group 1 includes all *DCs*;

Group 2 excludes Australia, Canada, New Zealand, and the United States from *DCs*;

Group 3 includes only the four *DCs* excluded from Group 2.

According formula:

$$\left(\frac{Y_d - Y_l}{Y_d}\right) = 0.10\left(\frac{a_d - a_l}{a_d}\right) + 0.25\left(\frac{s_d - s_l}{s_d}\right) + 0.15\left(\frac{f_d - f_l}{f_d}\right) + 0.10\left(\frac{m_d - m_l}{m_d}\right)$$

$$+ 0.40\left(\frac{E_d - E_l}{E_d}\right) + 0.15\left(\frac{U_d - U_l}{U_d}\right)$$

where *y, a, s, f, m,* are, respectively, output, land, livestock, fertilizer, machinery per male worker; *E* and *U* are, respectively, the general education (school enrollment ratio) and the technical education variable; lower case letter *d* denotes *DC* and *l* denotes *LDC*.

93.6 percent. The six variables included in the production function accounted for 95, 85, and 96 percent of the difference in agricultural output per worker between the LDCs and the three DCs groups.

In the comparison between the eleven LDCs and the thirteen DCs (group 1), each generalized category—internal resource accumulation (land and livestock), technical inputs from the industrial sector (fertilizer and machinery), and human capital (general and technical education in agriculture)—accounts for approximately one-third of the explained difference in labor productivity.

The main difference between group 1 and the other two groups is the amount of the difference explained by land. Difference in land accounts for only 2 percent of the difference in labor productivity between the LDCs and the older DCs, while it accounts for 19 percent between the LDCs and the new DCs. This implies that it should be feasible for the LDCs, even with the present land-labor ratios, to achieve levels of productivity per worker roughly equivalent to the labor productivity levels achieved by workers in the older DCs—that is, roughly four times as high as present LDC levels and well over half the level achieved by the DCs of recent settlement. The critical elements in achieving such increases in labor productivity are the supply of modern industrial inputs in which the new technology is embodied and the investment in general education and in research and extension which raises the capacity to develop and adopt a more productive technology. Comparison of group 2 and 3 results does indicate that resource endowments, particularly land, do represent a serious barrier to efforts of both the LDCs and the older DCs to achieve levels of output per worker comparable to the levels currently enjoyed in the more recently settled DCs. This is the first time, to our knowledge, that the economic advantage of the favorable resource endowments in these countries has been demonstrated quantitatively.

Individual Comparisons

The individual country comparisons presented in Table 4.4 were developed in order to provide somewhat deeper insight into the sources of differences in labor productivity between different "ideal type" DCs and LDCs and the United States. Each now compares the percentage difference in agricultural output per worker between each country and the United States with the linear combinations of percentage differences in input variables weighted by the specified production elasticities. Inside the parentheses is the index with the output-per-worker difference set equal to 100. In general, the results are consistent with the group comparisons.

In the four underdeveloped countries—India, the Philippines, the United Arab Republic, and Colombia—internal resource accumulation accounts for approximately one-third and technical inputs roughly one-fourth of the differences. Human capital accounts for more than one-third of the difference between the United States and India, the United Arab Republic, and Colombia. In the Philippines, which has achieved a relatively high level of schooling and produces a relatively large number of agricultural college graduates, human capital explains less than one-fourth of the productivity difference. The contrast between India and the Philippines in this respect is quite striking.

In the comparisons between the countries of Europe and the United States, differences in internal resource accumulation represent the most significant source of difference in labor productivity. The constraint of land on agricultural

Table 4.4 **Accounting for Labor Productivity Differences from the United States as Percent of U.S. Labor Productivity, 11 Selected Countries**

	Difference in output per worker from U.S. as percent of U.S.	Total	Percentage of difference explained by: Resource accumulation (land and livestock)	Technical iputs (fertilizer and machinery)	Human capital (general and technical education)
LDCs					
India	97.8	102.1	32.7	25.0	44.4
	(100)[a]	(104)	(33)	(26)	(45)
Philippines	96.2	82.1	33.4	24.9	23.8
	(100)	(85)	(34)	(26)	(25)
UAR	95.6	97.0	33.8	24.6	38.6
	(100)	(101)	(35)	(26)	(40)
Colombia	89.7	89.4	25.8	24.7	38.9
	(100)	(100)	(29)	(28)	(43)
Europe					
Denmark	52.3	51.0	20.4	13.2	17.4
	(100)	(97)	(39)	(25)	(33)
Netherland	56.6	51.7	25.0	15.0	11.7
	(100)	(91)	(44)	(26)	(21)
United Kingdom	55.8	50.2	18.2	13.4	18.6
	(100)	(90)	(33)	(24)	(33)
France	63.9	64.3	26.2	16.5	21.6
	(100)	(101)	(41)	(26)	(34)
Japan	89.2	66.0	34.1	22.4	9.5
	(100)	(74)	(38)	(25)	(11)
Pastoral farming					
Argentina	60.0	45.9	–4.8	24.3	26.4
	(100)	(76)	(–8)	(40)	(44)
New Zealand	–42.4	–49.1	–55.2	2.7	3.4
	(100)	(116)	(130)	(–6)	(–8)

[a] Inside of parentheses are percentages with output per worker differences set equal to 100.

productivity is relatively modest for the United Kingdom, which experienced the drastic agricultural transformation after the repeal of the Corn Laws; it is strongest for France, which preserved peasant farms by protective tariffs. Increases in the use of technical inputs and improvements in the quality of human capital can bring labor productivity of the several European countries closer to the U.S. level. Nevertheless, it seems apparent that major advances in labor productivity in European agriculture (especially in countries like France) toward the U.S. level are dependent on the absorption of a higher percentage of the agricultural labor force into the nonagricultural sector. The Japanese case is similar to the European, except that Japan, characterized by a stronger constraint of land, has moved further toward the exhaustion of productivity differentials associated with investment in education and research. In our judgment the model underestimates the significance of the land constraint in the Japanese case and, to a lesser degree, in the European case. Without a significant increase in land area per worker it would be impossible for Japanese agriculture to increase technical inputs (especially machinery) to the U.S. level.

The two pastoral farming cases are of particular interest. In spite of low levels of technical inputs, labor productivity in Argentina is roughly comparable to that in Europe. This is due almost entirely to a favorable man-land ratio comparable to that in the United States. Argentina has, as a result of underinvestment in technology and human capital, failed to fully exploit its favorable man-land ratio. New Zealand, in contrast, has achieved a level of labor productivity well above the U.S. level (the highest in the world) by complementing its favorable resource endowments with high levels of technical inputs and investment in education and research.

The results obtained in both group and individual comparisons are somewhat different than those obtained by Krueger (1968). Using a different methodology, Krueger found that human capital explained more than half the difference in income levels between the United States and a group of less developed countries. This is in contrast to our studies, in which human capital explains approximately one-third of the difference in labor productivity. Krueger's results apply to the entire economy and ours to only the agricultural sector. It seems reasonable to expect that resource endowments would be of relatively greater significance in the agricultural sector than in the total economy. We see, therefore, no inconsistency between our results and those obtained by Krueger. In general the consistency between the results presented in Tables 4.3 and 4.4, combined with our general knowledge of the economies being studied, strengthens our confidence in the methodology employed in this study.

4. Implications for Agricultural Development Strategy

The implications of this analysis for agricultural development strategy in the less developed countries have both encouraging and discouraging aspects. It is clear that output per worker in the several LDCs can be increased by several multiples, while land area per worker remains constant or even declines slightly. To achieve increases of this magnitude will require substantial investment (a) in rural education and (b) in the physical, biological, and social sciences. The latter is required for the technical and institutional infrastructure needed for the invention, development, and extension of a more efficient agricultural technology. It will also require the allocation of substantial resources to the production of the technical inputs supplied by the industrial sector, by which new technology is carried into agriculture. By and large, these changes achieve the higher levels of output per worker through increases in output per unit area.

A more discouraging aspect of this analysis is that in order to achieve levels of labor productivity comparable to the levels achieved in the DCs of recent origin, it will be necessary to complement those technical changes designed to increase output per unit area with technologies that reduce the labor input per unit area. Significant reduction in labor input per unit area is likely to occur, however, only in those economies in which urban-industrial development is sufficiently advanced not only to absorb the growth in the rural labor force but also to permit a continuous reduction in employment in rural areas (Dovring 1959). It should be noted that this has occurred in Japan only since World War II. In most LDCs it seems likely that the agricultural labor force will continue to expand more rapidly than the nonagricultural demand for labor from rural areas.

The implications for agricultural development strategy for most LDCs seem relatively clear. An attempt must be made to close the gap in the level of modern industrial inputs and in education and research. Agricultural surpluses generated by closing the gap, over and above the amount necessary to maintain the growth of agricultural productivity, must be used to finance industrial development.[15]

Maintenance of the rate of growth of agricultural productivity can be expected to impose a substantial drain on the savings that can be generated from the agricultural surpluses. Initially a substantial component of industrial capacity must be designed to provide technical inputs for the agricultural sector. Substantial investment will be needed to create the institutional infrastructure to improve general education in rural areas and to produce the technical and scientific manpower needed to bring about technical changes in agriculture. Investment in land development, such as irrigation and drainage, will also be necessary in a number of countries in order to obtain a full return from the new biological and chemical technology.

If successful, the effort would, over time, result in a rate of growth in the nonagricultural labor force sufficient to permit a reduction in the agricultural labor force and a rise in labor productivity toward the levels of the DCs of recent settlement. Clearly the process outlined here is inconsistent with the low-cost route to agricultural development that seemed to be opened up by the dual-economy models which have dominated much of the theoretical discussion of agricultural development during the last decade.

APPENDIX

A Test of Unitary Elasticity of Substitution

In the analysis in the text the production function was specified as being of the Cobb-Douglas type, thus assuming unitary elasticity of substitution among inputs. Here we attempt to test this assumption by estimating the parameters of the *CES* production function developed by Kenneth Arrow, Hollis Chenery, Bagicha Minhas, and Robert Solow (1961).

The basic models used for estimation are

$$log\,(Y/L) = a + b\,log\,W + c\,log\,Z$$

and

$$log\,(V/L) = a' + V\,log\,W + c'\,log\,Z$$

where Y and V are, respectively, gross output and value-added in agriculture; L is labor; W is the wage rate (measured by output); Z is the shorthand notation for nonconventional variables which shift the production function (general and technical education, in the case of this study). It is well known that under competitive factor markets b or b' measures the elasticity of substitution (between labor and the aggregate of other conventional inputs, including current inputs, in the case of b; or between labor and capital in the case of b'). Also, c or c' measures $k(l - b)$ where k is the exponential coefficient of Z, if Z is specified as a multiplicative shifter of the original CES production function (see articles by Arrow et al. [1961] and Hayami [1970]).

Therefore, in order to accept the hypothesis of unitary elasticity of substitution, (a) the estimated parameters of b and b' should not be significantly different from one, and (b) the estimated parameters of c and c' should not be significantly different from zero.

The results of estimation from the available data of twenty-two countries for 1960 (1957–62 averages) are summarized in Table 4.A. This analysis was conducted exclusively by the 1960 set of data because the value-added series were not available for 1955 and 1965. Availability of wage data limited the sample size to twenty-two. Finland, Norway, and Sweden were discarded from the sample in the value-added term analysis because of the implausible estimates of value-added for these three countries (see Hayami et al. 1970). Two sets of wage data were tried for estimation: current wage rate (W_t: 1957–62 averages) and lagged wage rate (W_{t-1}: 1952–56 averages).

The lagged wage rate was tried to determine whether the adjustment might not be instantaneous. The results are quite similar, however, because there is a high correlation between current wage and lagged wage. The Koyck-Nerlove type of distributed lag model was also tried. The results were implausible, however, probably because of high intercorrelation between the wage rate and the lagged dependent variables.

Both in gross output terms and in value-added terms the results of estimation are consistent with the unitary elasticity of substitution hypothesis: (a) the coefficients of wage rate are not significantly different from one and (b) the coefficients of shift variables, general and technical education, are not significantly different from zero at conventional significance levels. There is little evidence against the use of the Cobb-Douglas production function for the cross-country analysis of agricultural production. Such a conclusion seems consistent with the results derived from the cross-regional analysis of agricultural production in the United States by Griliches (1964) and in Japan by Hiromitsu Kaneda (1968), although their results are less conclusive, with some of the estimates of b being significantly different from one and some of the estimates of c significantly different from zero.

Table 4.A **Estimates of the Elasticity of Substitution Function on Cross-Country Data. 1957–62 Averages**

Regression number	*Dependent variable*	*Coefficients of:*						
		Wage		*General Education*				
		Current (1957–62 av.)	*Lagged (1952–56 av.)*	*Literacy ratio*	*Sch. Enrol. Ratio*	*Technical education*	*Coef. of det.*	*S.E. of estimate*
(A1)	Y/L	1.152 (0.094)					0.878	0.175
(A2)	Y/L		1.112 (0.145)				0.736	0.258
(A3)	Y/L	1.101 (0.159)		0.131 (0.331)			0.872	0.179
(A4)	Y/L	1.106 (0.151)			0.162 (0.408)		0.872	0.179
(A5)	Y/L	0.927 (0.196)		0.155 (0.322)		0.124 (0.085)	0.879	0.174
(A6)	Y/L	0.962 (0.180)			0.107 (0.400)	0.119 (0.086)	0.878	0.175
(A7)	V/L	1.047 (0.098)					0.864	0.171
(A8)	V/L		1.002 (0.149)				0.709	0.250
(A9)	V/L	1.039 (0.165)		0.018 (0.331)			0.855	0.176

(A10)	V/L	1.039 (0.165)		0.024 (0.411)		0.855	0.176
(A11)	V/L	0.886 (0.209)	0.050 (0.328)		0.102 (0.087)	0.858	0.174
(A12)	V/L	0.908 (0.194)	−0.006 (0.407)		0.101 (0.087)	0.858	0.175

Notes: Equations linear in logarithms are estimated by the least squares. The standard errors of coefficients are in parentheses.

Countries included in the sample are 22: Austria, Belgium, Canada, Ceylon, Denmark, Finland, France, Germany, India, Ireland, Japan, Mauritius, Mexico, New Zealand, Norway, Peru, Philippines, Portugal, Sweden, Turkey, United Kingdom and the United States. Finland, Norway, and Sweden are not included in the sample for the estimation of regressions A7-A12.

Definitions of variables are the same as in Table 4.1 except: *V*: Value-added in agriculture in thousand wheat units; Wage: Farm wage rate per day per male worker including board in *U.S.* dollars, converted from native currency by official exchange rates.

Source: Hayami and associates (1970).

Notes

Yujiro Hayami and Vernon W. Ruttan, *American Economics Review* 60 (December 1970): 895–911. The authors are indebted to Zvi Griliches, Richard Nelson, Willis Peterson, and Mathew Shane for suggestions and comments; and Miss Sachiko Yamashita and Mrs. Barbara Miller for computational assistance in the preparation of this paper. Minnesota Agricultural Experiment Station Miscellaneous Journal Series Paper No. 1387. The research on which this paper is based was financed through a grant from the Rockefeller Foundation.

1. J. R. Hicks (1968) has suggested that growth theory and development economics have no connection. This view would seem to be invalid in view of Hicks's own criteria. See Krueger 1968.
2. Countries included are Argentina, Austria, Australia, Belgium, Brazil, Canada, Ceylon, Chile, Colombia, Denmark, Finland, France, Germany, Greece, India, Ireland, Israel, Italy, Japan, Mauritius, Mexico, Netherlands, New Zealand, Norway, Peru, Philippines, South Africa, Spain, Surinam, Sweden, Switzerland, Syria, Taiwan, Turkey, the United Arab Republic, the United Kingdom, the United States, and Venezuela.
3. For a report on a preliminary attempt see Hayami 1969b, 1970. Major extensions from the previous study include: (a) a comprehensive revision of data; (b) introduction of the livestock variable; (c) analysis on a per farm basis in addition to a national aggregate basis; (d) test of stability of the production function over time; and (e) refinements in the procedures used to account for productivity differences.
4. The basic data were collected from publications by the United Nations (1960) organizations (FAO, ILO, and UNESCO), the Organization for Economic Cooperation and Development, and the governments of various countries. These data were processed by Hayami and associates (1970) to be consistent with the definitions of variables and, also, to be comparable among countries. Earlier estimates of agricultural outputs reported by Hayami and Inagi (1969) were substantially revised for this study.
5. Averages were taken for flow variables (output and fertilizer input). Stock variables were in principle measured by 1955, 1960, and 1965 levels. It would seem more consistent to have averages of 1953–57, 1958–62, and 1963–67, but the original estimates of agricultural output are of 1957–62 averages (see Hayami et al. 1970), and when we tried to extend the 1958–62 output series to 1955 and 1965, the FAO index of agricultural production was available only until 1966.
6. This procedure was applied for 1960 data. Output estimates for 1955 and 1965 were extrapolated from the 1960 estimates by using the FAO indexes of agricultural production by countries.
7. Perennial plants belong to the same category of inputs as livestock, but they are not included due to the lack of data.
8. In a sense this variable may be superior as the proxy for the level of research and extension to the "state average of public expenditure on research and extension per farm" used by Griliches (1964), because our variable reflects the research and extension activities in the private sector as well as in the public sector.
9. In the short run, in which substitution between capital and labor is circumscribed by the rigidity of existing capital and equipment, production relationships are best described by an activity with relatively fixed factor-factor and factor-product ratios. In the long run, in which the constraints exercised by existing capital disappear and are replaced by the fund of available technical knowledge, including all alternative feasible factor-factor and factor-product combinations, production relationships can be adequately described by the neoclassical production function. In the secular period of production, in which the constraints given by the available fund of technical knowledge are further relaxed to admit all potentially discoverable knowledge, production relationships can be described by a metaproduction function which describes all potentially discoverable technical alternatives. The metaproduction function can be regarded as the envelope of neoclassical production functions. Although the term is not employed, the metaproduction function concept is implicit in the work of Brown (1966) and of Salter (1960).

We have discussed the rationale for the metaproduction function concept in Japanese and U.S. agricultural development in greater detail elsewhere (see Hayami and Ruttan 1970a). The elasticity of substitution among factors increases continuously as the time period increases from the short run to the secular period.

10. In order to test the assumption that farmers in different countries face the same production function, the production function was estimated separately for the two different groups of countries (DCs and LDCs). The estimation was tried for various groupings of DCs and LDCs, but the results are all implausible, with most of the coefficients statistically nonsignificant or negative in sign. It seems that measurement errors in our observations (especially of nonconventional variables) are too large to make it possible to estimate the influences of variables for the groups of countries within which the ranges of data variations are relatively small. The basic assumption is therefore not testable on the presently available data. All we can claim is that differences in agricultural productivity among countries can be explained well with this assumption.
11. The *1960 World Census of Agriculture* provides the data of the number of farms for a large number of countries. Comparable data are available for only a small number of countries for 1955 and 1965. See also note 9.
12. Surinam was dropped from the sample except in regressions 1 and 6 because of the lack of technical education data.
13. This does not necessarily mean that such variables have no significant influence, but rather that the presently available data are too crude to estimate the influences of such variables.
14. The F-statistics calculated for testing the equality of the labor and education coefficients are 0.22 for regression 2 vs. regression 4; 0.31 for regression 3 vs. regression 5; 0.65 for regression 7 vs. regression 9; and 0 77 for regression 8 vs. regression 10.
15. Shigeru Ishikawa (1967) has suggested that achievement of national agricultural output and productivity objectives may, in some developing countries, require a net flow of savings from the nonagricultural to the agricultural sector. The possibility has been such a shock to some students of development economics that they recommend a "development without agriculture" policy (e.g., Flanders 1968).

PART

III

TECHNICAL CHANGE AND AGRICULTURAL DEVELOPMENT IN ASIA

CHAPTER 5

Korean Rice, Taiwan Rice, and Japanese Agricultural Stagnation

AN ECONOMIC CONSEQUENCE OF COLONIALISM

Yujiro Hayami and Vernon W. Ruttan

The impact of colonial development, or exploitation, on metropolitan or mother country economic growth remains a major unresolved issue in economic history and development economics. Conventional wisdom seems to assume a world in which agricultural and raw material surpluses of colonial areas are used to fuel metropolitan industrial development.[1]

This paper analyzes the impact of the very successful Japanese colonial development efforts in Korea and Taiwan on economic growth in Japan.[2] The results of our analysis suggest that the imports of rice from the two colonial areas to Japan as the result of colonial agricultural development were, to a substantial degree, responsible for the stagnation of Japanese agriculture during the interwar years, though they contributed to industrial growth by keeping the industrial wage low and the return to capital high without causing a serious drain on foreign exchange. The increased supply of colonial rice did not produce an agricultural transformation comparable to that of nineteenth-century England, but it produced agricultural stagnation and low farm income, which were to a large extent responsible for the general economic and political instability of the interwar period.

Following our analysis of the Japanese colonial experience, we suggest several hypotheses that should be considered in accounting for the difference between the Japanese and English colonial experience. We also discuss the implications of the Japanese experience for today's developing nations in Asia and other regions in connection with a massive agricultural technology transfer, the so-called Green Revolution.

The analysis is based on time-series data for the period 1890–1937. We deliberately chose 1890 as the starting year, because the data before 1890 are much less reliable, despite the recent attempts to correct official statistics in *The Long-Term*

Economic Statistics of Japan since 1868 (abbreviated as *LTES*; Ohkawa et al. 1965–67). Even the data after 1890 are subject to the criticism raised by J. I. Nakamura (1966).[3] Although the issue has not yet been settled, we resorted to *LTES* official statistics, since those are the only data that can be used for the kind of analysis we made. We feel that the adequacy of the data should be checked not only in terms of the deliberate text critique of original documents, but also in terms of the plausibility of the results of an analysis that uses the data in question.

1. Empirical Observation and Hypothesis

The rate of output and productivity growth in Japanese agriculture varied widely during the one hundred years of "modernization" following the start of the Meiji period (1868–1911). Four main periods, sometimes referred to as "technical epochs," are frequently identified (Table 5.1). The first was a period of rapid growth in output and productivity that ended prior to 1920. It was followed by a period of slower economic growth during the 1920s and 1930s. The third "epoch" was the period of decline and recovery associated with World War II. A fourth period of explosive growth in productivity began in the late 1940s or early 1950s.[4] Output and productivity trends, both for rice and for the total agricultural sector, appear to have followed the same general pattern, reflecting the dominant role of rice in the agricultural economy.

The two decades of agricultural stagnation that followed the rapid growth in agricultural output and productivity prior to World War I have been a major puzzle in the history of Japanese economic development.[5] It has been asserted by Japanese scholars that imports of rice from Taiwan and Korea, stimulated by the transfer of Japanese production technology to the two colonial areas, depressed rice prices and dampened the growth of productivity and farm incomes in metropolitan Japan.[6] An alternative hypothesis has also been suggested: that the potential of the Meiji period biological technology had been exhausted, and that the new biological technology, which has been so important in fueling Japanese agricultural growth during the last two decades, was not available in the interwar period (Evenson et al. 1969).[7]

The sharp changes in the rate of agricultural output and productivity growth following World War I are clearly reflected in the various indicators of rice production, productivity, and price in Table 5.2. From 1890 to 1920, the area planted in rice and the yield per hectare planted grew, respectively, by 0.44 and 0.94 percent per year. Total production increased by 1.38 percent per year. In contrast, the growth rates declined to 0.16 for area, 0.24 for yield, and 0.40 for production between 1920 and 1935.

Growth in production and productivity between 1890 and 1920 was accompanied by an increase in the price of rice from 42 yen per metric ton in 1890 to 242 yen in 1920, an annual compound rate of growth of about 6 percent. The internal

Table 5.1 **Annual Percentage Growth Rates of Output, Inputs, and Productivity in Japanese Agriculture in Four Periods**

	Phase I (1882–1917)	*Phase II (1917–1937)*	*Phase III (1937–1947)*	*Phase IV (1947–1957)*
	percent per year			
Output				
Gross	1.78	0.80	-2.79	4.51
Net	1.37	0.69	-1.78	2.14
Conventional inputs				
Total inputs	0.28	0.28	-0.03	1.41
Labor	0.20	0.01	1.83	-1.36
Fixed capital				
including building	0.43	0.52	-0.46	1.70
excluding building	1.66	1.24	-1.44	3.62
Variable inputs	2.93	1.15	-6.76	12.02
Land acreage total	0.60	0.15	-0.54	0.35
Paddy field	0.27	0.34	-0.43	0.31
Upland field	1.02	0.05	-0.67	0.39
Productivity per unit of-				
Conventional inputs	1.49	0.49	-2.77	3.05
Labor	1.86	0.81	-4.54	5.84
Fixed capital -				
including building	1.34	0.27	-2.35	2.76
excluding building	0.11	-0.44	-1.37	0.85
Variable inputs	-1.12	-0.45	4.25	-6.71
Land	1.17	0.64	-2.27	4.14

Source: Calculated from data in Tables 5.1 and 5.2 of Saburo Yamada (1967).

terms of trade, as measured by the rice price deflated by the general price index, were favorable for agriculture immediately after 1890 and were relatively stable between 1895 and 1915. The fact that the internal terms of trade remained stable, without an appreciable increase in rice imports, for 1900–1915 indicates a relative balance in the growth of agriculture and industry, in the Ohkawa-Rosovsky sense, during the "big spurt" period of industrialization in Japan from the Russo-Japanese War (1904–5) to World War I (Ohkawa and Rosovsky 1960).

Table 5.2 **Area, Yield, Production, Price, and Seed Improvement Indexes for Rice in Japan, 1890–1935**[a]

Year	*Area planted A*	*Yield per unit area Y = Z/A*	*Production Z*	*Price P = V/Z*	*Farm value of production V*	*General price index I*	*Deflated price P/I*	*Deflated value production V/I*	*Seed improvement index S*
	(1000 ha.)	*(m. ton/ha.)*	*(1000 m. ton)*	*(yen/m.ton)*	*(mil.yen)*	*(1934–36 =100)*	*(yen/m.ton)*	*(mil.yen)*	*(1890=100)*
1890	2717	2.16	5861	42	243	31.7	131	767	100.0
1895	2752	2.05	5651	57	323	35.8	160	902	100.8
1900	2813	2.27	6372	79	501	47.4	166	1057	101.6
1905	2862	2.43	6943	91	633	55.7	164	1136	104.3
1910	2933	2.59	7588	104	790	60.3	173	1310	105.1
1915	3029	2.74	8286	106	882	66.4	160	1328	105.8
1920	3094	2.86	8838	242	2140	131.3	184	1630	106.2
1925	3129	2.78	8700	224	1944	128.3	174	1515	105.8
1930	3203	2.83	9070	143	1297	104.5	137	1241	105.8
1935	3169	2.97	9414	179	1673	101.9	174	1642	107.4
Year Annual compound rate of growth (percent)									
1890–1920	0.44	0.94	1.38	6.09	7.47	4.95	1.14	2.52	0.20
1920–1935	0.16	0.24	0.40	–2.05	–1.65	–1.70	–0.35	0.05	0.07

Sources: A—Ministry of Agriculture and Forestry, *Norinsho Ruimento-keihyo* (Historical Statistics of Ministry of Agriculture and Forestry; Tokyo, 1955): 24. Z—Ohkawa et al. vol. 9 (1966): 166–68. V—Ohkawa et al., vol. 9 (1966): 146–47. I—Ohkawa et al., vol. 8 (1967): 134, Series 1, Table 1. S—Hayami and Yamada (1969).

a. Five years' averages centering the years shown. Rice in brown (husked but not polished) rice basis.

Farmers' real income from rice, measured as the total value of rice production at the farm deflated by the general price index, went up rapidly, mainly as a result of growth in physical production.

The Japanese economy experienced a sharp inflation during World War I. The wholesale price index in Tokyo more than doubled between 1913 and 1919. Rice prices rose to their highest level relative to the consumer price index in 1913 and to their highest absolute level in 1919.

Stagnation of production and productivity coincided with the decline in the price of rice after 1919. The terms of trade continued to deteriorate and real income from rice to fall. This trend continued until the catastrophe of Nogyo Kyoko (agricultural depression) in 1929–32. What were the factors that accounted for such an epochal change—from rapid development until approximately 1920 to the stagnation during the interwar period? The emergence of the stagnation phase can be ascribed partly to an unfavorable shift in the demand for agricultural products, especially such staple foods as rice. The demand for food as well as for other consumer goods declined as a result of the decline in consumer income, which in turn resulted from the deflation policy Japan adopted in order to return to the gold standard at the prewar parity. There is also evidence that the income elasticity of demand for rice and staple foods declined as a result of urbanization and of changes in the occupational distribution of the labor force (see the summary by Kaneda [1969]). Labor's share of income tended to decline (see Table 4 and Table 7 in Umemura 1961). Such factors should have worked to slow down the shift of the demand schedule to the right. We hypothesize, however, that events of greater magnitude, such as the exhaustion of technological potential or the importation of colonial rice, must be sought to explain changes of the magnitude observed between the two periods.

The process of exploitation and exhaustion of technological potential between the Meiji Restoration and 1920 has been analyzed elsewhere and will only be summarized briefly here (Hayami and Yamada 1968). The real key to the success of Japanese agricultural growth prior to World War I rests on the nationwide diffusion of the stock of improved techniques, which had previously been partially blocked by feudal barriers, following the breakdown of feudalism at the time of the Meiji Restoration. Before the Restoration such techniques as high-yielding varieties of seeds or better seedling preparation were, though discovered, restricted to small localities due to the lack of communication facilities and the regulations of Han (territory of the feudal lord) and the villages. With the reforms of Meiji, farmers were no longer bound to the land. Moreover, they were free to choose their own crops and methods of farming. The exchange of seeds and technical information between regions was encouraged by the government. The nationwide diffusion of better techniques brought a rapid rise in yield per hectare—the fruit of Rono Gijutsu (veteran farmers' technique), which was primarily oriented toward achieving increased land productivity, with an adequate supply of fertilizer and the irrigation networks inherited from the feudal Han system.

The diffusion of Rono Gijutsu thus brought about a rise in yield and production, but it caused the exhaustion of the initial backlog of technology, in the absence of an adequate flow of new technology. It is true that national and prefectural experiment stations were established before agriculture entered the stagnation phase and that they did have some impact on the supply of new technology. But it would be fair to say that the organized research in experiment stations in those days contributed to the growth of agricultural productivity by exploiting the traditional potential through testing, selecting, and advocating the Rono techniques, rather than by adding new potential.[8]

The exploitation and the consequent exhaustion of the technological backlog can best be visualized by the rapid increase in the percentage of area planted in Rono varieties (rice varieties selected by veteran farmers) for 1895–1915 and the saturation in the subsequent period (Figure 5.1). The seed improvement index in Table 5.2 was calculated in an attempt to quantify the influence of the diffusion of improved seeds on the national average yield. This index is based on the weighted averages of the areas planted in the respective varieties, using as weights the standard yields of various varieties. The standard yields, which are fixed by regions, were based on the reports of comparative yield tests at various experiment stations. The annual growth rate of this index declined drastically from 1890–1920 to 1920–1935, reflecting the saturation in the spread of improved varieties.

The exhaustion of the traditional technological potential and the consequent deceleration of growth in rice yields seem to have coincided with the increase in

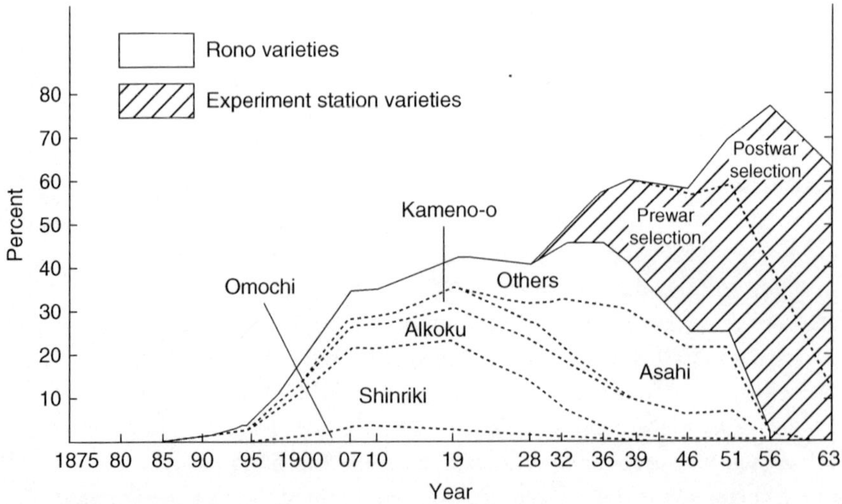

Figure 5.1 Percentages of Area Planted of Major Improved Varieties in the Total Area planted of Rice, All Perfectures. Source: Hayami and Yamada (1968), Appendix Table 5A: 159–60.

demand due to the boom of World War I. This forced the rice price to rise to an unprecedented level. The impact of inflation on the price of rice caused serious disruption in urban areas and culminated in the Kome Sodo (rice riot) of 1918.

The reaction of the government to the rice riot was to organize programs to import rice from the overseas territories of Korea and Taiwan. In order to create a rice surplus to export to Japan, short-run exploitation policies involved importing sorghum (milo) from Manchuria to Korea, forcing Korean farmers to substitute this lower-quality grain for rice in domestic consumption. A similar squeeze was practiced in Taiwan, forcing Taiwanese farmers to substitute sweet potatoes for rice in their diet. This policy was enforced by a squeeze on real income through taxation and government monopoly sales of such commodities as liquor, tobacco, and salt. The longer-run program was to introduce development programs designed to increase the yield and output of rice in those colonial territories. Under the program, titled Sanmai Zoshoku Keikaku (Rice Production Development Program), the Japanese government invested in irrigation and water control and in research and extension in order to develop and diffuse high-yielding Japanese rice varieties adapted to the local ecology of Korea and Taiwan.[9] The success of this effort created the tremendous rice surplus that flooded the Japanese market. As shown in Table 5.3, in the twenty years from 1915 to 1935 net imports of rice from Korea to Japan rose from 170 to 1,212 thousand metric tons per year, and net imports from Taiwan rose from 3 to 705 thousand metric tons. As a result of the inflow of colonial rice, the net import of rice rose from 5 to 20 percent of the domestic production.[10]

The success of the government program in developing Korea and Taiwan as major suppliers of rice to Japan should have had a major impact on rice prices and production in Japan. Such large-scale imports of rice, a commodity characterized by a relatively inelastic demand schedule, could be expected to lower the price and discourage the production of rice in Japan. A deterioration in the price and in the terms of trade for rice during this period would appear to be a logical consequence of the policies designed to increase imports from Korea and Taiwan.

Both the motivation and the consequences of the colonial rice development program are illustrated in Figure 5.2, which compares the trends of rice production and yield per hectare in Japan, Taiwan, and Korea.[11] Both production and yield per hectare in Korea and Taiwan began to take off in the 1920s, when growth decelerated in Japan. This seems to reflect the process we have discussed so far: (a) the Japanese government launched the colonial rice development program when pressed by the food problem arising from the exhaustion of technological potential in Japanese agriculture and the increase in demand for food from a growing nonagricultural population; (b) the success of the program in raising rice production and productivity in the two colonies permitted large-scale imports of rice from these territories, which in turn depressed the price and further discouraged the production of rice in Japan.

Table 5.3 **Production, Import, and Available Supply of Rice in Japan, 1890–1935**[a]

			Net import				Net import		
Year	*Supply Q = Z+K*	*Production Z*	*Total K*	*Korea K_k*	*Taiwan K_f*	*Production*	*Total k = K/Z*	*Korea $k_k = K_k/Z$*	*Taiwan $kf = K_f/Z$*
		(1000 m. tons)					percent		
1890	5813	5861	–48	–	–	100	–0.8	–	–
1895	5700	5651	49	–	–	100	0.9	–	–
1900	6578	6372	206	–	–	100	3.2	–	–
1905	7539	6943	596	–	–	100	8.6	–	–
1910	7923	7588	335	–	–	100	4.4	–	–
1915	8692	8286	406	170	113	100	4.9	2.1	1.4
1920	9720	8838	882	360	132	100	10.0	4.1	1.5
1925	10043	8700	1343	640	278	100	15.4	7.3	3.2
1930	10483	9070	1413	974	389	100	15.6	10.7	4.3
1935	11290	9414	1876	1212	705	100	19.9	12.9	7.5

Sources: *Z*—Ohkawa et al., Vol. 9 (1966), :166–68 ; *K*—Ohkawa et al., Vol. 6 (1967),: 150–52 ; K_k and K_f,—Bureau of Statistics Office of the Prime Minister, *Japan Statistical Yearbook* (1949).

a. Five years' averages centering the years shown. Rice in brown (husked but not polished) rice basis.

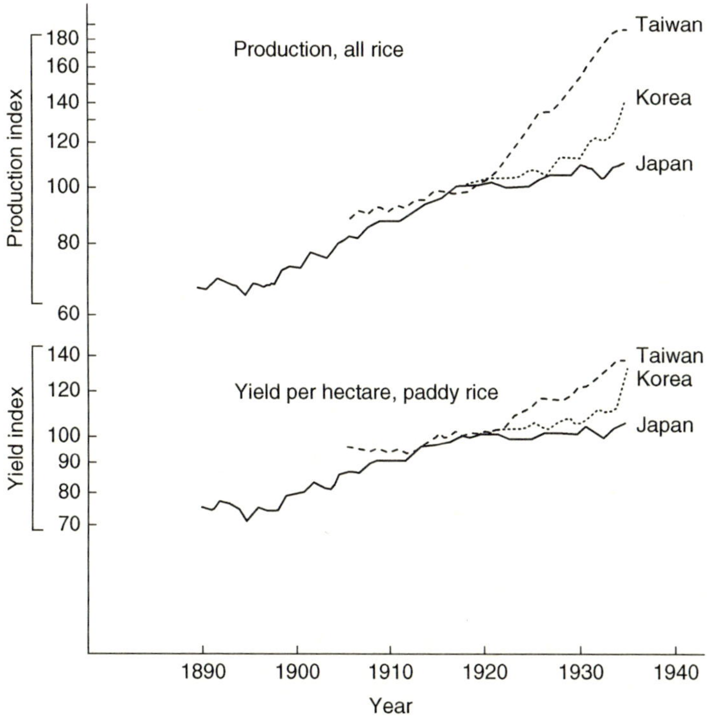

Figure 5.2 Indices of Total Production and Yield per Hectare of Rice, Japan, Korea, and Taiwan, Five-Year Moving Averages (1917–1922 = 100). Sources: Japan—Ohkawa et al., vol. 9 (1966): 166–67; *Norinsho Ruinen Tokeihyo* (Historical Statistics of Ministry of Agriculture and Forestry; Tokyo, 1945): 24. Korea—*Chosen Sotokutu Tokeihyo* (Statistical Yearbook of Government General of Korea), 1925 issue (p. 94), 1930 issue (p. 92). Taiwan—Joint Commission on Rural Reconstruction, *Taiwan Agricultural Statistic* (Taipei, 1966) : 23–27.

The data reviewed in this section appear to support the hypothesis that (a) the slowdown of technological progress, reflected in the slower rise in the seed improvement index, and (b) the increase in imports of rice from Korea and Taiwan were the two major factors underlying the epochal turn in the growth trend of rice production in Japan following World War I.[12] In the next section we attempt to assess the quantitative significance of these two factors.

2. Quantitative Analysis

In order to assess the relative influences of the two major causes, identified in the last section, of the epochal turn in the Japanese rice economy, we present two hypothetical or "counterfactual" calculations to illustrate how production and price could have changed after 1920. In Case 1 we assume that the ratio of net imports of rice to domestic production remained the same as in 1913–17. In Case 2 we assume, in addition to the constant import ratio, that the seed improvement index continued to grow at the 1890–1920 rate.

MODEL

The basic model for such calculations is the equilibrium of demand and supply. We will use the notation for the actual values of variables as specified in Tables 5.2 and 5.3, and identify the hypothetical values with a prime (').

Since the actual total supply of rice, Q, can be considered identical to total demand, the equilibrium of demand and supply can be written as

$$Q = (1+k)Z \tag{1}$$

where Q is total consumption, Z is domestic production, and k is the ratio of net import (and inventory change) to production. We assume that the above equilibrium relation holds at some actual price, P, and that an equilibrium level of consumption, imports, and production could be specified at some hypothetical price, P', as

$$Q' = (1+k')Z' \tag{2}$$

If we assume a typical constant elasticity demand function as

$$Q = Q_0 P^{\eta} \tag{3}$$

where income and other demand shifters are included in Q_0, the relation between Q and Q' is

$$Q' = Q\left(\frac{P'}{P}\right)^{\eta} \tag{4}$$

when η is the price elasticity of demand for rice. If we assume a constant elasticity supply function as

$$Z = Z_0 P^{\gamma} S^{\delta} \tag{5}$$

where supply shifters other than S are included in Z_0. The relation between Z and Z' is

$$Z = Z\left(\frac{P'}{P}\right)^{\gamma}\left(\frac{S'}{S}\right)^{\delta} \tag{6}$$

where γ is the price elasticity of supply, S is the seed improvement index, and δ is the elasticity of supply with respect to the seed improvement index. Since the following identity holds,

$$Z = A\,Y \tag{7}$$

where A is the area planted (in hectares) and Y is the yield per hectare (in metric tons). If we assume an area response function as

$$A = A_0 P^{\alpha} \tag{8}$$

and a yield response function as

$$Y = Y_0 P^{\beta} S^{\delta} \tag{9}$$

where α and β are, respectively, the elasticities of area response and yield response ($\gamma = \alpha + \beta$ and $Z_0 = A_0 Y_0$), the relations between A *and* A' and Y and Y' are

$$A' = A\left(\frac{P'}{P}\right)^{\alpha} \tag{10}$$

$$Y' = Y\left(\frac{P'}{P}\right)^{\beta}\left(\frac{S'}{S}\right)^{\delta} \tag{11}$$

Replacing equations (4) and (6) for Q and Z in equation (2), we have

$$Q\left(\frac{P'}{P}\right)^{\eta} = (1+k')Z\left(\frac{P'}{P}\right)^{\gamma}\left(\frac{S'}{S}\right)^{\delta} \tag{12}$$

From equations (1) and (12) we obtain the formula used to calculate the equilibrium price of rice in Japan under the hypothesized conditions:

$$P' = P\left(\frac{1+k'}{1+k}\right)^{\frac{1}{\eta-\gamma}}\left(\frac{S'}{S}\right)^{\frac{\delta}{\eta-\gamma}} \tag{13}$$

The hypothetical area, yield, and production can be calculated with P' by equations (10), (11), and (7), respectively.

ESTIMATION OF PARAMETERS

The problem now is to obtain empirical estimates of five parameters: the elasticity of area response to price (β), the elasticity of yield response to price (α), the elasticity of supply with respect to price (γ), the elasticity of supply with respect to the seed improvement index (δ), and the price elasticity of demand for rice (η).

The estimate of the price elasticity of demand (η) is available from Ohkawa's classical study on the food economy of prewar Japan (Ohkawa 1945). His estimates of the price elasticity of demand for rice were based on household survey data of 1931/32–1938/39 for the urban population, and on 1920–1938 market data for the rural population. Those estimates differ for different occupational, regional, and income groups, but cluster around the mode –0.2. We will adopt –0.2 as the elasticity of demand with respect to price (η), since this figure is also consistent with the various estimates of income elasticity of demand for rice.

The supply parameters represent our own estimates. Apparently no study of supply response of rice has been conducted in Japan. We chose to estimate area response and yield response separately and to obtain aggregate supply elasticity by adding the area and yield elasticities. An important consideration in using this approach is the difference in the time lag required to make adjustments in response to price changes between the area and yield responses. The yield response is essentially a short-run phenomenon, depending primarily on the time it takes to adjust various inputs, such as fertilizer, to a change in price. Area response involves a long-run adjustment period. In Japan, the area planted in upland rice is negligible (less than 5 percent of the total area planted in rice), and no competitive crop exists for rice on paddy land during the summer crop season. Therefore, the area planted in rice is almost completely determined by the available paddy field area. It requires substantial investment to expand the paddy field area (for example, by shifting upland crop fields to paddy fields), because such a change in land use must be accompanied by an extension of the irrigation system. Because of the large capital involved in paddy field development, the short-run response in the area planted in rice to a change in price is limited. The longer-run response may, however, be substantial. Because of the significance of lags in the response of area to price, we employ a distributed lag model of the Koyck-Nerlove type for the analysis of area response. The basic model used is

$$a_t{}^* = \alpha_0 + P_{t-1} + \alpha_0 P_{0(t-1)} \tag{14}$$

and

$$a_t - a_{t-1} = \lambda(a_t{}^* - a_{t-1}) \tag{15}$$

where a_t, p_t, and p_o are the logarithmic transformations of area planted in rice, rice price, and the price of competitive crops, respectively, and *at** is the long-run equilibrium area (in logarithm) for certain levels of p_t and p_{ct}. Equations (10) and (11) reduce to

$$a_t = \lambda\alpha_0 + \lambda\alpha P_{t-1} + \lambda\alpha_c P_{c(t-1)} + (1-\lambda)a_{t-1} \tag{16}$$

which we will use for regression analysis.[13] The prices of rice employed in the models estimated were deflated by the general price index, which to some extent reflects the changes in the cost of opening new paddy fields. An important variable lacking in our model is public investment in riparian and irrigation works.

We assume that such government investment is induced in the long run by price trends, and in that sense, it is incorporated into our distributed lag models.[14]

The yield response model is specified as

$$y_t = \beta_0 + \beta P_t + \delta s_t \tag{17}$$

where y_t, p_t, and s_t are the logarithmic transformations of rice yield per hectare, the rice price, and the seed improvement index, respectively. For purposes of estimation we deflated the rice price by the fertilizer price index in order to reflect the changes in the price of the major current input item.

The results obtained from estimating equations (16) and (17) by least squares are summarized in Table 5.4. In area response the coefficients of the price of competitive products were nonsignificant, and the estimation was repeated after dropping that variable. The estimates of the response of rice area with respect to the price of rice are significant at or near the 5 percent level. The magnitudes of the price coefficients are small and the coefficients of the lagged independent variable are close to one, indicating that the short-run response to price in area planted in rice is very small, but the long-run response is relatively large. This was the expected result, considering the long time required to adjust the paddy field area. The long-run elasticity, allowing infinite time adjustment, is in the order of 0.4–0.6. Such estimates are not incompatible with the results of estimation of area response elasticity in other Asian countries (Krishna 1967; Managahas et al. 1966).

The price coefficients in the yield response regressions are positive and significant at or near the 5 percent level. The seed improvement index variable is also highly significant. The price coefficients, especially in the case of (Y – 1), are very consistent with the results obtained in an earlier study of fertilizer demand by Hayami (1968b). In that study, the estimates of the elasticity of demand for fertilizer with respect to the price of fertilizer relative to the price of farm products center around 1.5, and the estimates of the production elasticity of fertilizer for rice center around 0.15. When one considers that the ratio of rice production to total agricultural production in value terms is about 0.55, those estimates imply that the price elasticity of rice yield response to rice price is around 0.12 ($= 1.5 \times 0.15 \times 0.55$), which is compatible with the results of direct estimation in Table 5.3.

From the results of the estimation of the yield response relation, we decided to adopt a yield response elasticity (β) of 0.1 and a seed improvement elasticity (δ) of 3.0. The problem of deciding on an appropriate area response parameter (α) from the results of estimation of the distributed lag area response model is more difficult. The model provides us with a short-run elasticity (allowing a one-year adjustment period) and a long-run elasticity (allowing an infinite adjustment period), neither of which is adequate for our purpose. The span of time that we are concerned with is the twenty years from 1915 to 1935. We chose ten years as the

Table 5.4 **Least Squares Estimates of Area and Yield Response of Rice Production to Price Based on 1890–1937 Annual Time Series Data**[a]

							Long-run price elasticity	
Regression Number	*Equations estimated*			*Coeff. of determination (adjusted)*	*Standard error of estimate (adjusted)*	*Durbin-Watson statistics*	*Infinite time adjustment*[a]	*Ten years adjustment*[b]
	Area response							
A–1	a_t=0.0529+0.0083 $P_{1(t-1)}$ (0.0691)	+0.0034 $P_{c(t-1)}$ (0.0107)	+0.9833 a_{t-1} (0.0223)	0.9872	0.00654	2.35	0.497	0.071
A–2	a_t =0.0691+0.0092 $P_{1(t-1)}$ (0.0058)		+0.9785 a_{t-1} (0.0163)	0.9874	0.00641	2.34	0.428	0.077
A–3	a_t =0.0719+0.0138 $P_{2(t-1)}$ (0.0076)	+0.0026 $P_{c(t-1)}$ (0.0101)	+0.9787 a_{t-1} (0.0219)	0.9876	0.00643	2.39	0.648	0.113
A–4	a_t =0.0848+0.0083 $P_{2(t-1)}$ (0.0070)		+0.9749 a_{t-1} (0.0162)	0.9878	0.00273	2.39	0.598	0.122
	Yield response							
Y–1	Y_t=–6.6713+0.1287P_{st} (0.0626)	+2.8219 s_t (1.1903)		0.6356	0.08731	2.28	–	–
Y–2	Y_t=–8.0034+0.0673P_{st} (0.0395)	+4.2887 s_t (0.8052)		0.7490	0.03112	2.18	–	–

Y–3	$Y_t = -6.6695+0.0911P_{st}$	$+3.5058\, s_t$	0.6199	0.03872	2.32	–	–
	(0.0615)	(1.1485)					
Y–4	$Y_t = -14.6023+0.0831P_{st}$	$+3.6244\, s_t$	0.6173	0.08346	2.34	–	–
	(0.0606)	(1.1672)					

Sources: Same as Table 5.1 except the following: Wholesale prices of rice (monthly prices at Fukagawa Rice Market in Tokyo)—
Nobufumi Kayo (1958). Fertilizer price index—Ohkawa et al., Vol. 9 (1966): 192–93. Price index of farm products except rice-price indexes by major commodity groups in Ohkawa et al., Vol. 8 (1967): 168–70; aggregated with 1934–1936 value weights, ibid.: 78.

a. "Variables are a_t = log A_t: area planted in rice (1000 ha.); y_t = log Y_t: rice yield per hectare planted (m. ton); p_1 = log (P/J): unit farm price of rice deflated by general price index (yen per m. ton); p_2 = log of calendar year average of wholesale price of rice deflated by general price index (yen per m. ton); p_3 = log of unit farm price of rice of previous year deflated by fertiliser price index of current year (yen per m. ton); p_4 = log of calendar year average of wholesale price of rice of previous year deflated by fertilizer price index of current year (yen per m. ton); p_5 = log of rice year (November of previous year to October of current year) average of rice deflated by fertilizer price index of current year (yen per m. ton); p_6 = log of January-July average of wholesale price of rice deflated by fertilizer price index of current year (yen per m. ton); p_c = log of price index of farm products except rice deflated by general price index; s = log of S: seed improvement index.

a. (Coefficient of p_{t-1}) ÷ (coefficient of a_{t-1}).

b. (Coefficient of p_{t-1}) x [1–(coefficient of a_{t-1})^9] ÷ (coefficient of a_{t-1}).

average adjustment period and selected an area response elasticity (α) of 0.1, based on the range of results shown in the last column of Table 5.3. It should be recognized that this is a convention adopted for computation ease. It has some intuitive appeal but little theoretical justification. The results of applying the specified parameters to the previous model are summarized in Table 5.5.

3. Findings and Implications

The results in Table 5.5 are plotted in Figures 5.3 and 5.4 in order to make comparisons between the actual and hypothetical growth paths of Japanese rice economy.

Figure 5.3 shows that the decline in the rate of growth in the seed improvement index and the increase in the imports of colonial rice explain most of the decline in the rate of growth in rice yield and production during the interwar period. The rates of growth in hypothetical yield and production declined slightly from 1890–1920 to 1920–35, but it is unlikely that anything resembling the "epochal" change in the rate of growth of actual rice production would have occurred if imports had been held at the 1913–17 level relative to production, and if the seed improvement index had continued to rise at the 1890–1920 rate (Case 2). The slight decline in the growth rates even in Case 2 could be accounted for by the structural changes affecting the demand for rice mentioned in Section 1. Neither is it necessary to invoke underestimation in rice production statistics in the earlier period, as claimed by Nakamura, nor to invoke failure of industrial capacity to produce inputs, as suggested by Rosovsky, to explain the decline in the rate of growth in rice production during the interwar period. It is also clear that imports of rice from the colonial areas (Case 1) is not, by itself, an adequate explanation for the decline in the rate of growth of rice production in the interwar period. The "technology gap" between the exploitation of the yield gains from the diffusion of the superior varieties of farmers' selections and the introduction of the new experiment station varieties also exerted a significant impact on dampening the rate of growth of rice production in Japan during the interwar period.

The influence of the rice imports did exert a sizable impact on rice prices and on the incomes of rice producers in Japan. Under the assumption of Case 1, production went up less rapidly than during 1890–1920, while the internal terms of trade for rice improved and the real income of farmers from rice rose after 1920 as rapidly as before 1920. Even in Case 2, where imports are held at the 1913–17 ratio and yield technology represented by seed improvement is assumed to continue at the earlier rate, the terms of trade improved gradually, except during the depression, and the real incomes of rice producers rose significantly over the period 1920–35, in contrast to almost no change under the condition that actually prevailed.

Table 5.5 **Actual and Hypothetical Paths of Growth of Area, Yield, Production, and Price of Rice in Japan, 1920–1935**[a]

Year	Area planted A	Yield per unit area Y	Production Z	Price P	Farm value of production V	Price deflated by general price index P/I	Value production deflated by general price index V/I
	(1000 ha.)	(m. ton/ ha.)	(1000 m. ton)	(yen/m. ton)	(mil.yen)	(yen/m. ton)	(mil.yen)
Actual							
1920	3094	2.86	8838	242	2140	184	1630
1925	3129	2.78	8700	224	1944	174	1515
1930	3203	2.83	9070	143	1297	137	1241
1935	3169	2.97	9414	179	1673	174	1642
Hypothetical, Case 1[b]							
1920	3116	2.87	8954	257	2307	196	1757
1925	3204	2.85	9126	284	2587	221	2016
1930	3280	2.90	9514	181	1726	173	1652
1935	3277	3.07	10064	250	2496	244	2450
Hypothetical, Case 2[c]							
1920	3116	2.87	8954	257	2307	196	1757
1925	3170	3.02	9335	254	2366	197	1844
1930	3219	3.10	9886	150	1480	143	1416
1935	3223	3.23	10402	212	2195	207	2164
Annual compound rate of growth from 1920 to 1935 (percent)							
Actual	0.16	0.24	0.40	−2.05	−1.85	−0.35	0.05
Case 1	0.34	0.44	0.78	−0.18	0.51	1.88	2.21
Case 2	0.21	0.79	1.00	−1.30	−0.30	0.40	1.40

a. Five years' averages centering the years shown. Rice in brown (husked but not polished) rice basis.

b. Case 1 assumes that the net import of rice stayed at the 1913–1917 level relative to domestic production.

c. Case 2 assumes, in addition to the assumption of Case 1, that the seed improvement index continued to grow at the 1880–1920 rate.

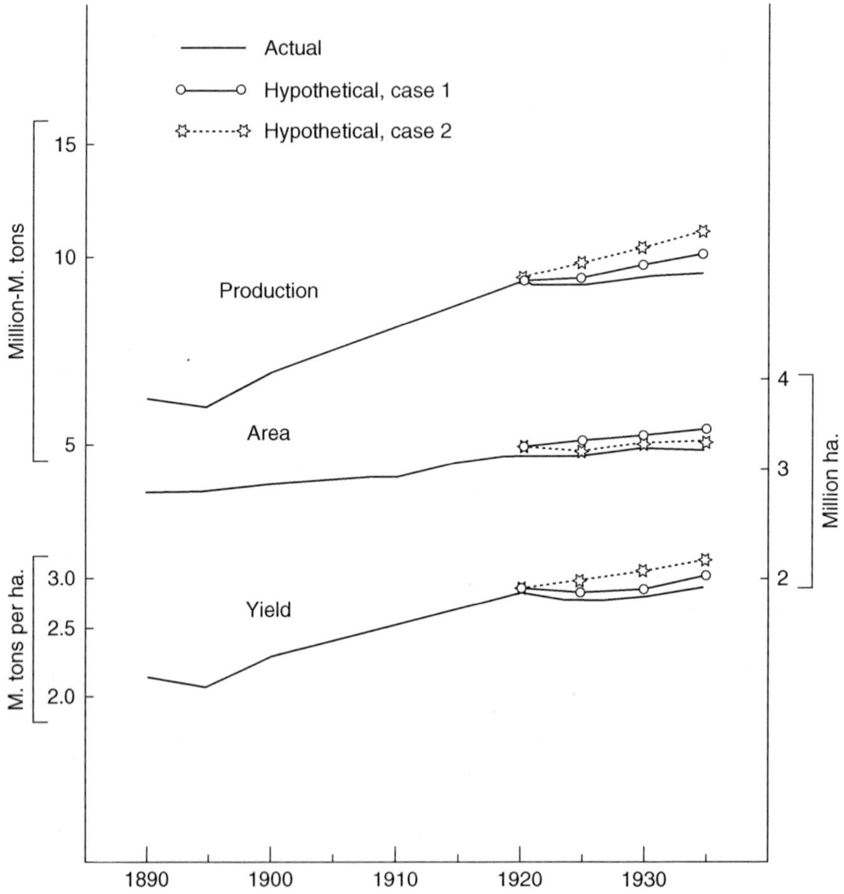

Figure 5.3 Area, Yield, and Production of Rice in Japan, 1890–1935.

In an economy which is closed, in the sense that there is no international trade, and in which there is no technological progress and no capital accumulation in agriculture, industrialization and economic growth will eventually lead to a point at which the terms of trade deteriorate for industry and the supply price of labor from agriculture to industry will rise in terms of industrial products, the "shortage point" of Ranis and Fei (1961). Japan was able to postpone the arrival of that point by exploiting the technological potential in the traditional peasant agriculture until World War I. Industrial development was supported by the very elastic supply of labor from agriculture.[15] Colonial policy seems to have been designed to postpone the arrival of the "shortage point" further and to make the progress of industrialization easier by expanding the supply of rice in the domestic market through imports from the colonies. The success of that policy kept the industrial wage low and the competitive position of industrial products strong in the international market. If the same amount of rice were supplied from foreign countries,

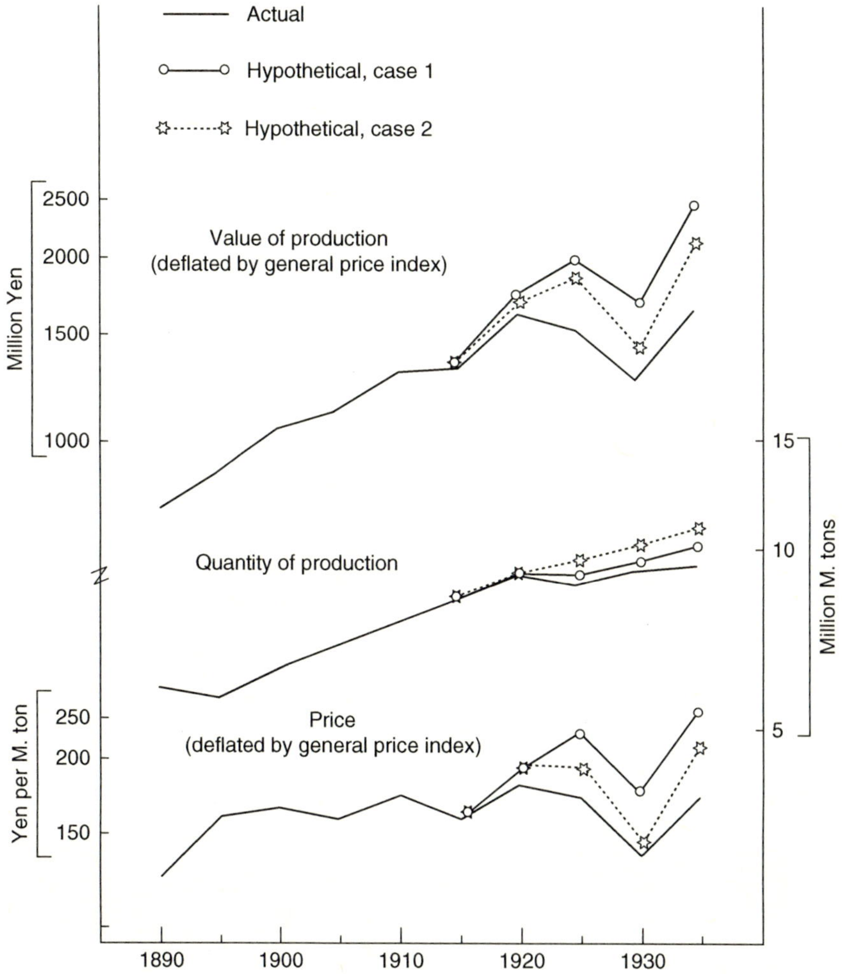

Figure 5.4 Production of Rice in Japan, 1890–1935.

precious foreign exchange would have been drained significantly, and the import of capital goods would have been curtailed.

This success was a mixed blessing for Japan. It depressed the price and the income of farmers and contributed to serious social disorders in the agricultural sector. The so-called military reformists made this social uneasiness and disorder among farmers the springboard for the invasion of Manchuria in 1931 and the other military adventures that followed. The policy decision concerning the rice supply after the rice riot in 1918 thus had not only economic but also vast social and political implications.[16]

Why did the economic effects of colonial development policy fail, in Japan, to produce the "classical" results associated with the importation of cheap grain into England from colonial areas and other areas of new settlement in the nineteenth century? The answer seems, at least in part, to be associated with the different structure of agriculture and the different pattern of industrial development in the two countries when the policies of dependence on overseas sources of food supply were initiated.

The inflow of cheap grain to England following the repeal of the Corn Laws in 1846 was accompanied by the continuing absorption of labor into the industrial sector and a transformation of the agricultural sector away from grain production and toward a more extensive system of livestock agriculture.[17] The transformation was facilitated by rising incomes in the industrial sector, which stimulated the demand for the products of animal agriculture (Dean and Cole 1962).

A number of obstacles impeded Japan's achieving a similar agricultural transformation in response to rising imports and declining prices of grain during the interwar period. Japanese agriculture was rigidly locked into a sophisticated labor-intensive system of crop production, highly dependent on irrigation and fertilizer as leading inputs (Ishikawa 1967). There was not a fully adequate basis, in either agricultural research or industrial infrastructure, for making a rapid transformation from grain production to a more diversified agricultural system. More critical was the fact that the rise in imports of grain was not accompanied in Japan by rapid growth in the demand for labor by the industrial sector. The demand for labor in the industrial sector slackened after 1920, as a result of (a) the contraction of world demand for the products of Japanese industry after World War I, (b) the contraction of domestic demand due to the deflation policy adopted to permit a return to the gold standard at a prewar parity, and (c) the adoption of an industrial rationalization policy in an attempt to stay competitive in world markets. This policy placed major emphasis on attempts to increase productivity and to save labor through more capital-intensive methods of production (Ohkawa and Rosovsky 1965). Finally, income levels in the urban industrial sector of the Japanese economy remained too low to create a large increase in the demand for the products of a more diversified agriculture.

The conditions which led to agricultural stagnation in Japan during the interwar period have been reversed since World War II. The application of modern biological science, particularly post-Mendelian genetics, in agricultural research has sharply raised agricultural productivity potentials. New technological potential, accumulated gradually under the Assigned Experiment System (initiated in 1926), began to exert a major impact on agricultural production in the post–World War II period. Japan emerged from World War II with an adequate industrial infrastructure to provide the fertilizer and other agricultural chemicals needed for a modern labor-intensive biological and chemical agricultural technology. Since World War II this infrastructure has been complemented by the capacity of the engineering and machinery industries to introduce an efficient small-scale mechanical technology suited to the factor proportions of Japanese agriculture. Incentives for rapid realization of the new agricultural potential have been reinforced by high price supports for agricultural commodities, particularly rice, and by modifications in the tenure system, which strengthen the impact of the price incentives on farm management decisions.

By the mid-1960s, evidence was emerging to support an argument that the shift in direction of agricultural policy may represent an overcompensation for the errors of the interwar period. The high price support for rice, at more than double the world price, and the subsidies for paddy development are resulting in surplus production at a time when the prices of rice and other food grains in the world market are declining. The restrictions on the growth of farm size under the land reform legislation have been discouraging the introduction of labor-saving mechanical technology, at a time when labor shortages are beginning to emerge as a permanent feature of the Japanese economy. It is too early to be overly confident of the long-run effect of these policies on Japanese agricultural development. The unique success of Japanese agricultural development, over the long run, has been due to the effective response of Japanese agricultural scientists, agricultural supply industries, and farm operators to price relationships that have accurately reflected the resource endowments and factor proportions of the Japanese economy (Hayami and Ruttan 1969). It appears that the present policies are inducing a significant malallocation of national resources. Today Japan should learn from the experience of free trade and agricultural transformation in nineteenth-century England.

The policies associated with Japanese agricultural stagnation during the interwar period are also of significance for many of the less developed economies of South and Southeast Asia. These nations are attempting to utilize the new agricultural production potentials associated with the "Green Revolution" as a basis for sustained economic growth (see Barker 1969). How to convert current or potential food surpluses into a basis for sustained economic growth poses an extremely difficult problem for most countries of South and Southeast Asia during the next decade. The continuing decline of export opportunities and prices sharply reduces the opportunity to use surplus production to earn the foreign exchange needed to finance domestic development. Furthermore, the relatively large share of the population engaged in agricultural production and the slow (absolute) growth in nonfarm employment opportunities limit the economic gains that can be realized by using the surpluses primarily to support employment in the urban-industrial sectors, unless the transfer of surpluses is also accompanied by lower food prices.

Thus, if Japan and other developed countries do not adopt less protectionist policies with respect to their domestic agriculture, the economies of Southeast Asia are likely to face difficulties during the 1970s similar to those faced by the Japanese economy during the interwar period. The main difference is that the downward pressure on rice prices in these countries will come from increased supplies generated from internal rather than colonial sources. The major problems are (a) maintaining sufficient equity in income distributions, both within the rural economy and between the rural and urban sectors, and (b) generating sufficient internal demand to absorb the productive capacity of an expanding urban sector, while simultaneously using lower rice prices as a device for transferring the gains of agricultural productivity into capital formation and economic growth in the urban-industrial sector. Solving them will require extreme skill. It may also generate more social tension than the political structures of many South and Southeast Asian economies seem able to absorb.

Notes

Yujiro Hayami and Vernon W. Ruttan, *Quarterly Journal of Economics* 84 (November 1970): 562–89. Minnesota Agricultural Experiment Station Journal Paper No. 7100. The research on which this paper is based was financed by a grant from the Rockefeller Foundation. The authors wish to thank W. P. Falcon, J. P. Houck, Shigeru Ishikawa, B. F. Johnston, Simon Kuznets, J. I. Nakamura, Kazushi Ohkawa, Gustav Ranis, P. M. Raup, A. M. Tang, and Sabro Yamada for suggestions and comments. They are indebted to Miss Sachiko Yamashita and Mrs. Barbara Miller for computational assistance.

1. The status of economic thought on imperialism, including the impact of colonial policy on metropolitan economies, is particularly unsatisfactory. For two recent reviews see Neisser 1960 and Blaug 1961. For a classical statement on the contribution of colonies to the economic development of metropolitan economies, see Friedrich List 1885. According to List (1885: 269), "The highest means of development of the manufacturing power, of the internal and external commerce proceeding from it . . . are colonies." This is essentially the view held by Marx and elaborated by his followers. See Bober 1940. Joan Robinson (1964: 45) has recently enunciated a postimperialist view: "the misery of being exploited by capitalists is nothing compared to the misery of not being exploited at all."
2. The English-language literature on Japanese colonial policy in Korea is less complete than that for Taiwan. The impact of colonial development policies on both Taiwan and Korea has been reviewed by Nakamura (1969). For two recent evaluations of Japanese colonial policy in Taiwan, see Pao-San Ho 1968 and Chang and Myers 1963. The Japanese-language literature is extensive. The two classical works which have special relevance to the present study are Kawano 1941 and Tobata and Ohkawa 1935.
3. The questions raised by Nakamura in regard to the official statistics have been widely discussed by Japanese and other scholars. For discussions by Japanese scholars, see Hayami 1968a, Hayami and Yamada 1969, and Nakamura 1968. Appraisals by other scholars include Rosovsky 1968 and Clark 1967.
4. Hayami and Yamada 1969; Yamada 1967; and Johnston 1966.
5. For example, see Johnston 1951 and Ohkawa and Rosovsky 1960.
6. "The years after 1920 were difficult years for Japanese agriculture. Cheap rice began to be imported from Korea and Taiwan, where rice cultivation had been encouraged by the Japanese government following the food shortage of World War I and the Rice Riots that resulted in 1918" (Sawada 1965: 334.) See also Ohkawa and Rosovsky 1960.
7. The Ohkawa-Rosovsky development model asserts that during the beginning of modernization the development of the modern economy depends on accelerated growth of the traditional economy, and that during later stages the transformation of the traditional sector depends on the ability of the modern sector to support the rationalization of the traditional sectors. Ohkawa and Rosovsky (1960) attribute the lag in the agricultural sector to the failure of the modern industrial sector to produce the capital and current inputs needed for the transformation of Japanese agriculture during the interwar period. In correspondence with the authors of the present article, Rosovsky places major importance on the limited development of a mechanical technology suited to the needs of agriculture. The authors place greater emphasis on the lag in the transition from the traditional biological technology of the Meiji era to modern biological and chemical technology.

8. The major improved varieties that achieved nationwide diffusion prior to 1930 were almost all selected by veteran farmers. For example, the Shinriki variety, which made by far the largest contribution to the growth in yield during the Meiji period, was selected in 1877 by Jujiro Maruo, a farmer in the Hyogo prefecture (the variety was called Shinriki, meaning "the power of God," by the farmers, who were surprised at the high yield of the variety). The Kameno-o variety, which contributed greatly to increasing and stabilizing the yield in northern Japan, was selected in 1897 by Kameji Abe, a farmer in the Yamagata prefecture. Organized research by experiment stations to create new varieties started in 1904, when Koremochi Kato and Kotaro Ando made the initial hybrid experiments in the Kinai Branch of the National Experiment station. The first major breakthrough in organized research was by Hiroshi Terao, with the development of Rikuu 132 in the Rikuu Branch. But the appreciable contributions of organized research in seed improvement to the national average yields occurred only after the establishment of a nationwide organized research system, Norinsho Shitei Hinshu Kairyoshiken Seido (System of Seed Improvement Experiments of Varieties Assigned by the Ministry of Agriculture and Forestry), in 1926, and after the creation and diffusion of Norin numbered varieties as the research result of this system (Norin No. 1 appeared in 1931). See Noringijutsu Kyokai 1952.
9. This reorientation of colonial agricultural development policy in response to the shortage of rice in Japan is clearly described by Tobata and Ohkawa (1935: 7) in reference to Korea: "Since the Rice Riot Japan has faced a so-called 'population-food problem.' Rapid increase in population and even more rapid increase in nonagricultural population, as the result of industrial development, have been pressing the need for an increase in rice production. In Japan, however, rice farming had already approached a technical limit of intensification, and economically there was little possibility of increasing rice production. Therefore, the solution of the population-food problem was sought in the direction of enlarging the rice production area. In this connection Korea represented the biggest hope, where extensive and underdeveloped farming have been practiced without progress for hundreds of years. It was anticipated that if Korean agriculture were to be developed by the weapons of modern science it would be possible to increase its intensity as well as to expand the paddy field area." The process of agricultural development in Korea and Taiwan under this policy orientation is described in the literature cited in note 2, page 562. Quantitative analysis of this process is now under way by the authors.
10. A somewhat similar phenomenon occurred during the 1890–1905 period. The increase in the supply (and presumably consumption) of rice outpaced domestic production, although the 1905 (1903–7 average) observation includes the abnormal years of the Russo-Japanese War (1904–5). The fact that Japan shifted from being a net exporter to being a net importer of rice during the last decade of the nineteenth century pressed the government to take measures to encourage agricultural production, including the establishment of the National Agricultural Experiment Station (1896), the Law of State Subsidy for Prefectural Agricultural Experiment Stations (1899), and the Arable Land Replotment Law (1899). With the existence of indigenous technological potential that was not being fully exploited, these government efforts were effective and contributed to the advances in rice production and in yield per hectare during the first two decades of this century (see Figure 5.2). As a result Japanese agriculture continued to supply about 95 percent of the rapidly growing domestic rice consumption during this period.
11. Data for Taiwan and Korea are plotted for the periods after cadastral surveys (completed in 1906 and 1918, respectively), for which the data are more reliable.
12. The data presented in Table 5.3 indicate that the rate of growth in the supply (and presumably consumption) of rice declined after 1920 (from the annual compound rate of 1.7 percent during the 1890–1920 period to 1.0 percent during the 1920–35 period). Population continued to grow at an annual rate of about 1.0 percent for both periods. This stagnation of per capita rice consumption, if due to a decline in demand, might be expected to have a significant influence on production and productivity trends, although in an open economy domestic consumption does not represent a direct constraint on domestic production. The analysis in the present paper indicates that the stagnation of domestic rice production and productivity in Japan can

be consistently explained by two major factors: the exhaustion of indigenous technological potential and the importation of colonial rice. This does not, however, refute the hypothesis that demand contraction may have also contributed to the decline. Quantitative analysis of the influence of demand contraction on domestic rice production during this period awaits future research.

13. Several variations of the area response model were tried, e.g., using net income or profit instead of price. The estimates of such models were inferior to the present model.
14. This assumption is based on the following reasoning: The government, whether democratic or not, would perceive and try to respond to the demand of the people. If the price of agricultural products went up, the benefit-cost ratio of irrigation and water control investment would improve. In that situation, farmers, landlords, and consumers would demand more such constructions. The government, sensitive to this demand, would allocate a larger amount of funds for irrigation and water control. This would increase national wealth and might also result in an increase in government revenue under an appropriate tax system. Whether the present distributed lag specification of geometric convergence is adequate for describing this process is, of course, open to challenge.
15. It is questionable if there existed an unlimited supply of labor in the sense of Ranis and Fei, but a recent study by Minami indicates that there was a situation that could well be identified as the unlimited supply of labor from agriculture to industry. See Minami 1968.
16. It is interesting to consider what could have happened if the colonial development policies had been accompanied by land reform and other economic democratization measures similar to those implemented during the U.S. occupation after World War II. Land reform might have (a) raised the rate of growth in agricultural production by increasing the incentives of farmers, (b) improved the level of income and living of farmers and contributed to the social and political stability of the rural sector, and (c) expanded the domestic market for industrial products through the increased consumption of farmers, and depressed incentives to the imperialistic expansion of overseas market. On the other hand, the improved level of income and consumption of farmers might have depressed industrial growth by (a) decreasing the net outflow of savings from agriculture to industry and (b) shifting upward the schedule of labor supply to industry, which was determined by the level of living in the rural sector, with a possible rise in the industrial wage rate. More extensive analysis is required to evaluate the overall effects of alternative land tenure policies on economic growth and social and political development.
17. The shift away from grain production toward mixed farming characterized by "high feeding" of livestock was pronounced during the two decades following the repeal of the Corn Laws. Prior to 1850 livestock feeding was justified primarily on the basis of the value to the grain enterprise of the manure produced by the livestock. After 1850 livestock production became profitable in its own right. For an excellent assessment of the changes in farming during this period, see E. L. Jones 1968, reprinted from *Agricultural History Review* 10 (1962). Jones summarizes the factors responsible for the shift as follows: "after the Repeal the altered relative value of wheat and livestock products due to imports which prevented a rise in the price of wheat, the growth of population, and rising real income of which an increasing proportion was spent on livestock products" (229). He also quotes an observation by James Caird, made in 1878: "Thirty years ago probably not more than one-third of the people of this country consumed animal food more than once a week. Now nearly all of them eat it, in meat or cheese or butter, once a day. . . . The leap which the consumption of meat took in consequence of the general rise of wages in all branches of trade and employment, could not have been met without foreign supplies" (227).

CHAPTER 6

Environmental, Technological, and Institutional Factors in the Growth of Rice Production

PHILIPPINES, THAILAND, AND TAIWAN

S. C. Hsieh and Vernon W. Ruttan

A basic premise of the technical assistance and agricultural development programs of the late 1940s and early 1950s was that rapid growth in agricultural productivity and output could be achieved by the transfer of technology, institutions, and capital from high-income to low-income countries. It was thought that agricultural production could be expanded rapidly as a result of (a) the transfer of known agricultural technology from the high-productivity to the low-productivity countries, (b) the development of more effective rural marketing, credit, and land tenure institutions, and (c) capital investment in irrigation and flood control, mechanization, and transportation. The diffusion of practices employed by the best farmers within the low-income countries was also regarded as an important source of productivity growth.

Such expectations have typically failed to materialize. The rate of growth of crop output in most developing countries has been disappointingly slow. Furthermore, a relatively large share of the recorded increases in production have been based on expansion of area planted rather than on increases in output per unit area (Hendrix et al. 1965).

Now, in the mid-1960s, a new consensus appears to be emerging that intensive investment in research and development designed to produce improvements in the quality of agricultural inputs represents the missing link in the agricultural development process in many countries (Hill 1965; Kellogg 1964; Schultz 1964a, 1964b). There is increasing recognition that traditional practices employed by the more successful farmers in each area do not have a sufficiently high payoff to provide an incentive for rapid growth in aggregate output. And there is growing agreement that much agricultural research and development is highly location specific—it must be done in biological and economic environments approximating those where the innovation will be employed.

There is danger that these insights may be contributing to a new set of oversimplifications regarding the requisites for rapid agricultural development. The evidence presented in this paper emphasizes the essential complementarity between (a) increased investment in research and development leading to higher rates of return on purchased inputs, (b) increased investment in land and water development, and (c) improved institutional and organizational systems for providing technical inputs and services to farmers.

Most countries in Southeast Asia have been, and continue to be, more dependent on increased area than on increased yield as a source of growth in rice production (Table 6.1). This is in contrast to the countries of Northeast Asia, where increases in yield have been more important than increases in area in recent years. Taiwan and Malaysia are the only countries, however, which seem to have achieved their total increase in output during the last decade from yield increases. The Philippines and Cambodia stand at the opposite extreme. Thailand occupies an intermediate position; changes in yield are somewhat more important than changes in area planted in accounting for increases in rice production in Thailand during the last decade.

Two hypotheses with respect to the factors affecting yield increases and yield differences are tested in this study.

The first is that the increases in yield of rice of the last decade and the differences in yield among major rice-producing areas within Southeast Asia at the present time primarily reflect variations in the environmental conditions under which rice is grown (soil, season, water, and weather differentials) rather than differences in variety or cultural practices.

The second hypothesis is that differences in rice yield between Southeast Asia and Northeast Asia reflect variations in the technological and institutional factors under which rice is grown, in addition to environmental factors.

In this paper, we test these two hypotheses with data from the Philippines, Thailand, and Taiwan. Major emphasis will be placed on factors associated with changes or differences in yield.[1]

Trends in Rice Production, Area, and Yield in Three Countries

The Philippines, Thailand, and Taiwan have all experienced relatively rapid growth in total rice production since the early 1900s. The pattern of growth over time and the relative contribution of area and yield are sharply different among the three countries (Figure 6.1; Table 6.2).

Table 6.1 **Production, Area, and Yield of Rice in Asia, 1961/62–1963/64 Average Compared with Ten Years Earlier***

Regions and countries	*Production, rough rice (thousand metric tons)*			*Area (thousand hectare)*			*Yield (tons per hectare)*			*Percentage contribution to change in production*	
	1951/52 to 1953/54	*1961/62 to 1963/64*	*Percent change*	*1951/52 to 1953/54*	*1961/62 to 1963/64*	*Percent change*	*1951/52 to 1953/54*	*1961/62 to 1963/64*	*Percent change*	*Change in area*	*Change in yield*
Northeast Asia											
Japan	12,043	16,880	40.2	3,013	3,286	9.1	4.00	5.14	28.5	26	74
Korea (Rep. of)	2,318	3,532	52.4	946	1,147	21.2	2.45	3.08	25.7	46	54
Taiwan[a]	1,947	2,586	32.8	784	775	–1.1	2.48	3.34	34.7	–4	104
Total	16,308	22,998	41.0	4,743	5,208	9.8	3.44	4.42	28.5	27	73
Southeast Asia[b]											
Burma	5,836	7,392	26.7	4,112[c]	4,637[c]	12.8	1.42	1.59	12.0	51	49
Cambodia	1,679	2,474	47.3	1,673	2,305	37.8	1.00	1.07	7.0	83	17
Indonesia	10,090	12,504	24.4	6,131	6,960	13.5	1.65	1.80	9.1	59	41
Malaysia	660	980	48.5	498[d]	474	–4.8	1.32	2.07	56.8	–13	113
Philippines	3,052	3,907	28.0	2,589	3,142	21.4	1.18	1.24	5.1	78	22

Table 6.1 ***(Continued)***

Regions and countries	*Production, rough rice (thousand metric tons)*			*Area (thousand hectare)*			*Yield (tons per hectare)*			*Percentage contribution to change in production*	
	1951/52 to 1953/54	*1961/62 to 1963/64*	*Percent change*	*1951/52 to 1953/54*	*1961/62 to 1963/64*	*Percent change*	*1951/52 to 1953/54*	*1961/62 to 1963/64*	*Percent change*	*Change in area*	*Change in yield*
Thailand	7,389	9,208	24.6	5,599	6,077	8.5	1.32	1.52	15.2	37	63
Total	28,706	36,465	27.0	20,602	23,595	14.5	1.39	1.55	11.5	57	43
South Asia[e]	49,874	69,756	39.9	40,441	45,741	13.1	1.23	1.53	24.4	37	63

* Data from FAO, *The World Rice Economy in Figures, 1901–1963* (Commodity Reference Series No. 3, Rome, 1965); FAO, *Production Yearbook 1965*; and FAO, *Monthly Bulletin of Agricultural Economics and Statistics*, June 1966. The author has computed the relative contribution of area and yield to the change in production on a logarithmic basis.

[a] Production and yield differ from figures used elsewhere in this paper, apparently due to conversion from brown to rough rice at 1.24 here rather than 1.312.

[b] Laos and Vietnam not included.

[c] Planted.

[d] Including approximation for Sarawak for comparability with production figures.

[e] Ceylon, India, Iran (unofficial), and Pakistan. Nepal not included.

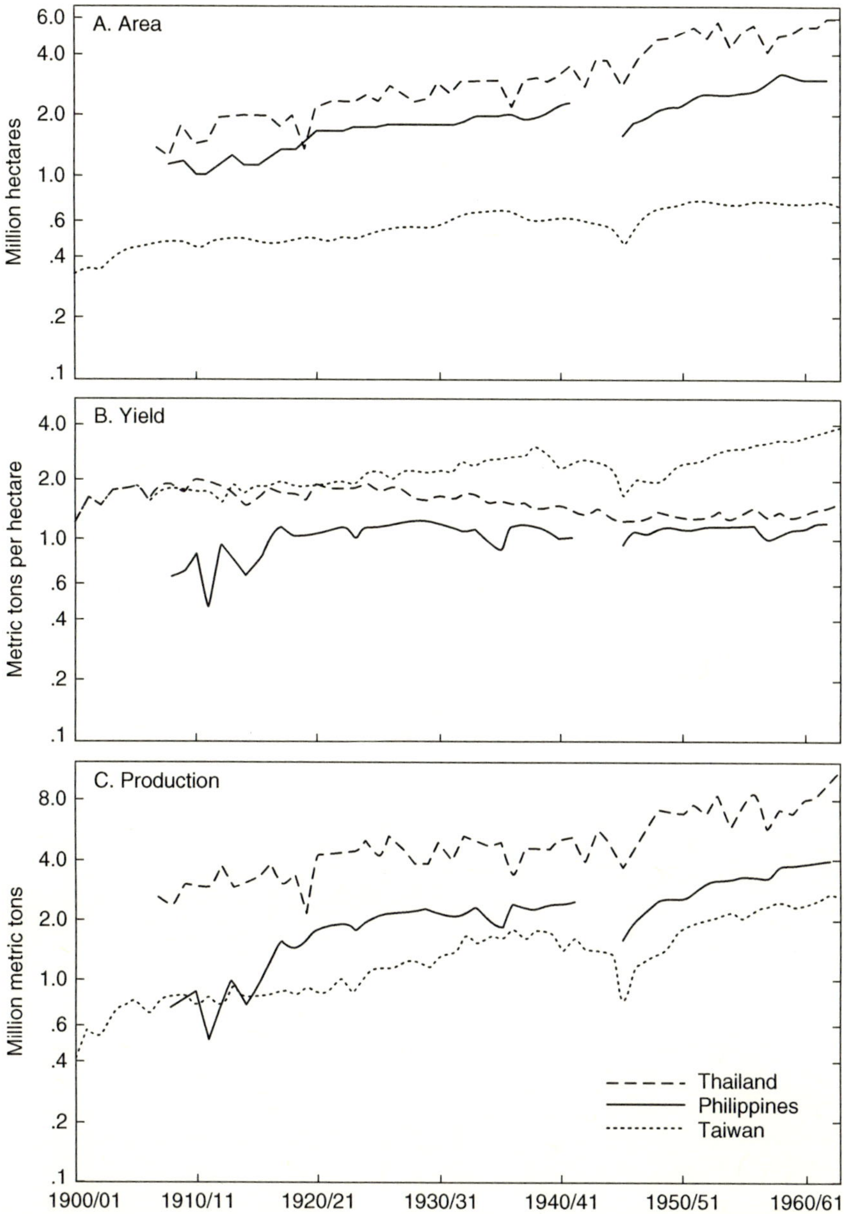

Figure 6.1 Area, Yield, and Production of Rice in the Philippines, Thailand, and Taiwan, from the Early 1900s to 1963/64.*

* See Appendix Note for sources of data. Area figures for the Philippines through 1952/53 are for area planted; all other area figures are harvested basis. All production and yield figures are in terms of rough rice.

Table 6.2 **Changes in Rice Production, Area, and Yield in the Philippines, Thailand, and Taiwan for Selected Periods (Rough Rice Basis)***

Period	*Production (thousand metric tons)*	*Area (thousand hectares)*	*Yield (tons per hectare)*	*Annual rate of change (percent)*		
				Production	*Area*	*Yield*
		PHILIPPINES[a]				
1908/09–1909/10	798	1,174	.68			
1925/26–1926/27	2,140	1,781	1.20	6.0	2.5	3.4
1952/53–1953/54	3,163	2,650	1.19	1.5	1.5	.0
1962/63–1963/64	3,905	3,124	1.25	2.1	1.7	.5
1908/10–1962/64				3.0	1.8	1.1
		THAILAND				
1907/08–1908/09	2,475	1,319	1.88			
1920/21–1921/22	4,250	2,298	1.85	4.2	4.4	.1
1946/47–1947/48	4,974	3,907	1.27	.6	2.1	1.4
1962/63–1963/64	9,711	6,288	1.54	4.3	3.0	1.2
1907/09–1962/64				2.5	2.9	.4
		TAIWAN				
1903/04–1904/05	735	415	1.75			
1919/20–1920/21	916	499	1.84	1.4	1.1	.3
1936/37–1937/38	1,761	670	2.63	3.9	1.7	2.1
1951/52–1952/53	2,004	787	2.55	.8	1.1	–.2
1962/63–1963/64	2,769	772	3.58	3.0	–.2	3.2
1903/05–1962/64				2.2	1.0	1.2
1919/21–1962/64				2.6	1.0	1.6

* See Appendix Note for sources of basic data. Area figures are harvested basis except as indicated for the Philippines in note a. Annual rates of change are the authors' computation.

[a] Area figures are area planted prior to 1953/54, area harvested thereafter, Yield figures reflect this change.

Throughout the entire period a substantial share of the total increase in output in both the Philippines and Thailand is accounted for by increases in the area devoted to rice production. Growth in area was particularly rapid in both countries prior to the early or mid-1920s. In Taiwan, however, the expansion of area planted was relatively slow throughout the entire period, although rather substantial increases were recorded during the 1920s and early 1930s.

There have also been sharp contrasts in yield. In the Philippines yield per hectare apparently rose rapidly, from an extremely low level in the early years of the century to approximately 1.20 metric tons per hectare, until the early 1920s.

Since the mid-1920s national average rice yields in the Philippines seem to have remained almost unchanged. In 1962/63–1963/64 the Philippine average yield was only 1.25 metric tons per hectare. The average yield in Thailand declined continuously from the early 1920s to the mid-1950s. During the late 1940s and early 1950s it was only slightly higher than in the Philippines. Although the long-term decline in yields was reversed by the late 1950s, the average yield in 1962/63–1963/64 was still only 1.54 metric tons per hectare–substantially below the levels achieved before the 1920s. During this same period Taiwan experienced a spectacular growth, with yield per hectare rising from 1.84 metric tons per hectare in 1919/20–1920/21 to 3.58 in 1962/63–1963/64.

Both the long-term stability in national average yield in the Philippines and the long-term decline in national average yield in Thailand are difficult to explain. The stability in national average yield in the Philippines may reflect the combined effect of expansion in area devoted to low-yielding upland and rain-fed rice and a stable or declining area devoted to rice production in the higher-yielding irrigated areas. In Thailand, it is possible that increases in area devoted to rice in the low-yielding provinces of the Northeast have more than offset the effect of stable or rising yields in the central and northern provinces.

In Taiwan, the higher yields seem to have been due primarily to favorable technological and institutional factors, which include the development and introduction of high-yielding *ponlai* rice varieties, increased use of chemical fertilizer, improved irrigation facilities and water management, improved cultural practices, reduced acreage of low-yielding upland and rain-fed rice, and the organization of farmers' associations and irrigation associations for fertilizer distribution, rice collection, storage, processing and marketing, and water use, distribution, and management at the local level. Among all these factors it appears that innovations associated with the introduction of the *ponlai* varieties beginning in the early 1920s have been particularly important. Data on the long-term yield trends for the several classes of rice grown in Taiwan is presented in Figure 6.2.

Differences in Yield among Regions in the Philippines, Thailand, and Taiwan

National average yields can be regarded as a weighted average of the yield obtained in the several rice-producing regions of each country. Differences in average yields among regions may reflect differences in the environmental conditions under which rice is grown—the proportion of rice grown under irrigated, rain-fed, or upland

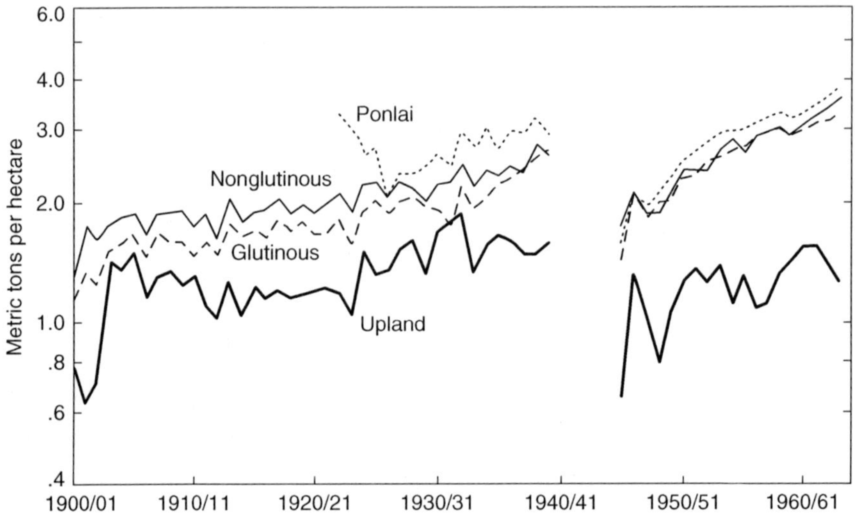

Figure 6.2 Changes in Average Yield of Different Types of Rice, Taiwan, 1900/01 to 1963/64.*

* See Appendix Note for sources of data. Yields are in terms of rough rice. For ease of reading, the vertical scale on this chart is double that on Figure 6.1.

conditions or during the wet and dry seasons, for example.[2] Differences in yield may also reflect differences in the level of technology employed in each region–cultural practices, varieties, use of technical inputs such as fertilizer, insecticides, and others. The level of technology itself may reflect differences in economic incentives such as factor and product prices; differences in institutional organization such as land tenure, credit, and marketing organization; and social and cultural differences that influence the adoption of new technology and use of technical inputs.

In this section, we examine the extent to which differences in yield among regions within each country reflect differences in the environmental conditions under which rice is grown. We include under environmental factors long-term infrastructure investment such as irrigation which modifies the natural environment and enables rice producers to achieve greater local environmental control.

In the Philippines, rice is produced under many situations. Each province grows some rice in the rainy (wet) season and some in the dry season, and in each some rice is grown under irrigated, rain-fed, and upland conditions. Regional or national average yields differ depending on season (wet or dry) and water treatment (irrigated, rain-fed, or upland).[3] Thus the average rice yield in each province or region (Figure 6.3), and in the Philippines as a whole, is determined by (a) the yield obtained under different production conditions, and (b) the percentage of the total area on which different production practices are employed.

The nonirrigated or rain-fed first crop (wet season) accounts for the largest share of rice area in almost all regions (Figure 6.4). Irrigated first crop areas are

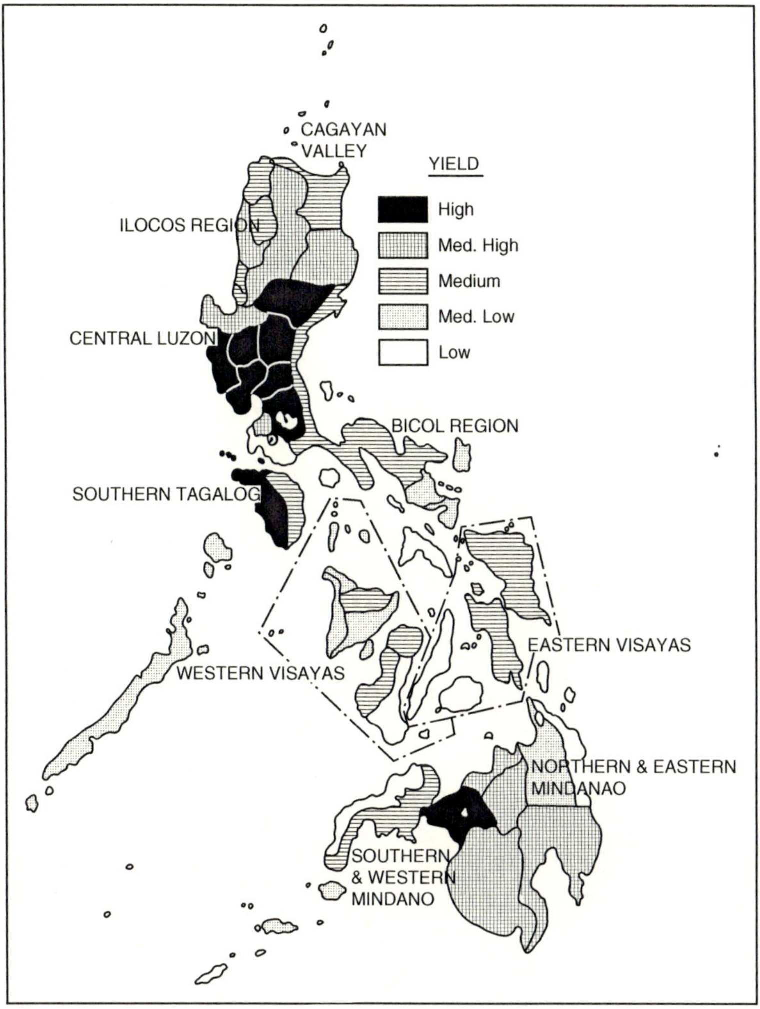

Figure 6.3 Distribution of Rice Yields among Philippines Provinces, 1956/57–1958/59 Average*

* See Appendix Note for source of basic data; 10 provinces are included in each category except medium which include 13. The categories represent yields in metric tons of rough rice per hectare harvested, and indexes with the Philippines national average of 1.10 tons = 100, as follows:

High	*Yield*	*Index*
High	1.28–2.13	116.4–193.6
Medium high	1.10–1.27	100.0–115.5
Medium	.92–1.09	83.6–99.1
Medium low	.77–.91	70.0–82.7
Low	below .77	below 70.0

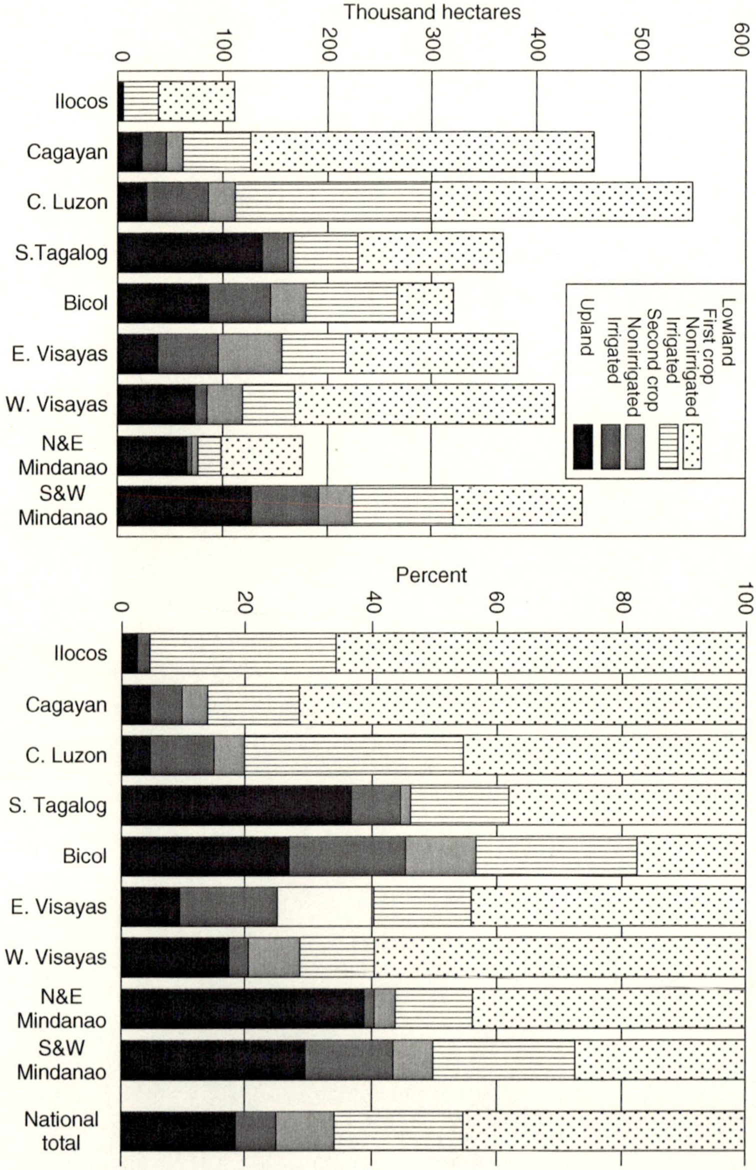

Figure 6.4 Regional Distribution of Rice Area Harvested in the Philippines, 1960/61.*
* See Appendix Note for source of data.

substantial only in a few regions, such as Central Luzon, Bicol, and southern and western Mindanao. The area devoted to the irrigated and rain-fed second crop (dry season) rice is relatively small in all regions. The area devoted to upland rice relative to lowland rice is relatively large in a few regions, such as southern Tagalog and southern and western Nindanao.

The data in Table 6.3 represent an attempt to estimate the effects of season (wet or dry) and water use (irrigated, rain-fed, or upland) on regional average yields. The data in column 1 are the actual average yields obtained in 1960/61 in each region. The data in column 3 are the average yields that would have been reported for the region if the distribution of rice area by season and water supply in the region had been the same as the national average. The only year for which sufficient data are available to make this calculation is 1960/61.

In Central Luzon, for example, the actual average yield in 1960/61 was 1.574 metric tons of rough rice per hectare, or almost 36 percent above the national average. If the distribution of area (a) between the wet and the dry season, and (b) among irrigated, rain-fed and upland areas had been the same as the national average, the 1960/61 average yields in Central Luzon would have been 1.382 metric tons or only 19 percent above the national average. This means that almost half of the difference between the actual average yield in Central Luzon and the average national yield is accounted for by the relatively favorable area distribution with respect to season and water treatment rather than by actual yield differences under similar environmental conditions. In the Ilocos region, about three-fifths of the margin of actual yield over the national average yield results primarily from the favorable area distribution.

In the Cagayan Valley, southern and western Mindanao, and southern Tagalog regions, the relatively high proportion of upland area accounts for the below-average yield obtained in each. If the distribution of area among different types of production had been the same as the national average, yields in these three regions would have approximated the national average.

The close agreement between the actual and standardized yield in western Visayas is particularly striking. This implies that the higher-than-average yields are primarily the result of higher real yields rather than area distribution. Similarly, in Bicol, eastern Visayas, and northern and eastern Mindanao yields are low although the distribution of production is close to the national average.

The limited fraction of the total area devoted to rice that is irrigated in both the wet and the dry seasons represents a major barrier to increased production and higher average yields in most regions. Even in Central Luzon, a region where yields are relatively high, a shift of one hectare from production of one crop of rain-fed rice to production of irrigated rice during both the wet and dry seasons would add almost 2.37 tons to the total production, assuming the cultural practices of 1961. This would represent a 168 percent increase in rice production per hectare per year.[4]

In Thailand the range in yield variation among provinces is similar to that in the Philippines (Figure 6.5). However, most of the rice is grown under irrigated or rain-fed conditions. The percentage of upland rice is low—probably not more than 1 percent in recent years. The second crop (dry season) production is also low. It accounts for less than 1 percent of the total area planted (or harvested). Most of the dry season crop is grown in the north and in the Central Plain. But the

Table 6.3 **Effect of Differences in Regional Production Patterns on Regional Average Yields of Rough Rice per Hectare Harvested in the Philippines and Thailand***

	Actual yield		*Standardized yield*[a]	
	Tons per hectare	*Index*	*Tons per hectare*	*Index*
Country and region	*(1)*	*(2)*	*(3)*	*(4)*
Philippines, 1960/61	1.159	100.0	1.159	100.0
Ilocos	1.278	110.3	1.201	103.6
Cagayan Valley	1.087	93.8	1.174	101.3
Central Luzon	1.574	135.8	1.382	119.2
Southern Tagalog	1.049	90.5	1.143	98.6
Bicol	1.025	88.4	1.013	87.4
Eastern Visayas	.891	76.9	.891	76.9
Western Visayas	1.263	109.0	1.289	111.2
Northern and Eastern Mindanao	.847	73.1	.851	73.4
Southern and Western Mindanao	1.127	97.2	1.176	101.5
Thailand, 1961/62–1963/64	1.514	100.0	1.514	100.0
Central Plain	1.766	116.6	1.394	92.1
Northeast	1.123	74.2	1.409	93.1
North	2.144	141.6	2.125	140.4
South	1.602	105.8	1.770	116.9

*See Appendix Note for sources of actual yield figures; for Thailand see text description of estimates for irrigated and nonirrigated areas. Tons are metric.

[a] In the Philippines, to obtain the standardized yields, regional yields of rough rice from first crop (1) irrigated, (2) nonirrigated; second crop (3) irrigated, (4) nonirrigated; and (5) upland areas are weighted by the national average distribution for the five categories. In Thailand the regional yields of rough rice, on a harvested area basis, for the irrigated and nonirrigated areas, were weighted by the national distribution of irrigated and nonirrigated area harvested to obtain the standardized yields.

Standardization for the differences among regions identified above reduces the coefficient of variation for yields among regions in both the Philippines and Thailand by about 20 percent (from .20 to .16 in the Philippines and from .26 to .21 in Thailand). It seems reasonable to expect that if data were available to permit standardization for differences in water control and season among provinces within regions and among villages within provinces, the coefficient of variation for the standardized yields would be even lower.

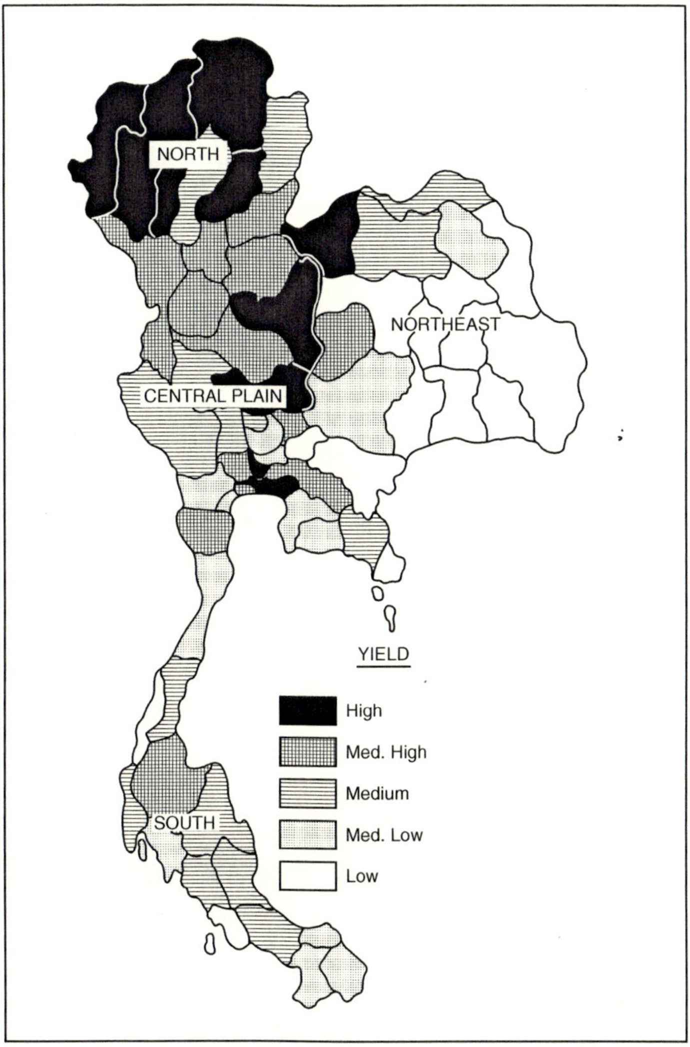

Figure 6.5 Distribution of Rice Yields among Thai Provinces, 1961/62–1963/64 Average.*
* See Appendix Note for source of basic data; 14 provinces are included in each category except medium which include 15. The categories represent yields in metric tons of rough rice per hectare harvested, and indexes with the Thai national average of 1.51 tons = 100, as follows:

High	*Yield*	*Index*
High	1.93–3.24	129.80–214.57
Medium high	1.68–1.95	111.26–129.14
Medium	1.52–1.67	100.66–110.60
Medium low	1.29–1.51	85.43–100.00
Low	.74–1.28	49.01–84.77

relative importance of irrigated and rain-fed areas varies sharply among provinces (Figure 6.6). In central Thailand almost half of the area planted and in the north more than one-fourth of the area planted is irrigated.[5]

The yields reported by the Royal Irrigation Department for irrigated areas are substantially higher than the yields estimated for nonirrigated areas by the residual method (Figure 6.7). Both the irrigated and nonirrigated areas have experienced increases in yield since 1958/59. The most dramatic increase occurred on irrigated land in the Northeast. Irrigated land represents such a small proportion of the total increases in the Northeast that the rice yield on irrigated land had a relatively minor impact in the average yield for the entire region. In the central plain, the estimated yield on nonirrigated land has risen more rapidly than on irrigated land.

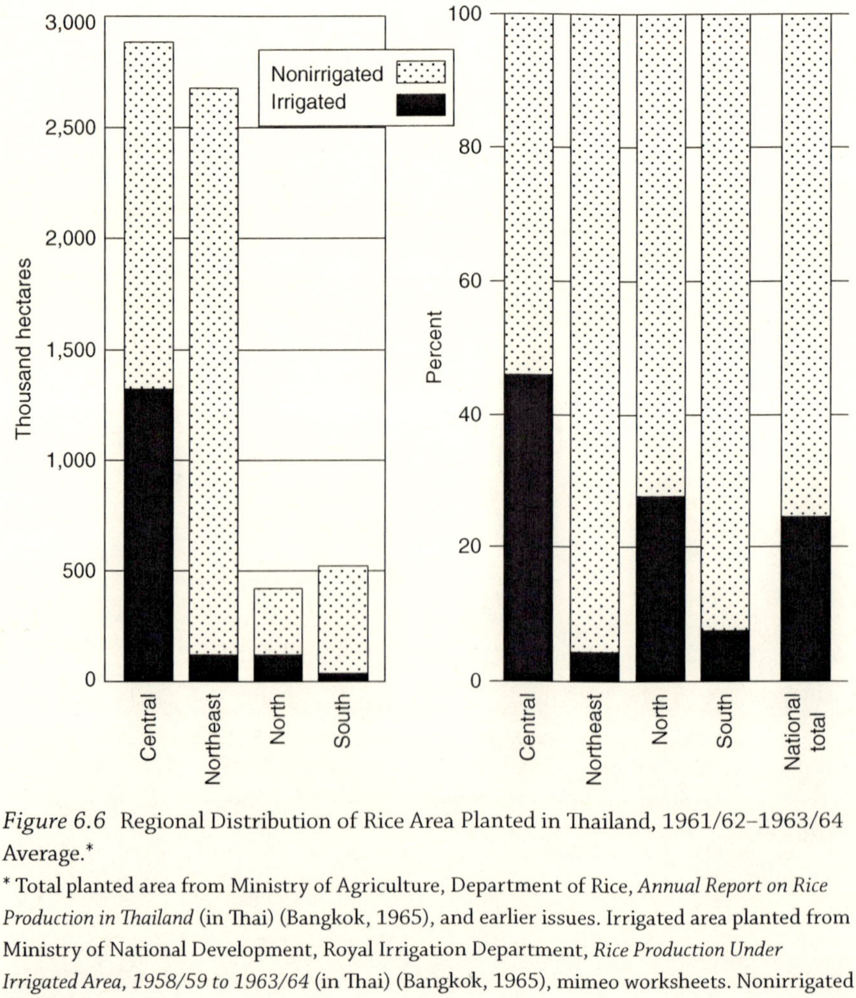

Figure 6.6 Regional Distribution of Rice Area Planted in Thailand, 1961/62–1963/64 Average.*

* Total planted area from Ministry of Agriculture, Department of Rice, *Annual Report on Rice Production in Thailand* (in Thai) (Bangkok, 1965), and earlier issues. Irrigated area planted from Ministry of National Development, Royal Irrigation Department, *Rice Production Under Irrigated Area, 1958/59 to 1963/64* (in Thai) (Bangkok, 1965), mimeo worksheets. Nonirrigated area approximated as the difference.

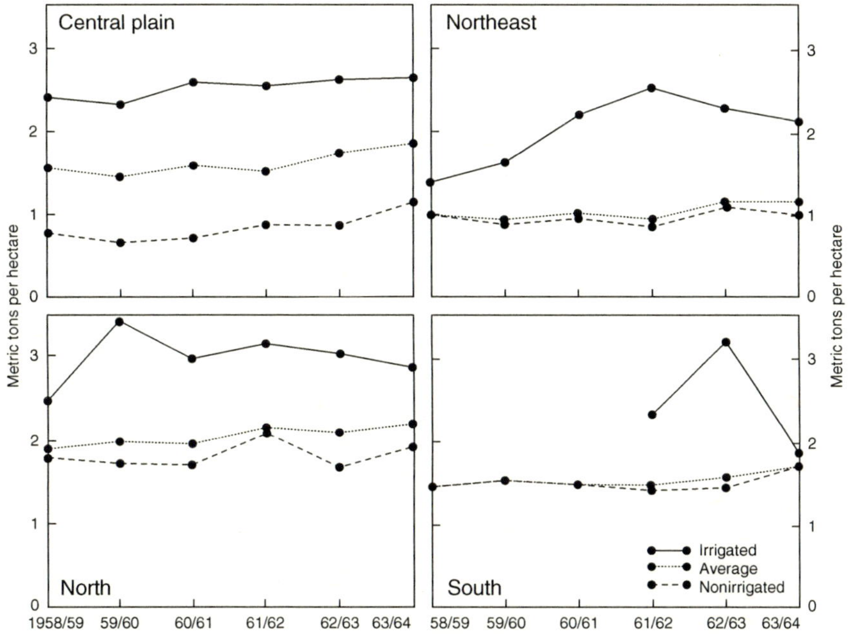

Figure 6.7 Regional Average Yield per Hectare Harvested in Irrigated and Nonirrigated Areas, Thailand, 1958/59–1963/64.*

* Based on data from sources cited for Figure 6.6, but using harvested-based area figures. See text for further description.

Differences in the proportion of area irrigated in each region have a substantial impact on the regional average yield. In those regions where only a small share of the land is irrigated, the average yield is close to the yield on nonirrigated land.

The data for Thailand in Table 6.3 attempt to measure the effect of different regional production patterns on regional yields. The data presented in column 3 are estimates of the average yields that would have been reported for the region if the distribution of area between irrigated and nonirrigated areas in the region had been the same as the national average. In the Central Plain, for example, the actual average yield in 1961/62–1963/64 was 1.766 metric tons of rough rice per hectare, or almost 17 percent above the national average. If the distribution of area between irrigated and rain-fed culture had been the same as the national average, the 1961/63 average yield in the Central Plain would have been 1.394 metric tons, or 8 percent below the national average.

The northern region is particularly striking because of the close agreement between the actual and standardized yield. This implies that the higher-than-average yields are primarily the result of higher rice yields under comparable conditions of water use rather than to a favorable distribution of irrigated area.

In Taiwan two crops of rice per year are grown in most areas. The rice crop harvested before August 15 is considered the first or dry season crop. The crop harvested after August 15 is considered the second or wet season crop. In each area and each season rice is grown under irrigated, rain-fed, and upland conditions. Taiwan differs from the Philippines and Thailand, however, in that a very high percentage of the rice area is served by irrigation systems designed to provide sufficient water for rice production during both the dry and wet seasons. Even in the mid-1920s, before the *ponlai* varieties were introduced, most rice land was fully irrigated. With further extension of irrigation during the last forty years the area devoted to rain-fed and upland rice has been further reduced. At present, upland rice accounts for less than 3 percent of the total rice area. It seems unlikely then that rain-fed rice accounts for more than 10 percent of the total area devoted to rice.[6]

It seems reasonable to hypothesize that the very high proportion of total rice area that is irrigated accounts for the small variation in yield among districts in Taiwan (Figure 6.8) as compared with the wide provincial yield variations in the Philippines (Figure 6.3) and Thailand (Figure 6.5). Measurement of the effect of differences in season and water treatment on differences in rice yields among geographic subdivisions (*Hsiens*) in Taiwan is more difficult than in the Philippines and Thailand. The differences in rainfall between the dry and wet seasons is not as pronounced. And the Provincial Food Bureau does not report yields separately for irrigated and rain-fed rice.

Certain data, however, permit alternative tests of the relationship between irrigation and yield differences. Regression analysis of the relationship between yield and area irrigated for the period 1922–38 and 1950–60 indicates a very high association between area irrigated and yield per hectare.[7] And the highest average yields are obtained in those *Hsiens* in western and southwestern Taiwan where irrigation is most highly developed.

Although the data from Taiwan do not permit the same degree of precision in identifying yield as in the Philippines and Thailand, it is organized to permit identification of the effect of differences in type of rice on yield differences among *Hsiens*. The highest-yielding rice varieties grown in Taiwan are of the *ponlai* type (Figure 6.2; Table 6.4). The *ponlai* varieties account for well over half of the rice area in each food district (Figure 6.9). The average yield in each region is a weighted average of the yield obtained from each type and the proportion of the area devoted to each type.

The effect of differences in area devoted to each type on regional average yields can be measured by comparing the actual average yield in each region with the standardized average yield that would have been obtained if the distribution of area in the region had been the same as for Taiwan as a whole. If standardization results in convergence (i.e., less variation in the standardized than actual yields), this would be consistent with the hypothesis that differences in the type of rice grown represent an important source of variations in yield among regions.

The results (Table 6.5) indicate that standardization of average yields among food districts in Taiwan, to reflect the effects of differences in area devoted to the

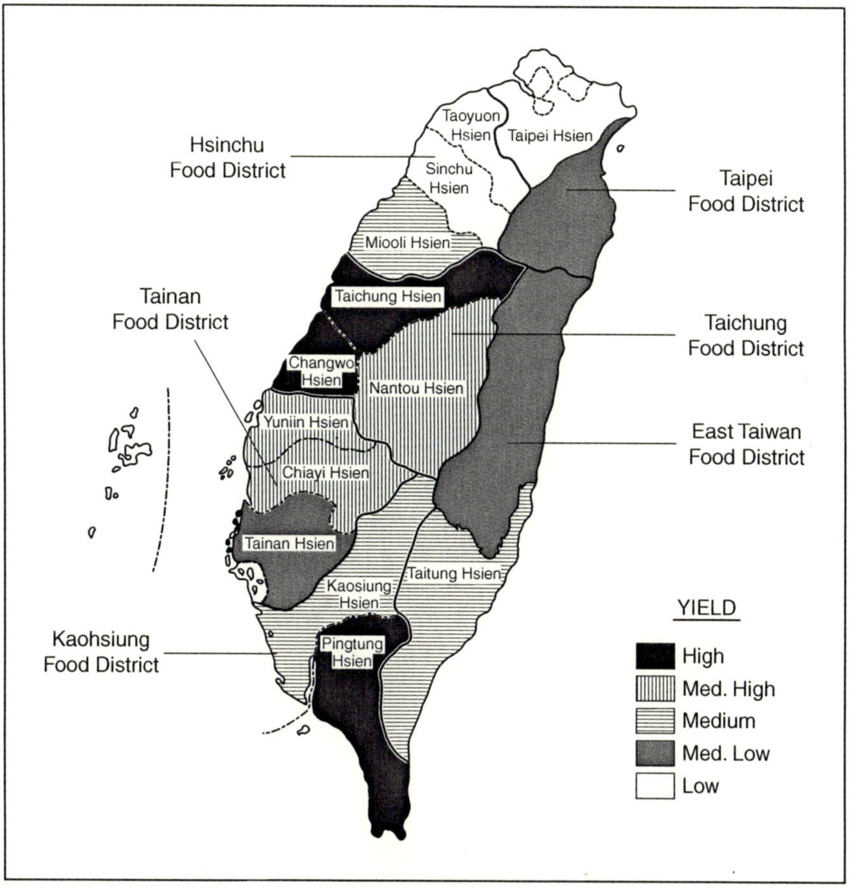

Figure 6.8 Distribution of Rice Yields among Hsiens in Taiwan, 1961/62–1963/64 Average.*

* See Appendix Note for source of basic data; 3 *Hsiens* are included in each category. The categories represent yields in metric tons of rough rice per hectare harvested, and indexes with the Taiwan national average of 3.52 tons = 100, as follows:

High	*Yield*	*Index*
High	3.91–3.98	111.13–111.92
Medium high	3.63–3.82	102.98–108.49
Medium	3.29–3.56	93.52–101.16
Medium low	3.09–3.24	87.62–92.08
Low	2.90–3.06	82.33–86.76

Table 6.4 **Actual Yields of Various Types of Rice in Taiwan, Selected Averages, 1926/27–1928/29 to 1961/62–1963/64* (*Metric tons rough rice per hectare*)**

	1926/27–1928/29		*1937/38–1939/40*		*1954/55–1956/57*		*1961/62–1963/64*	
Type of rice	*Yield*	*Index*	*Yield*	*Index*	*Yield*	*Index*	*Yield*	*Index*
National Average	2.15	100.0	2.77	100.0	2.90	100.0	3.52	100.00
Ponlai	2.24	104.2	3.06	110.5	3.11	107.2	3.64	103.4
Nonglutinous	2.23	103.7	2.60	93.9	2.85	98.3	3.45	98.0
Glutinous	2.01	93.5	2.62	94.6	2.81	96.9	3.27	92.9
Upland	1.50	69.8	1.52	54.9	1.18	40.7	1.47	41.8

* Yields from Taiwan Provincial Food Bureau, *Taiwan Food Statistics* 1964 (Taipei).

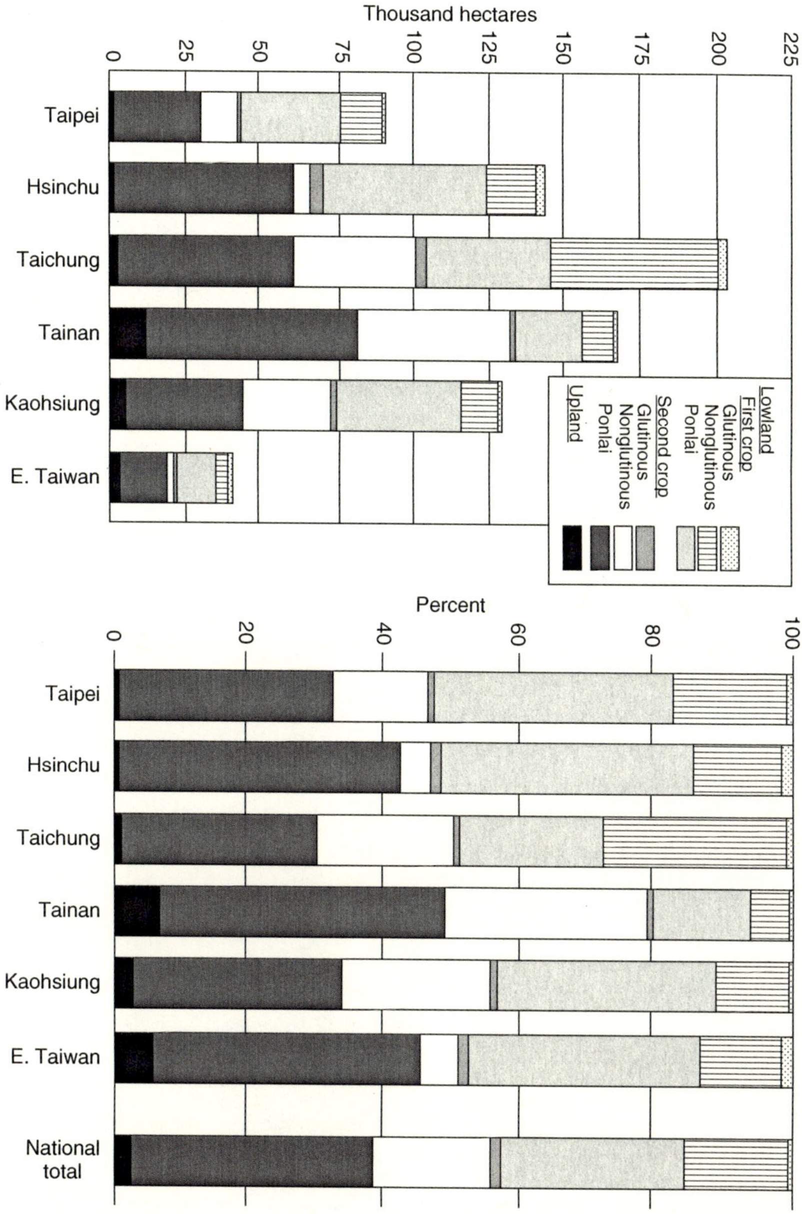

Figure 6.9 Distribution of Rice Area by Food Districts in Taiwan, 1961/62–1963/64 Average.*

* See Appendix Note for source data.

several classes of rice during the wet and dry seasons, tends to widen rather than narrow the yield dispersion among regions. That is, if each food region allocated exactly the same proportion of its rice area among types as the national average the yield variation among regions would be wider than at present—yields would decline in Taipei and rise in Kaohsiung, for example. Apparently there are

Table 6.5 **Effect of Differences in Regional Production Patterns on Regional Average Yield of Rough Rice in Taiwan, 1961/62–1963/64***

	Actual yield		*Standardized yield*	
Food district	*Tones per hectare*	*Index*	*Tons per hectare*	*Index*
Taiwan	3.520	100.00	3.520	100.00
Taipei	2.965	84.23	2.864	81.36
Hsinchu	3.158	89.71	3.021	85.83
Taichung	3.904	110.92	3.785	107.53
Tainan	3.530	100.28	3.762	106.88
Kaohsiun	3.793	107.76	4.378	124.38
East Taiwan	3.224	91.59	3.224	91.59

* Actual yields are from 1962, 1963, and 1964 issues of source cited for Table 6.4, Tons are metric.

substantial differences in yield for the same types in different food districts. It seems reasonable, therefore, to conclude that environmental differences continue to account for a substantial share of the variations in yield among districts in Taiwan.

The analysis of regional yield data for the Philippines, Thailand, and Taiwan reveals several significant differences. First, actual yield differences are less among regions in Taiwan than in the Philippines and Thailand. Second, standardization for differences in the type of rice grown among regions in Taiwan does not result in a convergence of yield differentials in the same way that standardization for the differences in season and/or water treatment resulted in convergence of yield differentials in the Philippines and Thailand.

Apparently the fact that most rice is grown under fully irrigated conditions in Taiwan imposed, by itself, a high degree of yield uniformity. In addition a very high proportion of the total rice area is planted to the *ponlai* varieties. The yield uniformity also reflects genetic improvements in the glutinous and nonglutinous *indica* (*Chailai*) varieties grown in Taiwan, which has permitted some convergence of yield differential among the *ponlai*, nonglutinous, and glutinous types (Table 6.5). Apparently only the upland varieties have failed to share in the yield improvements since the late 1930s.

In the previous section an attempt was made to determine the extent to which differences in the yield of rice among regions within each country are accounted for by environmental or technological factors. In this section an attempt is made to assess the relative importance of environmental and technological factors in determining yield trends in the major rice-producing regions of the Philippines, Thailand, and Taiwan. Taiwan is treated as a single region because of the relative uniformity of yields among regions and its small size relative to the other countries.

Clearly, national average yields per hectare are lower in the Philippines than in Thailand and are relatively lower today than a decade ago. Taiwan's average yields are higher than in either the Philippines or Thailand and are much higher relative to the other two countries today than in the early 1950s (Table 6.6).

Disaggregation to the regional level, in an attempt to achieve greater uniformity of environmental factors, reveals a somewhat different picture. Yields in central Thailand and the Central Luzon areas of the Philippines—the two regions in each country in which irrigation is most highly developed and which account for a relatively high percentage of the rice which enters the commercial market—are almost identical in most years and have risen at approximately the same rate over the last decade (Table 6.7). Moreover, the rate of yield increase in both Central Luzon and central Thailand has been approximately the same as in Taiwan. Thus the average yield in the two regions has remained at just slightly less than 50 percent of the Taiwan yield since the early 1950s (Table 6.7).

It is also of interest to compare yields in regions in which irrigation is least developed and where the area grown under rain-fed and upland conditions has been expanding rapidly. Northeastern Thailand has experienced a rapid expansion in rain-fed rice area. The Philippines has seen rapid expansion of both upland and rain-fed area in southern and western Mindanao and in the Cagayan Valley. In the early 1950s rice yields in southern and western Mindanao and in the Cagayan Valley were substantially higher than those in northeastern Thailand.

Table 6.6 **Comparison of National Average Yields of Rough Rice in the Philippines, Thailand, and Taiwan, 1953/54–1963/64***

	Philippines	*Thailand*	*Taiwan*		*Yield ratios*	
Year	*(1)*	*(2)*	*(3)*	*(1)/(3)*	*(2)/(3)*	*(1)/(2)*
1953/54	1.20	1.39	2.77	.43	.50	.86
1954/55	1.21	1.26	2.86	.42	.44	.96
1955/56	1.19	1.36	2.82	.42	.48	.88
1956/57	1.21	1.44	3.00	.40	.48	.84
1957/58	1.02	1.30	3.08	.33	.42	.78
1958/59	1.11	1.36	3.19	.35	.43	.82
1959/60	1.13	1.29	3.14	.36	.41	.88
1960/61	1.16	1.39	3.27	.35	.43	.83
1961/62	1.23	1.44	3.38	.36	.43	.85
1962/63	1.25	1.49	3.49	.36	.43	.84
1963/64	1.24	1.59	3.69	.34	.43	.78

* See Appendix Note for sources of yield figures.

Table 6.7 **Comparison of Yields of Rough Rice in Central Luzon, Central Thailand, and Taiwan, 1953/54–1963/64* *(Yields in metric tons per hectare harvested)***

	Central Luzon	*Central Thailand*	*Taiwan*		*Yield ratios*	
Year	*(1)*	*(2)*	*(3)*	*(1)/(3)*	*(2)/(3)*	*(1)/(2)*
1953/54	1.33	1.61	2.77	.48	.58	.83
1954/55	1.50	1.38	2.86	.52	.48	1.09
1955/56	1.61	1.53	2.82	.57	.54	1.05
1956/57	1.61	1.30	3.00	.54	.53	1.01
1957/58	1.41	1.46	3.08	.46	.42	1.08
1958/59	1.51	1.56	3.19	.47	.49	.97
1959/60	1.39	1.46	3.14	.44	.46	.95
1960/61	1.57	1.59	3.27	.48	.49	.99
1961/62	1.80	1.51	3.38	.53	.45	1.19
1962/63	1.82	1.73	3.49	.52	.50	1.05
1963/64	1.86	1.86	3.69	.50	.50	1.00

* See Appendix Note for sources of yield figures.

With the rapid expansion in area in southern and western Mindanao, yields have declined and are now only slightly higher than those in northeastern Thailand. Area expanded primarily through the addition of area in upland and rain-fed rice. Under this type of cultivation rice yields are low, and apparently differ little in northeastern Thailand, southern and western Mindanao, and the Cagayan Valley in spite of rather substantial differences in soil and climate (Table 6.8).

It would also be instructive to see whether the pattern of yield increases now occurring in Central Luzon and central Thailand are similar to those that occurred in Taiwan after the early or mid-1920s, when the rice yield "take-off" began. In Table 6.9 the decade 1924/25–1934/35 for Taiwan is selected for comparison with the decade 1953/54–1963/64 for central Thailand and Central Luzon. The absolute yields of rough rice in Taiwan during the 1924/25–1934/35 period were typically about 25 percent higher than in central Thailand and Central Luzon during 1953/54–1963/64. The relative yield remained roughly unchanged, indicating that the rate of yield increases in Central Luzon and in central Thailand from 1953/54 to 1963/64 was about the same as in Taiwan from 1924/25 to 1934/35 (Table 6.8). Inspection of the data would seem to indicate that rice yields in central Thailand and Central Luzon may have entered a take-off stage after the mid-1950s resembling that in Taiwan after the mid-1920s.

Table 6.8 **Comparison of Yields of Rough Rice in Philippines and Thailand, Regions with Rapid Expansion, 1953/54–1963/64* *(Yields in metric tons per hectare harvested)***

	Southern and Western Mindinao	*Cagayan Valley*	*Northeast Thailand*	*Yield ratios*	
Year	*(1)*	*(2)*	*(3)*	*(1)/(3)*	*(2)/(3)*
1953/54	2.04	1.59	1.08	1.89	1.47
1954/55	1.47	1.31	.93	1.58	1.41
1955/56	1.35	1.25	1.01	1.34	1.24
1956/57	1.36	1.25	1.13	1.20	1.11
1957/58	1.04	1.08	1.03	1.01	1.05
1958/59	1.04	1.28	1.01	1.03	1.27
1959/60	1.03	1.38	.93	1.11	1.48
1960/61	1.13	1.09	1.03	1.10	1.06
1961/62	1.14	1.21	.94	1.21	1.29
1962/63	1.26	1.28	1.16	1.09	1.10
1963/64	1.26	1.13	1.17	1.08	.97

* See Appendix Note for sources of yield figures.

A closer examination of the yield increases in Central Luzon and central Thailand indicates, however, that one should be cautious in accepting this conclusion. In Central Luzon the recent increases in yield are associated with a substantial decline in the area devoted to rice (Figure 6.10). Competition between rice and sugarcane for land has resulted in a shift of marginal rice land to other uses (Mangahas et al. 1966). At least part of the yield increases in Central Luzon over the last decade must be attributed to a transfer of lower-yielding upland and rain-fed rice hectarage to other uses.

In Thailand, natural disasters, typically excess flooding in the Central Plain and both excess flooding and extreme dry weather in the Northeast, frequently reduce sharply the percentage of the area planted that can be harvested. In some years, severe flooding or drought also reduces the yield on land that is harvested in areas that are not completely damaged.

The relationship between yield per hectare harvested and percentage of planted area reported damaged between 1947/48 and 1963/64 is presented in Figure 6.11. A relatively high percentage of the variation in yield from year to year can be explained by variations in the percentage of damaged areas in the Northeast and the Central Plain. In addition, most of the upward trend in yield in these two regions in recent years appears to result from a sequence of years in which the

Table 6.9 **Comparison of Yields of Rough Rice in Central Luzon and Central Thailand, 1953/54–1963/64, with Taiwan Yields 1924/25–1934/35*** ***(Yields in metric tons per hectare harvested)***

	Central Luzon	*Central Thailand*		*Taiwan*	*Yield ratios*	
Year	*(1)*	*(2)*	*Year*	*(3)*	*(1)/(3)*	*(2)/(3)*
1953/54	1.33	1.61	1924/25	2.14	.62	.75
1954/55	1.50	1.38	1925/26	2.19	.68	.63
1955/56	1.61	1.53	1926/27	2.05	.79	.75
1956/57	1.61	1.60	1927/28	2.21	.73	.72
1957/58	1.41	1.30	1928/19	2.18	.65	.60
1958/59	1.51	1.56	1929/30	2.14	.71	.73
1959/60	1.39	1.46	1930/31	2.25	.62	.65
1960/61	1.57	1.59	1931/32	2.21	.71	.72
1961/62	1.80	1.51	1932/33	2.52	.71	.60
1962/63	1.82	1.73	1933/34	2.32	.78	.75
1963/64	1.86	1.86	1934/35	2.55	.73	.73

See Appendix Note for sources of yield figures.

damaged area has declined continuously. If damage again rises to the range of 12 to 17 percent, as in 1958/59 and 1959/60, the average yield in the Central Plain could drop to around 1.5 metric tons per hectare. In the Northeast, damage in the range of 9 to 12 percent, as in 1957/58–1959/60, could again result in yields of around 1.0 metric ton per hectare.[8]

Technological and Institutional Factors in Taiwan

Despite numerous deficiencies, the data examined above are consistent with the first hypothesis—that both the yield increases of the last decade and the yield differences among major rice-producing regions in the Philippines and Thailand primarily reflect variations in the environmental factors under which rice is grown rather than differences in variety planted or cultural practices. After the effects of the environmental factors are taken into account, there is little yield increase or yield differential left to be explained by such factors as new varieties, better cultural practices, or more intensive use of technical inputs such as fertilizer and insecticides or by economic and social differences among regions and between Thailand and the Philippines.

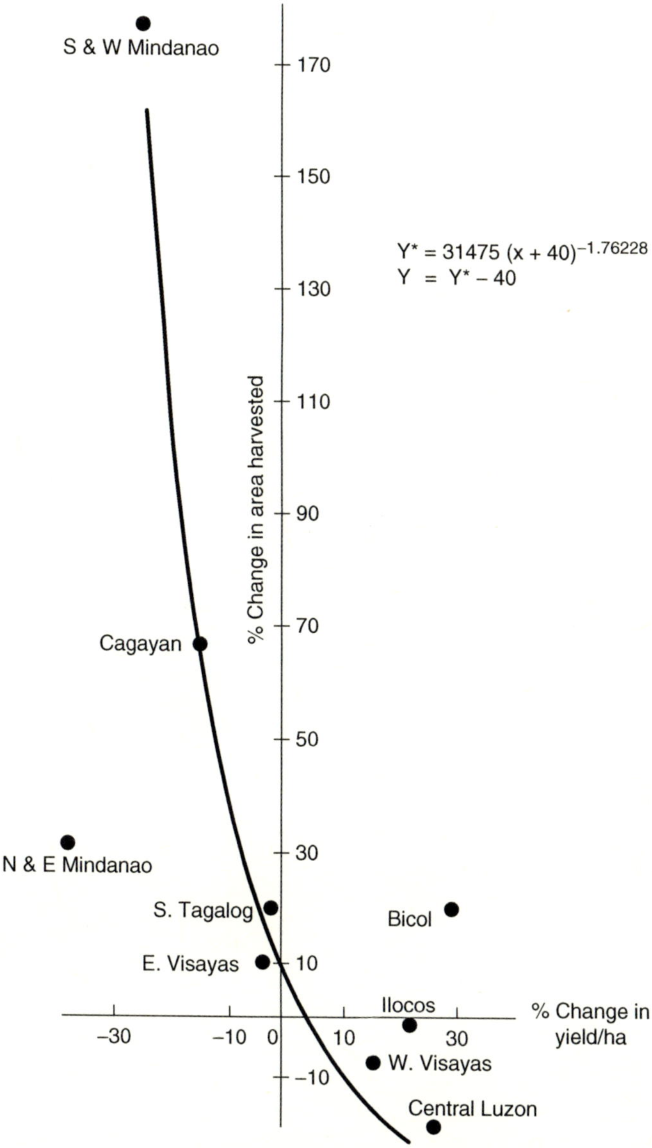

Figure 6.10 Interaction of Area and Yield Changes in Philippines Regions Between 1952/53–1954/55 and 1960/61–1962/63.*

* Data from Vengas and Ruttan (1964: 160, 176). See Appendix Note for source of basic data.

This conclusion would not have much significance if there had been no changes in varieties, cultural practices, or the use of technical inputs. Fertilizer is not widely used on rice in Southeast Asia. A major obstacle to higher levels of fertilizer use is the limited response to increased applications of nitrogen, particularly during the wet season, when most rice is grown (Herdt and Mellor 1964; U.S.

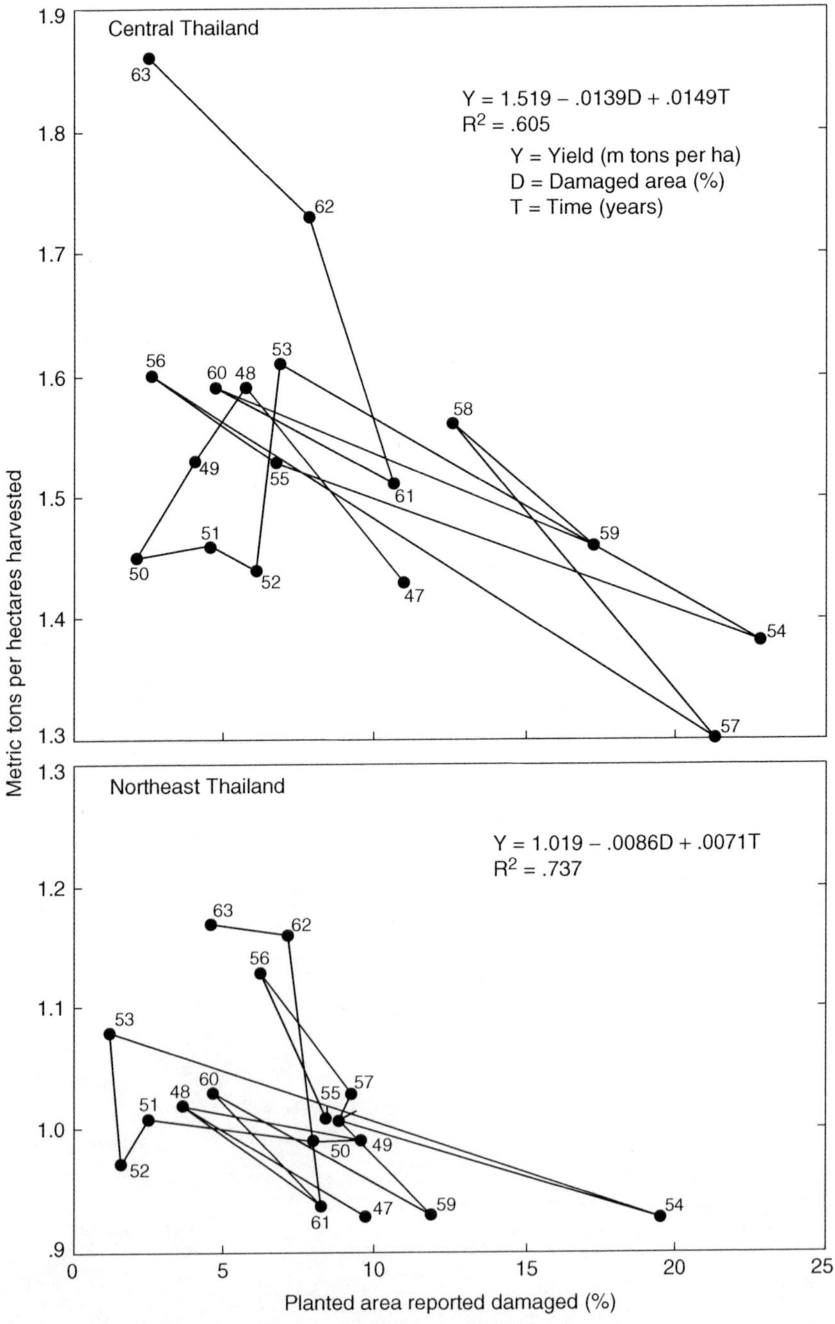

Figure 6.11 Relationship between Yield per Hectare Harvested and Percentage of Planted Area Reported Damaged, Thailand, 1947/48–1963/64.*

* See Appendix Note for source of basic data.

President's Science Advisory Committee 1967). There have been other significant changes in technology over the last decade and a half in both the Philippines and Thailand. Higher-yielding local varieties have been widely diffused; new varieties have been introduced from other Southeast Asian countries (principally Indonesia); and a number of new varieties based on local crosses have been developed and distributed. In the Philippines, straight row planting and use of the mechanical weeder has resulted in better weed control in substantial areas. Increasingly effective insecticides have been introduced in both countries. It seems apparent, however, that the innovations of the last several decades have not yet had any measurable impact on national average yields.

It is possible, however, that both the Philippines and Thailand may be entering the preliminary phase of a "yield take-off" similar to the situation in Taiwan in the mid-1920s. Some new technology has been introduced. New rice varieties are now being developed which resemble, in their fertilizer response and yield potential, the *ponlai* varieties that were introduced in Taiwan in the mid-1920s. Although the yield increases in Central Luzon and central Thailand since the mid-1950s appear to be based primarily on environmental factors, it is possible that some "real" yield increases have occurred. It is useful, therefore, to examine in greater detail the conditions under which the "yield take-off" in Taiwan actually occurred.

The simplest answer may lie in the fact that (a) the development and introduction of high-yielding *ponlai* varieties in Taiwan in the early 1920s provided an important breakthrough in the rice yield potentials in Taiwan, and (b) the substantial irrigation development that had already been completed or was completed within the next several years provided the essential infrastructure investment for rapid diffusion of the new technology. However, the answer is not really so simple. One can also ask, given the technology and infrastructure prerequisites, why it took roughly forty years—from the early 1920s to the early 1960s—to realize the yield potentials of the new varieties. An average yield of 3.78 metric tons of rough rice per hectare was achieved on the first 414 hectares of commercial *ponlai* production in 1922. The national average yield for *ponlai* varieties in 1961/63 was 3.64 metric tons of rough rice per hectare.

The Technological Conditions for Growth

By the mid-1920s Taiwan had acquired a number of essential elements for rapid development of its rice economy.[9] New and improved rice varieties had been introduced, and research and development institutions capable of making continuous improvements in varietal characteristics had been established. Much of the potential rice land was served by irrigation systems capable of delivering water to the land throughout the year. Technical inputs such as fertilizer were made available through economic integration with the Japanese economy. Economic integration also resulted in rapid development of the local transportation and marketing systems, opened up the Japanese markets, and created incentives to increase the marketable surplus of rice in Taiwan (Chang 1959).

HIGHER-YIELDING VARIETIES

Early efforts by the Japanese to improve rice varieties in Taiwan emphasized selection and diffusion of native *indica* varieties characterized by high yields (Chang 1959; Johnston 1962; Kung 1956). In spite of a large reduction in the number of inferior varieties grown and substantial diffusion of superior varieties, the national average yield showed only modest gains. Early efforts to introduce *Japonica* varieties from Japan were not successful. Even after substantial modifications in cultural practices the high yield potentials of the *japonica* varieties were only partially realized under Taiwan conditions. Efforts were then directed to breeding varieties of the *japonica* type which combined the desirable characteristics of the introduced *japonica* varieties (high fertilizer response, short growing period, nonsensitivity to photoperiod, and better quality) with the resistance to disease and the superior adaptation to the local ecology of the native *indica* varieties. The new *japonica-indica* crosses developed in Taiwan are referred to as *ponlai* varieties.

The first *ponlai* variety, Nakamaru, was introduced commercially in 1922 when it was planted on 414 hectares in the Hsinchu region. An exceptionally high yield of 3.78 metric tons per hectare was achieved. Later the planted areas were increased and extended to the Taipei and Taichung regions. With the diffusion, average yield declined. After 1925 an outbreak of rice blast disease, to which the new varieties were highly susceptible, sharply reduced the *ponlai* yields. Beginning in 1930, other *ponlai* varieties with greater resistance to the rice blast disease were introduced, and by 1940 half the total rice area was planted to *ponlai* varieties. Approximately twenty years had elapsed between the introduction of the first *japonica* varieties and the development of *ponlai* varieties which possessed sufficient advantages relative to local varieties to justify rapid diffusion.

Two characteristics of the new varieties were particularly important in establishing a high complementarity with other inputs. First, the higher yield potentials of the *ponlai* varieties could only be realized with high levels of fertilization and careful management of water. At low levels of fertilization and with inadequate or undependable control over irrigation water, the local *indica* varieties had higher yields than the *ponlai* varieties. Second, elimination of photoperiod sensitivity (flowering dependent on day length) and shortening of the number of days from transplanting to harvest made it possible to obtain two crops of rice per year, given a high level of crop husbandry and effective water control.

After World War II, strenuous efforts were made to develop new *ponlai* rice varieties to replace the old ones. Sixty-two improved varieties of *ponlai* rice were officially registered from 1946 to 1964. As a result the *ponlai* rice varieties released in the early period have been largely replaced by varieties developed in the postwar period. The new varieties developed feature early maturity, high-yielding capacity, short and sturdy straw (i.e., resistance to lodging), responsiveness to heavy fertilization, and resistance to most prevalent diseases.

Breeding efforts to increase yields of the native *indica* varieties were also emphasized after World War II. Efforts to develop *indica* varieties with such desirable characters as nonsensitiveness to day-length, lodging resistance, and responsiveness to fertilization have been successful. As a result large acreages are still planted to the native rice varieties. As the improved varieties of both types have demonstrated their superiority in increasing yield, a greater percentage of total area has been accounted for by a relatively limited number of varieties.[10]

IRRIGATION DEVELOPMENT

Rapid development of the irrigation system in Taiwan represented a major facet of the Japanese colonial policy designed to develop Taiwan into a major supplier of rice for the Japanese domestic market. Irrigation investment and irrigated area expanded rapidly from 1900 until completion of the Chianan system in the early 1930s (Table 6.10).

The major capital investments were in the form of grants, generated primarily out of internal revenues. Japanese government subsidies for Taiwan development extended only from 1896 to 1904 (Chang and Myers 1963). Development, maintenance, and operation of the irrigation systems was placed in the hands of farmers. Between the completion of the Chianan systems in the early 1930s and initiation of the Ta-Pu and Shihmen projects in the late 1950s, there was very little investment in expansion of system capacity. There was, however, very substantial investment by the irrigation associations and individual farmers in the improvement of the efficiency of the distribution systems—in canal development and maintenance, local storage and pumping facilities, and land leveling and development—to more effectively use the irrigation water.

TECHNICAL INPUTS

The relationship between fertilizer use and the yield of rice depends critically on two factors: (a) The rice variety must have the genetic capacity to respond to higher levels of fertilization in terms of higher grain yield. Vegetative response, typical of most *indica* varieties, tends to induce lodging and is competitive with higher grain yield. (b) Control of the timing and level of water application is also essential. Lack of water control, resulting in either excess or inadequate water, can sharply reduce the response of yields to fertilization. Lack of both fertilizer-responsive rice varieties and effective water control accounts for the fact that farmers in Southeast Asia have, in the past, rarely fertilized rice grown under rain-fed conditions even when fertilizer has been available (von Uexkull 1964).

Commercial fertilizers were introduced to Taiwan by the Japanese during the early years of colonization. Major efforts to induce farmers to use fertilizer on rice were not initiated, however, until the *ponlai* varieties were introduced. Use of

Table 6.10 **Irrigation in Taiwan, 1900–40***

	Irrigated land (thousand hectares)			*Costs[a] (thousand old Taiwan dollars at 1935–37 prices)*		
Period	*Total*	*Double paddy*	*Single Paddy*	*Total*	*Irrigation Investment*	*Irrigation operation*
1900	194.7	. . .	. . .			
1901–10				15.6	6.2	9.4
1910	332.4	. . .	. . .			
1911–20				28.5	9.5	19.4
1920	367.2	246.5	120.7			
1921–30				213.2	81.8	131.4
1930	396.3	292.1	104.2			
1931–40				118.3	24.7	93.6
1940	529.6	324.2	205.4			
1960	525.5	329.0	196.5			

* Data from E. L. Rada and T. H Lee (22): 33, 37.

[a] The data on irrigation investment and operating costs are presented in constant dollars in order to emphasize the absolute rise in irrigation investment. Another measure of the magnitude of the irrigation investment in Taiwan is obtained by comparing the current dollar value of irrigation investment with the current value of rice production. The results of this comparison are as follows in percent:

Investment and Operational Costs as a Percent of the Value of Rice Production in Current Dollars

	Total	*Irrigation investment*	*Irrigation operation cost*
1901–10	2.5	1.00	1.50
1911–20	3.55	1.22	2.33
1921–30	18.97	7.31	11.66
1931–40	6.86	1.44	5.42

The data on the current value of rice production is from Taiwan Provincial Food Bureau, *Taiwan Food Statistics* (Taipei), various years.

commercial fertilizers on rice increased by about 50 percent between the mid-1920s and 1938, remained relatively stable from 1938 until 1943, declined slightly during 1944–1947, and increased approximately five times between 1949 and 1960 (Rada and Lee 1963: 141). Except during 1946–1950 fertilizer has been available to farmers on relatively favorable terms (Hsieh and Lee 1966).

Rice yield per hectare did not reach the 1938 peak until 1956. This is clearly related to lack of fertilizer availability. It also seems reasonable to hypothesize that the level of fertilizer application limited the rate of growth of rice yields between the mid-1920s and 1938.

IMPROVED PRODUCTION PRACTICES

The emphasis on production practices has also shifted over time. Early efforts were directed toward diffusion of the better processes already in use. As early as 1908 government regulations with respect to the eradication and prevention of crop diseases and pests were promulgated. Closer spacing of rice seedlings to increase the plant population per hectare was emphasized. Deep plowing was introduced.

With the introduction of the *ponlai* varieties and the emphasis on fertilization in the mid-1920s special efforts were made to promote weed control and good practices of land preparation.

More recently the emphasis has fallen on the development and diffusion of an integrated set of practices ranging from land preparation to harvesting methods. As the yield potentials have continued to rise, greater emphasis has also been placed on plant protection, particularly with respect to control of stem borer and blast disease.

The Institutional Conditions for Growth

The essential technological and environmental elements for rapid development of the Taiwan rice economy were available by the mid-1920s. Introduction of these elements resulted in increases in yield per hectare of over 2.0 percent per year until 1938, when Japanese military efforts began to divert resources from development objectives. Since the early 1950s rice yields have again risen rapidly, even though the technological and environmental factors were not greatly different from those in the mid-1920s and early 1930s.

In spite of continued varietal development work, it appears that the yield potentials, under optimum environmental and management conditions, have not changed significantly since the late 1920s or early 1930s. It has previously been pointed out that greater fertilizer availability has been one factor permitting closer approximation of average to potential yields. It also seems clear that the evolution of the farmers' associations into effective extension and marketing organizations and the improvement in incentives resulting from the land reform of 1949–1952 have played a significant role in the achievement of higher rice yields.

FARMERS' ASSOCIATIONS

Approximately twenty years elapsed between introduction of the first Japanese rice varieties and the development of the *ponlai* varieties to the point where they were suitable for rapid diffusion. It looks roughly twice as long to develop fully effective institutional arrangements for rapid diffusion of new technology, the dissemination of credit, and marketing of agricultural supplies. The efforts to develop institutions to perform these functions have focused on the farmers' associations (Hsieh and Lee 1966).

The first farmers' association was established in Taipei Prefecture in 1900. By 1908 sixteen had been organized to provide a direct link with experiment stations in introducing seeds of new varieties and in dissemination of improved farm practices. The associations also purchased and distributed fertilizer. They came under formal government regulation in 1908, and membership and collection of dues became compulsory. The system was reorganized in 1927. Agricultural improvement stations were established in each prefecture with direct linkage to the prefectural associations. By the early 1930s the associations employed 1,148 agricultural technicians. Their responsibilities had expanded to include extension of new agricultural practices, handling of land rent disputes between landlords and tenants, seed multiplication, fertilizer distribution, and related activities. The associations were again reorganized in 1937 in order to strengthen them in the townships and villages.

While the system of farmers' associations was evolving, cooperatives were being fostered to provide credit to small business and to farms. By the early 1930s the cooperatives had added purchasing, marketing, and warehousing services. Considerable duplication had developed between the activities of the associations and the cooperatives, and in 1943 they were combined into a single organization.

After the establishment of Chinese administration, the farmers' associations and the cooperatives were first separated in 1946 and then reunified in 1949. Under the new reorganization, steps were taken to decentralize the administration of the associations and to give greater authority to the farmer members.

The period since 1950 has been one of continued development. The credit functions and the handling of farm supplies and marketing of farm products of the old cooperative system were fully integrated with the extension and technical advisory services of the farmers' associations. A combination of market power and efficient administration combined to make the association an efficient agent of technological change. Bothe market and nonmarket devices were coordinated to induce the cultivator to adopt the highest-yielding varieties, apply high levels of fertilizer, and adopt labor-intensive production practices directed at achieving rapid increases in yield.

The farmers' association system has evolved from a prewar pattern based very heavily on administrative control from the center down to the individual farmer to a system which relies primarily on a combination of technical information and market incentives in the factor and product markets to induce production decisions on the part of individual farmers.

LAND TENURE

A second factor in the rapid growth of yield per hectare during the last decade and a half has been the incentive for more intensive use of purchased inputs, family labor, and land associated with the land reform of 1949–1953. The first stage of the program involved a compulsory reduction in rent. The second stage involved purchase and resale of rented land to the tenant. Tenancy declined from 39 percent to 17 percent of families between 1949 and 1597. The land reform did not involve the breaking up of large estate but rather the transfer of tenant units from ownership of landlords to ownership of cultivators (Tang and Hsieh 1961).

The implications of the land reform for incentives to use purchased inputs and household labor is consistent with the empirical evidence. The rapid increase in fertilizer use on rice reviewed earlier was clearly a joint result of the availability of the fertilizer, a favorable rice-fertilizer barter ratio in relation to high potential response of rice output to fertilizer,[11] and the additional incentive associated with an owner-operator system as compared with a share tenure system. Dramatic increases in the multiple cropping index and in labor input per worker were probably even more closely associated with the increased incentives for more intensive use of family labor.[12]

The Taiwan experience is consistent with the proposition that institutional development has to be built up through a process of selection, trial and error, and adaptive research similar to the manner in which new varieties are evolved. Both the agricultural technology and the institutions must be developed, or at least tested and modified, in the location in which they are to be utilized (Long 1966).

Considerations in the Design of a Strategy for Increasing Rice Production in Southeast Asia

The analysis of the previous sections can be summarized as follows:

1 Prior to the mid-1920s differences in rice yields among the three countries—Philippines, Thailand, and Taiwan—and among regions within each country were due primarily to differences in the environmental conditions under which rice was grown rather than to technological, economic, and social differences. The dominant environmental factor was irrigation and the precision of water treatment control.

2 With the introduction of the *ponlai* varieties by the Japanese in Taiwan in the mid-1920s technology became a dominant variable in explaining the rapid increase in rice yields in Taiwan and in explaining differences in rice yields between Taiwan and the other two countries. An important factor in the rapid diffusion of the new varieties and the use of higher levels of technical inputs such as fertilizer was the rapid irrigation development in Taiwan which began shortly after 1900 and continued through the 1920s. Achievement of the yield potentials inherent in the new varieties was stimulated by institutional developments, such as (a) the organization of farmers' associations and irrigation associations during the period of Japanese occupation and (b) the successful implementation of the land reform program and the reorganization of the

farmers' associations into effective integrated farm supply, credit, and marketing cooperatives following the restoration of Chinese administration after World War II.

3 In the Philippines and Thailand differences in yield both between the two countries and among regions within each country are still primarily due to differences in environmental conditions under which rice is grown. When differences in season (wet or dry) and water treatment (irrigated, rain-fed, or upland) are taken into consideration very little difference in yield is left to be explained by such factors as new varieties, difference in cultural practice, more intensive use of technical inputs, or differences in economic and social institutions.

4 Both the Philippines and Thailand may now be approaching a yield take-off similar to that experienced in Taiwan in the mid-1920s. Yields in the major producing regions in both countries have been rising at about the same rate during the last decade as in Taiwan during the decade following introduction of the *ponlai* varieties. Furthermore, new higher-yielding varieties having a yield potential of at least 6.0 metric tons during the wet season and 8.0 metric tons during the dry season when grown under irrigation with an appropriate complement of technical inputs are now being introduced. (IRRI 1966)

Yet despite the yield potential inherent in the new varieties now being introduced there seem clearly to be basic deficiencies in the sequence of development programming which may prevent the Philippines and Thailand from repeating the experience of Taiwan. In Taiwan a major share of the basic investment in irrigation was already completed before the beginning of the biological revolution that led to the yield take-off in the 1920s. Furthermore, the irrigation development leading to effective water control was a prerequisite to the effective diffusion of the new higher-yielding, labor-intensive, "fertilizer-consuming" rice varieties. Institutional innovations such as extension work, farmers' associations, irrigation associations, and land reform followed and complemented both the investment in water control and the technological changes.[13]

In the Philippines and Thailand a reverse pattern is being followed. Efforts to develop agriculture following World War II have concentrated very heavily on institutional development. In the Philippines this effort is currently being supplemented by substantial efforts to develop and introduce high-yielding rice varieties responsive to fertilizer similar to the *ponlai* varieties introduced in Taiwan in the mid-1920s.

Neither the Philippines nor Thailand yet places major emphasis on the development of irrigation systems designed to provide a dependable water supply in both the wet and dry seasons to a major portion of the area devoted to rice production. It seems apparent that this lag of land and water resource development behind the institutional and technological changes will impose serious limitation on achievement of the output potential associated with the technological advances that are now being realized.

A high percentage of the lowland rice in the Philippines and Thailand is grown during the rainy season without irrigation. Under this rain-fed system of cultivation, village or provincial average yields rarely exceed 1.5 metric tons per hectare. In fully irrigated areas in both countries, however, in areas such as Cheingmai (Thailand) or Laguna (Philippines) average yields often exceed 3.0 metric tons in the wet season and 3.5 metric tons in the dry season, over fairly substantial areas. On such individual farms as those which participate in contests, or under experimental conditions, yields of the same varieties under irrigated conditions frequently fall in the range of 4.0–4.5 metric tons in the wet season and 5.0–6.0 metric tons in the dry season (Chandler 1962; IRRI 1964).

A major implication of this analysis is that the factors which permit a province or region to increase its yield from 1.5 metric tons per hectare in the wet season to the levels currently being achieved in the higher yielding areas of each country are primarily beyond the control of the individual farmer in the major rice-producing areas such as Central Luzon or central Thailand. Modifications in the environment necessary to achieve effective water control through irrigation and drainage during both the wet and the dry seasons will have to come primarily from public or semi-public agencies capable of organizing resources in a manner that is almost invariably beyond the capacity of individual tenants or farm owners.

A second major implication is that the limitations on environmental control that prevent farmers from achieving the yield potentials of existing varieties will be an equally severe limitation on achievement of the much higher yield potentials embodied in the new varieties now being introduced. These new varieties are even more sensitive than existing varieties to effective environmental control, technical inputs, and management.

The ecology of the monsoon tropics and the factor and product price relationships which characterize current development levels rule out the direct transfers of existing rice production technology from temperate region countries such as Japan and the United States. Even transfers within Southeast Asia, from Taiwan to the Philippines or Thailand, have not been successful.

But it is possible to transfer the propensity and the capacity to focus scientific manpower and other resources on technical problems of economic significance and the skill that comes from having solved similar problems although in a different environment. This involves skill (a) in breeding for fertilizer response, disease resistance, grain quality, and other elements, and (b) in using the local ecological information supplied by soil chemists, physiologists, entomologists, cereal chemists, geneticists, agronomists, economists, and others to select and achieve appropriate breeding objectives and breeding strategy.

The magnitude of the investment required to realize the production potential inherent in the new technology that is being created tends to be substantially underestimated. There will have to be massive investment in the industries that produce the inputs of fertilizer and insecticides; there will have to be massive investment in irrigation if the investment devoted to development of new varieties and production of the technical inputs is to achieve a reasonably high return; and it will be necessary to commit substantial increases in trained manpower to the tasks of management related to the direct investment and to educational work associated with rapid achievement of the production potentials.

Recognition of the complementarity between these infrastructure investments and the investments in research and development to create new production potentials raises a serious question about the validity of the assumption that primary emphasis on research and development could provide a relatively inexpensive route to rapid growth of agricultural production during the early stages of agricultural development.[14] These assumptions typically rest very heavily on analogies with the Japanese experience since the Meiji Restoration in 1868 and on the Taiwan experience after 1900 (Johnston 1966). In both Japan and Taiwan, however, a relatively high percentage of the rice-producing areas had already been brought under cultivation before the beginning of the "biological revolution" associated with the heavy use of natural and commercial fertilizer, the introduction of higher-yielding fertilizers and responsive rice varieties, and the intensive use of insecticides and other agricultural chemicals.

This failure to develop an effective water storage, transportation, and drainage system for rice production in the monsoon areas of Southeast Asia at an earlier stage in development was due to a major extent to the differences in physical geography. Both Japan and Taiwan are characterized by short river valleys and narrow coastal plains which lent themselves to locally organized, small-scale, labor-intensive irrigation and drainage works. Water typically did not have to be transported over long distances. In contrast to Japan and Taiwan, the major rice-producing areas of Southeast Asia are characterized by broad river valleys and plains. Under these conditions, the physical geography dictates the organization of large national systems. The construction of such systems lends itself to much more capital intensive patterns of investment in water storage, transportation, and drainage, in contrast to the relatively labor-intensive system employed during the early stage of development in Japan and even Taiwan.

Clearly, the investment requirements for growth of the agricultural input sectors and for infrastructure development in the rice-producing countries of South and Southeast Asia will be very high over the next several decades.[15] Furthermore, these investments will be competitive with other development goals. Unfortunately, investment in research and development has not opened up a new low-cost route to the rapid growth of agricultural output in those areas. It can provide one of the essential elements in a total program to achieve increases in agricultural production.

APPENDIX NOTE

Sources of Data for Rice Area, Production, and Yield

Philippines

Area figures through 1952/53 are for area planted, for area harvested thereafter. Yield figures reflect this change. Production figures are in terms of rough rice (paddy) all years; here shown in metric tons, but sometimes also officially reported in cavans (sacks) of 44 kilograms.

1902/03, Census Office of the Philippine Islands, *Census of the Philippine Islands*: 1918, vol. 3 (Manila, 1921); 1908/09, J. S. Camus, *Rice in the Philippines* (Dept. of Agr. and Natural Resources Bulletin No. 37, Manila, 1921). Data up to 1920 are also reported: 1909/10–1924/25, Bureau of Commerce and Industry, *Statistical Bulletin of the Philippine Islands* (Manila, 1926), No. 8 and earlier issues; 1925/26–1952/53, Dept. of Agr. and Natural Resources, *Philippine Agricultural Statistics*, vols. 1 and 2 (Manila, 1955 and 1956); 1953/54–1958/59, Dept. of Agr. and Natural Resources, *Crop and Livestock Statistics* (Quezon City, 1958/59), and earlier issues; 1959/60–1963/64, Dept. of Agr. and Natural Resources, Bureau of Agricultural Economics, Rice: *Area, Production and Yield per Hectare by Region* (Quezon City, mimeo, 1964), and earlier years. Data in Table 6.3 and Figure 6.7 are from the 1960/61 issue, the only issue to give this much detail.

Thailand

In all years area figures are for area harvested, and production in terms of rough rice.

Ministry of Agriculture, Department of Rice, *Annual Report on Rice Production in Thailand, 1965* [in Thai] (Bangkok), and earlier issues. Historical data for 1959 and earlier years in Figure 6.1 are from the 1959 issue.

Taiwan

Area figures are for area harvested all years. The authors have converted production and yield figures, officially reported in terms of brown rice, to rough rice (paddy) equivalent at 1.312 metric tons rough per metric ton brown, corresponding to an extraction rate of 76.2 percent.

Taiwan Provincial Food Bureau, *Taiwan Food Statistics, 1965* (Taipei), and earlier issues. Historical data for Figure 6.1 are from the 1964 issue: 2–3. Various issues give data for Hsiens (counties), Chens or Hsiengs (townships) by season (1st and 2nd crops) for 1952 and later years.

Notes

S. C. Hsieh and Vernon W. Ruttan, *Food Research Institute Studies* 7 (1967): 307–41. This paper draws heavily on several earlier reports by Ruttan et al. (1966a, 1966b), Hsieh and Lee (1966), and Abarientos (1966). The authors are indebted to M. K. Bennett and B. F. Johnson for helpful comments on an earlier draft of this paper.

1. We do not attempt, in this paper, to analyze the factors associated with the expansion or decline of area devoted to rice. Work has recently been completed relating the response of area devoted to rice and other crops to product and factor price behavior (Behrman 1966; Mangahas et al. 1966). In general the results indicate that the area planted to rice tends to be highly responsive to changes in produce prices relative to competing crops. These studies typically did not identify any significant response in yield to changes in relative prices.
2. Irrigated rice is typically grown in fields where water can be impounded by bunds or dikes and where water can be delivered to the field from surface storage, stream diversion, or wells. Rain-fed rice is grown in similar fields but without access to water from surface storage, stream diversion, or wells. Upland rice is grown in fields where water is not impounded. Production of rain-fed and upland rice is typically confined to the wet season in Southeast Asia. In areas where seasonal differences are not too pronounced, two crops of rain-fed or upland rice per year are sometimes obtained. Typically, however, two or more crops per year are obtained only where irrigation is available from surface storage or wells.
3. Yield is measured in terms of kilograms of palay or paddy (i.e., rough rice) per hectare per season. Thus if both a wet- and dry-season crop is grown on the same hectare, it is counted as two hectares and the average yield is the total production for both seasons divided by two.
4.

	Tons per hectare
Wet season irrigated	1.97
Dry season irrigated	1.81
Total irrigated	3.78
Wet season rain-fed	1.41
Increase from irrigation	2.37

This is clearly a conservative estimate of the increase in output that would accompany irrigation. The dry-season yield reflects a situation where there is inadequate water throughout the dry season. Experimental evidence from the IRRI and elsewhere indicates that with adequate irrigation water the dry season yield should exceed the wet season yield by 25 to 50 percent.

5. There are some difficulties in comparing the production, area, and yield of irrigated and nonirrigated land in Thailand. The Rice Department (Ministry of Agriculture) reports only total production, total area planted and harvested, and provincial, regional, and national average yields. It does not report separately production, area, and yield for irrigated, nonirrigated, and upland rice. Since 1958/59 data on production, area planted and harvested, and yield for irrigated land have been reported by the Royal Irrigation Department (Ministry of National Development). The data on production, area, and yield for nonirrigated land utilized in this report were obtained by subtracting the production and area estimates of the Royal Irrigation Department from the total production and area estimates of the Rice Department. Any bias in the Royal Irrigation department data would, therefore, result in an opposite bias in the residual estimates of production, area, and yield in nonirrigated areas. In both Thailand and the Philippines the definition of irrigated land is rather imprecise. Irrigation water is usually supplied by diversion dams in streams and is available only during the wet season. Thus in the Philippines and Thailand the area of the second (dry-season) crop that is irrigated may represent a better estimated area that is adequately irrigated than the area of the first (wet-season) crop that is irrigated. In Thailand, substantial areas classified as irrigated are subject to serious flooding and have inadequate drainage.
6. The Provincial Food Bureau (PFB) reports rice production statistics in terms of paddy rice and upland rice. While all upland rice is rain-fed, part of the paddy rice is also grown on rain-fed (without irrigation) or so-called weather-depending paddy land. However, the PFB data do not differentiate between irrigated rice and rain-fed rice on paddy land. The available data do indicate that even in the mid-1920s, the irrigation ratio (percentage of irrigated land to total cultivated land) was 42 percent in 1922 and 48 percent in 1928. Since irrigation was developed primarily in the lowland rice-producing areas, the area of irrigated land is even higher relative to the total rice area. Since most of the irrigated land is devoted to rice, and two crops of rice per year are typically grown in irrigation areas, the percentage of rice land that is irrigated is much higher than the percentage of total cultivated land that is irrigated. It seems likely that more than 75 percent of the area devoted to rice was irrigated by the mid-1920s.
7. The regression analysis by Rada and Lee (1963) can be summarized as follows:
   1922–38: $Y = 9.6196 + 0.2595F + 0.6232I + 0.0375P\ R^2 = 0.91$
   (0.1240) (0.2774) (0.1109) $S = 5.3643$
   1950–60: $Y = 186.5523 + 0.4971F + 2.4786I - 0.0047P\ R^2 = 0.97$
   (0.7273) (0.6880) (0.036) $S = 2.4918$
   Where I = rice yield per hectare
   F = total fertilizer application
   I = total area irrigation
   P = rice price
8. As long as the parameters for damaged area (d) in the equations presented in Figure 6.11 hold a decline in the area damaged by 10 percentage points, say from 15 to 5 percent, would result in a rise in yield of 139 kilograms (0.139 metric ton) per hectare in the Central Plain and 86 kilograms (0.086 metric ton) in the Northeast. In contrast, the parameter for time or trend (^{T}) indicates an average rise in yield of only 14.9 kilograms (.0149 ton) per hectare per year in the Central Plain and 7.1 kilograms (.0071 ton) per year in the Northeast. The effect is to produce a rather substantial increase in average yield during a period when the damage is declining, which could be sharply reversed by one or two bad years.
9. Mosher (1966) identifies (Abarientos 1966) five agricultural development essentials—(a) markets for farm products, (b) constantly changing technology, (c) local availability of supplies and equipment, (d) production incentives for farmers, and (e) transportation—and (Behrman 1966) five accelerators—(a) education for development, (b) production credit, (c) group action by farmers, (d) improving and expanding agricultural land, and (e) national planning for agricultural development. Our analysis leads us to classify irrigation development as an essential element for agricultural development in the rice-producing areas of the tropics.

10. The following percentage data illustrate the extent to which rice area was accounted for by a few varieties in 1963.*

	Ponlai rice		*Native rice*	
	1st crop	*2nd crop*	*1st crop*	*2nd crop*
Most popular variety	19.5	28.2	47.9	18.0
Seven most popular varieties	65.4	63.6	76.8	60.5
Total hectare	200,623	288,921	112,484	131,111

*Data from S. C. Hsieh and T. H. Lee 1966.

11. The fertilizer-rice barter ratio in Taiwan has been criticized as relatively unfavorable in comparison with some other developing countries. However, given the relatively steep slope of the physical output response relationship for the *ponlai* varieties under irrigated conditions, it has been profitable for Taiwan farmers to use relatively high levels of fertilizer on rice.
12. The changes in farm employment, labor input, and double cropping can be summarized as follows (1911–1915 = 100):*

	Number of agricultural workers	*Labor input in man days/worker*	*Multiple cropping index*
1911–1915	100	100	116
1921–1925	98	118	121
1946–1950	144	141	151
1956–1960	149	198	180

*Data from S.C. Hsieh and T. H. Lee 1966: 24, 41.

13. The Taiwan experience is also consistent with the Japanese experience where effective water control also has represented a significant factor in the diffusion of rice production technology (Kanazawa 1966).
14. B. F. Johnston and G. S. Tolley (1965: 369) indicate that "initial emphasis should be placed on innovations that do not require large increases in the use of purchased inputs. This means emphasis upon the development and introduction of innovations such as high-yielding varieties, improved crop rotation, optimum spacing and time of planting, and a better seasonal distribution of the work load." This advice does not appear relevant in the tropical rice-producing regions of South and Southeast Asia. Without massive investment in irrigation these innovations will not result in higher productivity.
15. For a discussion of irrigation costs in the Philippines and other Southeast Asian countries, see G. Levine 1966 and President's Science Advisory Committee 1967.

CHAPTER 7

Controversy about Agricultural Technology

LESSONS FROM THE GREEN REVOLUTION

Vernon W. Ruttan

1. Introduction

Concern about the unanticipated consequences of technical change is strongly rooted in public consciousness. Such concerns have emerged with particular force with respect to the potential adverse environmental effects of transgenically modified organisms and to the safety concerns about food products derived from transgenically modified crop or animal products.[1] These concerns have given rise to substantial tension in trade relations between the United States and the European Community (Paarlberg 2000; Victor and Runge 2002) and are viewed by some as a potential threat to food security in developing countries (Pinstrup-Anderson and Cohen 2001; Pinstrup-Anderson and Schioler 2001).

The development and introduction, in tropical Latin America and Asia, in the 1960s and the 1970s of high-yielding modern varieties (MVs) of wheat, maize, and rice, characterized by the press as a Green Revolution, was also controversial. Critics argued that the gains in production would be offset by losses in equity—that the new technology would make the rich richer and the poor poorer (Griffin 1974: 51–52; Lappe and Collins 1979: 121–68; Pearse 1980).

The view that modern agricultural technology is both subversive of traditional institutions and regressive in its impact on rural incomes has been supported by both Marxist ideology and populist sentiment. Much of the discussion on this issue is badly confused. There has often been a failure to distinguish between the different income distribution effects of mechanical-engineering and biological-chemical technology. There has also been a tendency to focus on single-factor explanations and to ignore the effects of such factors as the growing population pressure against land resources.

In this paper, I draw on my earlier research on the introduction of modern varieties of wheat, rice, and maize to explore whether there are lessons that are relevant to the current controversy about the new biotechnology revolution.

2. Technology and Agrarian Structure

The perspective that an inevitable consequence of both modern technology and capitalism is to polarize the peasantry into commercial farmers and wage laborers was advanced by Karl Marx and elaborated by Karl Kautsky and Vladimir Lenin (Marx 1967, 1968; Lenin 1964). In this perspective, the institutions of precapitalist village society, such as communal land ownership, mutual-help associations, and patron-client ties, were thought to assure the subsistence needs of the poorest members of the rural community. As those traditional institutions were replaced by modern market institutions, such as private property rights, village elites began to accumulate land for commercial production by encroaching on the commons, by evicting tenants, and by purchasing or appropriating the holdings of small peasants. The introduction of modern machine technology was viewed as further enhancing the efficiency of large-scale relative to small-scale operations, enabling large capitalist farms to displace the small peasants from their land and convert them into landless laborers. Those who were not able to find employment in agriculture owing to the labor-saving effect of modern agricultural technology were forced to migrate and join the urban lumpenproletariat or the reserve army of industrial workers.

2.1 WHY ARE FARMS SO SMALL?

The eighteenth- and early nineteenth-century Enclosure Movement in England and Scotland became the lens through which Marx viewed the effects of technical and institutional change in agriculture. The Marxian predictions did not materialize in the other early industrializing countries of Western Europe. In Western Europe, industrialization was accompanied by the persistence of small-scale peasant production units. Even in the United States, where the development of labor-saving technology proceeded most rapidly, family farms continue to account for a high share of agricultural production. Unlike the industrial sector, large farm firms characterized by hired labor and management has not yet become the dominant mode of production in the modern capital-intensive system of agriculture practiced in the United States (Johnson and Ruttan 1994).

Why did the Marx-Lenin prediction fail to materialize in the course of capitalist development? The primary reason seems to be that intensive polyculture systems require high levels of husbandry skill. Only a few crops, such as sugarcane and cotton, have lent themselves to production by gangs of laborers working under the direction of hired overseers. Unlike the industrial sector, in which the machine process makes work highly standardized and easy to monitor, the biological process of agricultural production is subject to infinite variations in response to ecological conditions. A very different crop or animal husbandry practice is often required in response to slight differences in temperature and soil moisture. It matters a great deal whether workers perform their work with care and judgment. The quality of such work is extremely difficult to monitor. The scattering of agricultural operations over a wide space adds to the difficulty of monitoring (Hayami and Kikuchi 1982).

This difficulty multiplies as the farming system becomes more complex, involving more intensive crop and animal husbandry:

> In areas more suitable for multiple enterprise farms, family operators have the advantage. Increasing the number of enterprises so multiplies the number of on-the-spot supervisory-management decisions per acre that the total acreage which a unit of management can oversee quickly approaches the acreage which an ordinary family can operate. (Brewster 1950: 331)

Thus, the development of biological technology geared to increase output per unit of land area by applying more labor, together with increased biological and chemical inputs for more intensive crop and animal husbandry, gives small family farms an advantage over large farms dependent on hired wage labor. Perhaps the strongest evidence of the relative inefficiency of the estate or plantation system, based on the use of large numbers of laborers carrying out standardized tasks under hired overseers, is its tendency to disappear whenever an urban demand for labor generates upward pressure on agricultural wage rates.

It is critical to recognize that modern technologies are not homogeneous in their effects on agrarian structure. Advances in mechanical technology are usually accompanied by scale economies, resulting in economy in management effort as well as in the use of labor in production. It is much easier to supervise one tractor driver than a large number of bullock teams. The development of mechanical technology has increased the relative efficiency of large farms, as Marx and Lenin envisaged. Biological technology, in contrast, is generally embodied in divisible inputs such as improved seed and fertilizer and requires intensive on-the-spot supervisory management decisions. Its effect is to raise the relative efficiency of small family farms and promote a unimodal farm-size distribution.

Marx and Lenin failed to predict the course of agrarian change primarily because they failed to understand the complexity of the biological production process and the potential contribution of advances in biological technology to productivity growth. The Marxian model of agrarian change remained a source of bias in efforts to interpret the productivity and distribution effects of the Green Revolution in the work of scholars such as Cleaver (1972), Griffin (1974), Palmer (1976), Pearse (1980), and Oasa (1987).

2.2 TECHNOLOGY AND POPULATION PRESSURE

The relation between new technology and income distribution is closely related to the characteristics of both the new technology and the structure of the economy into which it is introduced. The extent to which the income generated by a new technology, embodied in factors such as a new seed variety or a new machine, will augment the productivity and the income accruing to other factors will depend on the technical characteristics of the production function, the elasticity of supply of the several factors, and the institutional environment into which the new technology is introduced.

In rural communities in poor countries, a major cause of inequality in income distribution has often been the inequitable distribution of land ownership. Land-saving and labor-using technological changes that raise the economic return to labor relative to land have the effect of equalizing the income distribution between the landless and the land-owning classes. In contrast, labor-saving and land-using technological changes contribute to greater inequality.

Since biological technology saves land by applying labor and biological inputs more intensively, its diffusion might be expected to contribute to a more favorable income distribution in rural communities. Nevertheless, the new seed-fertilizer technology has often been blamed for benefiting landlords at the expense of tenants and laborers on the grounds that land rents increased while wage rates stayed the same or even declined in many areas where MVs and related inputs were introduced. These arguments have often ignored a critical factor coinciding with the MV diffusion—the growing pressure of population on the land. If this had not been partially offset by the adoption of land-saving technology, incomes would have fallen further, and a larger portion of agricultural income would have accrued to landlords.

3. Green Revolution Controversies

The discussions in the previous section should make it clear that the development of biological technology designed to increase agricultural output per unit of land area is a critical factor in offsetting tendencies toward a worsening of income distribution in the rural sector in response to growing population pressure on land. Yet, since its introduction, MV technology has frequently been viewed as a source of inequality in income distribution and of polarization in rural communities.

The critics of the Green Revolution have often argued that

- the new technology tends to be monopolized by large farmers and landlords who have better access to new information and better financial capacity even though MVs and related inputs are divisible and, hence, applicable to small farms,

- small farmers are unable to use MVs efficiently because financial constraints make it difficult for them to purchase cash inputs such as fertilizers and chemicals,
- favorable access to the new technology by large farmers enables them to use their profits to enlarge their operational holdings by consolidating small farmers' holdings,
- as farms' size increases, it becomes profitable to purchase large-scale machinery and reduce the cost of labor management (Griffin 1974; Pearse 1980; Cleaver 1972; Frankel 1971, 1974; Falcon 1970; Wharton 1969).

Tests of the several criticisms against experience suggest that the critics were wrong.

3.1 WAS MV TECHNOLOGY MONOPOLIZED BY LARGE FARMERS?

The available evidence indicates that neither farm size nor tenure was a serious constraint to MV adoption. The data on adoption of modern wheat varieties in Pakistan, presented in Table 7.1, are fairly typical of those available for other areas where MVs are technically well adapted. Similar results have been reported for wheat in India, rice in India, Indonesia, Malaysia, and the Philippines, and maize in Kenya (B. Sen 1974; Gerhart 1975; Mangahas 1974; Mangahas et al. 1976; Soejono 1976; Goldman and Squire 1982; Bliss and Stern 1982: 124–210; Barker et al. 1985).

There are, of course, cases in which small farmers lagged significantly behind large famers in MV adoption. One example was found in a rice village in Andhra Pradesh, India, covered by an international project and coordinated by the International Rice Research Institute (IRRI) to study the changes in rice farming

Table 7.1 **Mexican-Type Wheat Acreage as Percentage of all Wheat Acreage, by Size and Tenure of Holdings: 1969–1970 Post-Monsoon Season in Lyallpur, Sahiwal, and Sheikhupura Districts, Pakistan**

Number of acres in holding	*Owner holdings*	*Owner-cum-tenants*	*Tenant holding*	*All holdings*
Less than 12.5	71.0	80.4	66.7	72.5
12.5–25	63.3	71.7	69.2	68.0
25–50	71.9	92.7	81.9	82.0
50	73.2	87.3	57.3	78.6
All sizes	69.4	80.5	70.0	73.4

Source: (Azam 1973: 408), Original source (Government of the Punjab, Planning and Development Department, Statistical Survey Unit 1970: 38).

in selected areas of Asia (Parthasarathy 1975). This village was characterized by extremely skewed farm-size distribution. Its experience supports the hypothesis that the introduction of MV technology into a community in which resources are very inequitably distributed tends to reinforce the existing inequality.

However, this village is an exception rather than a norm. Of the thirty-six villages studied by the project, it was the only one where a significant differential in the MV adoption among farm-size classes was observed. On the average, small farmers adopted the MV technology even more rapidly than large farmers (see the upper diagram of Figure 7.1). The pattern of MV diffusion contrasts sharply with the pattern for the diffusion of tractors, in which large

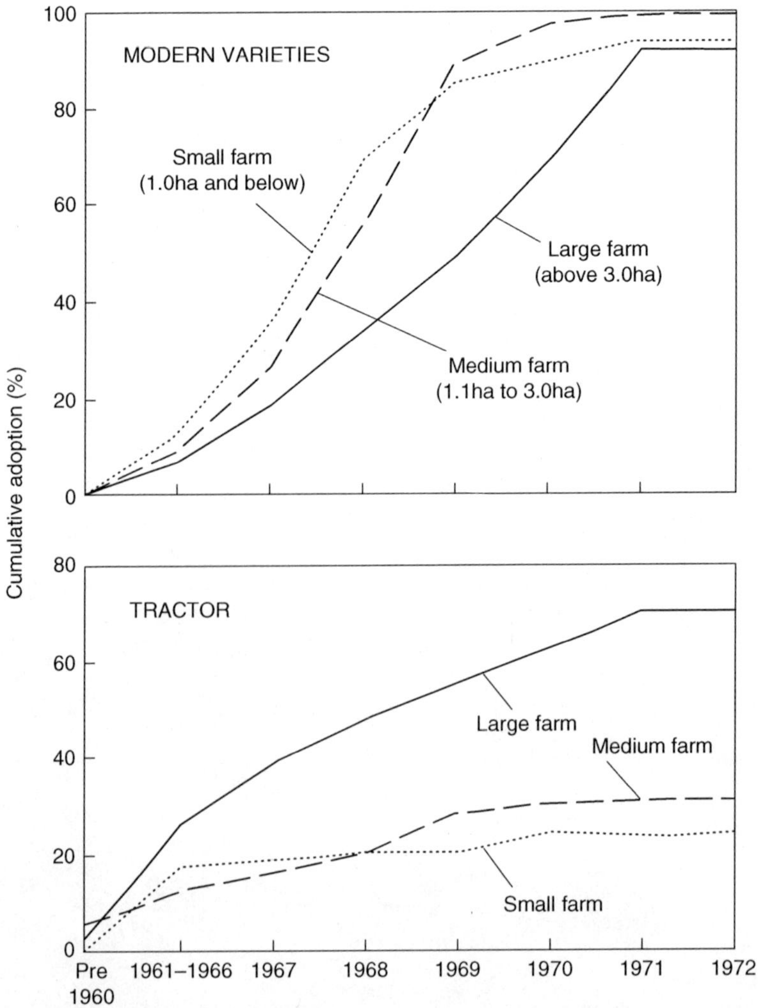

Figure 7.1 Comulative Percentage of Farms in Three Size Classes Adopting Modern Varieties and Tractors in 30 Villages in Asia. Source: (IRRI 1978: 9).

farmers achieved a distinctly faster and higher rate of adoption (lower diagram in Figure 7.1).

3.2 DID THE MV TECHNOLOGY MAKE LARGE FARMS RELATIVELY MORE EFFICIENT?

There is a large body of evidence suggesting that small farmers make more efficient use of available land than large farmers (Parthasarathy 1975; Cline 1975). They apply higher levels of labor input, particularly family labor, and they often have more livestock per unit of land than large farms do. A carefully conducted study of the adoption of modern wheat varieties in the Indian Punjab by Sidhu (1974a, 1974b) showed that MV wheat represented a neutral technological change with respect to farm scale—both small and large farms achieved approximately equal gains in efficiency.

A study in Pakistan by Azam (1973: 18) interpreted the data from the Pakistan Punjab to indicate that, although

> the smaller farmers do face relatively more severe constraints of irrigation water and credit, the difference in the severity of these constraints is not serious enough to have caused any significant differences in the yields obtained by the small farmers as compared with large farmers.

Similar results have been reported for rice from the Philippines by Mangahas (1974; Mangahas et al. 1976) and from Indonesia by Soqiono (1976). Among the thirty-two villages throughout Asia covered by the IRRI-coordinated project, significant differences in rice yields per hectare between large and small farmers were recorded in only eight villages (IRRI 1978: 96).

A major puzzle is why, in view of the evidence, political leaders and planners in developing countries and officials in national and international development assistance agencies remain skeptical about the efficiency of small farms. One reason may be that as a country develops and the opportunity cost of labor rises, the efficiency advantage of small farms tends to disappear. It thus becomes natural to associate large farms with a highly developed national economy. But this inference is irrelevant in most developing economies in which the absolute size of the agricultural labor force is continuing to increase.

3.3 DID THE MV TECHNOLOGY PROMOTE MECHANIZATION?

The popular perception that MV technology stimulates the introduction of labor-displacing machinery has not been borne out by careful analysis. The data in Figure 7.1 indicate that, throughout Asia, large farmers began to adopt tractors before the introduction of MVs. Nor was there any indication that adoption of tractors was accelerated by the dramatic diffusion of MVs from the late 1960s to the early 1970s.

Much of the early adoption of tractors in South and Southeast Asia can be attributed to distortions in the price of capital by such means as overvalued exchange rates and subsidized credits from national governments and international lending agencies. Also, the ease of supervising the operation of one tractor with an operator relative to that of supervising a large number of laborers and bullock teams seems to have worked as a strong inducement to tractorization on already large farms (Barker et al. 1972; McInerney and Donaldson 1975; Binswanger 1978). This factor should have been especially serious where regulation of land rent and tenure arrangements depressed the incentive of large landowners to rent out their holdings in small operational units.

3.4 DID THE MV TECHNOLOGY REDUCE LABOR EMPLOYMENT AND EARNINGS?

An extensive review of the literature by Bartsch (1977) indicates that the introduction of MVs into traditional wheat and rice production systems has typically resulted in substantial increases in annual labor use per unit of cropped area and, in some cases, in higher cropping intensity. Similarly, data assembled by Barker and Cordova (1978) from various areas in Asia show that labor input per hectare of area in rice was higher for MVs than for traditional varieties by 10–50 percent. The econometric investigation by Sidhu (1974a, 1974b) indicates a very substantial shift to the right of the labor demand function on wheat farms in Indian Punjab as a result of the introduction of MVs. Similar results were obtained by both Rao (1975: 227) and Staub (1973).

Increases in labor use associated with MVs were often realized despite the concurrent progress in mechanization. The data on labor use in rice production from the Laguna province in the Philippines, as presented in Table 7.2, are typical. This province experienced rapid diffusion of both modern rice varieties and tractors. Tractorization reduced the amount of labor needed for land preparation, but the reduction was more than compensated for by increases in labor use for weeding and in other areas of crop husbandry. The econometric test by Sidhu (1974a, 1974b) for Punjab wheat production shows that the new technology was neutral with respect to factor use, implying that labor's income rises proportionally with the incomes accruing to land and capital. A similar study by Ranade and Herdt (1978) on rice in the Philippines suggests that the MV technology is biased in the land-saving direction.

Several studies do indicate, however, that the labor share of income declined and the land share increased in some areas during the period of MV diffusion. Jha (1974) indicates that the factor share to land rose in India between 1960–61 and 1970–71. Data assembled by Mellor and Lele (1973) indicate that a disproportionately small percentage of the increased output attributable to MV adoption was allocated to labor. The data on relative shifts in factor shares cannot be interpreted without further analysis to indicate that landowners have gained

Table 7.2 **Percentages of Farms Adopting MVs and Tractors and Use of Labor Man-Days per hectare for Rice Production in Laguna, Philippines, 1966–1975, Wet Seasons**

	1966	*1970*	*1975*
MV adopters (percent of farms)[1]	0	76	94
Tractor adopters (percent of farms)[1]	26	71	90
Average paddy yield (metric tons/ha)	2.5	3.4	3.5
Labor input (man-days/ha)			
Land preparation	18.7	11.1	9.0
Transplanting	10.2	10.2	10.9
Weeding	13.8	17.8	31.3
Other preharvest operations	9.4	14.8	20.2
Harvesting and threshing	31.6	33.6	31.6
Postharvest operations	4.4	5.4	3.4
Total	88.1	92.9	106.4

[1] Averages for wet and dry seasons.
Source: (Rao 1975: 120, 127).

relative to tenants and laborers from the adoption of MVs. Considerable confusion has resulted from neglect of the fact that while the income share of land increased, as Jha's data clearly show, not only did technology change but labor supply also increased. If the labor supply increases faster than demand for labor, it is possible for the factor share of land to rise even if the technological change is biased in the land-saving and labor-using direction (Mellor and Lele 1973: 334–36).

Much of the data that indicated a rise in the factor share to land, such as that presented by Mellor and Lele, was obtained during the initial stages of MV adoption. At that time, MVs accounted for only a small percentage of area cultivated and of output. There was, therefore, only a modest shift in aggregate wheat or rice production or in aggregate factor demand. Early adopters were able to capture excess profits from the use of more efficient technology without forcing down product prices or bidding up factor prices appreciably. As the technology is diffused more widely, innovators' excess profit tends to be lost as product and factor prices move toward a new equilibrium. In the long run, the relative share of labor will return to the same level as before if the introduction of MVs represents a neutral technological change. It will become larger if the technology is biased in the land-saving and labor-using direction. This sequence is supported by a number of studies. For example, Bardhan (1970) found that in North India MV diffusion initially had no significant effect on the demand for rural labor. An analysis by D. Lal (1976) in the same region for a later period, however, shows clearly that as MV use diffused more widely, the net effect of the resulting increase in demand for labor was a significant rise in the real wage rates in Punjab and other parts of North India at a time when real wage rates were constant or declining in other parts of India, parts where MV diffusion was limited.

4. Perspective

How do we interpret the critical assessments of the effects of the Green Revolution on income distribution in view of the findings reported in this paper? First, it is apparent that many of the assessments that were made during the initial years of the Green Revolution were based on casual observation and on limited data (Hazel and Ramasamy 1991: 1–7). The initial concerns were largely resolved in the professional literature by more careful observation and analysis of the mid-1970s. But the less securely grounded early impressions of Green Revolution impacts have remained pervasive in the popular literature and in public consciousness, even though the private and social rates of return to the investment in research and development that led to the Green Revolution have been high by any standard (Alston et al. 1999; Evenson and Gollin 2003a).

Second, there was a general failure to understand that the impact of technical change on income distribution is a function both of the technology's character and of the economic and institutional environment into which it is introduced. When the Green Revolution technology was introduced into economies with relatively equitable income distribution, it reinforced that equity; when it was introduced into countries with inequitable income distribution in rural areas, it reinforced that inequity. There is no substantial evidence that the MV technology was heavily biased against labor. There is substantial evidence that in most areas where it has been adopted, it has increased the demand for labor. And there is a growing body of evidence that the impact on production and on demand for labor has had a positive effect on the quality of life in rural villages. In his study of a Punjab village, for example, Leaf (1983: 268) notes that farmers now

> grow more per hectare . . . and more per capita overall. As measured by food, medical care, educational facilities, and housing, there have been substantial improvements in general welfare. . . . The gains have gone at least as much to the poorer villagers as to the wealthier.

The critics of the biotechnology revolution in agriculture draw their inspiration from substantially different sources than those cited by the critics of the Green Revolution. European consumers, who were scarcely aware of the Green Revolution, have been a major source of opposition to food products derived from commodities produced using TGMO technology. Nongovernmental organizations (NGOs) have played a major role in focusing attention on potential adverse environmental and health effects associated with their production and consumption. And the environmental and health concerns—although unsupported by research and experience over many years—have served as a mask for implementation of protectionist trade policies advocated by developed countries' agricultural producers.

There have been important similarities, however, in the dynamics of popular perception of the impacts of the Green Revolution and of the new biotechnology revolution. In both cases, the substantial critical literature, both prior to and following introduction of the new biological technologies in crop and animal production, succeeded in creating considerable confusion about the potential economic benefits that farmers and consumers in developing countries could realize from the development, introduction, and diffusion of the new technologies. One effect has been to delay the realization by agricultural producers and consumers in developing countries of the benefits, first of the MVs, and more recently of the TGMO. A second effect was to draw very large scientific and technical resources into the assessment of MVs and TGMO impacts. It is not yet clear whether, in retrospect, we will judge that the resources devoted to TGMO assessment and regulation were productively employed, or whether they will be viewed as a diversion of technical and scientific resources from more productive employment.

Notes

Vernon W. Ruttan, *International Journal of Biotechnology* 6 (2004): 43–54. In this paper I draw heavily on earlier work with Yujiro Hayami (Hayami and Ruttan 1985: 330–62). I have benefited from editorial and substantive comment by Runge and by two anonymous reviewers.

1. The language used to describe the agricultural products produced by genetic engineering has been indelibly compromised. The health and environmental concerns with the products of genetic engineering are most appropriately focused on transgenically modified organisms (TGMOs)—that is, on organisms in which genetic material from an unrelated species has been inserted. All domestic crops and animals have been genetically modified since first being domesticated and are appropriately referred to as GMOs.

CHAPTER 8

The Peasant in Economic Modernization

Yujiro Hayami

Peasants—self-employed tillers of soil, whose farm production is based mainly on family labor as an integral part of household activities—have been for thousands of years and still are today the majority of mankind. Their production mode represents a sharp contrast with the large, internal organization of modern corporate firms characterized by a hierarchy of employees.

An apparently archaic style of peasant farming, relative to modern corporate activities, has often led to a presumption that the peasantry is a remnant of feudal society and bound to disappear as modernization proceeds. As a corollary it has been argued that consolidation of peasants into large farm enterprises is desirable or necessary for promoting agricultural productivity growth consistent with modern economic development.

This perspective has been waning recently, partly because of the disastrous experience of collective farming in former socialist economies, as well as repeated failures in the attempt to develop large farms as both state and private enterprises in developing economies (Eicher and Baker 1992; Johnson and Ruttan 1994). Concurrently, the high potential of peasants to achieve productivity growth has been recognized with the successful diffusion of modern high-yielding varieties and related inputs—the so-called Green Revolution in Asia. Yet, pessimism about peasant agriculture persists and tends to distort the development strategy of the Third World toward favoring large farm estates (Binswanger et al. 1995; Eicher et al. 1996).

More ambiguous is the role of peasants in industrial and commercial development. The traditional view from Karl Marx (1867) to W. Arthur Lewis (1969, 1970) has assumed peasants to be the source of an industrial reserve army for assuring the horizontal supply of labor to the emerging modern industrial sector. The possibility of peasants displaying entrepreneurship in industrial and commercial activities has been totally neglected. However, rural industrialization in the early modernization phase in Japan as well as recent developments in the village-township enterprises in post-reform China strongly suggest the possibility of rural-based economic development with proper exploitation of peasants' entrepreneurial abilities.

In this paper the major controversy concerning the nature and fate of the peasantry in the course of modern economic development is reviewed. Second, strengths and weaknesses of the peasant system are reviewed in comparison with the plantation system. Third, the impact of commercialization on peasants is investigated, with a focus on the relationship between peasants and middlemen. Finally, the possibility of rural-based economic development by mobilizing peasants' entrepreneurship in commerce and industry is examined and policies to enhance this process are explored.

The Agrarian Question

Since the outset of "modern economic growth" à la Kuznets (1966a), the nature and fate of peasantry have been the subject of a major controversy. Pessimism about peasant agriculture as being incompatible with modern development needs first found expression in the work of Arthur Young (1774) and other exponents of "new husbandry" in England from the time of the Agricultural Revolution in the eighteenth century to the era of "high farming" in the nineteenth century (Ernie 1961).

In their view, small peasant farmers were constrained by village-community regulations on crop rotation and, therefore, were unable to shift from the open three-field system to the Norfolk crop-rotation system. With the enclosure of peasants' plots into large, private farms leased to innovative tenant operators, the advantage of the new crop rotation could be properly exploited. By this arrangement, fallowed lands were planted with fodder crops, such as clover and turnips, which increased the livestock-carrying and, hence, the stable-manure-supplying capacity, which in turn augmented soil fertility and crop yields.

This popular view on the productivity-increasing effect of the Second Enclosure Movement in eighteenth-century England, together with the serious labor-displacement experienced in the First Enclosure Movement of the fifteenth to sixteenth centuries, by which peasants' holdings were consolidated into sheep farms for commercial wool production, provided the basis for Karl Marx's (1867) theory on the demise of peasantry. Marx predicted that peasants would be displaced by large capitalistic farm firms using labor-saving machinery and, therefore, would be forced to seek employment in the labor market. This was nothing but an extension of the general process of capitalist development in which the majority of self-employed, small producers owning small productive assets ("means of production") are proletarianized.

The subsequent German censuses of 1882 and 1895 were a shock for Marxists, because there was no indication in the census data that small farms had been displaced by large ones. This anomaly, which was called the "Agrarian Question," ignited a major controversy. Some tried to defend the Marxian orthodoxy. Karl Kautsky

(1899), among others, reasserted the superiority of large farms in Germany and other European economies, and argued that the eventual demise of peasantry was delayed because of peasants' desperate efforts to continue farming by working harder and reducing consumption against competition from capitalist farms.[1] In another effort, Vladimir Lenin (1960) tried to show that polarization of peasantry into large commercial farmers and landless laborers was, in fact, in progress in Russia.

In the other camp, so-called revisionists such as Eduardo Bernstein (1899) and Eduardo David (1903) argued that the Marxian theory of proletarianization does not apply to agriculture because of the inherent difficulty of labor enforcement in agricultural production. In urban industries, work is standardized and easy to monitor. The biological process of agricultural production, however, is subject to infinite ecological variations. Different ways of handling crops or animals are often necessary because of slight differences in temperature and soil moisture. The dispersal of agricultural operations over wide spaces adds to the difficulty of monitoring. Therefore, small family farms will continue to be more productive than large farms dependent on hired labor despite development of the capitalist system in other sectors of the economy.[2]

The Agrarian Question continued to fuel a major debate from the late nineteenth to the early twentieth century on the choice of socialist political programs (Mitrany 1951). Looking back from a century later there is little doubt about which side withstood the historical test. In all the advanced market economies in Western Europe, North America, and Japan, family farms have continued to be the dominant form of agricultural production organization. Their size of operation has increased in terms of farming area and capital input applied. However, corporate firm farms based on hired labor organized according to a management hierarchy have, until recently, been the exception.

Several production function studies have found significant scale economies in agriculture in advanced economies (Griliches 1964; Hayami and Ruttan 1985; Hayami and Kawagoe 1989). However, the continued dominance of family farms implies that the range of increasing returns has been limited within the size that could be managed mainly by family labor. The farm-size expansion has been motivated largely to equate the average income of family members engaging in farm production with that of nonfarm employees (Kislev and Peterson 1981), while being supported by technological innovation geared toward increasing the optimum farm size. The nuclear family farm has continued to be optimum because scale economies arising from the use of indivisible inputs such as large-scale machinery are countervailed by scale diseconomies from the use of hired labor, according to the logic of the revisionists.

In fact, the history of the Agricultural Revolution in England, on the basis of which the Marxian orthodoxy was formulated, has now been drastically redrawn. The iconoclastic study by Robert Allen (1992) convincingly shows that the enclosure in the eighteenth century resulted in no significant gain in agricultural productivity and that the major increase in land productivity had been brought about by yeomen (small independent farmers comprising an upper stratum of the British peasantry) during the seventeenth century before their lands were enclosed. Agricultural stagnation in former socialist economies under farm collectivization promoted by the Marxist doctrine might have been a bad replica of the true enclosure history.[3]

Peasants and Plantations

While the Agrarian Question has already been resolved for advanced market economies, it still resounds in developing economies. The issue has often been discussed around the relative efficiency of peasants versus plantations.[4]

The term "plantation" refers here to large firm farms based on hired wage labor, which were initially established in developing economies by Western colonizers for the purpose of extracting tropical agricultural products for export to home countries.[5] A traditional paradigm developed under colonialism had been to identify the plantation sector as a modern enclave geared for the international market and the peasant sector as dominated by subsistence orientation and irresponsive to profit incentives created by changes in market demands and technological opportunities (Boeke 1953). This stereotyped view has simultaneously been debunked by three great development economists: Theodore W. Schultz (1964), Hla Myint (1965), and W. Arthur Lewis (1969, 1970).

Schultz convincingly argued that peasants in traditional agriculture are rational and efficient in resource allocation and that they remain poor not because they are irresponsive to economic incentives but because only limited technical and market opportunities are available to which they can respond. Myint, drawing mainly on the experience of Southeast Asia, demonstrated how peasants responded vigorously to market incentives in opening new lands for cultivation of export cash crops while maintaining subsistence food crop production. This observation for the Southeast Asian case was found by Lewis to be no exception in tropical development from the late nineteenth to the early twentieth century.

A conventional explanation for the establishment of a plantation system is the scale economies inherent in the production of tropical export crops (Baldwin 1956). However, the crops subject to sufficiently strong scale economies at the farm level to make it necessary to use the plantation organization are few (Pim 1946; Wickizer 1951, 1960; Lim 1968; Hayami et al. 1990, chaps. 5 and 6). In fact, one can find an example of every so-called plantation crop being grown successfully by peasants somewhere in the world.

Significant increasing returns emerge only at the levels of processing and marketing activities. The vertical integration of a large farm unit with a large-scale central processing and/or marketing system is called for because of the need to supply farm-produced raw materials in a timely schedule. A typical example is fermented "black tea." The manufacturing of black tea at a standardized quality for export requires a modern machine plant into which fresh leaves must be fed within a few hours after plucking (Wickizer 1951, 1960). The need for close coordination between farm production and processing underlies the pervasive use of the plantation system for black tea manufacture. Unfermented "green tea," in contrast, remains predominantly the product of peasants in China and Japan.

In the case of bananas for export, harvested fruits must be packed, sent to the wharf, and loaded to a refrigerated boat within a day. A boatful of bananas that can meet the quality standards of foreign buyers must be collected within a few days (Hayami et al. 1990). Therefore, the whole production process from planting to harvesting must be precisely controlled so as to meet the shipment schedule. Although the plantation system has a decisive advantage for this export production, bananas for domestic consumption are usually produced by peasants.

On the other hand, for the crops for which centralized processing and marketing are not necessary, plantations have no significant advantage over peasants. Typical examples are cocoa and coconuts. The fermentation of cocoa and the drying and smoking of coconuts to make copra can be handled in small lots with no large capital requirement beyond small indigenous tools and facilities. These crops are grown predominantly by peasants.

Sugar is frequently cited as a classic case of scale economies stemming from the need of coordination between farm production and large-scale central processing (Binswanger and Rosenzweig 1986). Efficient operation of a centrifugal sugar mill requires the steady supply of a large amount of cane over time. Coordination of production from planting to harvesting with processing is required. This coordination, however, need not be as stringent as for tea and bananas. The rate of sugar extraction decreases as the processing of cane is delayed, but this loss is in no way comparable to the devastating damage that delayed processing has on the quality of tea and bananas. Sugar cane can be hauled from relatively long distances and stored for several days. Therefore, the need for vertical integration is not so large, and the necessary coordination can be achieved through contracts of a sugar mill with cane growers on the time and quota of cane delivery. In fact, an efficient sugar industry with small holders has developed in Australia and Taiwan. In tropical Asia, too, sugar production has been carried out in the peasant system in India and Thailand.

Another explanation for the use of the plantation system is the advantage of large estate farms in accessing capital. Because of this, it has been argued that plantations have an advantage in regard to tree crops characterized by long gestation periods from planting to maturity (Binswanger and Rosenzweig 1986). However, the opportunity costs of labor and capital applied to formation of the tree capital are not necessarily high for peasants. Typically, they plant the trees in hitherto unused lands. If such lands are located near their residence, they open new lands for planting by means of family labor at low opportunity cost during the idle season for the production of food crops on farm lands already in use. When they migrate to frontier areas, a typical process is to slash and burn jungles and plant subsistence crops such as maize, potatoes, and upland rice, together with tree seedlings. Such complex intercropping is difficult to manage with hired labor in the plantation system.

Therefore, even in the export boom of tropical cash crops under colonialism from the nineteenth century to the early twentieth century, the plantation system failed to make inroads in regions where indigenous populations have established family farms (Lewis 1970). Western traders found it more profitable to purchase tropical agricultural commodities from peasant producers in exchange for imported manufactured commodities than to produce these commodities themselves in the plantation system. This was particularly convenient during the nineteenth century, when the Industrial Revolution in the Western nations made it possible for these countries to produce and supply manufactured products at much lower cost than if these products were produced by the manufacturing sector in the tropical economies (Resnick 1970).

The establishment of plantations in less developed economies became a necessity when the demand for tropical products by the industrialized nations continued to rise, although the regions in the less developed economies physically suited for the production of these products had no significant peasant population that could produce and trade these commodities. Opening frontier lands for the production of new crops entailed high capital outlays. Virgin lands had to be cleared and developed, and physical infrastructure, such as roads, irrigation systems, bridges, and docking facilities, had to be constructed. Capital, in the form of machinery and other equipment, had to be imported and redesigned to adapt to local situations. Laborers were not only imported from the more populous regions but also had to be trained in the production of these crops.

The establishment of plantations thus requires huge initial capital investment. For the investors to internalize gains from investment in infrastructure, the farm size inevitably must be large. Viewed from this perspective, it follows that the plantation system evolved not because it was generally a more efficient mode of productive organization than the peasant mode, but because it was the most effective type of agricultural organization for extracting the economic benefit accruing from the exploitation of sparsely populated virgin areas. From this perspective, it is easy to understand why the same crop is grown mainly by peasants in one place and mainly by plantations in another. For example, for sugar cane production the peasant mode is more common in old settled areas of Luzon, and the plantation system predominates in the newly opened Negros, both in the Philippines (Hayami et al. 1990, chap. 5).

Thus, the efficiency of the plantation relative to the peasant system is high in the initial opening-up process of land-abundant and labor-scarce economies. However, several negative aspects of plantations become significant as tropical economies shift from the land-abundant to the land-scarce stage after the completion of the opening-up process.

First, the plantation system tends to substitute capital for labor. This is because of the inherent difficulty in supervising wage laborers in spatially dispersed and ecologically diverse farm operations.

Second, agricultural lands tend to be cultivated less intensively in the plantation system that employs mainly wage labor and produces essentially a monoculture crop. Complicated crop rotation and crop-livestock combinations are more difficult to manage in the command system. This implies that both labor input and income per hectare were lower in the plantations. In contrast, small-sized family farms tend to cultivate land more intensively.

Third, plantations usually specialize in a single crop. This bias for the production of a monocrop reduces the flexibility of these productive organizations to respond to changing demand by shifting to the production of other crops. Moreover, continual cropping of a single crop tends to result in soil degradation and an increase in pest incidence. Counterapplication of fertilizer and chemicals causes serious stress on the environment and human health.

Fourth, the specialization of plantation workers in specific tasks inhibits the development of their managerial and entrepreneurial capacity (Baldwin 1956; Myint 1965; Beckford 1972).

Fifth, the plantation system is the source of class conflict between laborers and managers/capitalists. The presence of a plantation enclave in rural economies where the peasant mode of production predominates has often strained relationships in rural communities. In terms of the criterion of social stability, therefore, the plantation system is no match for the system of relatively homogeneous small producers owning small assets, however small they might be.

These disadvantages can be mitigated if the plantation system is reorganized into the "contract farming" system. In contract farming, an agribusiness firm (or cooperative) manages processing and marketing but contracts for the supply of farm products with peasant farmers. The firm provides technical guidance, credit, and other services to peasants in return for their pledged production to the firm. In this way the system can take advantage of peasants in farm-level production without sacrificing scale economies in processing and marketing. A major advantage of this system is to tap not only the muscle labor but also the management ability of rural people in developing economies. The high efficiency of this system has been illustrated by the fact that Thailand, which began canned pineapple production relatively recently based on this system, has surpassed the Philippines, formerly the world's leading exporter, whose production is based on the plantation system.

While negative aspects of plantations have been looming larger over time, government direct controls on their operations will likely prove damaging to both national development and the well-being of rural people. The entrepreneurship and management capability of agribusiness enterprises, including multinational corporations, in the area of agricultural marketing and processing are very valuable inputs which can be dispensed with only at a very high cost. The rational approach, therefore, should be to design an inducement mechanism toward establishing an agrarian organization that adequately combines the entrepreneurial and managerial abilities of both peasants and agribusiness firms.

A policy designed in this direction might include the gradual phasing out of special treatments to agribusiness plantations such as public land leases at favorable terms and special allocation of import licenses and foreign exchange, and the stricter application of labor and environment codes to the corporate farms. At the same time, government must invest in education, research, and extension for developing the capability of small growers to operate the contract farming scheme effectively.[6]

Peasants and Middlemen

The same policy prescription can be envisaged for the relation between peasants and middlemen. It is a deeply rooted popular belief that middlemen exploit peasants by means of monopoly/monopsony pricing and usury. This suspicion against middlemen is common in the Third World but especially strong in East Africa and Southeast Asia, where the trading networks established during the colonial regime were such that export-import business in major port cities was mainly handled by European firms, while collection of tropical export products from inland villages and distribution of imported consumption goods there were largely carried out by non-European ethnic minorities (Indians and Chinese). Such an ethnic division of labor originally could have been based on the comparative advantage of the native population in primary production in the natural-resource-rich economies suddenly opened to international trade. However, it was inevitable for the natives to develop strong anti-middleman sentiment and ideology as they continued to be excluded from the main current of commercial activities. Thus, as Leon Mears (1981: 133) described for Indonesia, even after independence, "it is not unusual to hear judgment . . . that farmers or consumers are exploited by the market control exercised by ethnic Chinese middlemen. At times one even hears that all private traders are exploitative and discouraging to producers."This stereotype, however, has not stood up under empirical tests. Almost all substantive empirical studies, including the classic work for export cash crops in West Africa by Bauer (1954) and two major studies for food crops in India by U. J. Lele (1971) and in Africa by Jones (1972), have produced results inconsistent with the hypothesis of marketing inefficiency and middleman exploitation.[7] These studies unanimously show that entry to agricultural marketing activities is open and competition among middlemen is intense in developing economies in the absence of government control, so that marketing margins are largely consonant with the costs associated with marketing activities; wide price gaps across areas and fluctuation over seasons are not caused by monopolistic behavior by traders/speculators but arise mainly from the high costs of transport and storage as well as insufficient market information services.

In the past, the fundamental contribution of trading activities to the development of the peasant economy has been neglected, relative to the importance to such factors as capital formation, rural education, agricultural research, and land reform. It must be recognized that profitable opportunities created by new technology and improved infrastructure such as roads cannot be exploited without the activities of middlemen. While solely motivated for their own profit, middlemen, in effect, provide essential support for peasants:

> Traders both large and small create new opportunities. With their knowledge of the requirements of local, regional, and export markets, traders provide outlets for farm products. They buy the traditional products and at the same time acquaint farmers with new products and the methods of growing them. Further, they make available to them the necessary inputs such as seeds, fertilizers, and implements. Thus the traders encourage new wants, convey new opportunities, and help farmers to take advantage of them. The activities of traders set in motion and maintain the process by which participation in the exchange economy replaces subsistence production. (Bauer and Meier 1994: 193)

When governments attempted to constrain or even to replace private trading by state-trading based on the folklore of exploitative middlemen, disastrous consequences were inevitable, as evident from the experience of marketing boards and parastatals in several African economies (Bauer 1954; Hopkins 1973; Bates 1983; W. O. Jones 1987; Lele and Christiansen 1989).[8]

This does not mean that government necessarily should leave the existing system of marketing as it is. A wide scope exists to reduce transportation costs through government investment in roads and railways. Moreover, improvements in transportation and communication by public investments are critically important for reducing trade risk and transaction costs, and thereby promoting new entry and competition in marketing. Development of institutions for the service of market information, such as grading, standardization of measures and weights, commodity exchange, crop forecasting, and regular quotations of market prices through mass media, as well as more fundamental institutions for the protection and enforcement of property rights and contracts, can contribute much to reductions in trade risks and transaction costs.

If the activities of middlemen in the countryside of developing economies were supported by these government services, the healthy development of peasant economy would be greatly promoted. The problem is that most governments underinvest in this infrastructure and overinvest in their own enterprises and efforts to carry out agricultural marketing directly. If policymakers trusted their peasants more and feared middlemen less, this government bias could be reversed. Most policymakers have never met a peasant, much less one with entrepreneurial skills engaged in risky trading activities. (Timmer 1993: xi)

Peasant Entrepreneurship in Commerce and Industry

Indeed, the popular belief that peasants are exploited through the marketing process assumes implicitly that middlemen belong to a social group alienated from the peasantry. Peasants have been considered always to be passive to market forces and to have neither the desire nor the ability to participate in commercial and industrial activities.

This view found a typical expression in Clifford Geertz's (1963) anthropological study in Indonesia. Based on observations in East Java and Bali, he concluded that the entrepreneurship for nonfarm business activities that may induce social modernization cannot emerge from "the immediate purview of village social structure" but is limited to the population with "extra-village status," such as ethnic Arab traders in the East Javanese town and traditional rulers in the Balinese town (Geertz 1963: 148–49).

If the Geertz thesis is valid, the case of Indonesia represents a sharp contrast to the historical experience of Japan. In the initial stage of modern economic growth in Japan, wealthy peasants, who typically cultivate a part of their land by themselves and rent out the other part, actively participated in trading and manufacturing; this process had begun already in the feudal Tokugawa period in response to the gradual development of the market economy, and it accelerated with Japan's opening to foreign trade and national unification by the Meiji Restoration in 1868 (T. C. Smith 1956, 1959, 1988). Contributions of these small-scale, rural-based enterprises to the national economy were no less significant than those of large, modern corporations developed by urban entrepreneurs who emerged from the preindustrial merchant class (such as Mitsui and Sumitomo) and the ex-warrior class (such as Yataro Iwasaki, the founder of Mitsubishi). In fact, until the turn of the century, or even later until about World War I, rural and national economic development is considered to have been supported, to a large extent, by the commercial and industrial activities of those rural entrepreneurs (Rosovsky and Ohkawa 1961; Tussing 1966). This development of rural-based enterprises had made conditions for industrialization in modern Japan less capital intensive than in other latecomers to modern economic growth (T. C. Smith 1988: chap. 1).

What I myself observed in a field study of agricultural marketing in Indonesia during 1986–90, as reported in Hayami and Kawagoe 1993, was contrary to the image developed by Geertz (1963). Both in long-settled Java and newly opened Sumatra, indigenous entrepreneurs belonging to the upper peasantry actively engaged in the marketing and processing businesses. These village-based traders in upland Java have been overtaking town-based ethnic Chinese traders in the interregional transshipment of such commodities as corn and soybeans by effectively mobilizing a large number of small collectors who belong to the lower ranks of the peasantry. In the highly complicated and risky operation of commercial vegetable marketing for the metropolis, they have become dominant. Owner-operators of local tobacco factories have applied to their businesses modern marketing techniques, such as grading and the use of brand names, for reducing product quality uncertainty and transaction costs, without ever attending business school. In the transmigration area in Sumatra, too, peasant entrepreneurs have been following the developments in Java, in response to improvements in transportation and communication infrastructure. All these activities by the agents of peasant marketing in Indonesia resemble those of "rural capitalists" (Smith 1956) in Japan, who emerged from the *gono* (wealthy peasant) class and supported Japan's emergence as a modern industrial state.

The strength of these village-based traders is their ability to enforce contracts with farmers and lower-rank collectors by means of the village community tie. This advantage is especially large in connection with perishable commodities like vegetables, for which close coordination between farm-level collection and bulk shipment to urban markets is required (Hayami and Kawagoe 1993: chap. 4). This coordination is enforced by such means as long-term contracts involving credit tying, which are difficult for urban-based traders, lacking the community mechanism of enforcement, to organize.[9] Thus, if they are appropriately linked with international agribusiness or trading firms, while supported by public agricultural research and extension, they could well become an effective instrument for bringing Indonesian agriculture up to the status of a major supplier to the rapidly expanding world market for horticultural products.

There is little doubt that Geertz's (1963) pessimism about Indonesian peasants' entrepreneurship does not stand up under empirical tests today.

Toward Rural-Based Development

What will be the role of peasant entrepreneurs as economies continue to advance to higher stages? The question arises as to what their fate will be in the event of successful economic modernization. Their marketing organization, as documented in Japan's history and as observed in Indonesia today, is a decentralized hierarchy of many self-employed informal agents tied by customary trade practices and informal contracts, where vertical integration is typically absent. In the low-income stage of economic development, the system is highly efficient in economizing the use of scarce capital and management input while making intensive use of labor having a low opportunity cost. This system's efficiency depends, to a large extent, on the dualistic structure characterized by differentials in wage and interest rates across firm sizes. Will this system become inefficient and be replaced by vertically integrated large corporations when the economy advances to a stage at which the factor market dualism is eliminated?

The experience of the Japanese economy in the past three decades may shed some light on this question. Within a decade of high economic growth from the mid-1950s, the dualistic structure was largely eliminated (Minami 1973). Yet small-scale family enterprises have survived and have even been strengthened (Kiyonari 1980; Patrick and Rohlen 1987). Advantages of small- and medium-scale enterprises, such as high incentives for entrepreneurs and flexibility in employment and staffing, have increased corresponding to the increased need for small-lot production of differentiated products, as the Japanese economy has advanced to a stage characterized by high per capita income and diversified consumer demands.

Large corporations in Japan continue to prefer subcontracting to vertical integration. Coordination between parent company and small/medium firms has been developed with such precision that the subcontracting system is integrated inseparably in Toyota's famous *kanban* (just-in-time) system. In this system the subcontractors deliver the supply of their parts and materials to the assemblers precisely at the time when the parts are used, so that no inventory accumulates in the assembling plant even for small lot-production of many differentiated products. The improved subcontracting system is now considered a major organizational innovation that underlies the strength of Japanese industries, especially the automobile industry (Abegglen and Stalk 1985; Asanuma 1985, 1988; Wada 1991).

Is there any strong reason to doubt whether entrepreneurial and managerial skills now being learned in the countryside of Indonesia through the marketing of peasants' products will provide the basis of a modern subcontracting system and thereby support the advancement of the Indonesian economy to a higher regime of development? Indeed, the relationship between the transshippers of vegetables to metropolitan markets and their agents engaged in collection from farmers, which I observed in rural Indonesia, is very similar to the Toyota's *kanban* system (Hayami and Kawagoe 1993: chap. 4). Are there insurmountable cultural and social barriers for peasant entrepreneurs in Indonesia to follow the development of their Japanese counterparts?

If the emergence of peasant entrepreneurs in Indonesia has followed the same pattern as in Japan, is there any reason to suspect that they will be incapable of becoming a major carrier of modern commerce and industry when Indonesia advances to a regime of higher economic development? Does not the same question apply to other developing economies?

The iconoclasm of T. W. Schultz (1964) has established a consensus in our profession that peasants in developing economies are not tradition-bound, irrational creatures but are highly responsive to economic opportunities and perfectly capable of carrying out modern agriculture. We must now recognize that they also can be a basis of modern commerce and industry if appropriate policies will be taken to support, rather than constrain, their entrepreneurship.

Notes

Yujiro Hayami, *American Journal of Agricultural Economics* 78 (December 1996): 1157–67. Useful comments from Keijiro Otsuka and Vernon Ruttan are gratefully acknowledged.

1. Kautsky's argument is similar to the theory of Alexander Chayanov (1966) on the point of the strong resilience and viability of peasants due to the application of family labor to farm production beyond the equilibrium between market wage rates and labor's marginal productivities. However, unlike Kautsky, who reasserted the demise of peasantry along the Marxian orthodoxy, Chayanov argued its persistence, similar to the revisionists.
2. This perspective has been elaborated by a number of modern economists from John Brewster (1950) to Hans Binswanger and Mark Rosenzweig (1986), to the point that it has been established as a current orthodoxy.

3. Stalin collectivized family farms into *kolkhoz* partly based on the Marxian doctrine (Mitrany 1951) but more importantly with the intention of utilizing the collective farms for compulsory procurement of foodstuff at low prices for urban industrial workers (Tang 1967). The consequence was a shift of status for Russia from a major exporter of food grains to a major importer after World War II.
4. This section draws heavily on Hayami 1994.
5. In a broader definition, for example, by Jones (1968a, 1968b), farm estates based on forced labor, such as slavery, corvée, and serf, instead of free wage labor may also be called plantations. These estates based on forced labor were established typically before the onset of the Industrial Revolution in Europe and North America. They had a major impact on the southern United States and Latin America (hacienda), as well as Eastern Europe (such as the *Junker* estates in Prussia) but had little effect in Asia. The plantations dealt with in this paper are those established in tropical Asia in the late nineteenth to the early twentieth century. From the beginning their operations were based on wage laborers, even though many laborers were imported from densely populated economies such as China and India under long-term contracts, often tied by credit, akin to debt peonage.
6. In this connection the debate on the role of food versus cash crop, which has been heated especially in Africa, should be reconsidered. The traditional emphasis on export cash crop under the colonial regime was initially inherited by postindependent governments. However, since Africa shifted from the net food exporter to the importer in the early 1970s, the reallocation of resources to the food sector has been strongly (often emotionally) advocated (Rodney 1974; Lappe and Collins 1977; Twose 1984). Correspondingly, both international and national supports on cash crop research, which was relatively well developed in the colonial regime, have been drastically reduced (Eicher and Baker 1992; Eicher et al. 1996). While the importance of public research on food crops cannot be overemphasized, the total neglect of export crop research on the popular presumption that it serves for the profit of agribusiness alone is counterproductive to the benefit of small peasant producers, It is important to recognize that cash crop is an important source of earning for peasants in Africa as well as other developing regions and that peasants' participation in cash crop production increases their entitlement to foods, thereby enhancing their food security (Dreze and Sen 1989). Research on cash crops, especially nontraditional export crops such as flowers, fruits, and vegetables for which world demands have been expanding very rapidly (Islam 1990), would be highly effective to promote food security in low-income economies.
7. The same conclusion has been drawn from numerous individual commodity studies, including Hirsch 1961 on sugar in India, Ruttan 1969a on rice and corn in the Philippines, Mears 1971 on rice in the Philippines, G. J. Scott 1985 on potatoes in Peru, Hayami and Kawagoe 1993 on upland crops, and Akiyama and Nishio 1996 on cocoa in Indonesia.
8. For example, farm producers' shares of export FOB prices for cocoa for 1980–88 were less than 60 percent in the countries in which marketing was handled by state marketing boards, such as Ghana, Cameroon, and Côte d' Ivoire, whereas these of countries with no marketing board, such as Brazil and Indonesia, were higher than 80 percent. Within Indonesia, producers' shares were much higher for commodities with little government intervention, such as cocoa and coffee, than for sugar, which was controlled by the state procurement agency (BULOG) (Akiyama and Nishio 1996: 10–11).
9. I must caution, however, that the community mechanism can produce multiple equilibria depending on different social and cultural conditions, as predicted by Akerlof (1984). Unlike Indonesia and many other parts in Asia, close kinship relationships in African tribal communities are said to be working more strongly as a mechanism of tolerating poor villagers' defaults of credits from relatively rich ones rather than as the mechanism of enforcing repayment (Kennedy 1988; Platteau 1996). This tradition might be one of the major factors underlying poorer performances in capital accumulation and economic growth in sub-Saharan Africa than in East Asia for the past several decades.

CHAPTER 9

Ecology, History, and Development

A PERSPECTIVE FROM RURAL SOUTHEAST ASIA

Yujiro Hayami

The process by which different ecological conditions and historical trajectories interacted to create different social and cultural systems resulted in major differences in economic development performance within Southeast Asia. In the late nineteenth century, Indonesia, the Philippines, and Thailand commonly experienced vent-for-surplus development through exploitation of unused lands. Nevertheless, different agrarian structures were created. Indonesia's development was mainly based on the exploitation of tropical rain forest under Dutch colonialism. It resulted in the bifurcation of the rural sector between rice-farming peasant proprietors and large plantations for tropical export crops based on hired labor. In the Philippines, exploitation of the same resource base under Spanish rule resulted in pervasive landlessness among the rural population. Relatively homogeneous land-owning peasants continued to dominate in Thailand, where delta plains that were suitable only for rice production formed the resource base for development. These different agrarian structures associated with different social value systems have accounted for differential development performance across the three economies in the recent three decades.

Ecology and history have a fundamental impact on the course of economic development. Nevertheless, few studies have investigated how different ecological conditions and historical trajectories have interacted to forge different social and cultural systems, resulting in major differences in development performance across economies. This article aims to shed light on this process, drawing on agricultural development experiences in Southeast Asia. Relatively high growth performance in agriculture in the past three or four decades has been counted as one of the factors underlying the "economic miracle" of this region (World Bank 1993). Yet economic performance has varied within the region. Variations in the recent agricultural growth performance reflect differences in the agrarian structure, which were created through distinct colonial regimes under diverse ecological environments. As such, this study does not aim to conduct research for predicting the future course of rural development in Southeast Asia; rather, I intend to provide a broad telescopic guide to such research for this region as well as other regions.

Southeast Asia can be classified into two major ecological zones: the continental zone, including Thailand, Vietnam, and Myanmar, and the insular and peninsular zone (henceforth called the insular zone), including Indonesia, Malaysia, and the Philippines (see Figure 9.1). Major river deltas characterize the continental zone, and tropical rain forests characterize the insular zone. Before the 1860s, when new transportation technology integrated this region with the rapidly industrializing West, people in Southeast Asia lived on wet rice production in small valleys or shifting cultivation in upland forests. Many of the major deltas and thick rain forests were unused for agricultural production. When the region was faced with growing demand from the West for tropical products, this unused land became the basis of vent-for-surplus growth. Deltas were converted into paddy fields for commercial rice production, and rain forests were converted into plantations for export cash crops.

Corresponding to the different crops produced, peasants or small family farms continued to dominate the deltas, whereas the insular areas were bifurcated between peasants cultivating rice in small valleys and coastal plains, and large plantations based on hired labor. The different agrarian organizations were rooted in different ecological conditions and in land policies across different political regimes.

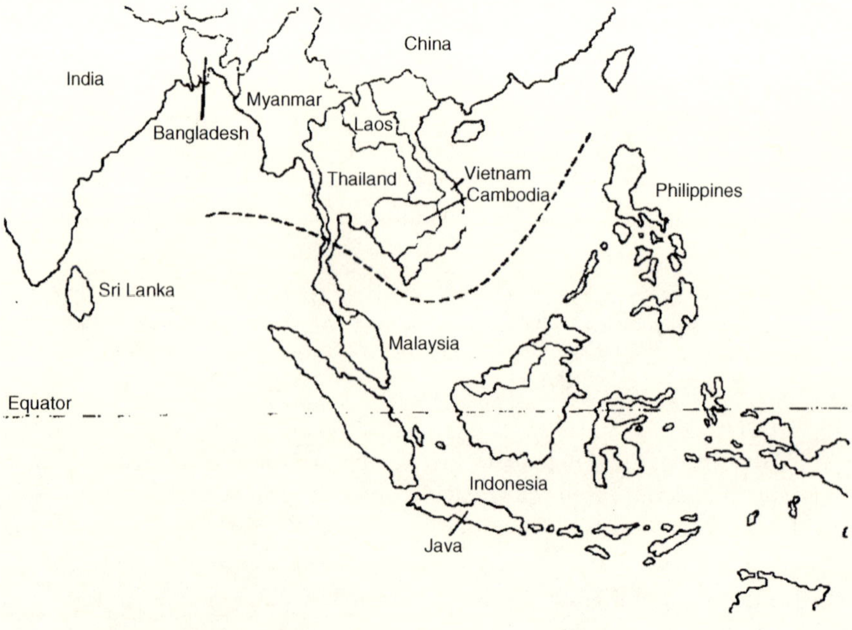

Figure 9.1 Map of Southeast Asia.

For example, the distribution of land ownership became far more skewed in the Philippines under Spanish colonialism than in Indonesia under Dutch colonialism, although both countries were in the insular zone. Differences in agrarian structure formed along different historical trajectories under different ecological conditions have had far-reaching influences on the performance of agricultural development across Southeast Asia. Several important variables other than the agrarian structure, including government policies, influence rural development. However, the agrarian structure is a major determinant of the political economy of the countries in the region, which exerts critical influences on their policy choices.

This article first outlines the characteristics of resource endowments, agrarian structures, growth in aggregate agricultural output, and changes in the shares of major export commodities in world markets in Indonesia, the Philippines, and Thailand in the past three decades. Second, it reviews the process of vent-for-surplus development in Southeast Asia in the late nineteenth century to the early twentieth, emphasizing the critical roles of major river deltas in the continental zone of Southeast Asia and tropical rain forests in the insular zone. Different agrarian structures evolved in the three economies in the vent-for-surplus development process under different ecological conditions and political regimes. The preemption of uncultivated but cultivable land by the power elite was the major force to have resulted in skewed land distributions. Finally, the article tries to explain differential agricultural growth performance across Indonesia, the Philippines, and Thailand in terms of different agrarian structures. It discusses how governments forged policy choices in terms of the structure of political economy, under unique ecological conditions and unique historical trajectories. Although this study is limited to comparisons within Southeast Asia, its approach may be applicable to comparisons across regions, such as Africa versus Asia, to draw insights on broader development issues.

Recent Developments

Table 9.1 compares the endowments of land for agricultural production relative to the population and the labor force in Indonesia, the Philippines, and Thailand in 1965 and 1996.[1] Land is measured by area of cropland, which is the sum of areas of arable land (used for annual cropping) and land under permanent cropping, using data from the Food and Agriculture Organization. Arable land is classified into lowland paddy fields and upland annual cropland. Data for these subcategories of arable land have not been enumerated in the Food and Agriculture Organization statistics, which are mainly based on the census of farm households. It was only recently that the data for lowland paddy fields, based mainly on aerial photography, began to be available in the official reports of national statistical agencies for some specific years, which are used for calculations in Table 9.1.[2]

Table 9.1 **Land Endowments for Agricultural Production in Inodonesia, the Philippines, and Thailand, 1965–96**

	Indonesia			*Philippines*			*Thailand*		
Indicator	1965	1996	*1996/65* ratio	1965	1996	*1996/65* ratio	1965	1996	*1996/65* ratio
NumberolTarm workers (1,000)	29,006	47,713	1.64	7,363	12,128	1.65	12,450	20,824	1.67
Croplandll									
Total (OOt)ha)	26,000	30,987	1.19	6,660	9,520	1.42	12,600	20,445	1.62
Percapita (ha)	0.24	0.15	0.63	0.21	0.14	0.67	0.41	0.35	0.85
Per farm worker (ha)	0.90	0.65	0.72	0.90	0.78	0.87	1.01	0.98	0.97
PercenliigL- ofcropland (%)									
Lowland paddy field	---	27	---	---	32	---	---	53	---
Upland annual crop land	---	31	---	---	22	---	---	31	---
Land under permanent crop	31	42	1.35	38	46	1.21	11	16	1.45

---, Not available.

a. Economically active population.

b. Arabic land area plus area under permanent crop.

c. Lowland paddy field areas pertain to 1995 in Indonesia. 1991 in the Philippines and 1993 in Thailand.

d. Arable land area minus lowland paddy field area.

Sources: FAOSTAT database (FAO 1999) except for lowland paddy field areas, which arc taken from 1996 Statistical Yearbook of Indonasia (Indonesia Biro Pusat Statistik 1996) for Indonesia (8.484.000 ha in 1995). Philippine Statistical Yearbook 1998 (Republic of the Philippines 1991) for the Philippines (3,001,000 ha in 19911), and Agricultural Statistics! 995/96 (Thailand Ministray of Agriculture 1996 for Thailand (10,934,000 ha in 1993).

The areas of upland annual cropland are measured as differences between arable land and lowland paddy field areas.

The data in Table 9.1 show that in per capita terms, cropland area in Thailand is more than twice as large as in Indonesia and the Philippines, but only marginally larger in per farmworker terms (in 1996). Between 1965 and 1996, cropland areas increased by about 20 percent in Indonesia, 40 percent in the Philippines, and 60 percent in Thailand. However, in all three economies, the rate of expansion in cropland area was lower than the rate of growth in population and in agricultural labor force. The cropland endowment relative to population decreased by 15 percent in Thailand and by more than 30 percent in Indonesia and the Philippines. Cropland relative to the agricultural labor force remained about the same in Thailand, decreased by 28 percent in Indonesia, and decreased by 13 percent in the Philippines. These data suggest that Thailand has been endowed with relatively favorable conditions for expanding land cultivation, compared with Indonesia and the Philippines.

For the analysis here, the important characteristic that distinguishes Thailand from Indonesia and the Philippines is the high share of paddy field area in total cropland. Relative paddy field area is greater than 50 percent in Thailand, compared with only about 30 percent in Indonesia and the Philippines (in 1996). Indonesia and the Philippines are characterized by high shares of area under permanent crops, amounting to more than 40 percent, in contrast to less than 20 percent in Thailand. Permanent crops in these economies consist mainly of tropical trees for cash crop production, such as coffee, coconuts, and rubber. Although data are not available for lowland paddy field area in 1965, the share of tree cropland was as much higher in Indonesia and the Philippines than in Thailand thirty years ago than it is today. The data reflect the ecological difference between the continental zone of Southeast Asia, as represented by Thailand, and the insular zone, as represented by Indonesia and the Philippines. The continental zone has major river deltas almost exclusively used for wet rice production. The insular zone was originally covered mainly by tropical rain forests that could be converted into profitable plantations of tropical cash crops.

The different types of agricultural production corresponding to different environmental conditions gave rise to different agrarian structures in the continental and insular zones. As is common in cereal-producing areas throughout the world, peasants or small family farms make up the organization of production. Thai agriculture, which has traditionally been dependent on rice, has been characterized by the dominance of peasants or small family farms as the organization of production. By contrast, a significant portion of tropical cash crop production has been carried out by plantations or large estate farms dependent on hired labor, although many peasants have also grown cash crops. Table 9.2 compares the distribution of farm size and the incidence of tenancy across Indonesia, the Philippines, and Thailand for the period before the influence of Philippine land reform became significant.

Table 9.2 **The Distribution of Operational Farm Size and the Incidence of Agricultural Tenancy in Indonesia, the Philippines, and Thailand 1970s**

Indicator act	*Indonesia 1973*	*Philippines 1971*	*Thailand 1978*
Average operational farm size (ha)	1.1	3.7	3.7
Percentage of farms and farmland			
Below 5 ha			
Farms	98	8 5	72
Land area	69	48	39
Above SO ha			
Farms	0[a]	0.2	0[a]
Land area	14	14	0.9
Gini coefficient of land concentration	0.56	0.51	0.45
Percentage of tenanted area in total farmland			
Pure tenancy	2	21	6
Total[b]	24	33	16
Percentage of share tenancy in tenanted land	60	79	29

[a] lless than 0.05 percent.

[b] Area in pure tenancy farms plus area in owncr-cum-tenant farms.

Sources: Hayami and Otsuka (1993) and U.N.-FAO (1971).

In all the three economies in the 1970s, small farms operating below five hectares were the majority, comprising 70–100 percent of farms and cultivating 40–70 percent of farmland. Large farms above fifty hectares, which were considered agribusiness plantations, were negligible in number: those estate farms operated on 14 percent of the land area in Indonesia and the Philippines and less than 1 percent in Thailand. Thus the agricultural sector in the insular zone was bifurcated between peasants subsisting on small parcels of land and large plantations with hired labor under the hierarchy of management. The continental zone was characterized by the unimodal distribution of self-employed family farms. These plantations were privately owned and managed in the case of the Philippines: those in Indonesia were mostly state enterprises expropriated from Dutch planters after independence. The incidence of tenancy also varied widely. Tenancy was distinctively higher in the Philippines than in the other two countries, especially in terms of percentage of area under pure tenancy. In fact, the central focus of this article is on the ecological factors and historical processes that resulted in such differences in agrarian structures in Southeast Asia.

Table 9.3 compares agricultural growth performances in Indonesia, the Philippines, and Thailand between 1965 and 1995. In terms of total agricultural output, the growth rate was about the same in Indonesia and Thailand, but in per capita and per farmworker terms, Indonesia's growth rates were somewhat higher. The Philippines had the lowest growth rates for those three measures. In terms of output per hectare of cropland, growth in the Philippines and Thailand was comparable and much slower than in Indonesia. The slow growth of land productivity in Thailand resulted partly because of a major expansion of the cultivation frontier in the Northeast, which was characterized by poor soil and unstable rainfall, and partly because of the relatively low rate in the diffusion of modern, high-yielding rice varieties. It was difficult to grow short-stature modern

Table 9.3 **Growth of Agricultural Production in Indonesia, the Philippines, and Thailand 1961–95**

	Index			*Growth rate (annual percent)*		
Country, indicator	*1961–65*	*1976–80*	*1991–95*	*1961–65 to 1976–80*	*1976–80 to 1991–95*	*1961–65 to 1991–95*
Indonesia						
Total	100	157	309	3.0	4.5	3.8
Per capita	100	111	165	0.7	2.6	1.7
Per farm worker	100	138	232	2.1	3.5	2.8
Per ha[a]	100	157	263	3.0	3.4	3.2
Philippines						
Total	100	177	239	3.8	2.0	2.9
Per capita	100	116	111	1.0	-0.3	0.3
Per farm worker	100	134	156	2.0	1.0	1.5
Per ha[a]	100	137	165	2.1	1.2	1.7
Thailand						
Total	100	190	277	4.3	2.5	3.4
Per capita	100	123	140	1.4	0.9	1.1
Per farm worker	100	145	199	2.5	2.1	2.3
Per ha[a]	100	129	163	1.7	1.6	1.6

[a] per hectare of cropland (arable land plus land under permanent crop).
Source: FAO (1999).

varieties in the flood-prone areas of the Chao Phraya delta, as well as in the drought-prone areas of the Northeast. In addition, farmers were slow to adopt modern varieties because of their low value in Thailand's export markets.

In terms of both environmental conditions and relative resource endowments, traditional comparative advantage in agricultural production in Thailand lay in rice and that of Indonesia and the Philippines lay in tropical cash crops. Table 9.4 shows that Thailand is a major rice exporter (the world's largest), and its world market share continued to rise between 1961–65 and 1991–95. Indonesia and the Philippines remained net importers of rice, although their import margins were significantly reduced owing to the success of the Green Revolution. This success was especially great in Indonesia, accounting for the high rate of growth in aggregate agricultural output despite the relatively slow growth in cropland area (Tables 9.1 and 9.3).

Surprisingly, Thailand has become an exporter of several tropical cash crops that have declined in importance for Indonesia and, more conspicuously, for the Philippines. Sugar represents a typical example. Thailand was a net importer of sugar before World War II and was barely self-sufficient in the early 1960s. Nevertheless, Thailand rose to become the third largest exporter in the world (behind Brazil and Australia) in the 1990s. By contrast, Indonesia and the Philippines, two traditional exporters of sugar in Asia, have nearly completely lost significance in the international market. By the 1990s, Thailand exceeded Indonesia in the export of rubber and exceeded the Philippines in the export of pineapple products. Indonesia was able to achieve a major increase in its world market share of coffee and also to maintain high shares of palm oil and rubber. After the 1970s, the Philippines lost out in world competition in most of the tropical cash crops in which it had a traditional comparative advantage. The market share data reveal the strengthened competitive position of Thai agriculture and the dwindled position of Philippine agriculture, although comparative cost data are not available.

Indonesia and Thailand belonged to high-performing economies in the East Asian economic miracle throughout the three decades ending in the outbreak of the financial crisis in 1997 (World Bank 1993). The Philippine economy staggered, especially during the so-called lost decade of the 1980s. Gross national product (GNP) per capita in Thailand, which was about the same as that of the Philippines in the 1970s, became twice as large by the early 1990s. During the same period, Indonesia's GNP per capita increased from only about one-half that of the Philippines to about the same level. It should be reasonable to expect that the different performance of agriculture in the three countries was a significant factor underlying the different GNP growth rates.

The Basis of Vent-for-Surplus Development

A basic framework of my perspective is the classification of Southeast Asia into continental and insular zones, characterizing the former by major river deltas and

Table 9.4 **Shares of Net Exports in World Total Export Value of Selected Agricultural Commodities in Indonesia, the Philippines, and Thailand. 1961–95**

	Share in world market (percent)		
Commodity, country	*1961–65*	*1976–80*	*1991–95*
Rite			
Indonesia	–11.0	–17.6	–3.5
Philippines	–3.1	0.5	–0.5
Thailand	19.4	18.7	26.1
Maize			
Indonesia	–0.1	–0.1	–0.8
Philippines	0	–0.2	–0.1
Thailand	3.6	2.9	0.5
Sugar[a]			
Indonesia	0.5	–1.4	–1.1
Philippines	7.5	4.0	0.6
Thailand	0.2	2.7	6.9
Coffee[b]			
Indonesia	1.0	4.5	4.9
Philippines	0	0.3	0
Thailand	–0.1	0	0.8
Coconut oil			
Indonesia	0	–1.0	15.8
Philippines	39.8	69.4	60.4
Thailand	–0.1	–0.2	0
Palm oil			
Indonesia	17.8	14.5	13.9
Philippines	–0.9	–0.1	–0.1
Thailand	0	–0.6	0
Rubber			
Indonesia	23.3	23.7	27.9
Philippines	–0.3	0.1	0.3
Thailand	8.8	12.9	32.6
Pineapple[c]			

(*continued*)

Table 9.4 ***(continued)***

	Share in world market (percent)		
Commodity, country	*1961–65*	*1976–80*	*1991–95*
Indonesia	0	0	7.8
Philippines	12.9	20.7	15.0
Thailand	0	16.9	45.9
Banana			
Indonesia	0	0	0. 1
Philippines	0	8.0	5.4
Thailand	0.1	0.1	0

[a] Sugar, raw equivalent.
[b] Coffee, green and roast.
[c] Canned pineapple.
Source: FAO (1991) database.

the latter by tropical rain forests. Of course, such a characterization is subject to the hazard of oversimplification, disregarding wide ecological variations within each region.[3] In Thailand, for example, the major delta of the Chao Phraya River encompasses only a part of the Central Plain, one of four regions in Thailand. The North is characterized by small river valleys amid hills and mountains rising toward the China-Laos-Myanmar border, where irrigated rice farming can be practiced by tapping the small streams on which early Thai dynasties were built. The Northeast bordering on the Lao People's Democratic Republic is characterized by an undulated plateau with sporadic rainfall and poor soil, which had remained as the last frontier until Lao migrants settled recently by means of risky rainfed farming. The South toward the border of Malaysia has an environment similar to the insular zone, which was originally covered by rain forest.

Ecological variations within the insular zone are equally large. Especially pronounced is the difference between Java (and Bali) and the Outer Islands, such as Kalimantan and Sumatra, in Indonesia. Though much of the latter area is typically covered by tropical rain forest, the environment of Java is categorically different, as it is characterized by volcanic slopes with fertile soil and steady water supply, which make much of this area uniquely suited for irrigated rice farming. The environment of the Philippines is largely similar to that of the Outer Islands in Indonesia but mixed with volcanic terrain similar to that of Java.

Despite the large variations within each region, in general major river deltas characterize the environment of the continental zone, and tropical rain forests characterize the insular zone. These two land types formed the basis of economic development in Southeast Asia from the late nineteenth century to the early twentieth. Myint's (1965, 1971) so-called vent-for-surplus theory focuses on the process of development of "empty land" with low population density, large tracts of unused land, and abundant natural resources, typically found in Southeast Asia and East Africa at the outset of Western colonization. When these economies were integrated into international trade, unused natural resources (hitherto having had no value to indigenous people) began to command market value. Those resources could produce primary commodities to meet the high export demand of Western economies. In this way, previously unused resources became a source of economic development. The deltas of major rivers, such as Chao Phraya in Thailand, Irrawaddy in Myanmar, and Mekong in Vietnam, became the basis of vent-for-surplus development in the continental zone of Southeast Asia. The rain forest provided the basis for the development of the insular zone.

Major river deltas in the continental zone are flat and low relative to sea level, so that the surface is almost completely submerged by floods in the rainy season, although it dries up in the dry season, with no reservoir to store water. As such, floodplains in the major deltas had defied human settlement until the mid-nineteenth century, literally remaining empty land. Major civil engineering work made it possible to control flooding so that the deltas were transformed into habitable and agriculturally productive land. In Thailand the water control work took the form of developing the network of canals connected with the Chao Phraya River. The canals guide floodwater more evenly over wider areas for rice production. The canal banks provide flood-proof spaces on which farmers can settle.

The government of enlightened King Mongkut (Rama IV of the Chakri dynasty) initiated canal construction in the Chao Phraya delta. Construction began shortly after the government and Great Britain signed the so-called Bowring Treaty in 1855, which opened the kingdom to trade with the West. Soon rapid increases in foreign demand for Thai rice, which significantly raised both the price of rice and the value of rice land, induced the mobilization of private investment. A group of influential courtiers and wealthy Chinese traders established the Siam Canals Land and Irrigation Company, a major builder of private canals. The company secured a concession in 1889 to dig canals in a vast tract of swampy land northeast of Bangkok, under the clause that the company was allowed to hold ownership over reclaimed land along the canals. Its operation was managed by the Chinese business elite and construction work was heavily based on Chinese migrant laborers hired for wages, unlike the corvée labor that was used in the king's prior projects.[4] However, the farmers who settled in reclaimed land as tenants were Thai who had migrated from other regions.

There is little doubt that the opening of the Chao Phraya delta for rice production was the basis of vent-for-surplus growth, which moved Thailand's economy toward specialization in rice production in the late nineteenth century. Although comparable data are not available for earlier years, the area planted in rice in the Central Plain was as large as 6.8 million rai (1 rai = 0.16 hectare) or 85 percent of total rice area in the kingdom in the 1905–9 period. That was larger than the national total of 5.8 million rai in 1850 (Ingram 1971). The opening for cultivation of the Irrawaddy Delta in Myanmar and the Mekong Delta in Vietnam were similarly important for those economies during the comparable period.

The tropical rain forests in Southeast Asia's insular zone played a comparable role in vent-for-surplus development. Since long before the mid-nineteenth century, rain forests had been the source of supply of valuable products for trade, such as cinnamon, cloves, bird nests, deer horns, and hides. However, the high incidence of malaria and other tropical diseases defied human settlement inside thick tropical forests at low elevation. Typically, native people lived on sea coasts and occasionally entered the forests for collection and extraction of natural products for sale to foreign traders or their agents who sailed to their coasts. In the late nineteenth century, Western capital and entrepreneurship began to convert the forests into plantations of tropical export crops, heavily relying on migrant labor from China. Before this period, Western colonial powers had attempted to collect tropical products from the natives by taxation and other coercive means.

The concurrent exploitation of continental deltas and insular forests occurred with the greater integration of Southeast Asia into the world economy in the late nineteenth century. Much greater integration than before resulted from the establishment of the free trade regime under the hegemony of Britain and the revolution in ocean transportation. The free trade system was imposed on native economies by force, either directly by Britain in its colonies or indirectly by forcing liberalization on local sovereign and other colonial powers. In the Bowring Treaty, Thailand not only conceded extraterritoriality to Britain but also lost financial autonomy. Export and import duties were fixed at the flat rate of 3 percent ad valorem, and internal taxes, such as exercise taxes, transportation tolls, and even land taxes, were not allowed to change by the will of the kingdom alone. Advisers from Britain carefully monitored public finance (Ingram 1971). As such, the kingdom of Siam for several decades after signing the Bowring Treaty was almost a protectorate of Great Britain. Great Britain imposed the free trade system on Thailand, both internationally and internally, in a way similar to Great Britain's other colonies, such as Burma and Malay.

Furthermore, Great Britain pressed the other Western colonies to adopt the free trade system. For example, the British occupation of Manila in 1762–64 during the Seven Years' War broke Spain's monopoly of the reexport trade in Manila of Chinese goods to Mexico by galleon ships, opening up the port of Manila to shipments and commerce by traders in other nations. Great Britain's continued pressure underlay the successive opening of other ports in the Philippines until the mid-nineteenth century (Larkin 1972).

The reason behind Great Britain's strong drive for free trade was its high manufacturing production capacity, which established the country as the "Workshop of the World" after the Industrial Revolution. British industries sought markets for their products and sources of raw material supplies. Having established the modern factory system that could produce industrial products at lower cost than local cottage industries in the tropics, Great Britain found it advantageous to trade its manufactured commodities for tropical agricultural products and minerals. Thus trade replaced the forced collection of tropical commodities through tax and other means, which were commonly practiced by earlier colonialists, such as the Spanish conquistadors in the Philippines and the Dutch East India Company in Indonesia. Soon other Western nations followed Great Britain in industrialization and in trade.

Corresponding to its expanded industrial production capacity, the West's demand for raw materials for processing—such as cotton, rubber, and tin—became very large. Moreover, as the level of income and wages rose, tropical delicacies—such as pepper, coffee, and tea, hitherto limited to the high-income elite—became common items on the tables of ordinary working people.

This tendency was further strengthened by major innovations in ocean transportation, consisting of the introduction of the steamship and the opening of the Suez Canal in 1869. These two innovations combined reduced the transportation cost of commodities from Bangkok to major ports in Europe, such as London, below that from Bangkok to Thailand's old capital, Chiang Mai (Ingram 1971). Without such innovations, it would have been impossible for bulky commodities like rice produced in Southeast Asia to find markets as far as Europe (Furnivall 1948).

Although the innovations in ocean transportation reduced the prices of commodities from Southeast Asia in the West, they also reduced the prices of Western commodities in Southeast Asia to a large extent. Thus under the liberal trade regime in the late nineteenth century, industrial commodities flowed into Southeast Asia, outcompeting local handicraft industries. Deindustrialization became a common feature in Southeast Asia (Resnick 1970). Thailand, which had been an exporter of cotton products before the 1850s, quickly became a major importer (Ingram 1971). Indigenous labor shifted from manufacturing to primary production for export. This shift, together with the migration of labor from China and India, provided the basis for exploiting unused natural resources, such as major river deltas and tropical rain forests, for vent-for-surplus development.

An example that clearly illustrates the impact of opening to international trade and specialization in primary production can be seen in the development of sugar production in Negros, Philippines. Prior to the opening of nearby Iloilo City as an international port in 1855, Negros Island was sparsely populated, and much of its area was uncultivated. When the port opened, the island was rapidly transformed into sugar plantations. Concurrently, the inflow of cheap British cloth played havoc on local weaving industries surrounding Iloilo, which had hitherto made textiles a major export item from this region (McCoy 1982).

In the global trade system created in the late nineteenth to the early twentieth centuries, the exchange was not simply between industrial commodities in the West and primary commodities in Southeast Asia. Rice produced in the continental zone was originally brought to Europe as cheap food for industrial laborers (some was reexported to Latin America). Later, as plantations developed in the insular zone, demand for rice as the basic subsistence need for plantation laborers expanded at a speed that could not be met by local supply. Correspondingly, the share of rice exported from the continental zone to the insular zone within Southeast Asia increased. Thus triangular trade flows emerged in this period—rice produced from the continental zone was brought to the insular zone, and tropical cash crops produced in the insular zone by laborers fed on the imported rice were exported to Europe in exchange for industrial products. In this triangular trade flow, comparative advantage dictated regional specialization. For example, the sugar industry, which appeared to be a promising industry for export in Thailand at the onset of trade opening, was soon destroyed by imports from Indonesia and the Philippines (Ingram 1971).

In this way, vent-for-surplus development in Southeast Asia based on the exploitation of hitherto unused land resources was reinforced by comparative advantage within the region, which was largely determined by ecological conditions. Comparative advantage based on natural resource endowments was also reinforced by colonial policies on farmland as well as public investments in physical and institutional infrastructure. For example, the strong sugarcane research program organized by the Dutch colonial government significantly contributed to strengthening the international competitiveness of the sugar industry in Indonesia (Evenson 1976).

Evolution of Agrarian Systems

This process of vent-for-surplus development would have influenced the formation of agrarian structures in Indonesia, the Philippines, and Thailand (Table 9.2). Thailand is characterized by the unimodal distribution of peasants or family farms, with an insignificant number of large estate farms or plantations and a relatively low incidence of tenancy. Indonesia and the Philippines are characterized by bifurcation between the peasant sector, which grows mainly subsistence crops, and the plantation sector, which grows tropical cash crops. Relative to the other two countries, the incidence of tenancy is high in the Philippines and, combined with the bifurcation of agricultural production, it implies that the share of landless population in the rural sector is highest in the Philippines.

It is common to explain the persistence of the peasant mode in contrast to the emergence of the plantation system in terms of different technological requirements for production between subsistence food crops and export cash crops. However, in my perspective, the bifurcated farm-size distribution and the problem of landlessness in Southeast Asia (as well as in other parts in the world) stemmed essentially from "preemption of land" by colonial and domestic elites rather than technological factors for agricultural production.

CONDITIONS OF THE PLANTATION SYSTEM[5]

A conventional explanation for the establishment of the plantation system is based on the scale economies inherent in the production of tropical export crops (Baldwin 1956). However, few crops are subject to sufficiently strong scale economies at the farm level to make the use of plantation organization necessary (Pirn 1946; Wickizer 1951, 1960; Lim 1968; Hayami et al. 1990).[6] In fact, there are examples of every so-called plantation crop being grown successfully by peasants somewhere in the world. Significant increasing returns emerge only at the levels of processing and marketing activities. The vertical integration of a large estate farm with a large-scale central processing and/or marketing system is called for because of the need to supply farm-produced raw materials on a timely schedule. A typical example is fermented black tea. The manufacturing of black tea at a standardized quality for export requires a modern machine plant into which fresh leaves must be fed within a few hours after plucking (Wickizer 1951, 1960). The need for close coordination between farm production and processing underlies the traditional use of the plantation system for black tea manufacture. By contrast, mainly peasants in China and Japan produce unfermented green tea. Even for the manufacture of black tea, it is not imperative to use the plantation system. This is evident in the case of Taiwan, where smallholders produce both black and green tea with small-scale equipment. The large fermentation plant has been used in plantations as a device enforcing the work schedule and standardizing product quality for the export market. In fact, farm production by smallholders based on the system of contract farming has developed relatively recently in Kenya (Lamb and Muller 1982).

In the case of bananas for export, harvested fruit must be packed, sent to the wharf, and loaded on a refrigerated boat within a day. A boatful of bananas that can meet the quality standards of foreign buyers must be collected within a few days. Therefore, the whole production process from planting to harvesting must be precisely controlled so as to meet the shipment schedule. Although the plantation system has a decisive advantage for this export product, bananas for domestic consumption are usually produced by peasants.

Plantations have no significant advantage over peasants for the crops for which centralized processing and marketing are not necessary. Typical examples are cocoa and coconuts. The fermentation of cocoa and the drying and smoking of coconuts to make copra can be handled in small lots with no large capital requirement beyond small indigenous tools and facilities. These crops are grown predominantly by peasants.

Sugar is frequently cited as a classic case of scale economies stemming from the need for coordination between farm production and large-scale central processing (Binswanger and Rosenzweig 1986). Efficient operation of a centrifugal sugar mill requires the steady supply of a large amount of cane over time. It requires coordination of production from planting to harvesting and processing. However, this coordination need not be as stringent as it is for tea and bananas. The rate of sugar extraction decreases as the processing of cane is delayed, but this loss is in no way comparable to the devastating damage to the quality of tea and bananas for export that may result from delayed processing. Sugarcane can be hauled from relatively long distances and stored for several days. Therefore, the need for vertical integration is not as large, and the sugar mill can achieve the necessary coordination through contracts with cane growers on the time and the quota of cane delivery. In fact, Australia, Taiwan, and more recently Thailand have developed an efficient sugar industry with smallholders.

Another explanation for the use of the plantation system is the advantage of large estate farms in accessing capital. Binswanger and Rosenzweig (1986) argue that this gives plantations an advantage with regard to tree crops characterized by long gestation periods from planting to maturity. However, the opportunity costs of labor and capital applied to formation of the tree capital are not necessarily high for peasants. Typically, they plant the trees in previously unused land. If such land is located near their residence, they open new land for planting by means of family labor at low opportunity cost during the idle season for the production of food crops on farm land already in use. Often, when peasants migrate to frontier areas, they slash and burn jungles and plant subsistence crops such as maize, potatoes, and upland rice, together with tree seedlings. Such complex intercropping is difficult to manage with hired labor in the plantation system because of the inherent difficulty in monitoring the work of hired wage laborers over spatially dispersed and ecologically variable farm operations (Brewster 1950; Binswanger and Rosenzweig 1986; Hayami and Otsuka 1993).

Therefore, even in the export boom of tropical cash crops under colonialism from the nineteenth century to the early twentieth, the plantation system failed to make inroads in regions where the indigenous population had established family farms (Lewis 1970). Western traders found it more profitable to purchase tropical agricultural commodities from peasant producers in exchange for imported manufactured commodities than to produce the tropical crops themselves by means of the plantation system.

The establishment of plantations in less developed economies increased as the demand for tropical products by the industrialized nations continued to rise and the regions physically suited for the production of these products had no significant peasant population that could produce and trade their commodities. Opening frontier land for the production of new crops entailed high capital outlays. Virgin land had to be cleared and developed, and physical infrastructure, such as roads, irrigation systems, bridges, and docking facilities, had to be constructed. Capital, in the form of machinery and equipment, had to be imported and redesigned to adapt to local situations. Laborers were imported from the more populous regions and trained in the production of these crops.

The establishment of plantations thus requires huge initial capital investment. For the investors to internalize gains from investment in infrastructure, farm size must be large. Viewed from this perspective, it follows that the plantation system evolved not because it was generally a more efficient mode of productive organization than the peasant mode. Instead, the system was adopted because it was the most effective type of agricultural organization for extracting the economic benefit accruing from the exploitation of sparsely populated virgin areas, typically in the process of vent-for-surplus development.

From this perspective, it is easy to understand why the same crop is grown mainly by peasants in one place and mainly by plantations in another. For example, for sugarcane production, the peasant mode is more common in the old settled areas of Luzon, and the plantation system predominates in the newly opened Negros, both in the Philippines (Hayami et al. 1990). Usually the share of peasants in the production of export cash crops rises when the initial land-opening stage is over and infrastructure is decently established with increased population density (Booth 1988).

Although the plantation system had an economic advantage in the vent-for-surplus stage, plantations could not have been established if governments had not granted concessions to hold large tracts of virgin land for the exclusive use of plantations. Typically colonial governments granted concessions to Western planters. For example, the Dutch colonial government had traditionally tried to prevent alienation of farmland from indigenous peasants by regulating against land purchase by foreigners, including the ethnic Chinese. However, in the late nineteenth century, demand for tropical cash crops rose sharply. The colonial government passed the Agricultural Land Law of 1870. which granted Dutch planters long-term contracts to lease wild land. The land was de jure owned by the government (although it was de facto used by native tribes). Although this new institutional arrangement should have accelerated the development of "empty land" for cash crop production, it served as an instrument to preempt land for the elite, closing smallholders' access to land. Similar public land-leasing arrangements were also practiced under the American colonial administration with frontier land in the Philippines, especially in Mindanao, which became the basis of large plantations under the management of multinational corporations (Hayami et al. 1990).

LAND PREEMPTION AND TENANCY

The incidence of land tenancy is closely related to the preemption of land. Of course, a land tenancy relationship can emerge as a practice among peasants in the absence of preemption. If external forces did not disturb a rural community, land tenure institutions would evolve gradually from communal to private ownership. Corresponding to the growing relative scarcity of land under mounting population pressure, it becomes necessary to intensify the utilization of land, typically from shifting cultivation with long fallow to that with short fallow, to annual cropping, and further to multiple cropping per year involving irrigation (Boserup 1965).

The process of agricultural intensification requires major investment for improving land infrastructure, from removing stones and roots from newly opened land, to land leveling and terracing, and further to irrigation and drainage. To secure incentives for such investment, it becomes necessary to give land users the right to use their land exclusively. Thus land tenure institutions normally evolve from communal ownership to private ownership, involving various steps from periodical reallotment of communal land among community members, to lifelong usufruct rights, to usufruct rights inheritable by heirs, and further to private property rights amenable for market transactions.

Land tenancy arrangements gradually develop as an institution to increase production efficiency by improving combinations of land and labor (including entrepreneurship) as individual land tenure becomes longer and more exclusive. When a farmer finds his family labor short for cultivation of a land parcel on which a long-term usufruct is established (because of sickness or some other reason), he may rent out a part of it to someone whose land endowment is short relative to their labor endowment. It is a Pareto improvement if the latter pays to the former a rent equivalent to the marginal productivity of the land. At the same time, land tenancy associated with private property rights on land can work as an institution to increase inequality in income distribution and social hierarchy within a community. A farmer endowed with superior muscular power or entrepreneurship may rent more land and increase income and may eventually buy the land. As he eventually accumulates more land than his family labor can efficiently cultivate, he may rent out a part of his land to someone who has become landless for whatever reason. Increased income from rent revenue added to farm income may motivate him to purchase more land for renting. This process should progress faster as the relative scarcity of land rises under increased population pressure.

Such autonomous evolution of land property rights and tenancy relationships does not usually result in the large-scale absentee landlordism observed in several developing economies. Rather, it tends to create stratification of peasantry along a continuous spectrum between landlord-cum-owner and owner-cum–tenant farmer. Although land tenancy is commonly practiced, a majority of farmland continues to be under owner cultivation, and both noncultivating landlords and pure tenants are the minority.

Such an agrarian structure is typically found in the peasant sector in Indonesia. Unlike other colonial powers, the Dutch did not try to impose Western institutions, such as private property rights in land. Rather, they preserved or even strengthened traditional community institutions and organizations. The Agrarian Law of 1870 granted long-term lease of wild public land to foreign planters, but did not allow them to purchase or rent cultivated land from native peasants individually. Instead, sugar planters were allowed to lease rice land through contracts with the heads of villages. The contracts normally extended for less than twenty years. The lessee was allowed to occupy only one-third of the village land, which had to be rotated over three crop seasons. This rotation was designed to prevent planters from gaining a permanent hold on village land. Periodic reallocation of village land under the direction of village headmen strengthened traditional tendencies toward communal landholding (Pelzer 1945).

The situation in the Philippines provides a sharp contrast. At the time of conquest, the Spaniards introduced the notion of legal title to land (McLennan 1969). They applied to the Philippines the same principle they applied to other new territories—that all the lands except those officially proved to be private or communal possessions belonged to the Spanish Crown. The Crown's property rights were established over vast areas of uncultivated land, including areas used as commons by native people. Much of the royal domain was granted to conquistadors and monastic orders, such as Augustinian and Franciscan friars. This institutional development in the early Spanish era represented a wholesale preemption of usable land, closing access by native people. Later, the population increased, and foreign demand for Philippine products increased through trade liberalization. Large landholdings created from earlier royal grants became plantations in the upland areas and rice haciendas with tenant labor in the lowland areas.

Native peasants were even deprived of the opportunity to establish ownership by opening new lands for cultivation. For example, the inner part of Central Luzon had been covered by jungle and used only for cattle ranching. When it was finally converted into large rice haciendas in the late nineteenth century, many peasants migrated from the north, believing that they had settled in no-man's-land. After the peasants opened the jungle, landowners' agents visited and notified the peasants that they had to pay rent as tenants on haciendas (Hesters and Mabun 1924).

Pervasive landlordism in the Philippines was also rooted in the relatively free land transactions under the Spanish regime. Chinese and Chinese mestizos, who engaged in internal trade along littorals, where native peasants held traditional land rights, acquired land through money lending using land as collateral. A common arrangement was that the borrower continued to cultivate his land as a sharecropper of his creditor during the loan period. If the borrower became unable to repay the loan at the end of the period, the land title shifted to the creditor and the borrower usually continued sharecropping (McLennan 1969). The scale of landholding accumulated in this commercial process in the coastal area was typically much smaller than that of haciendas in the inner part of Central Luzon (Hayami and Kikuchi 1981). Thus, before the Marcos land reform in the 1970s, rice area in the Philippines was predominantly cultivated by share tenants, who typically owned no land of their own. The pervasive landlordism in the rice sector and plantations in the cash crop sector that characterized the traditional agrarian structure in the Philippines were both rooted in the preemption of land in the Spanish period.

In Thailand, preemption occurred in the vent-for-surplus stage through the granting of land concessions to private canal builders in the Chao Phraya delta. As a result, the incidence of tenancy is significant in the Central Plain, especially in the Rangsit area northeast of Bangkok, where the private company intensively dug canals. Yet, taking Thailand as a whole, tenancy is of minor importance compared with Indonesia and the Philippines, partly because of relatively abundant land endowment and, more important, because of government policy.

The country's ancient custom was to give every man the right to take as much land from the state as he and his family could cultivate, which was normally considered to be 25 rai (equivalent to 4 hectares). This institution was maintained even after opening trade with the West. The Consolidated Land Act of 1908 did not specify an exact area of land, but gave people the right to take as much land as they could profitably cultivate. In practice these areas ranged between 20 and 50 rai. The Land Act of 1936 specified 50 rai as the maximum that one could take. These laws kept access to land wide open for ordinary Thai, making the situation diametrically different from that of the Philippines.[7] Both of these Thai laws incorporated the old custom that the cultivator could receive title to the land only after he cultivated it for three years. This clause together with land taxation, which applied to not only cultivated but also uncultivated holdings, discouraged holding land idle for speculation (Ingram 1971).

The basic factor underlying the major difference in land policy between the Philippines and Thailand was the difference in the culture or the value system between the Spanish colonial rulers and the rulers of the independent kingdom. The Dutch colonial rulers tried to preserve traditional village institutions, thereby avoiding alienation of land from peasants in Indonesia. Their motivation might have been to maintain social stability for the sake of extracting tropical agricultural products from this colony at minimum administrative cost, as argued by Furnivall (1944, 1948).

It is also important to observe that the preemption of rice land through canal construction in Thailand resulted in the emergence of large-scale landlordism, but not in the formation of plantations. This was similar to the case of the Philippines. In Thailand, large holdings of landlords were usually subdivided into small parcels for rice cultivation by the family labor of landless peasants under tenancy contracts. The owners of large tracts of rice land established titles through land preemption, such as obtaining concessions for canal digging in the Chao Phraya delta. They preferred tenancy to plantation operations, perhaps at least in part because of the difficulty of standardizing tasks of rice production and, hence, of monitoring the efforts of workers.

Another reason the owners preferred tenancy may have been because paddy is storable. Unlike black tea and bananas, paddy does not require close coordination between farm production and processing/marketing. Although rice milling and marketing for export involved significant scale economies, the operators could secure adequate supply of paddy through ordinary market transactions. As the result, they could dispense with efforts to vertically integrate farm production with processing and marketing by means of the plantation system or the contract farming system. Therefore it may not be unreasonable to postulate the counterfactual hypothesis that, if the nature of rice-milling technology were such as to require close coordination with paddy production, large rice plantations would have been established in the Rangsit area, where territorial concessions were granted to private canal builders.

Outside the newly opened delta area, the practice of tenancy is fairy common in the old settled northern region. The agrarian structure in northern Thailand, which did not experience preemption, is similar to that of the peasant sector in Indonesia. It is characterized by a continuous spectrum from landlord-cum-owner to owner-cum–tenant farmer.

Agrarian Structure and Agricultural Growth Performance

This section discusses whether the different agrarian structures that emerged along different historical paths under different ecological conditions explain, at least in part, the different agricultural growth performance across Indonesia, the Philippines, and Thailand. The analysis focuses on two questions. First, why did Indonesia and the Philippines, which had strong comparative advantage in tropical cash crops such as sugar before World War II, lose ground to Thailand in world market competition in recent years (Table 9.4)? Second, why was the agricultural output growth of the Philippines so slow relative to growth in Indonesia and Thailand (Table 9.3)?

DECLINE IN THE ADVANTAGE OF PLANTATIONS

The previous section argued that the efficiency of plantations relative to the peasant system is high in the initial opening-up process of land-abundant and labor-scarce economies. However, several negative aspects of plantations grow large as tropical economies shift from the land-abundant to the land-scarce stage after the completion of the opening-up process. Correspondingly, the relative advantage of the peasant system increased.

Negative aspects of the plantation system

First, the plantation system tends to substitute capital for labor because of the inherent difficulty in supervising wage laborers in spatially dispersed and ecologically diverse farm operations. In addition, plantations have relatively easy access to both the private credit market and concessional loans from the government. The substitution of capital for labor is socially inefficient in many developing economies, which are characterized by the abundant endowment of labor relative to capital.

Second, agricultural land tends to be cultivated less intensively in the plantation system, which employs mainly wage labor and usually practices monoculture. Complicated intercropping and crop-livestock combinations are more difficult to manage in the command system, implying that both the labor input and income per hectare are lower on the plantations.[8] This is a source of inefficiency in the plantation system, where land becomes scarce relative to labor under the pressure of population growth. By contrast, small-sized family farms tend to cultivate land more intensively.

Third, plantations usually specialize in a single crop. This monocrop bias reduces the flexibility of productive organizations to respond to changing demand by shifting to the production of other crops. Moreover, continual cropping of a single crop tends to result in soil degradation and an increase in the incidence of pests. Counterapplication of fertilizer and chemicals causes serious stress on the environment and human health and incurs high costs.

Fourth, the specialization of plantation workers in specific tasks inhibits the development of their managerial and entrepreneurial capacity (Baldwin 1956; Myint 1965; Beckford 1972).

Fifth, the plantation system is a source of class conflict between laborers and managers/capitalists. The presence of a plantation enclave in rural economies where the peasant mode of production predominates has often strained relationships in rural communities. Therefore, in terms of the criterion of social stability, the plantation system is no match for the system of relatively homogeneous small producers that own small assets.

Increased advantage of the peasant system

Although Southeast Asia had traditionally been endowed with relatively abundant land resources ready for exploitation, frontiers for new land opening were progressively closed under the explosive population growth that characterized developing economies after World War II. It seems reasonable that the advantage of the plantation system declined and that of the peasant system increased correspondingly. Therefore it is not surprising that Thai agriculture, which predominantly consisted of smallholders, began to perform better than that of Indonesia and the Philippines, which were characterized by large plantation sectors.[9] Major increases in the export of nonrice agricultural commodities, such as rubber, kenaf, and cassava tips from Thailand, were totally based on the production of smallholders. To a significant extent, the expansion in the production of nonrice export crops in Thailand was supported by the existence of open land frontiers, which enabled relatively fast increases in the area under cultivation (Table 9.1). The important point in the present context, however, is that the exploitation of cultivation frontiers was carried out by smallholders and not by plantations.

Relative increases in the efficiency of the peasant system were not limited to Thailand. The dramatic rise in Indonesia's share in world coffee and cocoa markets was entirely based on smallholders (Akiyama and Nishio 1996). The production of coconut oil in the Philippines, for which the country was able to maintain its high world market share, was extracted predominantly from copra made by smallholders, although some coconut plantations continued to operate, especially in Mindanao.

The advantage of the plantation system is better coordination between large-scale marketing/processing and farm-level production. Yet the disadvantage of the peasant system in this aspect could be overcome by organizing contract farming. In contract farming, an agribusiness firm manages processing and marketing but contracts for the supply of farm products with peasant farmers. The firm provides technical guidance, credit, and other services to peasants in return for their pledged production to the firm. In this way, the system can take advantage of peasants in farm production without sacrificing scale economies in processing and marketing. An advantage of this system is that it taps not only the manual labor but also the management ability of rural people in developing economies. Thailand used this system when it began production of canned pineapple relatively recently; Thailand has surpassed the Philippines, formerly the world's leading exporter, whose production is based on large plantations in Mindanao.[10]

THE DILEMMA OF LAND REFORM

The Philippine government has attempted to mitigate the social unrest rooted in pervasive landlessness and landlordism. Redistributive land reform extends back to the American colonial regime. However, the framework of the reform applied in the past four decades was established by the Agrarian Land Reform Code of 1963, which was enacted under President Diosdado Macapagal (Hayami et al. 1990).

The major thrust of the code was the creation of owner-cultivatorship on rice and corn land. This involved two steps. First, "Operation Leasehold" converted share tenancy to leasehold tenancy, with rent fixed at the rate of 25 percent of the average harvest for three normal years preceding the operation. Second, "Operation Land Transfer" transferred land ownership to tenants. In the latter operation, the government expropriated land in excess of landlords' retention limit (75 hectares). It compensated the landlords with 10 percent of the land value in cash and the rest in interest-free redeemable Land Bank bonds. The land was resold to the tenants for annual amortization payments within twenty-five years.

The code was amended in 1971 under President Marcos to extend land reform to the whole nation, with automatic conversion of all share tenants to leaseholders. The 1971 code was enforced by Presidential Decrees No. 2 and No. 27 under the martial law proclaimed in 1972. The landlord's retention limit was reduced successively from 75 to 7 hectares. The period of amortization payments was shortened to fifteen years. It is easy to enumerate the shortcomings of the land reform programs in the Philippines, yet there is no denying that large haciendas in Central Luzon were broken down. Most tenants established their status as leaseholders or amortizing owners, although sizable areas remain under the direct administration of landlords.

The beneficiaries of land reform have captured a large economic surplus. Rice yields have increased significantly due to the development of irrigation and the application of new varieties and fertilizers, while rent and amortization payments have been fixed. Thus, land reform has been successful in transferring much of the economic return to land from absentee landlords to former sharecroppers. However, the reform has created serious income inequality within village communities. The income of landless laborers has not risen (or may have declined) because the strong population pressure on land has prevented their wages from rising despite agricultural productivity increases.

Major distortions in resource allocations occurred because reforms were applied in a discriminatory manner to a certain sector of agriculture. By limiting program application mainly to tenanted land, the reforms created a strong incentive for landlords to evict their tenants and cultivate their land directly. However, labor inputs and, hence, agricultural output and labor income per hectare are usually higher in small family farms than in large farms. This is because of the inherent difficulty large farms have in supervising wage laborers. Therefore, the exemption of land under the direct administration of landlords had the effect of reducing labor input per hectare below an optimum level, thereby reducing the income of the laborers.

The impact of the regulations on tenancy contracts (especially the prohibition of share tenancy and the control of land rent) were equally serious. They reduced the incentive of large landholders to rent out their land in small parcels, resulting in a reduction in social product and labor income. This behavior applied not only to landlords but also to land reform beneficiaries. As the income of former sharecroppers, who were converted into leaseholders or amortizing owners, rose significantly, many of them retreated from arduous farmwork, leaving it to landless laborers. Yet they hesitated to subrent their holdings to landless laborers because their formal titles might be transferred. The land reform laws said that formal titles would be transferred to sublessees if they could prove to the agrarian reform office that they were the actual tillers of the land. Thus land reform beneficiaries have to continue to cultivate their land based on hired labor, even if they are not able to work because they are sick, old, or engaged in nonfarm activities. The reforms inevitably resulted in inefficient combinations of land and labor.

Significant negative effects of land reform on agricultural production efficiency also occurred outside the rice and corn sector. The cash crop sector has not been covered by reform programs. The Comprehensive Agrarian Reform Law of 1988 intended to cover the cash crop sector, but it has not been significantly implemented. However, plantation owners fear that their land will eventually be expropriated. It is only natural that they have stopped investing in improvements in their land infrastructure, including planting and replanting trees. Some landowners even preferred to keep their land idle rather than use it for agricultural production. This was often the case in frontier regions like Mindanao.

Such fears and lack of investment might underlie, to a significant extent, the low rate of expansion in cropland area in the Philippines as compared with Thailand (Table 9.1). The poor performance of the Philippines in competition for world export market shares is at least partly rooted in the uncertainty of the planters of tropical cash crops concerning the future course of land reform (Table 9.4).

Toward Political Economy

Different agrarian structures developed in Indonesia, the Philippines, and Thailand along different historical paths and under different ecological conditions. From the late nineteenth to the early twentieth century, development of the three economies followed a typical pattern along the vent-for-surplus theory. Vent-for-surplus development is based on the exploitation of unused natural resources corresponding to their integration into the world market. Thailand represents the continental zone of Southeast Asia, whose resource base for vent-for-surplus development was the major delta of the Chao Phraya River. Indonesia and the Philippines represent the insular zone, whose resource base was the tropical rain forest. This difference in the resource base underlay the major difference in farm-size distribution—the unimodal distribution of peasants or family farms in Thailand as compared with the coexistence of peasants and large estate farms or plantations specializing in tropical export crops in Indonesia and the Philippines.

Different land policies, especially with respect to preemption of unused land by the elite, under different political regimes resulted in major differences in the pattern of land ownership. The preemption was wholesale in the Philippines under Spanish colonialism. It provided the base for the highly skewed land distribution, which was characterized by the bifurcation between noncultivating landlords and sharecroppers in lowland rice areas and between plantation owners and wage laborers in upland areas. In Indonesia, the preemption took place as the Dutch colonial government granted long-term lease of uncultivated public land to foreign planters. However, the government tried to prevent the alienation of cultivated land from native peasants to avoid social instability. As a result, the peasant sector continued to consist mainly of landlord-cum-owners and owner-cum–tenant cultivators, and both noncultivating landlords and the pure landless remained a minority. In Thailand the preemption occurred through the grant of concessions for private canal building. However, the incidence of tenancy did not become serious because the government of the independent kingdom preserved the traditional institution of giving land to anyone who could open and cultivate it. Relatively homogeneous landowning peasants continued to dominate the rural sector of Thailand.

It appears that major differences in the agrarian structure have been significant factors in the differences in agricultural growth performance across the three economies in recent years. As frontiers for opening new land for cultivation were progressively closed, the initial advantage of the plantation system in large-scale land development began to be outweighed by its disadvantage in monitoring hired labor. At the same time, the advantage of the peasant system increased with respect to the use of family labor needing no supervision. This tendency seems to be manifest in Thailand's growing share in world exports of tropical cash crops in recent years. Furthermore, the land reform programs in the Philippines that called for reducing inequality in the distribution of land ownership have made land markets inactive, resulting in major distortions in resource allocations and serious underinvestment in agriculture.

Many factors in addition to the agrarian structure have contributed to the differential performances in agriculture. For example, one factor that is commonly cited in explaining the poor growth performance of Philippine agriculture is the prolonged continuation of the country's industrial protection policy geared for import substitution. Under this policy regime, the agricultural sector was penalized by high tariffs on manufactured commodities and overvalued exchange rates (Ariff and Hill 1985; Bautista 1987; Intal and Power 1989). Another factor was the state's trade monopoly on sugar and coconut products, which was heavily tinted with cronyism in the late stage of the Marcos regime (Hayami et al. 1990). The political instability in the 1980s from the downfall of the Marcos administration throughout the succeeding Aquino regime discouraged both domestic and foreign investments in agriculture as well as in other sectors.

By contrast, Thailand began to shift from the import-substitution to the export-oriented strategy in the 1970s, almost two decades ahead of the Philippines (Warr 1993; Warr and Nidhiprabha 1995). In addition, the government of Thailand intervened little in the activities of private traders in agricultural marketing. The government's control of trade was largely limited to indirect measures, such as the imposition of an export tax on rice (the rice premium). A large number of traders of various sizes, ranging from small collectors of farm produce at the village level to large exporters to the foreign market, were well coordinated through free competition. They made up a highly efficient channel to deliver overseas demands to farmers. Their activities were facilitated by major public investment in infrastructure, especially highways. This free trade system, supported by the government's provision of public goods, created remarkable diversification of agricultural resources to new export crops. The agricultural diversification was achieved while Thailand continued to strengthen its competitive position in rice production (Siamwalla et al. 1990; World Bank 1987).

It is unlikely that such differences in government policy are independent of differences in the agrarian structure and value system in society that are deeply rooted in different ecological conditions and historical paths. For example, Hara (1994) advances a hypothesis on the reason why import-substitution industrialization was pursued more strongly for a longer period in the Philippines than in Thailand and other Association for Southeast Asian Nations economies. He argues that in the Philippines the business elite who benefited from industrial protection originated from the landed oligarchy, therefore little countervailing power was mobilized against the industrial protection policy. By contrast, the rural countervailing power against industrial protection was comparatively high in Indonesia, Malaysia, and Thailand because the urban business elite were predominantly ethnic Chinese. Also, the rather harmonious division of labor that developed between Thai farmers and Chinese traders in the kingdom of Siam may have prevented the modern Thai government from adopting antimarket and antitrader interventions.

Another example is the remarkable success of the Green Revolution in Indonesia. The country's high growth of land productivity was, to a large extent, based on the strong support of the rice sector during the three decades of the Soeharto administration. It invested in irrigation and agricultural research and extension, plus subsidies for inputs and credits. This support was effective in overcoming the "Dutch disease effects" that seriously damaged agriculture in some oil-producing countries, such as Nigeria in the 1970s and early 1980s (Hayami 1997). It seems that Soeharto's policy choice was not independent of the tradition in Indonesia of protecting peasants as the stabilizing block of society.

In the Philippines in the 1970s, the Masagana-99 Program promoted the Green Revolution by means of distributing to farmers packages of new seeds, subsidized fertilizers, and other modern inputs, in a manner similar to Indonesia's Bimas Program. However, in the absence of "peasant fundamentalism" in the Philippines comparable to that of Indonesia, the Masagana Program lasted only about a decade (Hayami and Kikuchi 2000). Thus rice self-sufficiency in the Philippines, which had been achieved during the 1970s, could not be sustained in the 1980s. Indonesia rose from the world's largest importer of rice in the 1970s to achieve self-sufficiency in the 1980s. However, the country again became a major importer with the recent economic crisis associated with the downfall of the Soeharto regime. Unlike Indonesia and the Philippines, in Thailand's liberal trade regime, the role of government policy in promoting fertilizer application was not very significant and effective (World Bank 1987).

For now, such political-economy theorizing is largely conjectural. Yet the agrarian structure of a nation and the value system in its society have been created along a unique historical trajectory, under unique ecological conditions. These should have a far-reaching influence on the organization of political economy and, hence, on policy choices. The positive analysis of this relationship presents a major challenge for future research. The analysis might be extended beyond the comparison within a region, as attempted here, to comparisons across regions. It might shed light on major questions in world development. For example, it might help in analyzing why Africa lags behind in achieving innovations in agricultural technology comparable to the Green Revolution in Asia.

Notes

Yujiro Hayami, *World Bank Research Observer* 16 (Fall 2001): 169–98. The author wishes to gratefully acknowledge helpful comments from Takamasa Akiyama, Robert Allen, Gershon Feder, and Yair Mundlak, as well as technical assistance from Kei Kajisa and Yue Yaguchi.

1. For a more comprehensive assessment of agricultural growth performance in Asia, including Southeast Asia, see the five-volume report of the Asian Development Bank's project titled "Study of Rural Asia." Especially relevant to the context of this section are its overview (Asian Development Bank 2000), volume 1 by Rosegrant and Hazell (2000), and volume 2 by Kosa-ard and Rekasem (2000). Another major study specifically addressed to Southeast Asian agriculture is in progress by the Development Economics Research Group at the World Bank, titled "Dynamism of Rural Sector Growth: Policy Lessons from East Asian Countries."
2. Huke and Huke (1997) estimate paddy field areas in Indonesia, the Philippines, and Thailand in the mid-1990s as being 9,441,000, 3,456,000, and 9,806,000 hectares, respectively. However, they do not specify the years for these data. The substitution of Huke and Huke's estimates for the data used in Table 9.1 does not change the conclusion of this article.
3. Descriptions of ecological and environmental conditions in Southeast Asia in this article are mainly based on Takaya 1985.
4. Though the corvée obligation was replaced by tax in kind or money, slavery was also phased out gradually over the reigns of Kings Mongkut and Chulalongkorn, ending in its abolishment in 1905 (Ingram 1971; Feeny 1982). The elimination of slavery and the corvée should have been an important factor for allocating a greater share of Thai labor to rice cultivation.
5. This section draws heavily on Hayami 1994, 1996.
6. Absence of scale economies in agriculture is also attested by the estimation of aggregate production functions based on intercountry cross-section data (Hayami and Ruttan 1985).
7. All forestlands were de jure state-owned, but were de facto open-access, except valuable teak forests that were an important source of the kingdom's revenue (Feeny 1999).
8. Official statistics often record that yields per hectare of cash crops such as coffee and rubber are higher in plantations than in smallholders. However, these statistics do not take into account various products intercropped with principal cash crops by smallholders, whereas monoculture is the common practice of plantations.
9. In addition to this disadvantage, the plantation sector in postindependence Indonesia that expropriated the estates of Dutch planters seems to have suffered from inefficiency common to state enterprises. Several attempts to cure this problem include the "nuclear estate" scheme, in which a state plantation acts as a marketing/processing center with a demonstration farm for technical extension, along which smallholders are organized in a manner similar to contract farming. These attempts have often been marred by the direct application of the technology and practice of plantations without due understanding of the conditions of smallholders (Barlow and Tomich 1991). The case of Indonesia represents a contrast to the relatively high efficiency of plantations in Malaysia under private entrepreneurship. Private plantations in Malaysia arc also well supported by the cooperative research and extension system that has been organized since the colonial period.
10. However, it needs a high degree of entrepreneurship and managerial skill to organize and operate the efficient contract farming system. It is not easy to enforce contracts with a large number of smallholders concerning the quantity, quality, and time of their product delivery to processing plants and/or marketing centers. Insufficient ability and effort of agribusiness firms in this regard have often resulted in failure in the operation of contract farming. Thus the performance of contract farming has so far been mixed even in Thailand (Siamwalla 1992). The same applies to other areas, including Africa, where it is reported that contract farming organized by government agencies is usually inefficient (Jaffee and Morton 1995).

PART

IV

INDUCED TECHNICAL AND INSTITUTIONAL CHANGE

CHAPTER 10

Factor Prices and Technical Change in Agricultural Development

THE UNITED STATES AND JAPAN, 1880–1960

Yujiro Hayami and Vernon W. Ruttan

The United States and Japan are characterized by extreme differences in factor endowments and in price ratios among factors. Furthermore, these differences have widened over time. In spite of these differences, both countries have attained high and sustained rates of growth in agricultural output and productivity. Indeed, the two countries are frequently identified as alternative "agricultural development models." There is considerable discussion regarding the "lessons," the "relevance," or the "transferability" of the Japanese and United States agricultural development experiences to presently developing countries.

The purpose of this paper is to explore the hypothesis that a common basis for rapid growth in agricultural output and productivity lies in a remarkable adaptation of agricultural technology to the sharply contrasting factor proportions in the two countries. It is hypothesized that an important aspect of this adaptation was the ability to generate a continuous sequence of induced innovations in agricultural technology biased toward saving the limiting factors.[1] In Japan these innovations were primarily biological and chemical (hereafter referred to as biological). In the United States they were primarily mechanical. Only in the last several decades has there been what appears to be the initial stage of convergence in patterns of technological change in the two countries, with the United States beginning to experience rapid advances in biological technology and Japan experiencing a rapid adoption of mechanical technology.

We will first review the trends in factor prices and in several significant factor-product and factor-factor ratios in the United States and Japan for the period 1880–1960. After presenting this background material we will specify a hypothesis precisely. We will then subject the hypothesis to a statistical test.

The data on which it has been necessary to draw in conducting this study are subject to substantial limitations (see appendixes).[2] Since much of the data is admittedly crude and comparability of the data for the two countries is less adequate than we would prefer, of necessity the analysis must deal only with the broadest trends in the comparative growth experience of the two countries.

1. Factor Endowments, Prices, and Productivity

In this section we attempt to characterize the differences and similarities in agricultural growth patterns in the United States and Japan for 1880–1960. First, we point to the extreme differences in factor endowments and factor prices in the two countries. We then compare changes in factor productivity ratios in the two countries. Finally, we contrast the different pace of mechanical and biological innovations in the two countries.

FACTOR ENDOWMENTS AND PRICES

Japan and the United States are characterized by extreme differences in relative endowments of land and labor (Table 10.1). In 1880, total agricultural land area per male worker was thirty-six times larger in the United States than in Japan, and arable land area per worker was ten times larger in the United States than in Japan. The difference has widened over time. By 1960, total agricultural land area per male worker was ninety-seven times and arable land area per male worker was forty-seven times larger in the United States than in Japan.

The relative prices of land and labor also differed sharply in the two countries. In 1880, in order to buy a hectare of arable land (compare row 10 and row 18 in Table 10.1), it would have been necessary for a Japanese hired farmworker to work nine times as many days as a U.S. farmworker. In the United States the price of labor rose relative to the price of land, particularly between 1880 and 1920. In Japan the price of land rose sharply relative to the price of labor, particularly between 1880 and 1900. By 1960 a Japanese farmworker would have to work thirty times as many days as a U.S. farmworker in order to buy a hectare of arable land.

PRODUCTIVITY GROWTH

In spite of these substantial differences in land area per worker and in the relative prices of land and labor, both the United States and Japan experienced relatively rapid rates of growth in output per worker throughout the entire eighty-year period (Figure 10.1). For expository purposes it seems useful to partition the

Table 10.1 **Land-Labor Endowments and Relative Prices in Agriculture: United States and Japan, Selected Years**

		1880	*1900*	*1920*	*1940*	*1960*
United States:						
1.	Agricultural land area (million ha)	202	319	363	411	435*
2.	Arable land area (million ha)	76	129	189	187	181*
3.	Number of male farm workers (thousands)	7,959	9880	10.221	8,487	3,973
4.	(1)/(3) (ha. Worker)	25	32	36	48	109
5.	(2)/(3) (ha. Worker)	10	13	18	22	46
6.	Value of agricultural land ($/ha.)	47	49	171	78	285*
7.	Value of arable land ($/ha.)	163	129	352	180	711*
8.	Farm wage rate ($/day)	0.90[a]	1.00[b]	3.30	1.60	6.60
9.	(6)/(8) (days/ha.)	52	49	52	49	43
10.	(7)/(8) (days/ha.)	181	129	107	113	108
Japan:						
11.	Agricultural land area (thousand ha)	5,507	6,031	6.957	7,100	7,043
12.	Arable land area (thousand ha)	4,748	5,200	5,997	6,121	6,071
13.	Number of male farm workers (thousands)	7,842	7,680	7,593	6,365	6,230
14.	(11)/(12) (ha. Worker)	0.70	0.79	0.92	1.12	1.13
15.	(11)/(13) (ha. Worker)	0.61	0.68	0.79	0.96	0.97

(*continued*)

Table 10.1 **(*continued*)**

		1880	*1900*	*1920*	*1940*	*1960*
Japan:						
16.	Value of arable land (yen/ha.)	343	917	3,882	4,709	1,415,000
17.	Farm wage rate (yen/day)	0.22	0.31	1.39	1.90	440
18.	(16)/(17) (days/ha.)	1,559	2.958	2,793	2,478	3,216

Note – See the sources of data in Appendix II. Agricultural land areas in Japan are estimated by multiplying arable land areas by 1.16, the ratio of agricultural land area to arable land area in the 1960 Census of Agriculture.

* 1959.

[a] 1879 or 1880.

[b] 1899.

growth in output per worker among two components, land area per worker and land productivity, as in the following identity:

$$\frac{Y}{L}=\frac{A}{L}\frac{Y}{A},$$

where Y = output, L = labor, A = land area, Y/L = labor productivity, A/L = land area per worker, and Y/A = land productivity. Given the differences in the prices of land and labor in the United States and Japan, we would expect that growth of output per worker (Y/L) in the United States would be closely correlated with changes in land area per worker (A/L), and in Japan with changes in land productivity (Y/A).

These expectations are confirmed by the data on land area per male worker and output per hectare plotted on Figure 10.1. In the United States, land area per worker (A/L) rose much more rapidly than in Japan. In Japan land productivity (Y/A) rose much more rapidly than in the United States.

CONTRASTS IN INNOVATIONS

In agriculture it appears consistent with the technical conditions of production to consider growth in land area per worker (A/L) and output per hectare (Y/A) as "somewhat independent, at least over a certain range" (Griliches 1968: 242). If this view is accepted, the major source of increase in the land area per worker would be mechanical innovations which facilitate the substitution of other sources of power for human labor. Similarly, the major source of increase in land productivity would be biological innovations which permit conversion of a higher percentage of the solar energy falling on an area into higher levels of plant and animal production through the increased supply and utilization of plant nutrients.

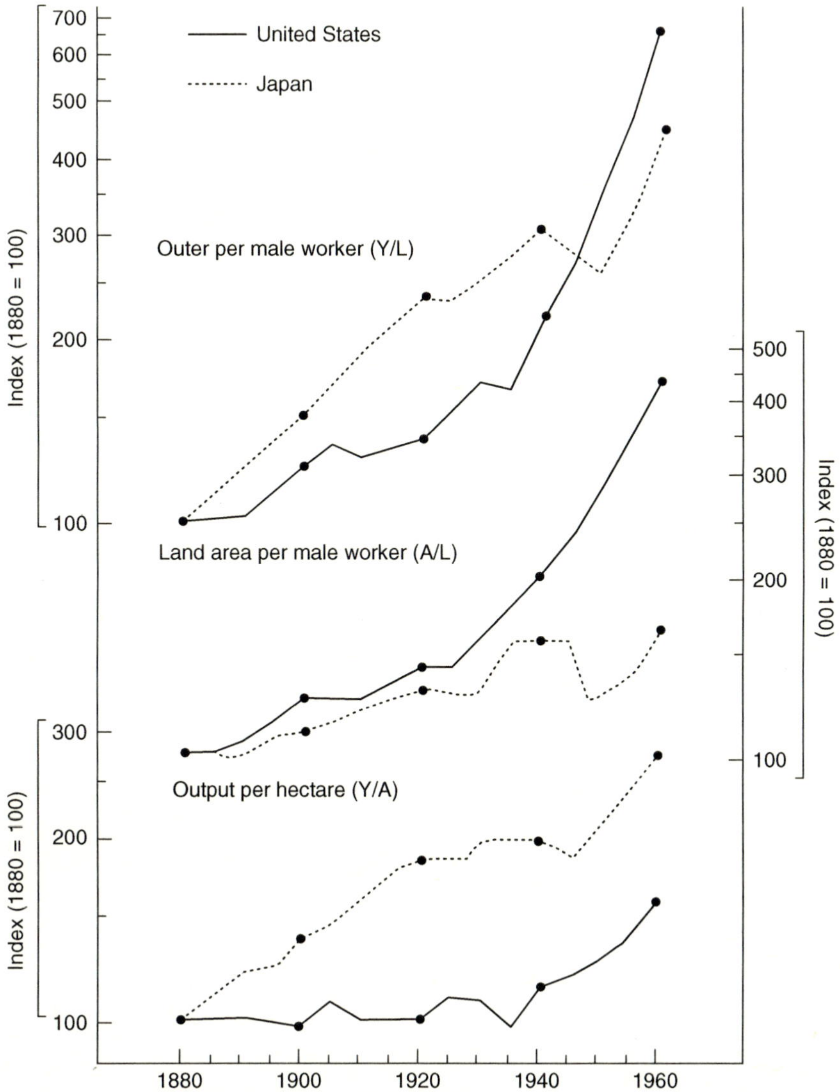

Figure 10.1 Changes in labor productivity, land-labor ratio, and land productivity (1880 = 100), the United States and Japan, 1880–1960.

The association between mechanical and biological innovations and the contrasting growth patterns in land area per worker (*A/L*) and in the land productivity (*Y/A*) in the United States and Japan are shown in Figures 10.2 and 10.3. In Figure 10.2, the three indicators of the land-labor ratio (*A/L*) are compared with the number of work animals (horses, mules, and work cattle) and tractor horsepower per worker.[3] Although there are considerable differences in the three

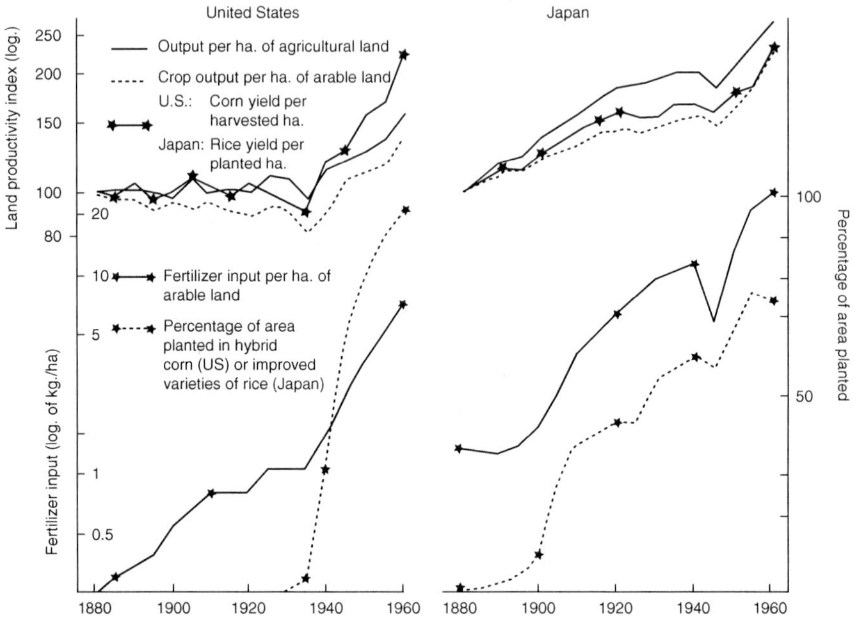

Figure 10.2 Land-labor ratio and power-labor ratio, the United States and Japan, 1880–1960.

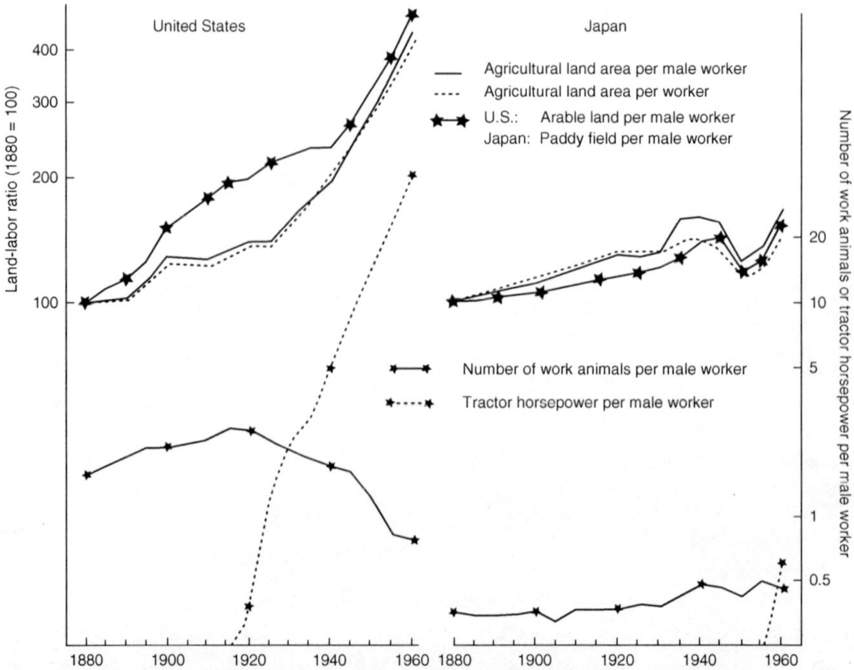

Figure 10.3 Land productivity, fertilizer input per hectare, and progress in the improvements of plant varieties, the United States and Japan, 1880–1960.

indicators of land area per worker (*A/L*), when comparing the United States and Japan, their differences are relatively minor, and the general pattern is not altered by the choice of indicator. In the United States the number of work animals increased up to the 1920s, and then began to decline. The increase in tractor horsepower more than compensated for the decline in work stock. Overall, it seems that the nonhuman power per worker moved more or less parallel with land area per worker (*A/L*). These increases in power per worker would represent a convenient index of the adoption of mechanical innovations. For example, the substitution of the self-raking reaper for the hand-rake reaper and, also, the substitution of the binder for the self-raking reaper required more horses per worker. Those innovations also involved the substitution of power for labor, thereby causing an increase in the land area used per worker in agriculture.

In Japan, corresponding to the slow rate of growth in land area per worker (*A/L*), the number of work animals increased slowly, and the introduction of the tractor started only after the Second World War.

Figure 10.3 illustrates the contrasting relationship between land productivity (*Y/A*) and the progress of biological innovations in the United States and Japan. Here, again, three indicators of land productivity (*Y/A*) are shown in order to check whether any different conclusion is implied by the different choices of data. The percentage of total corn area planted to hybrid corn, and of total rice area planted to improved varieties are treated as proxy variables representing an index of biological innovation in the United States and Japan, respectively.

Although the evidence from these two crops is certainly not conclusive (the percentages are poor proxies even for corn and rice improvements), from a comparison of the corn and rice adoption ratios with the trends in fertilizer inputs, it seems fairly safe to say that in Japan the significant yield-increasing innovations date from the 1880s, while in the United States they began only in the 1930s. The yield-increasing varieties are almost invariably associated with high levels of plant nutrient utilization. Biological innovations of the yield-increasing type involve the creation of crop varieties which can respond to higher levels of fertilization. The parallel increases in fertilizer input per hectare and in the percentage of area planted in improved rice varieties in Japan indicate that the significant biological innovations started in Japan as early as the 1880s. In the United States the introduction of hybrid corn (and other high-yielding crop varieties) is closely associated with the growth of fertilizer consumption. A major factor in the development, introduction, and adoption of hybrid corn and other new crop varieties was greater responsiveness to the higher application of commercial fertilizers which were becoming available at continuously lower real prices.[4]

In connection with the complementarity between fertilizer input and the development of yield-increasing varieties, it is suggestive that Japan's level of fertilizer input per hectare in the 1880s was almost identical to the level of the United States in the 1930s. Furthermore, these dates represent the beginning of periods in which significant advances in biological innovations accompanied by rapid growth in fertilizer consumption were initiated in both countries.

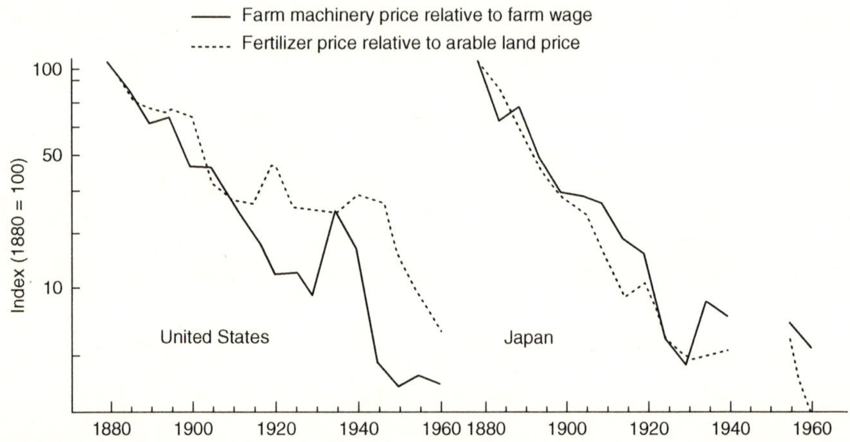

Figure 10.4 Farm machinery price relative to farm wage and fertilizer price relative to arable land price (1880 = 100), the United States and Japan, 1880–1960. Prices are the averages of the five years preceding the year shown.

Increases in power per worker and in fertilizer input per hectare were accompanied by dramatic declines in (a) the price of machinery (a proxy for the price of power and machinery) relative to the wage rate and (b) the price of fertilizer relative to the price of land (Figure 10.4). These trends in factor-price ratios, along with the trend in the price of land relative to labor (Table 10.1), are consistent with the hypothesis that the differential development of mechanical and biological innovations in the United States and Japan represented a process of dynamic factor substitution in response to the changes in relative factor prices.

2. The Induced Innovation Hypothesis

In this section we outline in greater detail the manner in which differences in factor-price movements in Japan and the United States have influenced the process of technical change and the choice of inputs in the two countries. The argument is developed that the contrasting patterns of productivity growth and factor use in U.S. and Japanese agriculture can best be understood in terms of a process of dynamic adjustment to changing relative factor prices—dynamic in the sense that production isoquants change in response to the changes in relative factor prices.[5]

A decline in the prices of land and machinery relative to wages encouraged the substitution of land and power for labor in the United States. This substitution generally involved mechanical innovations. With fixed technology represented by a certain type of machinery, there is little possibility of factor substitution. For example, an optimum factor combination with the hand-rake reaper (such as the McCormick or Hussey) was more or less determined as two workers, one reaper, four horses (two horses for original models), assuming two shifts of horses and 140 acres of wheat. Only when a new technology was introduced in the form of the self-rake reaper was it possible for the farmer to change this proportion to one worker, one reaper, four horses, and 140 acres.[6] Although we do not deny the possibility of substitution within a limited range (for example, through change from two shifts to three shifts of horses), such enormous changes in factor proportions as observed in Figure 10.2 could hardly occur with fixed technology.

Dramatic increases in land area and power per worker of the magnitude that occurred in the United States indicate a response to mechanical innovations which raised the marginal rate of substitution in favor of both land and power for labor.[7] This is a continual process. The introduction of the tractor, which can be considered as the single most important mechanical innovation in agriculture, greatly raised the marginal rate of substitution of power for labor by making it much easier to command more power per worker. Substitution of higher-powered tractors for low-powered tractors has a similar effect.

In Japan the supply of land was inelastic, and the price of land rose relative to wages. Therefore, it was not profitable to substitute land and power for labor. Instead, the opportunity arising from the declining price of fertilizer relative to the price of land was exploited through biological innovations. Seed improvements were directed to the selection of varieties more responsive to fertilizers. At a lower level of fertilization, traditional varieties have equal or higher yields than improved varieties, but do not respond to a higher application of fertilizer. With fixed biological technology represented by a certain variety of seed, the elasticity of substitution of fertilizer for land was low. And such enormous changes in fertilizer input per hectare as observed in Japan since 1880, and in the United States since the 1930s, reflect not only the effect of a decline in the price of fertilizer but the development of more fertilizer-responsive crop varieties to take advantage of the decline in the real price of fertilizer.

In Japan, where expectations have been formed from past trends that not only would wages rise but fertilizer prices fall drastically relative to land price, the motivation of farmers and experiment station workers to develop the biological innovations of high-yielding fertilizer-responsive crop varieties has been very strong. It is suggestive that in the United States the biological innovations represented by hybrid corn began about ten years after the rate of increase in arable land area per worker decelerated (around 1920), and that biological innovations and fertilizer application were accelerated after acreage restrictions were imposed by the government. It seems that the changes in the land supply conditions coupled with a dramatic decline in fertilizer price induced a more rapid rate of biological innovation in the United States after the 1930s. It may be that when the increase in fertilizer input per hectare resulting from this relative price decline exceeded the amount of natural fertility depleted from the soil, demand for biological innovations became a pressing need, which, coupled with the change in the supply condition of arable land, brought about the dramatic biological innovations in the United States since the 1930s.

Our basic hypothesis is that such adjustments in factor proportions in response to changes in relative factor prices represent movements along the isoproduct surface of a "metaproduction function" or "potential production function." This is illustrated in Figure 10.5. In Figure 10.5, *U* represents the land-labor isoquant of the metaproduction function which is the envelope of less elastic isoquants, such as u_0 and u_1 corresponding to different types of machinery or technology. A certain technology represented by u_0 (for example, a reaper) is created when a price ratio, p_0, prevails for a certain length of time. When the price ratio changes from p_0 to p_1, another technology represented by u_1 (for example, a combine) is induced in the long run, which gives the minimum cost of production for p_0.

The new technology represented by u_1, which enables enlargement of the area operated per worker, generally corresponds to higher intensity of power per worker. This implies the complementary relationship between land and power, which may be drawn as a line representing a certain combination of land and power (*A*, *M*). In this simplified presentation, mechanical innovation is conceived as the substitution of a combination of land and power (*A*, *M*) for labor (*L*) in response to a change in wage relative to an index of land and machinery prices, although, of course, land and power are substitutable to some extent in actual practice.

In the same context, the relation between the fertilizer-land price ratio and biological innovations represented by the development of crop varieties more responsive to application of fertilizers is illustrated in Figure 10.5. *V* represents the land-fertilizer isoquant of the metaproduction function, which is the envelope of less elastic isoquants such as v_0 and v_1 corresponding to varieties of

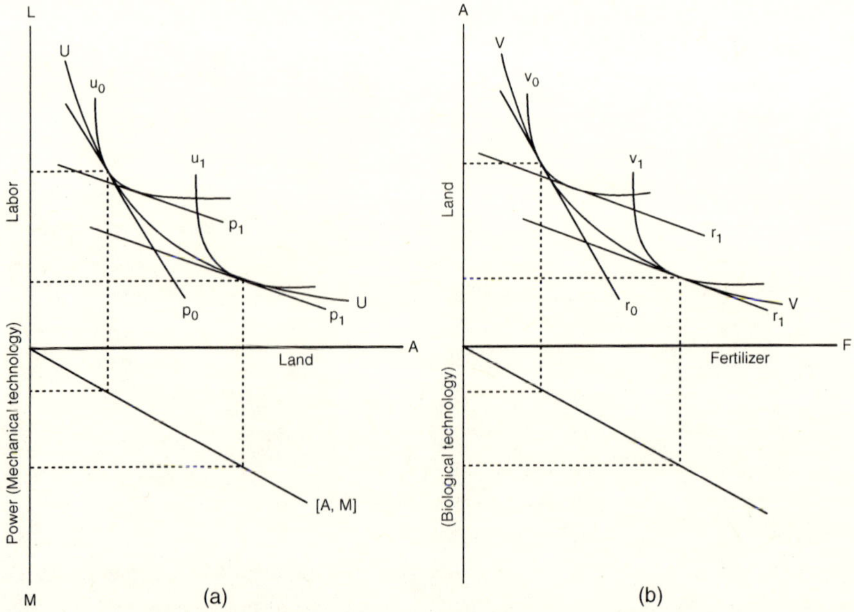

Figure 10.5 (a) Labor-land-power isoquants; (b) land-fertilizer isoquants.

different fertilizer responsiveness. A decline in the price of fertilizer relative to the price of land from r_0 and r_1 makes it more profitable for farmers to search for crop varieties described by isoquants to the right of v_0. They also press public research institutions to develop new varieties (Schultz 1969). Through a kind of dialectic process of interaction among farmers and experiment station workers, a new variety, such as that represented by v_1, will be developed.

Such movements along the metaproduction function may be inferred from Figure 10.6, which plots U.S. and Japanese data on the relation between fertilizer input per hectare of arable land and the fertilizer-land price ratio. Despite the enormous differences in climate and other environmental conditions, the relation between these variables is almost identical in the two countries. This suggests that the U.S. and Japanese agricultural growth has involved a movement along a common metaproduction function.[8]

All mechanical innovations are not necessarily motivated by labor-saving incentives, nor are all biological innovations necessarily motivated by land-saving incentives. In Japan, horse plowing was propagated as a device to cultivate more

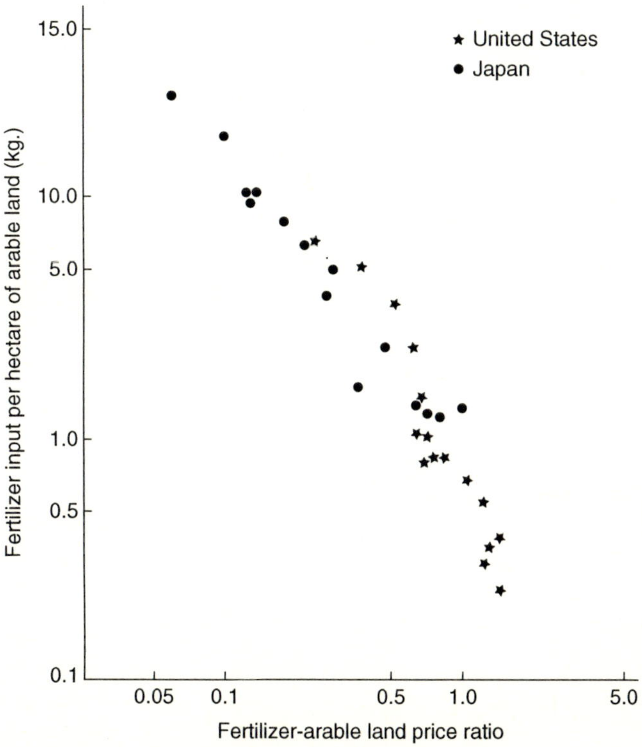

Figure 10.6 Relation between fertilizer input per hectare of arable land and fertilizer–arable land price ratio (= hectares of arable land which can be purchased by one ton of N + P_2O_5 + K_2O contained in commercial fertilizers), the United States and Japan: quinquennial observations for 1880–1960.

deeply to increase yield per hectare. The mechanical-powered threshing machine was introduced long before the Second World War. This innovation was motivated to divert labor from rice threshing to the preparation for the second crop, which resulted in an increase in the double-cropping ratio and the increase in total yield per hectare of land area. In the United States, in recent years, attempts have been made to develop crop varieties more suitable for mechanical harvesting. For example, tomatoes have been developed which have sturdier skin and ripen at the same time, so that they are susceptible to harvesting machinery. This shows that mechanical innovations could be land saving and biological innovations could be labor saving, depending on the conditions of factor-supply and factor-price trends. Historically, however, it appears that the dominant factor for saving labor has been the progress of mechanization, and the dominant factor for saving land has been the biological innovations.

3. The Statistical Test

The hypothesis developed in the previous section can be summarized as follows: Agricultural growth in the United States and Japan during the period 1880–1960 can best be understood when viewed as a dynamic factor-substitution process. Factors have been substituted for each other along a metaproduction function in response to long-run trends in relative factor prices. Each point on the metaproduction surface is characterized by a technology which can be described in terms of specific sources of power, types of machinery, crop varieties, and animal breeds. Movements along this metaproduction surface involve innovations. These innovations have been induced, to a significant extent, by the long-term trends in relative factor prices.

As a test of this hypothesis, we have tried to determine the extent to which the variations in factor proportion, as measured by the land-labor, power-labor, and fertilizer-land ratios, can be explained by changes in factor-price ratios. This is not, in a rigorous sense, a test of the so-called induced innovation hypothesis.[9] In a situation characterized by a fixed technology, however, it seems reasonable to presume that the elasticities of substitution among factors are small, and this permits us to infer that innovations were induced, if the variations in these factor proportions are consistently explained by the changes in price ratios. The historically observed changes in those factor proportions in the United States and Japan are so large that it is hardly conceivable that these changes represent substitution along a given production surface describing a constant technology.

In order to have an adequate specification of the regression form, we have to be able to infer the shape of the underlying metaproduction function and the functional form of the relationship between changes in the production function and in factor-price ratios. Because of a lack of adequate a priori information, we have simply specified the regression in log-linear form with little claim for theoretical justification.[10] If we can assume that the production function is linear homogenous, the factor proportions can be expressed in terms of factor-price ratios alone and are independent of product prices.

Considering the crudeness of data and the purpose of this analysis, we used quinquennial observations (stock variables measured at every five-year interval and flow variables averaged for five years) instead of annual observations for the regression analysis.[11] A crude form of adjustment is built into our model, since our data are quinquennial observations and prices are generally measured as the averages of the past five years preceding the year when the quantities are measured (for example, the number of workers in 1910 is associated with the 1906–10 average wage).

The results of the regression analyses are summarized in Tables 10.2–10.5. Table 10.2 presents the regressions for land-labor and power-labor proportions for the United States. In those regressions we originally included the fertilizer-labor price ratio as well. But, probably due to high intercorrelation between machinery and fertilizer prices, the coefficients for the fertilizer-labor price ratio either were insignificant or resulted in implausible results for the other coefficients.[12] This variable was dropped in the subsequent analysis.

In Table 10.2 more than 80 percent of the variation in the land-labor ratio and in the power-labor ratio is explained by the changes in their price-ratios. The coefficients are all negative and are significantly different from zero at the standard level of significance, except the land price coefficients in regressions 2 and 4. Such results indicate that the marked increases in land and power per worker in U.S. agriculture over the past eighty years have been closely associated with declines in the prices of land and of power and machinery relative to the farm wage rate. The hypothesis that land and power should be treated as complementary factors is confirmed by the negative coefficients. This seems to indicate that, in addition to the complementarity along a fixed production surface, mechanical innovations which raise the marginal rate of substitution of power for labor tend to also raise the marginal rate of substitution of land for labor. Estimates of elasticity of substitution close to one in regressions 5 and 6 seem to suggest that the observed factor substitution was not restricted to a fixed production surface describing a constant technology.[13]

The results of the same regressions for Japan (Table 10.3) are much inferior in terms of statistical criteria. This is probably because the ranges of observed variation in the land-labor and power-labor ratios are too small in Japan to detect any significant relationship between the factor proportions and price ratios. It may also reflect the fact that the mechanical innovations developed in Japan were motivated by a desire to increase yield rather than as a substitute for labor.

The results of the regression analyses of the determinants of fertilizer input per hectare of arable land for the United States are presented in Table 10.4. The results indicate that variations in the fertilizer-land price ratio alone explain almost 90 percent of the variation in fertilizers. It is also shown that the wage-land price

Table 10.2 **Regressions of Land-Labor Ratio and Power-Labor Ratio on Relative Factor Prices: United States, 1880–1960 Quinquennial Observations**

Regression Number and Dependent Variables	Coefficients of Price of: Land Relative to Farm Wage	Coefficients of Price of: Machinery Relative to Ram Wage	$\bar{R}^2$	$\bar{S}$	d
Land-labor ratio:					
1. Agricultural land per male worker	−0.451 (0.215)	−0.486 (0.120)	.828	.0844	1.29
2. Arable land per male worker	−0.035 (0.180)	−0.708 (0.101)	.882	.0706	1.37
3. Agricultural land per worker	−0.492 (0.215)	−0.463 (0.120)	.828	.0789	1.34
4. Arable land per worker	−0.077 (0.182)	−0.686 (0.102)	.879	.0713	1.41
Power-labor ratio:					
5. Horsepower per male worker	−1.279 (0.475)	−0.920 (0.266)	.827	.1865	1.33
6. Horsepower per worker	−1.321 (0.474)	−0.898 (0.265)	.828	.1863	1.36

Note – Equations are linear in logarithms. Standard errors of the estimated coefficients are in parentheses. Data from Appendix II: number of workers (a), number of male workers (a), agricultural land area (a), arable land area (a), power in horsepower equivalents = number of work animals (a) + tractor horsepower (a), farm wage (c), land price (c), machinery price (c).

ratio is a significant variable, indicating the substitutionary relationship between fertilizer and labor. Over a certain range, fertilizer input can be substituted for human care for plants (for example, weeding). A more important factor in Japanese history would be the effects of substitution of commercial fertilizer for labor allocated to self-supplied fertilizers.

A comparison of Table 10.5 with Table 10.4 indicates a striking similarity in the structure of demand for fertilizer in the United States and Japan. The results in these two tables seem to suggest that despite enormous differences in climate and initial factor endowments, the agricultural production function, the inducement mechanism of innovations, and the response of farmers to economic opportunities have been essentially the same in the United States and Japan.

The possibility of structural changes in the metaproduction function over time, as suggested by some of the low Durbin-Watson statistics in Tables 10.2–10.5,

Table 10.3 **Regressions of Land-Labor Ratio and Power-Labor Ratio on Relative Factor Prices: Japan, 1880-1960 Quinquennial Observations**

Regression Number and Dependent Variables		Coefficients of Price of		$\bar{R}^2$	$\bar{S}$	d
		Land Relative to Farm Wage	*Machinery Relative to Ram Wage*			
Land-labor ratio:						
7.	Arable land per male worker	0.159 (0.110)	−0.219 (0.041)	.751	.0347	1.17
8.	Arable land per worker	0.230 (0.049)	−0.155 (0.019)	.914	.0156	1.71
Power-labor ratio:						
9.	Horsepower per male worker	−0.665 (0.261)	−0.299 (0.685)	.262	.2191	0.60
10.	Horsepower per worker	−0.601 (0.236)	−0.228 (0.620)	.266	.1982	0.61

Note – Equations are linear in logarithms. Standard errors of the estimated coefficients are in parentheses. Data from Appendix II: number of workers (a), number of male workers (a), arable land area (a), power in horsepower equivalents = number of work animals (a) + tractor horsepower (a), farm wage (c), land price (c), machinery price (c).

was tested by running regressions separately for 1880–1915 and 1920–60. The results summarized in Table 10.6 do not suggest that any significant structural change occurred between those two periods. The inference from this test is relatively weak, however, because of the small number of observations involved.

Overall, the results of the statistical analysis are consistent with the hypothesis stated at the beginning of this section.

4. Conclusion

The results of this study indicate that the enormous changes in factor proportions which have occurred in the process of agricultural growth in the United States and Japan are explainable in terms of changes in factor-price ratios. In spite of strong reservations regarding the data and the methodology, when we relate the results of the statistical analysis to historical knowledge of the progress in agricultural technology, we conclude that such changes in input mixes represent a process of dynamic factor substitution accompanying changes in the production surface induced by the changes in relative factor prices.

Table 10.4 **Regression of Fertilizer Input per Hectare of Arable Land on Relative Factor Prices: United States, 1880–1960 Quinquennial Observations**

	Coefficients of Price of					
Regression Number	*Fertilizer Relative to Land*	*Labor Relative to Land*	*Machinery Relative to Land*	$\overline{R}^2$	$\overline{S}$	*d*
11	−1.622 (0.200)	1.142 (0.275)	0.014 (0.286)	.950	.1042	2.08
12	−1.615 (0.134)	1.138 (0.255)	.....	.954	.0968	2.09
13	−1.951 (0.166)	....	....	.895	.1406	0.77
14	−1.101 (0.184)	1.134 (0.173)	-0.350 (0.214)	.969	.0816	1.38
15	−1.357 (0.102)	1.019 (0.168)	....	.970	.0832	1.15
16	−1.707 (0.154)	....	....	.884	.1481	0.84

Note – Equations are linear in logarithms. Standard errors of the estimated coefficients are in parentheses. Data from Appendix II: fertilizer input (b), arable land area (a), In the cases of 11, 12, and 13, farm wage (a), land price (a), machinery price (c), fertilizer price (b); In the cases of 14, 15, and 16, farm wage (c), land price (c), machinery price (c), fertilizer (c).

Table 10.5 **Regression of Fertilizer Input per Hectare of Arable Land on Relative Factor Prices: Japan, 1880–1960 Quinquennial Observations**

	Coefficients of Price of					
Regression Number	*Fertilizer Relative to Land*	*Labor Relative to Land*	*Machinery Relative to Land*	$\bar{R}^2$	$\bar{S}$	*d*
17	−1.437 (0.238)	0.662 (0.244)	0.236 (0.334)	.973	.0865	2.45
18	−1.274 (0.057)	0.729 (0.220)	.....	.974	.0810	2.45
19	−1.211 (0.071)	....	....	.958	.1036	1.52
20	−1.248 (0.468)	1.217 (0.762)	-0.103 (0.708)	.878	.1820	1.76
21	−1.313 (0.131)	1.145 (0.556)	....	.888	.1670	1.79
22	−1.173 (0.126)	....	....	.860	.1794	1.52

Note – Equations are linear in logarithms. Standard errors of the estimated coefficients are in parentheses. Data from Appendix II: fertilizer input (b), arable land area (a), In the cases of 17, 18, and 19, farm wage (a), land price (a), machinery price (c), fertilizer price (b); In the cases of 20, 21, and 22, farm wage (c), land price (c), machinery price (c), fertilizer price (c).

Table 10.6 **Test for Structural Change of Regression Relations between 1880–1915 and 1920–1960**

	Residual Sum of Squares			*Number of Parameter p*	*Sample Size*		*F Statistics*	
Regression Number	*1880–1915* s_1	*1920–1960* s_2	*1880–1960* s		*1880–1915* n_1	*1920–1960* n_2	*Computed* F_c	*Theoretical F*
1	0.00314	0.07898	0.08719	3	8	9	0.23	3.59
2	0.00123	0.05539	0.06099	3	8	9	0.28	3.59
3	0.00282	0.07788	0.08709	3	8	9	0.29	3.59
4	0.00103	0.05443	0.06233	3	8	9	0.45	3.59
5	0.00284	0.39095	0.42588	3	8	9	0.30	3.59
6	0.00277	0.38936	0.42512	3	8	9	0.31	3.59
7	0.00052	0.00865	0.01241	3	8	7	1.06	3.86
8	0.00146	0.00046	0.00250	3	8	7	0.93	3.86
9	0.00344	0.46381	0.49381	3	8	7	0.17	3.86
10	0.00346	0.38035	0.40415	3	8	7	0.16	3.86
11	0.01295	0.03399	0.11470	4	8	9	3.25	3.63
12	0.01856	0.06597	0.11472	3	8	9	1.37	3.59
13	0.07902	0.09521	0.27809	2	8	9	2.43	3.80
14	0.00582	0.03278	0.07027	4	8	9	1.85	3.63

15	0.01578	0.03771	0.08473	3	8	9	2.14	3.59
16	0.02107	0.23481	0.30829	2	8	9	1.33	3.80
17	0.01602	0.03085	0.06462	4	8	7	0.66	4.12
18	0.01872	0.03859	0.06754	3	8	7	0.54	3.86
19	0.05996	0.04582	0.12952	2	8	7	1.01	3.98
20	0.11286	0.01408	0.28639	4	8	7	2.20	4.12
21	0.11312	0.06828	0.28694	3	8	7	1.75	3.86
22	0.12274	0.15434	0.38845	2	8	7	2.21	3.98

Note. – $F_c = (s - s_1 - s_2) / (s_1 + s_2) \times (n_1 + n_2 - 2_p) / p$; F = theoretical value at 5 percent level.

This conclusion, if warranted, represents a key to understanding the success of agricultural growth in the two countries. The basis for the contrasting patterns of factor-price changes are the differences in factor-supply conditions. In the United States, land supply to agriculture has been more elastic than labor supply. In Japan, land supply has been either as elastic as labor supply, or less elastic. With the increased demand for farm products in the course of economic development, the price of the less elastic factor tends to rise relative to the prices of the more elastic factors. Given the differences in supply elasticities, agricultural growth in both countries accompanied contrasting changes in land-labor price ratios. Prices of agricultural inputs such as fertilizer and machinery supplied by the nonfarm sector tended to decline relative to the prices of land and labor. Such trends induced farmers, public research institutions, and private agricultural supply firms to search for new production possibilities that would offset the effects of the relative price changes. Thus, mechanical innovations of a labor-saving type were induced in the United States and biological innovations of a yield-increasing type in Japan. After the 1930s the decline in fertilizer price was so dramatic that innovation in U.S. agriculture shifted from a predominant emphasis on mechanical technology to the development of new biological innovations in the form of crop varieties highly responsive to the lower-cost fertilizer.

Rapid growth in agriculture in both countries could not have occurred without such dynamic factor substitution. If factor substitution had been limited to substitution along a fixed production surface, agricultural growth would have been severely limited by the factor of inelastic supply. Development of a continuous stream of new technology which altered the production surface to conform to long-term trends in factor prices was the key to success in agricultural growth in the United States and Japan.

Such inducement of technological change was not attained without cost. The United States and Japan are among the few countries which have made a substantial national effort in agricultural research and extension for the past hundred years. The history of agricultural research and extension in the United States is relatively well known (see Moseman 1968 and U.S. Department of Agriculture 1962).

Japan's efforts to develop agricultural techniques were no less significant than those of the United States.[14] Beginning with the trial importation of Western farming techniques in the 1870s, the itinerant agricultural instructor system started as early as 1885, and the National Agricultural Experiment Station was established in 1893, only five years after the Hatch Experiment Station Act was enacted. Farmers, also, responded vigorously to exploit the opportunities opened by the Meiji Reforms by organizing Nodankai (Agricultural Discussion Societies) or Hinshukokankai (Societies for Exchanging Seeds).[15]

The important point in the context of this paper is that such efforts were directed appropriately in terms of factor-supply conditions. It is suggestive that in the 1870s the Japanese government tried to develop a mechanized agriculture of the Anglo-American type by importing machinery and implements from the United States and inviting British agronomists to the newly established Komaba Agricultural School. This trial represented one of the general efforts to borrow technology from the Western world at the outset of modern economic growth. But, unlike the case in industry, this trial was entirely unsuccessful in agriculture (except in Hokkaido). The government quickly realized the failure and reoriented its effort to the development of a biological technology by replacing British agronomists with German soil scientists and hiring veteran farmers as itinerant instructors during the 1880s. Thereafter, the main current of agricultural research has been to develop veteran farmers' techniques (with the primary motivation to raise the yield per hectare) on the scientific basis of German agricultural chemistry.[16]

In both the United States and Japan, vigorous growth in the industries which supplied machinery and fertilizers at continuously declining relative prices represented an essential source of agricultural growth. Equally important were the efforts in research and extension to best exploit the opportunities created by industrial development. Without the creation of fertilizer-responsive crop varieties, the benefit from the lower fertilizer price is limited. The success in agricultural growth in both the United States and Japan seems to lie in the capacity of their farmers, research institutions, and farm supply industries to exploit new opportunities according to the information transmitted through relative price changes.

Agriculture in the United States and Japan under entirely different initial factor endowments and factor-supply conditions attained rapid growth. There is little reason that presently developing countries cannot attain the same success if they exploit the opportunities available to them. Their patterns of growth would likely be different from the United States or Japan, as their factor-supply conditions are different from those two countries. Efforts must be directed to create a unique pattern of growth for each developing country. An important element in this effort appears to be a system which accurately reflects the economic implications of factor endowments to producers, public institutions, and private industry.

Appendix I

QUALITY ADJUSTMENTS IN THE FARM MACHINERY PRICE INDEX

Quality adjustment factors for the farm machinery price index (USDA index of prices paid) were calculated for 1915–60 on the basis of Fettig 1963. The adjustment factors we calculated are originally for tractor prices, not for the prices of farm machinery in general. The basic assumption we have to make in order to use those factors for farm machinery prices is that the quality improvement in all farm machinery can be represented by or is parallel with quality improvement in wheel-type tractors.

The basic approach used by Fettig to construct the quality adjusted index of farm tractors for 1950–62 is (a) to estimate the regression of tractor price on the two quality variables (average horsepower per tractor and a dummy variable for the diesel engine) on cross-section data and (b) to discount the price changes due to the changes in these quality variables from the actual changes in tractor prices by the estimated regression equations.

Our quality adjustment factors for 1955–60 are based on the ratios of changes in the USDA index. The ratios calculated are 0.99 from 1950 to 1955 and 0.94 from 1950 to 1960. For 1915–50 we calculated the adjustment factors using Fettig's linear regression equation on 1950 cross sections. Since the numbers of diesel-powered tractors are negligible before 1950, and data are unavailable, we dropped the diesel dummy from the equation. The equation we used is $Y_t = 176.02 + 43.81\ X_t$, where X_t and Y_t are the average horsepower per tractor and the estimate of tractor price (1950 U.S. dollars) for the corresponding horsepower in year t. Then, Y_t divided by *Y1915* can be interpreted as the degree of tractor quality improvement from 1915 to year t. We made the inverse of (Y_t/*Y1915*) the quality adjustment factor (k_t) as in Table Al. Here for 1955 and 1960 k is calculated by multiplying k for 1950 by the ratios of Fettig's index to the USDA index (0.99 and 0.94), as explained earlier.

Data for average horsepower per tractor are calculated from the USDA, Farm Cost Situation 36 (November 1965), for 1940–60, and, Demand for Farm Tractors in the United States, Agriculture Economics Report No. 103 (1966), 1925–35. For 1915–20, the average horsepower is extrapolated from the 1925 value by the quinquennial growth rate of 7 percent (average rate for 1925–40).

Table 10.A **Tractor Quality Adjustment Factors**

Year	X_t *(HP)*	Y_t *($)*	k_t *(1008/*Y_t*)*
1915	19	1,008	1.00
1920	20	1,052	0.96
1925	22	1,140	0.88
1930	24	1,227	0.82
1935	25	1,271	0.79
1940	27	1,359	0.74
1945	27	1,359	0.74
1950	27	1,359	0.74
1955	....	....	0.73
1960	....	....	0.70

Appendix II

BASIC STATISTICAL SERIES

All data are quinquennial. Series marked as (a) are measured in single years at every five-year interval beginning with 1880. Series marked (b) and (c) are five-year averages centering on those quinquennial years and ending in these quinquennial years, respectively.

1. U.S. Data

Agricultural output (b): gross output net of seed and feeds, Changes in Production and Efficiency, 1964, USDA Statistical Bulletin (hereafter Statis. Bull.) 233, 1964.

Crop production index (b): crop production index, USDA Statis. Bull. 233, extrapolated by 1910–14 constant price aggregate of nine major crops.

Number of male workers (a) and number of workers (a): economically active population adjusted by D. L. Kaplan and M. D. Kasey, Occupational Trends in the United States 1900–1950, U.S. Bureau of Census Working Report 5, 1958, linked with the number of gainful workers adjusted by A. M. Edwards, Comparative Occupational Statistics for the United States, 1870–1940, U.S. Department of Commerce, 1943.

Arable land area (a): cropland in U.S. Bureau of the Census, U.S. Census of Agriculture (various issues) with minor modifications.

Agricultural land area (a): land in farm in the Census of Agriculture with minor modifications.

Number of work animals (a): oxen, horses, and mules of all ages. Horses and mules from A Century of Agriculture in Charts and Tables, USDA Agriculture Handbook 318, 1966. Oxen from W. M. Hurst and L. M. Church, Power and Machinery in Agriculture, USDA Miscellaneous Publication 157, 1933.

Tractor horsepower (a): Farm Cost Situation 36, 1965, and Demand for Farm Tractors in the United States, USDA Agriculture Economics Report 101, 1966.

Fertilizer input (b): (N + P_2O_5 + K_2O) series in USDA Statis. Bull. 233 linked with series 160 of U.S. Dept. of Commerce, Historical Statistics of the United States, Colonial Times to 1957, 1961 (hereafter Hist. Stat.).

Corn yield per harvested hectare (b): USDA Agriculture Handbook 318.

Percentage of corn area planted in hybrid seed (b): USDA, Agricultural Statistics 1963.

Farm wage (a): farm wage per day without board, series K80 of Hist. Stat.

Farm wage index (c): composite index of farm wage rates, series K76 of Hist. Stat.

Arable land price (a): total value of farm real estate, series K4 of Hist. Stat. divided by arable land area.

Land price index (c): index of average value of farm real estate per acre of land in farm, series K5 linked with K7 of Hist. Stat.

Farm machinery price index (c): quality-adjusted index of farm machinery prices (Appendix I) extrapolated by the BLS and Warren-Pearson wholesale price index of metal and metal products, series E7 and E20 of Hist. Stat.

Fertilizer price (b) (c): current farm expense for fertilizer, USDA, Farm Income Situation 207, 1967, per ton of (N + P_2O_5 + K_2O), linked with the index of fertilizer prices at Connecticut market compiled by E. E. Vail, Retail Prices of Fertilizer Materials and Mixed Fertilizers, New York Agricultural Experiment Station Bull. 545 (1932).

2. JAPAN DATA

Most Japanese data are taken from vol. 9 of *Estimates of Long-Term Economic Statistics of Japan since 1868*, edited by Kazushi Ohkawa et al. Tokyo, 1966 (hereafter *LTES* 9), supplemented by vol. 3 and vol. 8 of the *LTES* series.

Agricultural output (b): gross output net of agricultural intermediate goods. The index of gross agricultural production (series 10 of Table 35, *LTES* 9) multiplied by 1 minus the ratio of agricultural intermediate goods to agricultural production calculated from 1934–36 aggregates.

Crop output (b): series 10 of Table 4, *LTES* 9.

Number of male workers (a) and number of workers (a): gainful workers, series 1 and 3 of Table 33, *LTES* 9.

Paddy field area (a) and arable land area (a): series 13 and 14 of Table 32, *LTES* 9.

Number of work animals (a): horses and draft cattle of all ages, Table 7, *LTES* 3.

Tractor horsepower (a): estimated from the number of garden tractors or cultivators, Table 10, *LTES* 3, by assuming the average horsepower is 5.

Fertilizer input (b): (N + P_2O_5 + K_2O), series 1 of Tables 20–22, *LTES* 9.

Rice yield per planted hectare (b): in terms of brown rice. Data from Ministry of Agriculture and Forestry, Norinsho Ruinen Tokei-hyo, 1955. Yields before 1890 are adjusted as in *LTES* 9, p. 37.

Percentage of rice area planted in improved varieties (a): estimated in Hayami and Yamada 1968.

Farm wage (a): wage of male daily contract workers. Series 24 of Table 25, *LTES* 9.

Farm wage index (c): index of male daily contract workers' wages. Series 24 of Table 25, *LTES* 9.

Arable land price (a): weighted average of the price of paddy fields and upland fields. Series 9–10 of Table 34, *LTES* 9.

Land price index (c): simple average of paddy field price index and upland field price index. Series 9–10 of Table 34, *LTES* 9.

Machinery price index (c): index of farm machinery prices (paid by farmers) from Bank of Japan, Hundred-Year Statistics of the Japanese Economy, 1966, linked with the index of machinery prices, series 21 of Table 8, *LTES* 8.

Fertilizer price (b) (c): current farm expense for fertilizer, series 1 of Table 19, *LTES* 9, per ton of ($N + P_2O_5 + K_2O$).

Notes

Yujiro Hayami and Vernon W. Ruttan, *Journal of Political Economy* 78 (September/October 1970): 1115–41. Minnesota Agricultural Experiment Station Scientific Journal Paper Series 6944. We are indebted to W. K. Bryant, Zvi Griliches, J. M. Henderson, D. G. Johnson, B. F. Johnston, Hideo Kanemitsu, A. O. Krueger, Takashi Negishi, R. R. Nelson, Kazushi Ohkawa, W. L. Peterson, Gustav Ranis, T. W. Schultz, A. M. Tang, and G. S. Tolley for suggestions and comments. We thank Mrs. Barbara Miller and Miss Sachiko Yamashita for computational assistance. The research on which this paper is based was financed through a grant from the Rockefeller Foundation.

1. This problem of induced bias in innovations represents a frontier of development economics. Hypotheses have been postulated on historical observations (Habakkuk 1967), and significant theorems deducted (Fellner 1961, 1966; Kennedy 1964; Samuelson 1965). Yet little work has been done to subject those theorems to quantitative tests. Even in Schmookler's major contribution (1966) to the quantitative economic analysis of innovations, the aspect of factor-saving bias was not treated.
2. The reliability of agricultural production statistics in Meiji, Japan, has been strongly questioned, particularly by Nakamura (1966). For reactions to Nakamura's criticisms see Hayami 1968a, Hayami and Yamada 1969, and Rosovsky 1968.
3. When it is difficult to choose a single data series to represent a single variable adequately, it is reasonable to try several alternatives and to accept the results as conclusive only if the several results are consistent with one another.
4. The parallelism does not hold, however, for the period before the 1930s. Initially, increases in fertilizer input were not accompanied by increases in yield per hectare in the United States. This contradiction was apparently due to the use of commercial fertilizer primarily to offset the declining yields due to depletion of soil fertility. Prior to 1930, use of commercial fertilizer was concentrated in the South, in the production of cotton and tobacco, crops which were classified as soil depleting. The depletion of natural fertility from virgin land progressed considerably in the newly opened Great Plains. The increase in commercial fertilizer input per hectare and the stagnant or even declining land productivity (*Y/A*) between 1880 and 1935 is consistent with the inference that the supply of plant nutrients from all sources (including both natural and commercial sources) was stagnant or even declining during this period.
5. Our concept is similar to Fellner's "weak but general proposition" that the anticipated rise in the price of a factor relative to other factor prices induces firms to develop and adopt innovations which save that factor (Fellner 1961).
6. See Rogin 1931 for an excellent historical description.

7. This is consistent with the emphasis on the importance of the effect of mechanical innovations on the substitution between new and old machineries in terms of relative price changes as analyzed by P. A. David (1966). In fact, in efficiency terms the decline in the price of new machines (relative to old machines) represents a measure of the contribution of the farm machinery industry to technical changes in agriculture.
8. Griliches (1958) has shown, using a distributed lag model, that increase in fertilizer input by U.S. farmers can be explained solely in terms of decline in fertilizer price. The relation he estimated can be identified as the movement along the metaproduction function. The decline in the prices of fertilizer to farmers is a reflection of technical change in the fertilizer industry (Sahota 1967).
9. A direct test of the induced innovation hypothesis would involve a test for nonneutral change in the production surface. A possible approach is suggested by David and van de Klundert (1965).
10. Derivation of factor demand functions from a multifactor production function with different elasticities of substitution (Griliches 1969a, 1969b) seems to suggest a possibility for improving the present specification. Our regressions are similar to Griliches's, but our factor prices do not measure the costs of factor services other than fertilizer (see note 11).
11. See appendixes for the nature of the data. The power and power prices series present the most serious limitations. Instead of resorting to existing estimates of power and machinery (Tostlebe 1957; U.S. Department of Agriculture 1947) which seem to underestimate seriously the growth in power and machinery inputs in efficiency terms because they do not consider quality change, we constructed a series on farm power by aggregating the number of work animals and tractor horsepower in terms of the estimated power they would generate. One horse is assumed equivalent to 1 h.p. based on F. R. Jones 1938: 8 and Hunt 1964: 23. This assumption was consistent with a statistical test made to examine the adequacy of this conversion factor. The results of the test are available in mimeographed form. All we have for the price of power is the conventional price index of farm machinery, and even this does not exist for Japan before the Second World War. We have adjusted the conventional price index in the United States for quality changes based on Fettig's (1963) work (Appendix I). The results obtained from such data should of course be taken with the greatest reservations. Ideally it would have been desirable to prepare data treating factor prices as the costs of factor services, that is, wage for labor, rent for land, and rental for power and machinery. We could not obtain this kind of data for land and machinery. Our analysis is based on the assumption that changes in the prices of land and machinery in stock terms are an adequate reflection of changes in the costs of their services.
12. Some of the coefficients of own prices turned positive—for example, the coefficients of land price relative to wage in regressions 1 and 2. An exponential time trend was also included. The results were totally implausible due to multicollinearity (the simple correlation between time and the machinery price relative to wage was as high as 0.95).
13. Biological innovations represented by improvements in crop varieties characterized by greater response to fertilizer tend to be land saving and labor using. For example, traditional rice varieties in Southeast Asia are equally productive as or more productive than improved varieties under low levels of nutrition and poor cultural practices. The yield potential of the improved varieties is achieved only when high levels of fertilization are combined with high levels of crop husbandry and water management. On this score, the introduction of high-yielding varieties enhances the substitution of fertilizer and labor for land. On the other hand, commercial fertilizers have significant labor-saving effects as they substitute for self-supplied fertilizers. In Japan the production of such self-supplied fertilizers as manure, green manure, compost, and night soil has traditionally occupied a significant portion of farmers' work hours. With the increased supply of commercial fertilizers, farmers could divert their labor to the improvements in cultural practices in such forms as better seed bed preparation and weed control.
14. See Ogura 1963. Those who know Japanese are advised to consult Nogyo Hattatsushi Chosakai 1953–73 (*Nihon Nogyo Hattatsushi* [History of Japan's Agricultural Development], 10 vols.).
15. This process is described by Hayami and Yamada (1968).

16. Adjustments of production techniques to factor-price ratios are not confined to agriculture. In the early phase of Japan's modern economic growth we see a continuous sequence of modifications of "borrowed techniques" to conform to the factor-price ratios which were different from those in Western countries (see Ranis 1957).

CHAPTER 11

Social Science Knowledge and Institutional Change

Vernon W. Ruttan

Over the last several decades agricultural economists have made major contributions to our understanding of the impact of advances in natural science knowledge on technical change and of the impact of technical change on economic growth. We have also significantly advanced our understanding of the sources of demand for and supply of technical change. Work carried out within the framework of the induced technical change paradigm has demonstrated that technical change can be treated as largely endogenous to the development process (Hayami and Ruttan 1971; Binswanger and Ruttan 1978).

We have made less progress in our attempts to understand the contributions of advances in social science knowledge to institutional innovation or of the contribution of institutional innovation to economic, political, or social change. And our knowledge of the sources of demand for and supply of institutional change remains rudimentary. In this paper I suggest an approach to thinking about the sources of demand and supply for institutional change. I then proceed to explore the use of social science knowledge, and the role of social scientists, in the design and evolution of institutional innovations. Finally, I examine the contribution of agricultural economics research and of agricultural economists to the design and evolution of the "direct payment" approach to farm price and income policy.

I follow the lead of Commons (1950) and Knight (1952) and define institution to include both the behavioral rules that govern patterns of relationships and action as well as decision-making units such as government bureaus, firms, and families. The term "institutional change" will at times be used to refer to both institutional innovation and changes in institutional performance.[1]

Institutional Innovation and the Demand for Social Science Knowledge

The basic concept on which the evaluation of the returns to agricultural production research rests is that the demand for knowledge is derived from the demand for technical change in commodity production.[2] Once the output of research was clearly conceptualized as an input into the process of technical change in commodity production, processing, and distribution, this link made it possible to develop models to measure the ex post returns to research. It then became possible to make ex ante estimates of the relative contribution of alternative uses of research resources and to attempt to begin to specify rules that research managers might follow in the allocation of research resources.

Social scientists have only begun, perhaps somewhat reluctantly, to conceptualize adequately the contribution of knowledge in the social sciences (Stigler 1982: 60).[3] The first step in an attempt to value new knowledge in economics, and in the social sciences generally, is to specify the sources of demand for that knowledge. It is clear that the demand for knowledge in economics is not derived primarily from either private or public demand for technical change in commodity production. The demand for knowledge in economics and in the other social sciences—as well as in related professions such as law, business, and social service—is derived primarily from a demand for institutional change and improvements in institutional performance. Shifts in the demand for institutional innovation or improvements in institutional performance may arise from a wide variety of sources. The Marxian tradition has emphasized the importance of technical change as a source of demand for institutional change. North and Thomas (1970, 1973) attempted to explain the economic growth of Western Europe between 900 and 1700 primarily in terms of innovation in the institutional rules that governed property rights. A major source of institutional innovation was, in their view, the rising pressure of population against increasingly scarce resource endowments. Schultz (1968), focusing on more recent economic history, identified the rising economic value of labor during the process of economic development as a primary source of institutional innovation. North and Thomas would apparently have agreed with Schultz (1968: 1120) that "it is hard to imagine any secular economic movement that would have more profound influence in altering institutions than would the movement of wages relative to that of rents." It also seems more apparent today than a decade ago that in nonmarket environments, or in environments where prices are severely distorted, the shadow prices that reflect the real terms of trade among factors and products (or the gap between shadow and market prices) convey information to economic and political entrepreneurs that leads to shifts in the demand for institutional innovation and performance.

Conceptualizing the demand for institutional change in this manner opens up the possibility of a more precise identification of the link between the demand for institutional change and the demand for knowledge in economics and in the social sciences generally. Advances in knowledge in the social sciences offers an opportunity to reduce the costs of institutional innovation, just as advances in knowledge in the biological sciences and agricultural technology have reduced the costs of technical innovation in agriculture. The demand by policy makers for advances in knowledge about price and market relationships is, for example, appropriately viewed as derived from demand for improved performance on the part of market or nonmarket institutions.

What evidence can be brought to bear against the hypothesis that the demand for social science knowledge is derived from the demand for institutional innovation? Let me refer to two examples that tend at least to establish the plausibility of the hypothesis. The first example draws on U.S. historical experience. During the last one hundred years, the United States has experienced three major waves of institutional reform. The first was the Progressive era, which spanned the last decade of the nineteenth century and continued until the U.S. entry into World War I. The demands for reform were induced by the rapid technical and economic changes that had dramatically altered the conditions of American life since the Civil War.[4] The unifying theme that underlay the reform proposals of the Progressive era was a rejection of unregulated free-enterprise capitalism. Reforms reflecting this perspective were initiated in the areas of income distribution, labor relations, social services, financial markets, transportation, industrial organization, and resource conservation. Popular demands for "direct democracy" were translated into expansion of women's suffrage, direct election of senators, and more active participation of voters in the legislative process through the initiative, referendum, and recall. A major consequence of these reforms was to widen substantially the participation of the federal government in economic affairs and in areas previously reserved to the states. The second major wave of institutional innovation and reform was during the New Deal period in the 1930s. The question of whether the New Deal reforms represented a drastic new departure in American reformism (Hofstadter 1955) or primarily the realization of reforms proposed originally during the Progressive era (Scott 1959; J. R. T. Hughes 1977: 146–98) and incubated during the 1920s (Chambers 1963) has been debated by political scientists and historians. But the New Deal reforms are not too difficult to characterize. They were in defense of security of property, of work, and of income—a reshuffle of the cards that had too long been stacked against the working man, the farmer, and the small businessman (Commager and Morris 1963: xii). But the acceptance by the federal government of responsibility for maintaining economic life represented a radical break with tradition. The result was a period of six years, 1933 to 1938, that represented the most rapid period of institutional change since the Civil War (Leuchtenberg 1963: xv).

The third wave of institutional reform occurred during the Kennedy and Johnson administrations—the New Frontier (1960–63) and Great Society (1964–68) years. The Kennedy and Johnson administrations sought to complete the liberal agenda. They sought to eradicate racial discrimination in voting, housing, jobs, and schooling. And they sought to eliminate poverty—both black and white and urban and rural (Matusow 1984: 180–271). These reforms were followed in the late 1960s and early 1970s by rapid innovation in new forms of property rights in natural resources induced by a rising concern about the impact of technology on both material resources and environmental amenities (Ruttan 1971).

During each of these periods there was rapid growth in the demand for social science knowledge. The first period drew on a broad range of intellectual capacities and expertise in law, in economics, and in the newer social science disciplines—but there was relatively little theory and even less research on which to draw. During the second period economists played a much larger role in policy design. Unfortunately, lack of an adequate understanding of macroeconomic relationships and a pervasive pessimism about the prospects for growth led to a structuralist reform agenda. But the demands for institutional innovation did lead to substantial growth in the resources devoted to social science research and to strengthening the statistical services of the federal government. By the late 1930s new theory and new information were being brought to bear on institutional innovation and reform. A new class of "service intellectuals" emerged in policy roles in the federal government.[5] During the 1960s social science research played an even larger role in program design than it had in the two earlier periods. This was in part because of a greatly expanded body of social science knowledge, a large social research capacity, and improvements in capacity to generate, process, and analyze social science data. Attempts were made to introduce experimental design as a stage in program development. But in spite of the advances in theory and method, the policy-relevant social science knowledge on which the Kennedy and Johnson administrations were forced to draw in the design of the poverty programs of the 1960s was too weak to respond effectively to the demands that were placed on it (Matusow 1984: 217–76).

The second example draws more broadly on comparative experience. Stop for a minute and ask, which societies tend to draw most extensively on social science knowledge, and which societies draw least on social science knowledge, in policy design and reform? It seems clear that societies in which the design of social institutions is strongly determined by ideology or religion exhibit a very weak demand for social science knowledge. The USSR, for example, tends to draw primarily on that narrow range of economics most closely related to engineering-input/output analysis, mathematical programming, and sector modeling. In China much of the capacity of economics is devoted to clarifying the implications of shifts in economic ideology (Calkins 1984). Relatively little capacity is devoted to institutional design.

It also seems clear that the demand for social science knowledge is strongest in those societies and in those historical periods in which the burdens of ideology, religion, and tradition impose relatively weak constraints on institutional design. And within any society it seems apparent that the demand for social science knowledge is strongest when the society is attempting to confront the problems of the present rather than when it is attempting to recapture romantic memories of the past or pursuing utopian visions of the future. In the 1960s it was possible to believe that the exhaustion of the ideologies that had dominated social thought for the previous century and a half had permanently shifted the demand for social science knowledge to the right (Bell 1960). But this vision is somewhat more clouded when viewed from the perspective of the 1980s. It is difficult to avoid the conclusion that budget reductions have at times been used to reduce the accumulation of social science knowledge in order to reduce the challenge to ideology in policy design.

Social Science Knowledge and the Supply of Institutional Innovation

If one accepts the notion that the demand for knowledge in economics, and in the social sciences generally, is derived from the demand for institutional change, it then becomes necessary to consider the sources of supply of institutional change.

The view that emerges from my own work is that advances in social science knowledge act to shift the supply of institutional change to the right. Throughout history, improvements in institutional performance have occurred primarily through the slow accumulation of successful precedent or as a by-product of expertise and experience. Institutional change was traditionally generated through the process of trial and error much in the same manner that technical change was generated prior to the invention of the research university, the agricultural experiment station, or the industrial research laboratory. With the institutionalization of research in the social sciences it is becoming increasingly possible to substitute social science knowledge and analytical skill for the more expensive process of learning by trial and error.

But how responsive are advances in social science knowledge to demands arising out of social conflict or economic growth? Is the supply of social science knowledge for institutional innovation relatively elastic? Or is society typically faced with a situation wherein the demand for institutional innovation shifts against a relatively inelastic supply curve? Stigler has argued that the supply of knowledge in the social sciences is relatively impervious to the impact of economic events (Stigler 1965). He also has argued the opposite position (Stigler 1982). My own perspective is consistent with Stigler's more recent view that economists respond rapidly to changes in the economic and political environment. Advances in economic thought are becoming an increasingly effective substitute for trial and error in the design and reform of economic institutions and economic policy.

If we accept the arguments that (a) the value society places on social science research is derived primarily from its contribution to institutional change and performance and (b) advances in social science knowledge are responsive to demands generated by social and economic change, we are then forced to consider several additional questions. How much freedom does a society have in choosing the path of institutional change that it will follow? Is society as free to design new institutions as planners frequently assume? Or is institutional change so dominated by historical or evolutionary forces that rational design has a relatively small role to play in the process?[6] The response by economists to these questions can be grouped in two major intellectual traditions. One tradition can be characterized as the design tradition, the other the evolutionary tradition. The strategy adopted in the design literature is to attempt to distinguish between the institutional mechanism, over which the designer or planner can exercise some degree of analytical control, and the institutional environment, in which changes are treated as exogenous (Hurwicz 1972a, 1972b, 1977; Reiter 1977). The research agenda is then to study the performance characteristics of different institutional mechanisms under a wide class of institutional environments. My own work (with Hayami and Binswanger) on induced institutional innovation falls more within the evolutionary tradition. In this work we have attempted to test and examine empirically how changes in the institutional environment have been induced by long-term changes in resource endowments and changes in technology.[7]

The history of agricultural economics suggests a strong commitment to the design tradition. Agricultural economists have been intimately involved in the process of institutional design almost since the origin of the field. We have been involved both through our research and through personal involvement in the design and reform of land tenure, credit, and marketing institutions. And our leading practitioners have contributed both to the agricultural policy debates and to the design of agricultural policies and programs. The history of our successes and failures suggests that we have been less sensitive to the constraints placed on design by changes in the economic and social environment. And we have often been insensitive to the design opportunities made possible by changes in resources and cultural endowments or by changes in technology.

I would now like to turn to review the history of a major institutional innovation in which agricultural economists have played active roles in both the advancement of knowledge and in institutional design. My purpose will be to examine the relative contributions of the design logic and of external political and economic forces to the evolution of policies and programs. The area I have selected for examination is the development of direct payment approaches in programs to support commodity prices and farm incomes.

The Compensatory Payments Approach to Farm Income Support

The late 1950s and early 1960s were a period of remarkable vigor in agricultural policy research and in the design of agricultural commodity policy. Much of the professional discussion during this period was dominated by the "supply management" proposals developed and championed by Willard Cochrane (1945, 1946, 1947, 1958, 1984). Cochrane served as an adviser to Kennedy during the 1960 campaign, assisted in the drafting of a campaign "white paper" on agricultural policy, and was brought into the Kennedy administration as director of agricultural economics. The design of the commodity program provisions of the proposed Food and Agriculture Act of 1962 was based on the supply management ideas that Cochrane had worked out over the previous decade and a half.[8] But the most significant policy innovations in the new legislation that finally emerged out of this period drew more heavily on the compensatory or direct payment ideas that were first formally proposed to the Congress in 1949 by Secretary of Agriculture Charles F. Brannan than on the supply management proposals developed by Cochrane.

How did the direct or compensatory payment ideas incorporated in the 1949 Brannan plan emerge? Proposals for a program of countercyclical compensatory payments based on the differences between market prices and some percentage of the price that prevailed during a pre-depression period had been suggested by Theodore W. Schultz in a book in 1943 and in an article in 1944. The proposal was substantially elaborated in his 1946 study for the Committee for Economic Development, Agriculture in an Unstable Economy. Direct payments were also discussed in a number of the papers submitted to the 1945 American Farm Economic Association essay contest titled "Price Policy for Agriculture."[9] By 1948 practically all leading agricultural economists were favorably disposed toward direct payments as an essential element of an effective farm commodity policy (Christenson 1959: 28; Brandow 1977: 238–39). It was generally agreed that a system that could provide income support without distorting market prices would more effectively meet both equity and efficiency objectives than policies that attempted to meet income objectives through price supports.

In putting the emergence of proposals for direct or compensatory income payments into perspective, it is useful to recall the environment in which the earlier agricultural programs of the 1930s were initiated. The designers of commodity price programs during the first Roosevelt administration were not able to draw on an extensive body of either program experience or professional analysis and discussion comparable to that available to the designers of the farm credit programs. Agricultural economists, particularly Joseph Davis, M. L. Wilson, Mordecai Ezekiel, John D. Black, Howard Tolley, and George F. Warren, had played an active role in the debates about the merits of the McNary-Haugen and Federal Farm Board proposals of the late 1920s and early 1930s and in the design of the Agricultural Adjustment Act of 1933 (Kirkdendall 1966).[10] But their arguments drew on limited data about and weak understanding of the agricultural sector implications of macroeconomic policy. The extent to which the behavior of agricultural commodity and financial markets reflected the dramatic increase in unemployment and the decline in national income was not clearly understood.

It was not until the 1940s that the dialogue between theory, method, and data had advanced to the point at which the agricultural economics literature began to reflect adequately an understanding of what today can be recognized as the Schultz-Cochrane paradigm on the macroeconomic basis for the farm crisis of the 1930s or the implications of macroeconomic policy for the design of agricultural programs.[11]

Farm policy did not emerge as a major issue until late in the 1948 presidential campaign. With the support of the two major farm organizations, the Republicans and Democrats had joined forces to pass the 1948 Hope-Aiken bill that extended the high wartime price support levels for one year, to be followed by a program of flexible price supports. As the election approached, however, the consensus tended to break down. The breakdown was stimulated by the southern Democrats' unwilling support of the Hope-Aiken bill, falling farm prices, farmers' favorable response to Truman's "give'em hell" campaign rhetoric, and Brannan's vigorous emphasis on a policy of abundance in speeches in support of the Truman candidacy (Matusow 1984: 170–93; Cochrane and Ryan 1976: 26–28).

Following the election both Truman and Brannan agreed that farmers had played a critical role in the Truman victory. Brannan then set in motion steps to translate his commitment to a policy of abundance into the design of a farm program. As an initial step, Brannan assigned Oris V. Wells, then head of the Bureau of Agricultural Economics (BAE), to chair a departmental seminar on national agricultural policy. The regular members of the seminar included the senior policy officers of the department and several of the leading economists of the BAE—John Baker, Louis Bean, O. C. Stein, and Karl Fox. Other economists were involved in the presentation of seminar papers and in some of the individual seminars (Christenson 1959: 26). The seminars continued twice a week from January to early March of 1949, while the Congress impatiently pressed Brannan for his policy proposals.

The topics covered included problems of supporting perishable commodities, multiple price systems, income parity as an alternative to price parity, the food stamp plans, modernization of parity, and compensatory payments. Brannan's role in the seminars came close to approximating the textbook example of the appropriate role of policy makers in drawing on economic analysis. He "said little until the sixth meeting. He knew that if he were to tip his hand on how his thinking was running, it would dry up or deflect the contributions of the more timid—or ambitious—members" (Christenson 1959: 27).

At the sixth meeting, on March 3, the secretary concluded the seminars and formed a smaller technical group to work on the final formulation of department policy. On April 6 Brannan met with President Truman to review the economic and political implications of the program. On the same day he also met with the leaders of the major farm organizations to explain the program. And on April 7 he presented his recommendations to a joint hearing of the House and Senate agriculture committee.

The plan that Brannan presented to the Congress reflected "his philosophy of positive government and his goals of income equity to farmers and . . . cheap food for all consumers. Supply and demand were allowed to determine market prices but acceptable incomes for family farmers were to be guaranteed by supplemental payments" (Cochrane and Ryan 1976: 29). The proposal represented a major break with the scarcity orientation of the agricultural policies of the 1930s. The Branan proposals included "(1) the use of an income standard, based on a ten-year moving average . . . as a method of computing price support levels for farm products; (2) support for major products . . . at full income standard levels; (3) support of the incomes of growers of perishable commodities by direct payments by the government of the difference between the prices received in the market and the support price established; (4) restriction of supports to large-scale farmers to what efficient family farm units could produce; and (5) requirement of compliance with approved conservation practices and production or marketing controls in order to receive benefits" (Rasmussen 1983: 360).

In retrospect, Brannan's interpretation of the 1948 election as a mandate for his program of abundance was exaggerated (Ryan 1980). The plan was greeted with a storm of protest. The early proponents of direct payments objected to the revisions in the parity formula that had the effect of raising support levels (Schultz 1949: 176–90). The supporters of high support prices objected to the regimentation implied by production controls. Only the Farmers Union supported the payment limitations and the AFL-CIO the cheap food provisions. Initial support for the plan eroded rapidly throughout the 1949 and 1950 legislative sessions. When the Korean War broke out in June 1950, farm prices surged upward, and the problems for which the Brannan Plan was designed appeared to disappear (Christenson 1959: 143–70; Matusow 1984: 201–21).

The attraction of the compensatory payments concept did not die with the Brannan Plan. In 1954 the Congress authorized, with the approval of Secretary of Agriculture Ezra Taft Benson and supported by the votes of most Republican congressmen, a compensatory payments program for support of the income of wool growers, "the Brannan Plan in sheep's clothing," funded with tariff receipts on wool imports (Christenson 1959: 167; Benedict and Stein 1956: 352–55). It emerged again in the feed grain provisions of the Agricultural Act of 1962 in the form of production payments based on the difference between the price support level and the price that would allow wheat to move into international trade without a direct subsidy. In the Agricultural Act of 1964 this provision was extended to maize and cotton (with payments going to handlers in the case of cotton). In the Agricultural Act of 1965 the mandatory features of the earlier supply management program were completely abandoned—"voluntary production control programs with low levels of price supports and direct payment to producers had carried the day in the major commodities. And these program features . . . remained essentially unchanged for five years" (Cochrane and Ryan 1976: 82). In the Agricultural Act of 1973 the concept of a "target price" was introduced as a device for determining the size of the income support payment. The target price concept had the effect of further institutionalizing the direct or deficiency payment approach (Cochrane 1984).

It seems apparent that increased reliance on direct payments in agricultural commodity programs, beginning in the mid-1960s, was induced at least in part by the growing integration of U.S. agriculture into world commodity markets. The effects of the overvaluation of the dollar, which began in 1949 when a number of European countries undertook major devaluations, were initially masked by the Korean War. By the mid-1960s program costs, from acquiring stocks or removing land from production, had become excessively burdensome (Schuh 1974). The wheat referendum gave policy makers license to lower support levels gradually to a level consistent with the overvalued dollar. A program which permitted agricultural commodities to move into world markets without direct subsidies was more consistent with the opportunity to participate in the growth of agricultural trade. The benefits from a direct payments program when initially proposed by Brannan were primarily in terms of agricultural adjustment and income distribution. By the mid-1960s the gains could also be measured in terms of economic growth and higher farm income (Lopes and Schuh 1976; Schuh 1984; Cochrane 1984). After the initial defeat of the supply management proposals the Freeman-Cochrane-Schnittker team in the department responded skillfully and effectively to design and manage program changes that, by the late 1960s, brought agricultural commodity production and prices closer to equilibrium levels than they had been since the end of the Korean War.

Some Lessons

What does the case study reviewed in this paper reveal about the demand for and supply of social science knowledge and how such knowledge contributed to institutional design and innovation? Clearly, one case study is too limited to do more than suggest hypotheses to guide further research. It would also have been useful, for example, to examine institutional innovations such as (a) the "rural free delivery" of mail, which arose out of the farmer protest movement of the late nineteenth century with no assistance from social science analysis or research;[12] (b) the cooperative farm credit system in which agricultural economists played a preeminent role in the reform and management of the system;[13] and (c) the food stamp program, in which agricultural economists played a dominant role in both program design and the mobilization of political resources.[14]

A first lesson is that deficiencies in social science knowledge relevant to institutional design have at times imposed a substantial burden on the design of effective policy. The production control proposals advocated by department economists such as Wilson, Ezekiel, and Tolley reflected the pervasive deficiency in the understanding of macroeconomic relationships in the early 1930s.

In spite of advances in the understanding of the macroeconomic relationships during the 1940s, it seems apparent that the limited ability to translate that understanding into a system of demand and supply relationships, and to estimate empirically the parameters of commodity and sector models, imposed a severe burden on both the design and the acceptance of the Brannan Plan. For example, except for a few illustrative estimates for individual perishable commodity programs (for hogs, eggs, potatoes, and milk and milk products), Secretary Brannan was not able to present to the Congress overall cost estimates for implementing his proposals.

The first comparative estimates of alternative program costs using a consistent supply-and-demand framework were synthesized in 1950 for the 1949 crop year by George Mehren (1951). Mehren's estimates suggested, somewhat surprisingly, that the costs of the Brannan Plan would not have been significantly different than costs incurred under the programs that were mandated by the Agricultural Act of 1948 and the Agricultural Act of 1949. But it was not until the research programs of Karl Fox (1953) and his associates at the U.S. Department of Agriculture (USDA) in the early and mid-1950s and of George Brandow (1961) and his colleagues on the Interregional Committee on Agricultural Policy in the late 1950s were completed that reasonably consistent estimates of program costs and impact became possible. And it was not until the early 1960s that a substantial body of literature on program costs and impacts became available to policy analysts (Cochrane and Ryan 1976: 359–82).[15]

By the early 1960s the theory and method for the preparation of such estimates had become fully institutionalized in the USDA and were consistently referred to in debates over commodity policy. It had become customary by the time Cochrane became director of agricultural economics at the USDA to estimate the farm price and income effects, the consumer price effects, the federal budget impact, and the income distribution impact of the farm policy alternatives that received serious administrative or legislative attention. And I am prepared to argue that these estimates contributed to both the quality of the policy debates and to better policy than would have emerged in the absence of the advances in analytical capacity that occurred over the previous two decades.

A second major lesson that emerges from the cases examined in this paper is that short-run economic and political events can exert a major impact on the effectiveness of social science contributions to institutional design or reform. The depression of the early 1930s generated a dramatic increase in demand for social science knowledge for the design of policies and programs.

But the capacity of social scientists to respond to such opportunities with effective program design is itself dependent on the state of social science knowledge. Roosevelt's election resulted in a discrete shift to the right in the demand for institution innovation. The department economists who contributed to the design of the commodity and price policies of the 1930s were clearly among the most brilliant members of the profession. But the economic theory and economic research on which they were forced to draw for policy design was underdeveloped. The policies that were designed in the 1930s have imposed a continuing burden on professional dialogue in the field of agricultural policy and heavy social costs on both farmers and consumers.

A third inference is that the agricultural commodity programs were induced by fundamental economic forces associated with the development of the American economy and the agricultural economy in particular.

Before the beginning of this century, the gains in productivity in American agriculture were almost entirely a consequence of increased mechanization. The technological revolution of the nineteenth century contributed to increasing output per worker but contributed very little to growth in aggregate output (Hayami and Ruttan 1971: 138–52). The period immediately after the turn of the century was a period of technological stagnation. But by the mid-1920s a new biological technology capable of enhancing output per acre and output per unit of breeding stock was beginning to come onstream. It was becoming possible to increase aggregate output more rapidly than aggregate demand.

In the absence of public intervention in agricultural commodity markets, the gains from the new technology would have been transferred almost immediately from agricultural producers to consumers. In this environment it should not have been surprising that farmers would be unsatisfied with policies that protected them only from the effects of cyclical fluctuations in economic activity. Although farmers and farm leaders articulated these demands in different terms, it seems clear in retrospect that they were demanding economic policies that would dampen the transfer of productivity gains from farm producers to consumers.

I have not in this review presented any formal estimates of rates of return to agricultural economics research. It is quite clear, however, that lack of economic knowledge has at times imposed very heavy costs on American farmers and the American economy. As the participation of American agriculture in world markets has grown, our capacity to expand the knowledge relevant to institutional reform and design has not kept pace. Private sector research on this issue is almost nonexistent. The 6 percent or 7 percent of the public agricultural research budget now allocated to economic research represents a substantial underinvestment when evaluated against the gains that can be achieved by substituting economic analysis for trial and error in research policy, financial policy, commodity policy, trade policy, resource policy, and the other areas of applied economics that are amenable to the analytical skills of agricultural economists.

In concluding, I would like to add an important qualification to my enthusiasm about the value of agricultural economics research. One of our major deficiencies, both in the modern tool-using epoch and in the earlier epoch when we operated primarily with the use of principles unencumbered by significant tool-using capacity, has been our lack of sensitivity to the major sources of economic and social change that have shaped our policies and our institutions. The literature suggests that we have believed that institutional design is simply a matter of analytical skill and political will. We have given relatively little attention to an attempt to understand the rate and direction of the broader historical forces that influence the demand for institutional change. As a result, we have often found it difficult to escape the impact of short-run changes in the economic and political environment, or of the often volatile changes in the intellectual environment.

Notes

Vernon W. Ruttan, *American Journal of Agricultural Economics* 66 (December 1984): 549–59 (American Agricultural Economics Association 1984 Fellows Lecture). The author is indebted to Dale Adams, Peter J. Barry, John R. Brake, Harold Breimyer, Karen Brooks, Emery N. Castle, Willard W. Cochrane, James P. Houck, Glenn Fox, C. Edward Harshbarger, Yujiro Hayami, Forest F. Hill, Emanuel Melichar, Glenn L. Nelson, George W. Norton, Wayne D. Rasmussen, C. Ford Runge, Lyle P. Schertz, G. Edward Schuh, and Theodore W. Schultz, and to members of the University of Minnesota Agricultural Development Workshop for comments on an earlier draft of this paper.

1. This usage is consistent with my earlier work (Binswanger and Ruttan 1978: 327–57; Ruttan and Hayami 1984), where the term "institution" is used to include that of organization. The term "institutional innovation" will be used to refer to innovations that lead to changes (a) in the behavior of a particular organization, (b) in the relationship between such organization and its environment, or (c) in the rules that govern behavior and relationships in an organization's environment. This definition is more inclusive than Veblen's (Seckler 1975: 61) but is consistent with that used by Commons (1950: 26) and Knight (1952: 51). The definition used here also encompasses the several classes of institutional entities and behavior employed by Davis and North (1971).
2. This section and the next section, on the supply of institutional innovation, draw on earlier discussions in Binswanger and Ruttan 1978: 337–40, Ruttan 1982a: 304–8, and Ruttan and Hayami 1984.
3. For two initial attempts see Hayami and Peterson 1972 and Norton and Schuh 1981b. See also the reviews by Norton and Schuh (1981a) and Norton and Norris (1984).
4. For a very useful review of thought regarding the Progressive era see A. M. Scott 1959. For the intellectual, political, and social origins of many of the reforms of the Progressive era in the earlier farmer protest movements see Hicks 1961, chap. 15 and J. R. T. Hughes 1977.
5. The term "service intellectual" is from Kirkendall 1966. Kirkendall (1966: 1–7) traces the rise of the service intellectual back to origins in the Progressive era, when Governor Robert M. LaFollette actively encouraged the movement of academics from the University of Wisconsin into service of the state government.
6. This issue has been of concern since the origin of modern social science. In 1744 Giambattista Vico, whose role in the origins of political science is comparable to that of Adam Smith in economic thought, argued that it is "naive to regard political and social institutions as owing their origins to acts of rational planning . . . motivated either by considerations of enlightened self-interest or by respect for an abstract concept of justice" (Gardiner 1959: 10).
7. This perspective was initially outlined in Hayami and Ruttan 1971: 59–61. It will be elaborated more fully in the forthcoming revised edition of Hayami and Ruttan 1985. See also Binswanger and Ruttan 1978: 227–357 and Ruttan and Hayami 1984. The complementarity between the design and induced innovation perspectives was explored in a seminar at the University of Minnesota in February 1983 (see Runge 1983).
8. Cochrane's perspectives on aggregate economic relations for the agricultural sector began with a series of papers published in the 1940s (Cochrane 1945, 1946, 1947) and were articulated most completely in his book *Farm Prices: Myth and Reality* (1958). For a discussion of Cochrane's role in the design of the Food and Agricultural Act of 1962, see Hadwiger and Talbot 1965.

9. The American Farm Economic Association essay contest "Price Policy for Agriculture" reflected an exceptional interest in the design of postwar agricultural policy. Over three hundred essays were submitted. The major theme of the award papers was greater freedom in pricing of individual commodities combined with some form of "forward pricing" to guide production and minimum or flexible price support guarantees. Direct payments for farm income support represented a subsidiary theme. For the award papers see Nicholls 1945, Johnson 1945, and Waugh 1945. The Cochrane honorable mention paper (Cochrane 1945), which drew on his 1945 Harvard Ph.D. thesis, emphasized production adjustment, equilibrium market prices, and abundant and inexpensive food supplies for consumers. The food abundance theme became an important issue in the Brannan proposal in 1948.
10. John D. Black (1939) would give somewhat less credit (or blame) to the department economists. According to Black (1939: 26), "A little contemplation will convince anyone that in the great surge toward collective action in the agricultural economy of this and other nations since the World War, the economists have generally been considerably behind the lines of battle—many of them engaged in rear guard fighting. Not only the drive toward action but also the major part of the thinking about effective lines of action has come from outside the strictly professional ranks—from men like the two Wallaces, George Peck, Chester Davis, Governor Lowden, Alexander Legge, Edward O'Neal, even Rexford Tugwell if you like. This is in spite of the fact that in this particular case an unusual amount of aid has been rendered by several professional agricultural economists—Dr. H. C. Taylor in the days when he served with the elder Wallace, M. L. Wilson, H. R. Tolley and L. C. Gray; in the field of agricultural credit W. I. Myers and F. F. Hill. 'Cock-eyed' and 'screwy' though we economists may dub some of the ideas of some of these men, they have nevertheless set the stage and written many of the parts of the drama of agriculture in the last 16 years" (see also Gaus and Wolcott 1940: 65–66).
11. The weakness of agricultural policy analysis and discussion by economists before the 1940s has been noted by Wilcox (1963). Brandow (1977: 241) notes that by the early 1950s there was "a group of economists who tended to approach policy analysis in a particular way and who came to similar policy conclusions; this group . . . included T. W. Schultz, D. G. Johnson, W. H. Nicholls, O. H. Brownlee, and R. Schickele. A group in the USDA Bureau of Agricultural Economics . . . owed much to the leadership of H. R. Tolley and included, among others, B. W. Allin, W. W. Cochrane, J. G. Maddox, O. C. Stine and O. V. Wells. J. D. Black in his pragmatic way worked closely with the Tolley group, S. E. Johnson, J. P. Cavin, and others in the USDA." Brandow (1977: 219) also comments, "Though in retrospect Cochrane's analysis seems to be generally consistent with ideas presented . . . by Schultz, it is instructive to note that Cochrane's first articles did not present it in that context and that Schultz so severely criticized the details and emphasis of Cochrane's analyses as to appear to reject it. This was not the first or last time that economic ideas subsequently seen to be closely related were initially thought of as sharply different." In retrospect, it appears that the major difference between Schultz and Cochrane was not so much a difference in their analysis of the sources of the farm problem or the behavior of the agricultural economy but in their policy proposals. Schultz was more concerned with the protection of farm incomes from the effects of macroinstability. Cochrane was more concerned with protecting farm income from the effects of overcapacity associated with rapid technical change. See Cochrane's critical discussion of income payments (1946).
12. Legislation authorizing an experimental program of free mail delivery in rural areas was passed by the U.S. Congress in 1892. The program was not initiated, however, until 1896. The service grew rapidly during its first decade but it was not until 1926 that the system was fully developed. Legislation extending rural delivery of parcel post was passed in 1912 (Fuller 1964). Fuller (1964: 35) suggests that rural free delivery was almost the only positive accomplishment of the farmers' protest movement of the 1890s.
13. The draft of this paper presented at the AAEA annual meetings at Cornell University on August 7, 1984, contained a discussion of the political and economic forces that led to the initial development of the farm credit system during the 1916–29 period and the role of agricultural economists in the reform of the system in the 1930s. It was necessary, in order to conform to space requirements, to drop this section in the published version of the paper.

A copy of the paper containing the omitted section can be obtained by writing to the author at the Department of Agricultural and Applied Economics, University of Minnesota, St. Paul MN 55108.

14. The food stamp program was first initiated in 1939. It was discontinued in 1943 and revised again in the early 1960s (Benedict 1956: 289–94).
15. The definitive reports in these two efforts were Fox 1951 and Brandow 1961.

CHAPTER 12

Toward a Theory of Induced Institutional Innovation

Vernon W. Ruttan and Yujiro Hayami

The interpretation of technical and institutional change as endogenous rather than exogenous to the economic system is a relatively new development in economic thought. In work published in the early 1970s we extended the theory of induced technical change and tested it against the history of agricultural development in the United States and Japan (Hayami and Ruttan 1971; Binswanger and Ruttan 1978; Wade 1981). It is now generally accepted that the theory of induced technical change provides very substantial insight into the process of agricultural development for a wide range of developed and developing countries. And economic historians are increasingly drawing on the theory of induced technical change in attempting to interpret differential patterns of productivity growth among countries and over time (Cain and Paterson 1981; Phillips 1982).

The demonstration that technical change can be treated as largely endogenous to the development process does not imply that the progress of either agricultural or industrial technology can be left to an "invisible hand" that drives technology along an "efficient" path determined by relative resource endowments. The capacity to advance knowledge in science and technology is itself a result of a product of institutional innovation—"the great invention of the nineteenth century was the invention of the method of invention" (Whitehead 1925: 96).

In the case of agriculture, for example, in both Japan and the United States, much of the technical change that has led to growth of output per hectare has been produced by public sector institutions. These institutions—state (or prefectural) and federal (or national) agricultural experiment stations—obtain their resources in the political marketplace and allocate their resources through bureaucratic mechanisms. The success of the theory of induced technical change gives rise, therefore, to the need for a more careful consideration of the sources of institutional innovation and design.

In this paper we elaborate a theory of institutional innovation in which shifts in the demand for institutional innovation are induced by changes in relative resource endowments and by technical change. We also consider the impact of advances in social science knowledge and of cultural endowments on the supply of institutional change. After examining the forces that act to shift the demand and supply of institutional innovation, we then present the elements of a more general model of institutional change. The perspective on the role of institutional innovation in the process of economic development presented in this paper is much more positive than the views that were held by the American institutional school or in the recent literature on social choice and collective action (Zingler 1974; Seckler 1975; Olson 1982).

What Is Institutional Innovation?

Institutions are the rules of a society or of organizations that facilitate coordination among people by helping them form expectations each person can reasonably hold in dealing with others. They reflect the conventions that have evolved in different societies regarding the behavior of individuals and groups relative to their own behavior and the behavior of others.[1] In the area of economic relations they have a crucial role in establishing expectations about the rights to use resources in economic activities and about the partitioning of the income streams resulting from economic activity—"institutions provide assurance respecting the actions of others, and give order and stability to expectations in the complex and uncertain world of economic relations."[2]

In order to perform the essential role of forming reasonable expectations in dealings among people, institutions must be stable for an extended time period. But institutions, like technology, must also change if development is to occur. Anticipation of the latent gains to be realized by overcoming the disequilibria resulting from changes in factor endowments, product demand, and technical change represents a powerful inducement to institutional innovation (North and Thomas 1970; Schultz 1975). Institutions that have been efficient in generating growth in the past may, over time, come to direct their efforts primarily to protecting the vested interests of some of their members by maintaining the status quo and thus become obstacles to further economic development.[3] The growing disequilibria in resource allocation due to institutional constraints generated by economic growth create opportunities for political entrepreneurs or leaders to organize collective action to bring about institutional change.

Our perspective on the sources of demand for institutional change is similar to the traditional Marxian view.[4] Marx considered technological change the primary source of institutional change. Our view is somewhat more complex: we believe that changes in factor endowments and product demand are equally important sources of institutional change. Nor is our definition of institutional change limited to the dramatic or revolutionary changes of the type anticipated by Marx. Rather, we share with Lance Davis and Douglass North (1971: 9) the view that basic institutions such as property rights and markets are more typically altered through the accumulation of "secondary" or incremental institutional changes such as modifications in contractual relations or shifts in the boundaries between market and nonmarket activities.

There is a supply dimension as well as a demand dimension in institutional change. Collective action leading to changes in the supply of institutional innovations involves struggles among various vested interest groups. Clearly, the process is much more complex than the clear-cut, two-class conflict between the property owners and the propertyless, as assumed by Marx. In our view, the supply of institutional innovations is strongly influenced by the cost of achieving social consensus (or of suppressing opposition). How costly a form of institutional change is to be accepted in a society depends on the power structure among vested interest groups. It also depends critically on cultural tradition and ideology, such as nationalism, that make certain institutional arrangements more easily accepted than others.

Advances in knowledge in the social sciences (and in related professions such as law, administration, planning, and social service) can reduce the cost of institutional change in a somewhat similar manner as advances in the natural sciences reduce the cost of technical change. Education, both general and technical, that facilitates a better understanding among people of their common interests can also reduce the cost of institutional innovation. Our insistence that important advances in the understanding of the processes of institutional innovation and diffusion can be achieved by treating institutional change as endogenous to the economic system represents a clear departure from the tradition of modern analytical economics.[5] This does not mean that we abandon analytical economics. On the contrary, we try to expand the scope of modern analytical economics by treating institutional change as endogenous.

Demand for Institutional Innovation—Property Rights and Market Institutions

In some cases the demand for institutional innovation can be satisfied by the development of new forms of property rights or more efficient market institutions, or even by evolutionary changes arising out of direct contracting by individuals at the level of the community or the firm. In other cases, where externalities are involved, substantial political resources may have to be brought to bear to organize nonmarket institutions in order to provide for the supply of public goods.

In this section we illustrate, from the agricultural history of a number of countries, how changes in factor endowments, technical change, and growth in product demand have induced change in property rights and contractual arrangements in order to promote more efficient resource allocation through the market.

The agricultural revolution that occurred in England between the fifteenth and the nineteenth centuries involved a substantial increase in the productivity of land and labor. It was accompanied by the enclosure of open fields and the replacement of small peasant cultivators, who held their land from manorial lords, by a system in which large farmers used hired labor to farm the land they leased from the landlords. The First Enclosure Movement, in the fifteenth and sixteenth centuries, resulted in the conversion of open arable fields and commons to private pasture in areas suitable for grazing. It was induced by expansion in the export demand for wool. The Second Enclosure Movement, in the eighteenth century, involved conversion of communally managed arable land into privately operated units. It is now agreed that it was largely induced by the growing disequilibrium between the fixed institutional rent that landlords received under copyhold tenures (with lifetime contracts) and the higher economic rents expected from adoption of new technology, which became more profitable as a consequence of higher grain prices and lower wages. When the land was enclosed, there was a redistribution of income from farmers to landowners, and the disequilibrium was reduced or eliminated.[6]

In nineteenth-century Thailand, the opening up of the nation for international trade and the reduction in shipping rates to Europe resulted in a sharp increase in the demand for rice. The land available for rice production, which had been abundant, became more scarce. Investment in land development for rice production became profitable. The response was a major transformation of property rights. Traditional rights in human property (corvée and slavery) were replaced by more precise private property rights in land (fee-simple titles) (Feeny 1982).

In Japan, at the beginning of the feudal Tokugawa period (1603–1867), peasants' rights to cropland had been limited to the right to till the soil, with the obligation to pay a feudal land tax in kind. As the population grew, commercialization progressed and irrigation and technology were developed to make intensive farming more profitable. Some peasants divided their holdings into smaller units and leased them out to ex-servants or extended family members. Some accumulated land through mortgaging arrangements that made other peasants de facto tenants. As a result of the accumulation of illegal leasing and mortgaging practices, peasants' property rights in land approximated those of a fee-simple title by the end of the Tokugawa period. These rights were readily converted to the modern private-property system in the succeeding Meiji period (Hayami and Kikuchi 1981: 28).

Research conducted by Yujiro Hayami and Masao Kikuchi in the Philippines during the late 1970s has enabled us to examine a contemporary example of the interrelated effects of changes in resource endowments and technical change on the demand for institutional change in land tenure and labor relations (Kikuchi and Hayami 1980; Hayami and Kikuchi 1981). The case is particularly interesting because the institutional innovations occurred as a result of private contracting among individuals. The study is unique in that it is based on a rigorous analysis of microeconomic data in a village over a period of about twenty years.

CHANGES IN TECHNOLOGY AND RESOURCE ENDOWMENTS

Between 1956 and 1976, rice production per hectare in the study village rose dramatically, from 2.5 to 6.7 metric tons per hectare per year. This was due to two technical innovations. In 1958, the national irrigation system was extended to the village. This permitted double-cropping to replace single-cropping, thereby doubling the annual production per hectare of rice land. The second major technical change was the introduction in the late 1960s of the modern high-yielding varieties. The diffusion of modern varieties was accompanied by increased use of fertilizer and pesticides and by the adoption of improved cultural practices such as straight-row planting and intensive weeding.

Population growth in the village was rapid. Between 1966 and 1976 the number of households rose from 66 to 109 and the population rose from 383 to 464, while cultivated area remained virtually constant. The number of landless laborer households increased from 20 to 54. In 1976, half of the households in the village had no land to cultivate, not even land for rent. The average farm size declined from 2.3 hectares to 2.0 hectares.

The land is farmed primarily by tenants. In 1976, only 1.7 hectares of the 108 hectares of cropland in the village were owned by village residents. Traditionally, share tenancy was the most common form of tenure. In both 1956 and 1966, 70 percent of the land was farmed under share tenure arrangements. In 1963, a new agricultural land reform code was passed which was designed to break the political power of the traditional landed elite and to provide greater incentives to peasant producers of basic food crops.[7] A major feature of the new legislation was an arrangement that permitted tenants to initiate a shift from share tenure to leasehold, with rent under the leasehold set at 25 percent of the average yield for the previous three years. Implementation of the code between the mid-1960s and the mid-1970s resulted in a decline in the percentage of land farmed under share tenure to 30 percent.

INSTITUTIONAL INNOVATION

The shift from share tenure to lease tenure was not, however, the only change in tenure relationships that occurred between 1966 and 1976. There was a sharp increase in the number of plots farmed under subtenancy arrangements. The number increased from one in 1956 to five in 1966 and sixteen in 1976. Subtenancy is illegal under the land reform code. The subtenancy arrangements are usually made without the formal consent of the landowner. All cases of subtenancy were on land farmed under a leasehold arrangement. The most common subtenancy arrangement was 50-50 sharing of costs and output.

It was hypothesized that an incentive for the emergence of the subtenancy institution was that the rent paid to landlords under the leasehold arrangement was below the equilibrium rent—the level which would reflect both the higher yields of rice obtained with the new technology and the lower wage rates implied by the increase in population pressure against the land.

To test this hypothesis, market prices were used to compute the value of the unpaid factor inputs (family labor and capital) for different tenure arrangements during the 1976 wet season. The results indicate that the share-to-land was lowest and the operators' surplus was highest for the land under leasehold tenancy. In contrast, the share-to-land was highest and no surplus was left for the operator who cultivated the land under the subtenancy arrangement (Table 12.1). Indeed, the share-to-land when the land was farmed under subtenancy was very close to the sum of the share-to-land plus the operators' surplus under the other tenure arrangement.

The results are consistent with the hypothesis. A substantial portion of the economic rent was captured by the leasehold tenants in the form of operators' surplus. On the land farmed under a subtenancy arrangement, the rent was shared between the leaseholder and the landlord.

A second institutional change, induced by higher yields and the increase in population pressure, has been the emergence of a new pattern of employer-labor relationship between farm operators and landless workers. According to the traditional system called *hunusan*, laborers who participated in the harvesting and threshing activity received a one-sixth share of the paddy (rough rice) harvest. By 1976, most of the farmers (83 percent) adopted a system called *gamma*, in which participation in the harvesting operation was limited to workers who had performed the weeding operation without receiving wages.

The emergence of the *gamma* system can be interpreted as an institutional innovation designed to reduce the wage rate for harvesting to a level equal to the marginal productivity of labor. In the 1950s, when the rice yield per hectare was low and labor was less abundant, the one-sixth share may have approximated an equilibrium wage level. With the higher yields and the more abundant supply of labor, the one-sixth share became larger than the marginal product of labor in the harvesting operation.[8]

To test the hypothesis that the *gamma* system was adopted rapidly primarily because it represented an institutional innovation that permitted farm operators to equate the harvesters' share of output to the marginal productivity of labor, imputed wage costs were compared with the actual harvesters' shares (Table 12.2). The results indicate that a substantial gap existed between the imputed wage for the harvesters' labor alone and the actual harvesters' shares. This gap was eliminated if the imputed wages for harvesting and weeding labor were added.

Those results are consistent with the hypothesis that the changes in institutional arrangements governing the use of production factors were induced when disequilibria between the marginal returns and the marginal costs of factor inputs occurred as a result of changes in factor endowments and technical change. Institutional change, therefore, was directed toward the establishment of a new equilibrium in factor markets.

Table 12.1 **Factor Shares of Rice Output per Hectare, 1976 Wet Season**

	Number of Plots	Area (ha)	Rice Output	Factor shares[a]						
				Current Inputs	Land-owner	Sub-tenancy	Total	Labor	Capital[b]	Operators' Surplus
			kg/ha							
Leasehold land	44	67.7	2,889	657	567	0 (0)	567	918	337	410
			(100.0)	(22.7)	(19.6)		(19.6)	(31.8)	(11.7)	(14.2)
Share tenancy land	30	29.7	2,749	697	698	0 (0)	698	850	288	216
			(100.0)	(25.3)	(25.4)		(25.4)	(30.9)	(10.5)	(7.9)
Subtenancy land	16	9.1	3,447	801	504	801[c]	1,305	1,008	346	–13
			(100.0)	(23.2)	(14.6)	(23.2)	(37.8)	(29.3)	(10.1)	(–0.4)

[a] Percentage shares are shown in parentheses.

[b] Sum of irrigation fee and paid and/or imputed rentals of carabao, tractor and other machines.

[c] Rents to subleasors in the case of pledged plots are imputed by applying the interest rate of 40 percent crop season (a mode in the interest rate distribution in the village).

Source: Hayami and Kikuchi (1982): 111–13.

Table 12.2 **Comparison between the Imputed Value of Harvesters' Share and Imputed Cost of *GAMMA* Labor**

	Based on employers' data	*Based on employees' data*
No. of working days of *gamma* labor (days/ha)[a]		
Weeding	20.9	18.3
Harvesting/threshing	33.6	33.6
Imputed cost of *gamma* labor (P/ha)[b]		
Weeding	167.2	146.6
Harvesting/threshing	369.2	369.6
(1) Total	536.8	516.0
Actual share of harvesters: In kind (kg/ha)[c]	504.0	549.0
(2) Imputed value (P/ha)[d]	504.0	549.0
(2) – (1)	–32.8	33.0

[a] Includes labor of family members who worked as *gamma* laborers.

[b] Imputation using market wage rates (daily wage = P8.0 for weeding, P11.0 for harvesting).

[c] One-sixth of output per hectare.

[d] Imputation using market prices (1 kg = P1).

Source: Hayami and Kikuchi (1982): 121.

EFFICIENCY AND EQUITY IMPLICATIONS

It is important to recognize that subtenancy and *gamma* contracts were the institutional innovations to facilitate more efficient resource allocations through voluntary agreements by assigning more complete private property rights. The land reform laws gave tenants strong protection of their tenancy rights, with the result that a part of land property rights, which is the right to continue tilling the soil at a rent lower than the marginal product of land, was assigned to tenant operators. But the laws prohibited tenants from renting their land to someone else who might utilize it more efficiently—when they became elderly or found more profitable off-farm employment, for example. Subtenancy was developed to reduce such inefficiency due to the institutional rigidity in the land rental market based on the land reform programs. Likewise, the *gamma* system was developed to counteract the institutional rigidity in the labor market based on the traditional custom in the rural community in the form of a fixed harvester's share.

It might appear that these institutional innovations increased efficiency at the expense of equity. But if the subtenancy system had not been developed, the route would have been closed for some of the landless laborers to become farm operators and use their entrepreneurial abilities more profitably. If the implicit wage rate for harvesting work had been raised in the absence of the *gamma* contract, it might have encouraged mechanization in threshing and thereby reduced employment and labor earnings. It must be recognized that the institutional innovations to develop more efficient markets by assigning more complete private property rights do not necessarily impair equity, as is often argued by Marxist and populist critiques against private market institutions.

In the case reviewed here the induced innovation process leading toward the establishment of equilibrium in factor markets occurred very rapidly in spite of the fact that many of the transactions—between landlords, tenants, and laborers—were less than fully monetized. Informal contractual arrangements or agreements were utilized. The subleasing and the *gamma* labor contract evolved without the mobilization of substantial political activity or bureaucratic effort. Indeed, the subleasing arrangement evolved in spite of legal prohibition. Where substantial political and bureaucratic resources must be mobilized to bring about technical or institutional change, the changes occur much more slowly, as in the cases of the English enclosure movements and the Thai and Japanese property rights cases referred to at the beginning of this section.

The Demand for Institutional Innovation—Nonmarket Institutions for the Supply of Public Goods

The examples of institutional change advanced in the previous section, such as the enclosure in England and the evolution of private property rights in land in Japan and Thailand, have contributed to the development of a more efficient market system. Institutional changes of this type are profitable for society only if the costs involved in the assignment and protection of rights are smaller than the gains from better resource allocation. If those costs are very high, it may be necessary to design nonmarket institutions in order to achieve more efficient resource allocation.[9]

For example, in Japan, although the system of private property rights was developed on cropland during the premodern period, communal ownership at the village level permitted open access to large areas of wild and forest land which were utilized for the collection of firewood, leaves, and wild grasses to fertilize rice fields. However, over time more detailed common property rules were stipulated for the use of communal land in order to prevent resource exhaustion.[10]

Detailed stipulations of the time and place of utilization of communal land as well as rules for mobilizing village labor to maintain communal property (such as applying fire to regenerate pasture) were often enforced with religious taboos and rituals. Those communal village institutions remained viable because it was much more costly to demarcate and partition wild and forest land than cropland among individuals and to enforce exclusive use. Any villager's use of communal land involves externality. For example, his collection of firewood reduces the availability of the firewood for other villagers. If property rights are not assigned, there may be only limited incentive for resource conservation. This is not a serious problem if the resource that is subject to open access is abundant relative to population. However, as population pressure begins to rise, a common understanding regarding appropriate use, reinforced by social sanctions, may act to limit excessive exploitation. But as population growth continues to press against limited land resources and the market value of the resource product rises, it becomes necessary to impose more formal regulations regarding the access of individual villagers to communal land.

Group action to supply public goods, such as the maintenance of communal land, may work effectively if the size of group involved is small, as in the case of a village community. However, if a large number of people are involved in the use of a public good, as in the case of marine fisheries, it is more difficult to regulate their resource use or to prevent free riders by means of voluntary agreements.[11] Action by a higher authority with coercive power, such as government, may be required to limit free riding.

The "socialization" of agricultural research is common not only in socialist economies but also in market economies (Hayami and Yamada 1975: 224–49). This can be explained by the failure of the market in allocating resources efficiently for the supply of public goods for a large, unidentifiable clientele group. New information or knowledge resulting from research is typically endowed with the attributes of a public good characterized by nonrivalness or jointness in supply and utilization, and nonexcludability or external economies.[12] The first attribute implies that the good is equally available to all. The second implies that it is impossible for private producers to appropriate through market pricing the full social benefits arising directly from the production (and consumption) of the good—it is difficult to exclude from the utilization of the good those who do not pay for it. A socially optimal level of supply of such a good cannot be expected if its supply is left to private firms. However, present institutional arrangements are such that much information resulting from basic research is nonexcludable. This is the major reason why it has been necessary to establish nonprofit institutions to advance basic scientific knowledge.[13]

A unique aspect of agricultural research, particularly that directed to advancing biological technology, is that many of the products of research even in the applied area are characterized by nonexcludability. Protection by patent laws is either unavailable or inadequate. The nature of agricultural production to be conducted would make it difficult to restrict information about new technology or practices. Furthermore, even the largest farms are relatively small units and would not be able to capture more than a small share of the gains from inventive activity. Private research activities in agriculture have been directed primarily toward developing mechanical technology for which patent protection is established.[14]

Another important attribute of the research production function is that it has a stochastic form. Research, by nature, is characterized by risk and uncertainty. Success in a research project is like hitting a "successful oil well": any number of dry holes may be bored before the successful one is found. Richard Nelson (1959: 304) has pointed out that this stochastic nature of the research production function, which is especially strong in the case of basic research, contributes to the failure of the market in attaining optimum resource allocation over time:

> The very large variance of the profit probability distribution from a basic research project will tend to cause a risk-avoiding firm, without the economic resources to spread the risk by running a number of basic-research projects at once, to value a basic-research project at significantly less than its expected profitability and hence . . . at less than its social value.

The public-good attributes of the agricultural research product together with the stochastic nature of the research production function make public support of agricultural research socially desirable. It does not necessarily follow, however, that agricultural research should be conducted in governmental institutions financed by tax revenue. The social benefit produced by agricultural research can be measured as the sum of increases in consumers' and producers' surpluses due to the downward shift in the supply function of an agricultural product. If the benefit consists primarily of producers' surplus, agricultural research may be left to the cooperative activities of agricultural producers (that is, to the activities of such institutions as agricultural commodity organizations and cooperatives). Research on a number of tropical export crops grown under plantation conditions such as sugar, bananas, and rubber is often organized in this manner.

However, most agricultural commodities are produced by a number of small producers. Under these conditions voluntary cooperation to support research would be very costly to organize. Furthermore, most agricultural commodities, except those intended for export, are characterized by low price elasticity of demand. As a result, a major share of the social benefit produced by research tends to be transmitted to consumers through lower market prices. In such a situation the cost of agricultural research should be borne by the general public.

If agricultural research were left entirely to the private sector, the result would be serious bias in the allocation of research resources. Resources would flow primarily to those areas of mechanical technology that are adequately protected by patents and to those areas of biological technology where the results can be protected by trade secrets (such as the inbred lines used in the production of hybrid corn seed). Other areas, such as research on open pollinated seed varieties, biological control of insects and pathogens, and improvements in farming practices and management, would be neglected. The socialization of agricultural research or the predominance of public institutions in agricultural research, especially in the biological sciences, can be considered a major institutional innovation designed to offset what would otherwise represent a serious distortion in the allocation of research resources.

The Supply of Institutional Innovation

We have identified the disequilibria in economic relationships associated with economic growth, such as technical change leading to the generation of new income streams and changes in relative factor endowments, as important sources of demand for institutional change. But the sources of supply of institutional innovation are less well understood. The factors that reduce the cost of institutional innovation have not been widely studied by economists or by other social scientists.

In the Philippines village case discussed earlier, changes in tenure and labor market institutions were supplied, in response to the changes in demand generated by changing factor endowments and new income streams, through the individual and joint decisions of owner-cultivators, tenants, and laborers. But even at this level it was necessary for gains to the innovators to be large enough to offset the risk of ignoring the land reform prohibitions against subleasing and the social costs involved in changing traditional harvest-sharing arrangements. While mobilization of substantial political resources was not required to introduce and extend the new land and labor market institutions, the distribution of political resources within the village did influence the initiation and diffusion of the institutional innovations.

The supply of major institutional innovations necessarily involves the mobilization of substantial political resources by political entrepreneurs and innovators. It is useful to think in terms of a supply schedule of institutional innovation that is determined by the marginal cost schedule facing political entrepreneurs as they attempt to design new institutions and resolve the conflicts among various vested interest groups (or suppression of opposition when necessary). We hypothesize that institutional innovations will be supplied if the expected return from the innovation that accrues to the political entrepreneurs exceeds the marginal cost of mobilizing the resources necessary to introduce the innovation. To the extent that the private return to the political entrepreneurs is different from the social return, the institutional innovation will not be supplied at a socially optimum level.[15]

Thus, the supply of institutional innovation depends critically on the power structure or balance among vested interest groups in a society. If the power balance is such that the political entrepreneurs' efforts to introduce an institutional innovation with a high rate of social return are adequately rewarded by greater prestige and stronger political support, a socially desirable institutional innovation may occur. However, if the institutional innovation is expected to result in a loss to a dominant political bloc, the innovation may not be forthcoming even if it is expected to produce a large net gain to society as a whole. And socially undesirable institutional innovations may occur if the returns to the entrepreneur or the interest group exceed the gains to society (Tullock 1967; Krueger 1974; Tollison 1982).

The failure of many developing countries to institutionalize the agricultural research capacity needed to take advantage of the large gains from relatively modest investments in technical change may be due, in part, to the divergence between social returns and the private returns to political entrepreneurs. In the mid-1920s, for example, agricultural development in Argentina appeared to be proceeding along a path roughly comparable to that of the United States. Mechanization of crop production lagged slightly behind that in the United States. Grain yields per hectare averaged slightly higher than in the United States. In contrast to the United States, however, output and yields in Argentina remained relatively stagnant between the mid-1920s and the mid-1970s. It was not until the late 1970s that Argentina began to realize significant gains in agricultural productivity. Part of this lag in Argentine agricultural development was due to the disruption of export markets in the 1930s and 1940s. Students of Argentine development have pointed to the political dominance of the landed aristocracy, to the rising tensions between urban and rural interests, and to inappropriate domestic policies toward agriculture (de Janvry 1973; P. H. Smith 1969, 1974; Cavallo and Mundlak 1982). The Argentine case would seem to represent a case where the bias in the distribution of political and economic resources imposed exceptionally costly delays in the institutional innovations needed to take advantage of the relatively inexpensive sources of growth that technical change in agriculture could have made available.

Cultural endowments, including religion and ideology, exert a strong influence on the supply of institutional innovation. They make some forms of institutional change less costly to establish and impose severe costs on others. For example, the traditional moral obligation in the Japanese village community to cooperate in joint communal infrastructure maintenance has made it less costly to implement rural development programs than in societies where such traditions do not prevail. These activities had their origin in the feudal organization of rural communities in the pre-Meiji period. But practices such as maintenance of village and agricultural roads and of irrigation and drainage ditches through joint activities in which all families contribute labor were still seen in well over half of the hamlets in Japan as recently as 1970 (Ishikawa 1981). The traditional patterns of cooperation have represented an important cultural resource on which to erect modern forms of cooperative marketing and joint farming activities. Similar cultural resources are not available in South Asian villages where, for example, the caste structure inhibits cooperation and encourages specialization.

Likewise, the aspiration of new ideology may reduce the cost to political entrepreneurs of mobilizing collective action for institutional change. For example, the Jeffersonian concept of agrarian democracy provided ideological support for the series of land ordinances culminating in the Homestead Act of 1862, which established the legal framework designed to encourage an owner-operator system of agriculture in the American West (Cochrane 1979: 41–47, 179–88). Strong nationalist sentiment in Meiji Japan, reflected in slogans such as "A Wealthy Nation and Strong Army" (*Fukoku Kyohei*), helped mobilize the resources needed for the establishment of vocational schools and agricultural and industrial experiment stations (Hayami and Kikuchi 1981). In China, communist ideology, reinforced by the lessons learned during the guerrilla period in Yenan, inspired the mobilization of communal resources to build irrigation systems and other forms of social overhead capital (Schran 1975). Thus, ideology can be a critical resource for political entrepreneurs and an important factor affecting the supply of institutional innovations.

Advances in social sciences that improve knowledge relevant to the design of institutional innovations that are capable of generating new income streams or that reduce the cost of conflict resolution act to shift the supply of institutional change to the right. Throughout history, improvements in institutional performance have occurred primarily through the slow accumulation of successful precedent or as by-products of expertise and experience. Institutional change was generated through the process of trial and error much in the same manner that technical change was generated prior to the invention of the research university, the agricultural experiment station, or the industrial research laboratory. With the institutionalization of research in the social sciences and related professions the process of institutional innovation has begun to proceed much more efficiently; it is becoming increasingly possible to substitute social science knowledge and analytical skill for the more expensive process of learning by trial and error.

The research that led to advances in our understanding of the production and consumption of rural households in less developed countries represents an important example of the contribution of advances in social science knowledge to the design of more efficient institutions (Schultz 1964; Nerlove 1974; Binswanger et al. 1981). In a number of countries this research has led to the abandonment of policies that viewed peasant households as unresponsive to economic incentives. And it has led to the design of policies and institutions to make more productive technologies available to peasant producers and to the design of more efficient price policies for factors and products.

Similarly, the diffusion of education designed to raise the intellectual level of the general public and to facilitate better understanding of the private and social costs of institutional change may reduce the cost to political entrepreneurs of introducing socially desirable institutions and raise the cost of biasing institutional change in a manner that is costly to society.

Toward a More Complete Model of Induced Innovation

We illustrate, in Figure 12.1, the elements of a model that maps the general equilibrium relationships among resource endowments, cultural endowments, technologies and institutions.[16] The model goes beyond the conventional general equilibrium model in which resource endowments, technologies, institutions, and culture (conventionally designated as tastes) are given.[17] In the study of long-term social and economic change the relationships among the several variables must be treated as recursive. The formal microeconomic models that are employed to analyse the supply and demand for technical and institutional change can be thought of as "nested" within the general equilibrium framework of Figure 12.1.

One advantage of the "pattern model" outlined in Figure 12.1 is that it helps to identify areas of ignorance. Our capacity to model and test the relationships between resource endowments and technical change is relatively strong. Our capacity to model and test the relationships between cultural endowments and either technical or institutional change is relatively weak. A second advantage of the model is that it is useful in identifying the model components that enter into other attempts to account for secular economic and social change. Failure to analyze historical change in a general equilibrium context tends to result in a unidimensional perspective on the relationships bearing on technical and institutional change.

For example, historians working within the Marxist tradition often tend to view technical change as dominating both institutional and cultural change. In his book, *Oriental Despotism*, Karl Wittfogel (1957) views the irrigation technology used in wet rice cultivation in East Asia as determining political organization. In terms of Figure 12.1 his primary emphasis was on the impact of resource endowments and technology on institutions (C) and (B).

A serious misunderstanding can be observed in contemporary neo-Marxian critiques of the Green Revolution. These criticisms have focused attention almost entirely on the impact of technical change on labor and land tenure relations.

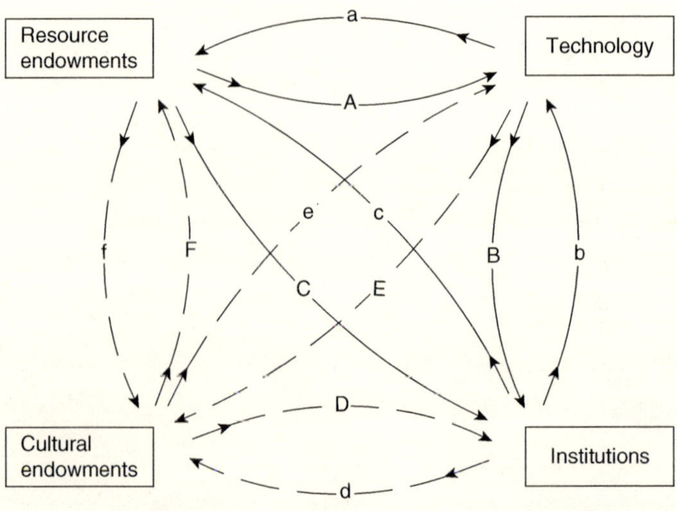

Figure 12.1 Interrelationships between Changes in Resource endowments, Cultural endowments, Technology and Institutions.

Both the radical and populist critics have emphasized relation (B). But they have tended to ignore relationships (A) and (C).[18] This has led to repeated failure to identify effectively the separate effects of population growth and technical change on the growth and distribution of income. The analytical power of the more complete induced innovation model was illustrated in the work by Hayami and Kikuchi (1982), discussed earlier in this paper, on the impact of both technical change and population growth on changes in land tenure and labor market relationships in the Philippines.

Armen Alchian and Harold Demsetz identify a primary function of property rights as guiding incentives to achieve greater internalization of externalities. They consider that the clear specification of property rights reduces transaction costs in the face of growing competition for the use of scarce resources as a result of population growth and/or growth in product demand (Demsetz 1967; Alchian and Demsetz 1973).

North and Thomas, building on the Alchian-Demsetz paradigm, attempted to explain the economic growth of Western Europe between 900 and 1700 primarily in terms of changes in property institutions.[19] During the eleventh and thirteenth centuries the pressure of population against increasingly scarce land resources induced innovations in property rights that in turn created profitable opportunities for the generation and adoption of labor-intensive technical changes in agriculture. The population decline in the fourteenth and fifteenth centuries was viewed as a primary factor leading to the demise of feudalism and the rise of the national state (line C). These institutional changes in turn opened up new possibilities for economies of scale in nonagricultural production and in trade (line b).

In a more recent work Mancur Olson (1982) has emphasized the proliferation of institutions as a source of economic decline.[20] He also regards broad-based encompassing organizations as having incentives to generate growth and redistribute incomes to their members with little excess burden. For example, a broadly based coalition that encompasses the majority of agricultural producers is more likely to exert political pressure for growth-oriented policies that will enable its members to obtain a larger share of a larger national product than a smaller organization that represents the interests of the producers of a single commodity. Small organizations representing narrow interest groups are more likely to pursue the interests of their members at the expense of the welfare of other producers and the general public. In contrast, an even more broadly based farmer-labor coalition would be more concerned with promoting economic growth than an organization representing a single sector. But large groups, in Olson's view, are inherently unstable because rational individuals will not incur the costs of contributing to the realization of the large group program—they have strong incentives to act as free riders. As a result, organizational "space" in a stable society will be increasingly occupied by special interest "distributional coalitions." These distributional coalitions make political life more divisive. They slow down the adoption of new technologies (line b) and limit the capacity to reallocate resources (line c). The effect is to slow down economic growth or in some cases initiate a period of economic decline.

What are the implications of the theory of institutional innovation outlined in this paper for the research agenda on the economics of institutional change? In our research on the direction and rate of technical change we were able to advance significantly our knowledge by treating technical change as endogenous—as induced primarily by changes in relative resource endowments and the growth of demand. We have also attempted to develop a theory of induced institutional innovation in which we treat institutional innovation as endogenous. There is now a significant body of evidence that suggests that substantial new insights on institutional innovation and diffusion can be obtained by treating institutional change as an economic response to changes in resource endowments and technical change.

We also insist on the potential significance of cultural endowments, including the factors that economists typically conceal under the rubric of tastes and that political scientists include under ideology. But our capacity to develop rigorous empirical tests capable of identifying the relative significance of the relationships between cultural endowments and the other elements of the model outlined in Figure 12.1 is quite unsatisfactory. Until our colleagues in the other social sciences provide us with more helpful analytical tools, we are forced to adhere to a strategy that focuses primarily on the interactions between resource endowments, technical change, and institutional change. The strategy suggested here does have the clear advantage of allowing us to explore how far a strategy based on the rather straightforward extension of standard microeconomic theory will take us in the analysis of both technical and institutional change.

Notes

Vernon W. Ruttan and Yujiro Hayami, *Journal of Development Studies* 20 (July 1984): 203–23. We are indebted to Margaret Andrews, Robert Bates, David Feeny, Elizabeth Hoffman, Robert Keohane, James Roumasset, and Ford Runge for comments on an earlier draft of this paper.

1. There is considerable disagreement regarding the meaning of the term "institution." A distinction is often made between the concepts of institution and organization. We find the broad view which includes both concepts most useful for our purpose. This is consistent with the view expressed by both Commons (1950: 24) and Knight (1952: 51). Our definition also encompasses the classification employed by Davis and North (1971: 8–9). We employ the more inclusive definition in order to be able to consider changes in the rules or conventions that govern behavior (a) within economic units such as families, firms, and bureaucracies, (b) among economic units as in the cases of the rules that govern market relationships, and (c) between economic units and their environment, as in the case of the relationship between a firm and a regulatory agency.
2. See Runge 1981b: xv. Formal analysis of the role of institutions in providing assurance of stability in economic relationships emerged from dissatisfaction with the implications of the assumption of strict dominance of individual strategy in modern welfare economics. See A. K. Sen 1967 and Runge 1981a. In a less formal treatment, North (1981: 45–58) argues, in a chapter on "Ideology and the Free Rider Problem," that shared ideological and ethical perspectives provide assurance that is lacking in models built on the dominance of individual strategies.

3. The role of special interest "distributional coalitions" in slowing society's capacity to adopt new technology and reallocate resources in response to changing conditions is the central theme in Olson 1982 (see esp. p. 74).
4. At a certain stage of their development, the material forces of production in society come in conflict with the existing relations of production, or—what is but a legal expression for the same thing—with the property relations within which they had been at work before. From forms of development of the forces of production these relations turn into their fetters. Then comes the period of social revolution. With the change of the economic foundation the entire immense superstructure is more or less rapidly transformed (Marx 1913: 11–12). For a discussion of the role of technology in Marxian thought see Rosenberg 1982: 34–54.
5. The orthodox view of a generation ago was expressed by Samuelson (1948: 221–22): "The auxiliary (institutional) constraints imposed upon the variables are not themselves the proper subject of welfare economics but must be taken as given." Contrast this with the more recent statement by Schotter (1981: 6): "We view welfare economics as a study . . . that ranks the system of rules which dictate social behavior." There are now five fairly well-defined "political economy" traditions that have attempted to break out of the constraints imposed by traditional welfare economics and treat institutional change as endogenous. These include (a) the theory of property rights, (b) the theory of economic regulation, (c) the theory of interest-group rent seeking, (d) the liberal-pluralist theories of government, and (e) the neo-Marxian theories of the state. In the property rights theories the government plays a relatively passive role; the economic theory of regulation focuses on the electoral process; the rent-seeking and liberal-pluralist theories concentrate on both electoral and bureaucratic choice processes; and the theory of the state attempts to incorporate electoral, legislative choice, and bureaucratic choice processes. For a review and criticism see Rausser, Lichtenberg, and Lattimore 1982.
6. There has been a continuing debate among students of English agricultural history about whether the higher rents that landowners received after enclosure was (a) because enclosed farming was more efficient than open field farming, or (b) because enclosures redistributed income from farmers to landowners. See Chambers and Mingay 1966, Dahlman 1980, and Allen 1982.
7. Although the passage and implementation of the Land Reform Code of 1963 was exogenous to the economy of the village, the land reform of the 1960s has been interpreted as the result of efforts by an emerging industrial elite to break simultaneously the political power of the more conservative land-owning elite and to provide incentives to peasant producers to respond to the rapid growth in demand for marketable surpluses of wage goods, primarily rice and maize, needed to sustain rapid urban industrial development. Thus, the Land Reform Code can be viewed as an institutional innovation designed to facilitate realization of the opportunities for economic growth that could be realized through rapid urban industrial development. See Ruttan 1969b.
8. Real wages for agricultural labor declined significantly in the Philippines between the mid-1950s and the mid-1960s. See Khan 1977. Thus, while we cannot be certain that the labor market was in equilibrium in the 1950s, it is clear that the degree of disequilibrium widened, as a result of both higher yields and lower wage rates, prior to the introduction and diffusion of the *gamma* system.
9. Harold Demsetz (1964) has pointed out that the relative costs of using market and political institutions is rarely given explicit consideration in the literature on market failure. An appropriate way of interpreting the "public goods vs. private goods" issue is to ask whether the costs of providing a market are too high relative to the cost of nonmarket alternatives. A similar point is made by Leonid Hurwicz (1972b).
10. For the distinction between open access and common property, see Ciriacy-Wantrup and Bishop 1975. In the case of open access use rights have not been fully established. In the case of common property rules have been established that govern joint use. Common property is therefore a form of land use that lies between the extremes of open access and fully exclusive private rights. The problem of resource exhaustion in open access properties was elaborated in Demsetz 1967 and Alchian and Demsetz 1973.

11. See Olson 1968. Several students of institutional change have emphasised that coordinated or common expectations resulting from the assurance provided by traditional institutions or common assumptions about equity or ideology have permitted much larger groups to engage in either implicit or explicit voluntary cooperation than implied by Olson's model. See Runge 1981b: 189–99 and North 1981: 54. North (ibid.) notes that "the premium necessary to induce people to become free riders is positively correlated with the perceived legitimacy of the existing institution."
12. For a characterization of the nonrivalness and nonexcludability attributes of public goods see Samuelson 1954, 1955, 1958 and Musgrave 1959.
13. Nonrivalness is an essential attribute of information. The use of information about a new farming practice (contour plowing, for example) by a farmer is not hindered by the adoption of the same practice by other farmers. There is no capacity limit for its utilization. Nonexcludability, by contrast, is not a natural attribute of information but rather is determined by institutional arrangements. In fact, patent laws are an institutional arrangement that make a certain kind of information (called an "invention") excludable, thereby creating profit incentives for private creative activities. Retention of trade secrets is another legally sanctioned method of retaining control over inventions or other forms of new technical knowledge. These arrangements are the ones designed to promote more efficient resource allocation through market arrangements as discussed in the previous section.
14. In a number of countries "breeders' rights" and "petty patent" legislation has induced rapid growth in private sector R&D related to agriculture. See Ruttan 1982b and Evenson and Evenson 1983.
15. See, for example, Frohlich, Oppenheimer, and Young 1971. For a review and extension of concepts of political entrepreneurship see Guttman 1982.
16. Fusfeld (1980: 33) uses the terms "pattern" or "Gestalt" model to describe a form of analysis that links the elements of a general pattern together by logical connections. The recursive multicausal relationships of the pattern model imply that the model is always "open"—"it can never include all of the relevant variables and relationships necessary for a full understanding of the phenomenon under investigation."
17. In economics the concept of cultural endowments is usually subsumed under the concept of "tastes" which are regarded as "given"—that is, not subject to economic analysis. Our use of the term "culture" is consistent with the definition suggested by Leslie A. White (1974: 1158): "When things and events are considered in the context of their relation to the human organism, they constitute behavior, when they are considered . . . in their relationship to one another, they become culture." We use the term "cultural endowments" to capture those dimensions of culture that have been transmitted from the past. Contemporary changes in resource endowments, technology, and institutions can be expected to result in changes in cultural endowments.
18. A major limitation of the Marxian model is the emphatic rejection of a causal link between demographic change and technical and institutional change (North 1981: 60–61). This blindness to the role of demographic factors, and to the impact of relative resource endowments, originated in the debates between Marx and Malthus. An attempt to correct this deficiency represents the major innovation of the "cultural materialism" school of anthropology. See Harris 1979.
19. See North and Thomas 1970: 1–17; 1973. For a critical perspective on the North-Thomas model see Field 1981. Field is critical of the attempt by North and Thomas to treat institutional change as endogenous.
20. For a review of the Olson work see North 1983: 163–64.

PART

V

PERSPECTIVES

CHAPTER 13

The Transition to Agricultural Sustainability

Vernon W. Ruttan

The institutional and cultural foundations of the modern world began to emerge in Western Europe in the seventeenth and eighteenth centuries. The material basis for the agricultural and industrial revolutions was established during the eighteenth and nineteenth centuries. These advances were initially limited to a few countries in Western Europe and their offshoots. For most countries of the world, the transition did not begin until well into the twentieth century. These institutional and technical changes combined to generate unprecedented growth in population, in resource use, and in human welfare. Since midcentury alone, global population has doubled, energy production has more than tripled, and economic output has increased by a factor of five.

The challenge of the twenty-first century will be to make the transition to sustainable growth in both presently developed and low-income countries. It will involve a transition to a stable global population, it may involve a transition to a stable level of material consumption, and it will involve a transition to a largely urban society. Whether the transition will be accompanied by levels of material and energy consumption in presently poor countries comparable to the levels that have been achieved by the industrial countries is the subject of intense debate. How much land will be left to nature after meeting the demands for agricultural commodities and the demands for environmental services arising out of population and income growth is even more problematical.

Sustainability Scenarios

It will be useful to discuss the transition to agricultural sustainability within the context of broader visions of global sustainability.[1] One thing we can be certain of is that, in the future, we will be continuously confronted by surprise. One approach to the exploration of plausible futures is the construction of integrated assessment models. An early, and highly controversial, example was the Club of Rome's report titled *Limits to Growth* (Meadows et al. 1972). The report depicted a world entering an "era of limits" in which even low rates of growth would no longer be sustainable. More recent integrated assessment models have emphasized the specification of more realistic model structures and parameter values. There also has been a shift away from prediction and toward exploration of the sensitivity to alternative parameter values and policy regimes. Integrated assessment models are increasingly employed in addressing global climate change issues (Weyant et al. 1996; Rotmans and Dowlatabadi 1998).

A second approach employed in attempts to reach beyond the analytical constraints of the more formal integrated models has been to construct plausible scenarios of alternative development paths that could arise from the forces that will drive the world system across the twenty-first century. Scenarios are stories told in the language of words as well as numbers. There are usually four major steps in formulating a scenario (Gallopin and Raskin 1998). The current state of the system is first described and quantitatively represented in sufficient detail to clarify the key issues that will be addressed. Next, the "driving forces" that govern the system and move it forward are identified and characterized. A third step involves identifying the forces that can redirect beliefs, behaviors, and policies away from some visions of the future toward others. Finally, an attempt can be made to impose surprising events on the scenario trajectory.

Recent examples include the World Resources Institute–Santa Fe Institute–Brookings Institution "2050 Project" (Hammond 1998) and the Stockholm Environmental Institute (Raskin and Gallopin et al. 1998). The Stockholm group presented three basic scenarios: Conventional Worlds, Barbarization, and Great Transitions. The Conventional Worlds Reference Scenario assumes that economic trends will, with minor variations, continue along the historical trajectory of the twentieth century without fundamental changes in institutions and values. "These include markets, private investment, and competition as the fundamental engine for economic growth and wealth allocation; free trade and unrestricted capital and financial flows to foster globalization of product and labor markets, rapid industrialization and urbanization; possessive individualization as . . . the basis of the 'good life'; and the nation-state and liberal democracy as the appropriate form of governance" (Raskin et al. 1996: 3).

The Reference Scenario implies a kinder and gentler world than projected in *Limits to Growth*. Population increases from 6 billion to a peak of 10 billion in 2050, with nearly all the increase in the presently poor countries. The economies of the developing countries grow more rapidly than those of the developed (Organization for Economic Cooperation and Development) countries—3.6 percent as compared with 2.0 percent per year. The ratio of per capita gross domestic product between the rich Organization for Economic Cooperation and

Development countries and the rest of the world declines from twenty in 1990 to fifteen in 2050—but the absolute difference continues to widen. Structural shifts in economic activity—from agriculture to industry to services—continues. Trends toward dematerialization and decarbonization also continue. Although energy use grows far less rapidly than gross domestic product, due to structural and technological changes, the greater scale of human activity results in rising environmental stress on the assimilative capacity of the air, water, and soil. Oil and gas become increasingly scarce, but price increases are contained by development of backup technologies.

The world described by the Reference Scenario is richer but dirtier than the world we live in at the threshold of the twenty-first century. There are also substantial risks associated with the Reference Scenario. "First, the cumulative loads on Earth's geochemical cycles and ecosystems could exceed natural assimilative capacities. . . . Second, heightened pressure on natural resources could lead to economic and social disruptions or even conflicts" (Gallopin and Raskin 1998: 11). The persistence of poverty in poor resource countries experiencing rapid population growth could become a serious source of social, political, and economic stress.

These concerns lead to construction of a Policy Reform variant of the Conventional Worlds Scenario. The Policy Reform variant assumes that, within the context of current values and institutional structures, governments act vigorously to achieve rapid economic growth, greater distributional equity, and serious protection of environmental quality. The policy reform variant would require major institutional changes, including substantial transfer of resources from rich to poor countries, and major technological changes, including a more rapid shift toward dematerialization and decarbonization than implied in the Reference Scenario. It would also require a more active public role in environmental management. The benefits, as compared with the Reference Scenario, would be realized in terms of improvements in environmental quality, greater equity, and a reduction in sociopolitical conflict.

Fundamental Change

The Stockholm Environmental Institute studies present two alternative scenarios, each with two variants, that assume more fundamental changes. In the Great Transitions New Sustainability variant, governance and economic systems reflect a stronger sense of global community and place a higher value on environmental amenities. The flow of energy and material through the economy is drastically reduced even as incomes continue to rise. Incomes in the poorer regions of the world converge more rapidly toward those in the developed countries. Growth in cultural consumption emerges as a substitute for growth in material consumption. This new postindustrial culture can emerge only from successful efforts to design the technical and institutional changes that will be necessary to respond to challenges that will be confronted in attempting to provide an improved quality of life for the people who will be living in the increasingly urbanized world.

The Barbarization Scenarios arise out of failure to realize the institutional reforms necessary to achieve either the Conventional Worlds or the Great Transitions scenarios. "The most significant element of these scenarios is that the number of people living in poverty increases while the gap between rich and poor grows—both within and among countries" (Gallopin and Raskin 1998: 26). Local and regional environments come under increasing stress, and conflict over access to natural resources intensifies. The Breakdown and Fortress World variants differ primarily in the degree to which the prevailing power structure—governments, transnational corporations, international organizations, and the armed forces—manages to maintain some semblance of order.

Scientific and Technical Constraints[2]

The half-century since World War II has experienced unprecedented rates of growth in population, in per capita income, and in agricultural production. World population increased from 2.5 billion in 1950 to 6.0 billion in the late 1990s. The global annual population growth rate peaked at slightly higher than 2.0 percent in the mid- to late 1960s (Cohen 1995). The production of cereal crops more than tripled during the same period. In spite of rapid population growth, global average per capita food availability rose from less than 2,400 to more than 2,700 calories. Projections of future population and income growth are notoriously uncertain. Population growth will likely add 3.0–5.0 billion people to the world population by 2050. The contribution of income growth to growth in food demand will depend importantly on whether the decline in the rate of per capita income growth in the low- and middle-income countries since 1980 is reversed in the early years of the twenty-first century. While income growth in rich countries imposes very little burden on per capita food consumption, the very poor often spend as much as one-half of any increase in per capita income on food.

In the 1950s and 1960s, it was not difficult to anticipate the sources of the increase in agricultural production over the next several decades. Advances in crop production would come from expansion in irrigated area, from more intensive application of fertilizer and crop protection chemicals, and from the development of crop varieties that would be more responsive to fertilizer and management. Advances in animal production would come from genetic improvements and advances in animal nutrition. At a more fundamental level, increases in grain yields would occur from changes in plant architecture that would make possible higher plant populations per hectare and by increasing the ratio of grain to total dry matter. Increases in production of animals and animal products would come about by decreasing the proportion of feed devoted to animal maintenance and increasing the proportion used to produce usable animal products.

I find it much more difficult to tell a convincing story about the sources of increase in crop and animal production over the next half-century than it was a half-century ago. There are severe physiological constraints to increasing the grain-to-drymatter ratio or to reducing the percentage of animal feed devoted to animal maintenance.[3] These constraints will impinge most severely in those areas that have already achieved the highest levels of output per hectare or per animal unit—in Western Europe, North America, and East Asia. The constraints are already evident in terms of a reduction in the incremental yield increases from fertilizer application and smaller incremental reductions in labor input from the use of larger and more powerful mechanical equipment.

There are also preliminary indications of declines in agricultural research productivity. As average grain yields, under favorable conditions, have risen from the 1.0–2.0 to 6.0–8.0 metric tons per hectare, the share of research budgets devoted to maintenance research—the research needed to maintain existing crop and animal productivity levels—has risen relative to the total research budget (Plucknett and Smith 1986). As a result, the scientist years required to achieve incremental yield increases in wheat and maize have been rising more rapidly than the yield increases (Maredia and Eicher 1995). And the cost per scientist has been rising more rapidly than the general price level (Pardy et al. 1989; Huffman and Evenson 1993). I find it difficult to escape a conclusion that agricultural research, in the countries that have achieved the most rapid gains in agricultural technology over the last half-century, has begun to experience diminishing returns to both public and private sector agricultural research. The good news is that there remains a substantial gap between the more technically advanced regions and the lagging regions that can be narrowed if sufficient effort is devoted to adaptive research and diffusion.

It is possible, within another decade, that advances in molecular biology and genetic engineering will reverse the urgency of the above concerns. The use of genetic engineering is enabling plant breeders to manipulate genetic materials with greater precision and to speed the pace of crop breeding. The applications of genetic engineering that are presently available in the field, however, are primarily in the area of plant protection and animal health. They are enabling producers to push crop and animal yields toward their genetic potential, but they have not yet raised the biological ceilings above the levels that have been achieved by researchers employing the older methods based on Mendelian biology.[4] The advances that are most likely to be introduced over the next decade are likely to be the result of efforts to realize higher value added—as in neutraceuticals and pharmaceuticals—rather than from efforts to break the constraints on yield ceilings. The excessively broad patent rights being granted in the field of biotechnology may become a serious institutional constraint on the transfer of plant protection and animal health biotechnology products to farmers in developing countries.

Resource and Environmental Constraints

A second set of concerns about the capacity of the agricultural sector to respond to the demands that will be placed on it focuses on resource and environmental constraints. Part of this concern is with the feedback of the environmental impacts of agricultural intensification on agricultural production itself. These include the degradation and loss of soil resources due to erosion, the waterlogging and salinity associated with irrigation, the coevolution of pests and pathogens associated with use of chemical controls, the impact of global climate change, and the loss of biological diversity.

SOIL EROSION

Soil erosion and degradation have been widely regarded as a major threat to sustainable growth in agricultural production in both developed and developing countries (Bennett 1931; Kellogg 1948; Pimentel et al. 1976; Pimentel et al. 1995a).[5] It has been projected to become an even more severe constraint into the future (Pimentel et al. 1995a). It has been suggested, for example, that, by 2050, it may be necessary to feed "twice as many people with half as much topsoil" (Harris 1990: 115).[6]

Attempts to assess the implications of erosion on agricultural production confront serious difficulties. Water and wind erosion estimates are measures of the amount of soil moved from one place to another rather than the soil lost to agricultural production. Most studies do not provide the information necessary to estimate yield loss from erosion and degradation. Even in the United States, credible national soil erosion measures are available only for three years (1982, 1987, and 1992). These studies, conducted by the U.S. Department of Agriculture Soil Conservation Service, now the Natural Resources Conservation Service, indicate that the rate of soil erosion had declined by 24 percent between 1982 and 1992, presumably because some 30–35 million acres of highly erosive land was put in the Conservation Reserve. Only the 1982 studies included estimates of the yield loss from erosion. The estimates indicated that, if the 1992 erosion rates continued for one hundred years, the yield loss at the end of the period would amount to only 2–3 percent (Crosson 1995a, 1995b).

The extent of soil degradation and loss and its impact on crop production in developing countries is even less well understood than in the United States. The estimates of soil erosion and degradation for developing countries that appear in the literature are typically based on expert opinion rather than carefully designed and adequately monitored experiments. R. Lal (1984) indicated fifteen years ago that the information needed to assess the productivity effects of soil erosion in developing countries was not available for major soils and crops. As far as I have been able to determine, information on the effects of soil loss and degradation is still lacking (Anderson and Thompapillia 1990). Studies conducted by Peter Lindert (1996, 1998, 1999) in China and Indonesia provide the only long-term evidence I have been able to identify on the impact of soil loss in developing countries. These studies indicate, somewhat surprisingly, that, while there has been some decline in soil organic matter and nitrogen, there has been little or no loss of topsoil or in productive capacity over the fifty-plus years covered by his study (Lindert 1996, 1998, 1999). A careful review of the international literature by Crosson suggests that yield losses at the global level might be roughly double the rates estimated for the United States (Crosson 1995a).

The fact that the data is so limited should not be taken to suggest that soil erosion is not a serious problem. But it should induce some caution in accepting some of the more dramatic pronouncements about the inability to sustain agricultural production (National Research Council 1993). The impact of human-induced soil degradation and loss is not evenly distributed across agroclimatic regions, either in developed or developing countries. What I do feel comfortable in concluding is that the impacts on the resource base and on regional economies from soil erosion and degradation are local rather than global. It is unlikely that soil degradation and erosion will emerge as important threats to the world food supply in the foreseeable future. Where soil erosion does represent a significant threat to the resource and the economic base of an area, the gains from implementation of the technical and institutional changes necessary to reclaim degraded soil resources, or at least to prevent further degradation, can be quite substantial.

WATER

During the last half-century, many countries have been undergoing a transition in which water is becoming a resource of high and increasing value. In the arid and semiarid areas of the world, water scarcity is becoming an increasingly serious constraint of growth of agricultural production.[7] The change in the economic value of water is the result of the very large increases in withdrawal of water for domestic and industrial purposes and, most importantly, for irrigation. The International Water Management Institute lists sixteen countries, with a total population of 361 million, located primarily in the Middle East and North Africa, that were experiencing absolute water scarcity in 1990. The Institute projected that, by 2025, an additional twenty-three countries, primarily located in Africa, with a 1990 population of 345 million, plus Northern China and Western India, where another 360 million people live, will experience either absolute or severe water scarcity.[8] The International Water Management Institute projects a decline in withdrawals of water for irrigation in almost all of these areas between 1990 and 2025.

During the last half-century, irrigated area in developing countries more than doubled, from 100 million to almost 200 million hectares. About half of developing country cereal production is grown on irrigated land (Alexandratos 1995). The issue of the relationship between water scarcity and food production has generated a substantial debate. It has been suggested that impending water shortages in northern China will be so severe by 2025 that China will need to import between 210 and 370 million metric tons of grain per year to meet the demand arising out of population and income growth (Brown and Halweil 1998). The International Water Management Institute studies indicate that northern China will experience absolute water scarcity, while southern China will have surplus water.

Much of public sector irrigation investment has been devoted to the development (and rehabilitation) of gravity irrigation systems. In most arid regions, the topography that is best suited to the development of large-scale irrigation systems has already been exploited. Investment costs of adding surface irrigation capacity have risen by several multiples during the last half-century. It is unlikely that there will be substantial new investment in large-scale, gravity-fed irrigation systems in the foreseeable future unless there is a substantial long-term rise in food prices.

In spite of the large public investment in gravity irrigation systems, the area irrigated by using tube wells to pump groundwater has expanded even more rapidly. In many respects, pump irrigation from aquifers is an ideal form of irrigation. The water is stored underground with no loss from evaporation. Water is generally available during the dry season even during drought years, when reservoirs for surface irrigation may be dry. Access to water is under the control of individual producers rather than of an often inefficient and corrupt irrigation bureaucracy.

There are substantial spillover effects or externalities in both surface and groundwater systems that impact directly on agricultural production. One of the most common problems of surface water systems is waterlogging and salinity resulting from excessive water use and poorly designed drainage systems. In the Aral Sea Basin in Central Asia, the effects of excessive water withdrawal for cotton and rice production, combined with inadequate drainage facilities, has resulted in waterlogging and salinity in irrigated areas and contraction of the Aral Sea, which threatens the economic viability of the region.[9] Another common externality results from extraction of water from aquifers in excess of recharge, resulting in lowering of the groundwater level and rising pumping costs. In some countries, these spillover effects are sufficient to offset the contribution of expansion of irrigated area to agricultural production.

The institutional arrangements under which producers obtain access to water contribute to inefficient water use. They not only are an important source of negative spillover effects but also have failed to induce the development and adoption of technology that would lead to growth of water productivity comparable to the increases that have occurred in output per hectare or output per worker in agriculture. The design of effective institutional arrangements to induce improvements in water efficiency and productivity will not be easy. The reforms that are typically suggested include elimination of subsidies, design of "constructed markets" to allocate surface water more efficiently, and a system of quotas, charges, and taxes to reduce groundwater withdrawals to a sustainable level (National Research Council 1992; Easter et al. 1998). It is possible to identify some successes from such efforts, but in general it has been difficult to design reforms that are both economically and politically viable. Transaction costs in constructed markets are often high. Water use typically involves a wide variety of public values that involve third parties. It seems clear, however, that the rising economic value of water and the constraints on water withdrawals that can be anticipated can be expected to induce more intensive institutional reform efforts.

PEST CONTROL

Pest control has become an increasingly serious constraint on agricultural production in spite of dramatic advances in pest control technology over the last half-century. The major pests of crops and animals include insects, pathogens, and weeds. Strategies include cultural control, biological control, pest-resistant crop varieties, and chemical control (Conway 1997; Palladino 1996; Ruttan 1982a).

Before the latter decades of the nineteenth century, farmers relied almost exclusively on cultural methods such as crop rotation in their efforts to control pests. Chemical controls began in the 1870s with the development of arsenical and copper-based insecticides. Use of biological control dates from the late 1880s with the introduction of the vedelia beetle (from Australia) to control a California citrus pest, the cottony cushion scale. Efforts also were made to identify, develop, and introduce pest-resistant crop varieties and animal breeds.

Pest control strategies changed dramatically as a result of the development of dichlorodiphenyl-trichlorethane (DDT) in the late 1930s and its use, during World War II, to protect American troops against typhus. Early tests found DDT to be effective against almost all insect species and relatively harmless to humans, animals, and plants. It was effective at low application levels and was relatively inexpensive. The effect was to direct the research efforts of economic entomologists, and the attention of funding agencies, away from fundamental research on insect biology, physiology, and ecology, as well as from the development of alternative methods of insect pest control. Chemical companies rapidly expanded their research on synthetic organic insecticides as well as chemical approaches to the control of pathogens and weeds.

Problems of negative externalities were encountered shortly after the introduction of DDT. When DDT was introduced in California to control the cottony cushion scale, its introduced predator, the vedelia beetle, turned out to be more susceptible to DDT than the scale. In 1947, just one year after its introduction, citrus growers, confronted with a resurgence of the scale population, were forced to restrict the use of DDT. In Peru, the cotton boll worm quickly built up resistance to DDT and other chlorinated hydrocarbon pesticides. Producers then turned to the more recently developed, and much more toxic, organophosphate insecticides, which again selected for resistant strains of the boll worm. In the meanwhile, natural predators were almost completely exterminated. Cotton production collapsed and was revived only after a program to regulate insecticide use was implemented (Palladino 1996). Concerns about the externality effects of the new pesticides emerged first in the United States and other developed countries. The adoption of the high-yielding Green Revolution cereal varieties in developing countries was associated with a dramatic increase in pesticide use. When yields were low, there was little benefit from pest control. As yields rose, the economic incentive to adopt chemical pest control technologies also rose.

During the 1950s, an increasing body of evidence suggested that the benefits of the pesticides introduced in the 1940s and early 1950s were obtained at a substantial cost. The costs included not only the increase in resistance to pest control chemicals in target populations and the destruction of beneficial insects, but also the direct and indirect effects on wildlife populations and on human health. In the early 1960s, public concern about these effects was galvanized by Rachel Carson's dramatic revelations of the effects of the new insecticides (Carson 1962). During the 1960s and early 1970s, the view emerged to the effect that a coalition of chemical manufacturers, agricultural interests, and economic entomologists at public universities were engaged in a "pesticide conspiracy" to block the technical and institutional changes necessary to achieve a more economically viable and ecological benign pest control strategy (Van den Bosch 1978; Perkins 1982).

The solution to the pesticide crisis offered by the entomology community was Integrated Pest Management (IPM). IPM involved the integrated use of some or all of the pest control strategies referred to above. It is more complex for the producer to implement than spraying by the calendar. It requires skill in pest monitoring and understanding of insect ecology. And it often involves cooperation among producers for effective implementation.[10] At the time IPM began to be promoted as a pest control strategy in the 1960s, there was very little IPM technology available to be transferred to farmers. IPM represented little more than a rhetorical device to paper over the differences between economic and ecological entomologists. By the 1970s, sufficient research had been conducted to provide the knowledge to successfully implement a number of important IPM programs (Conway and Pretty 1991). However, exaggerated expectations about the possibility that dramatic reductions in pesticide use could be achieved without significant decline in crop yields as a result of adoption of IPM have not been realized (Curtis et al. 1991; Pimentel et al. 1991; Gianessi 1991).

Integrated approaches to weed management evolved later than for insect pests, in part because emergence of resistance to chemical herbicides occurred much more slowly than resistance by insect pests to insecticides. By the mid-1990s, however, the development of genetically engineered herbicide-resistant crop varieties resulted in a new set of concerns. In some cases, herbicide-resistant crops may have beneficial effects on the environment—when, for example, a single broad-spectrum herbicide that breaks down rapidly in the environment is substituted for several applications of preand postemergence herbicides, or for a herbicide that is more persistent in the environment. When a single herbicide is used repeatedly, however, it does pose the danger of selecting for herbicide-resistant weeds. The impact of agricultural intensification and the coevolution of pathogens, insect pests, and weeds will continue to represent a major factor in directing the allocation of agricultural research efforts to maintenance research (Plucknett and Smith 1986).

CLIMATE CHANGE

In the late 1950s, measurements taken in Hawaii indicated that carbon dioxide (CO_2) was increasing in the atmosphere. Beginning in the late 1960s, computer model simulations indicated possible changes in temperature and precipitation that could occur due to human-induced emission of CO_2 and other "greenhouse gases" into the atmosphere. By the early 1980s, a fairly broad consensus had emerged in the climate change research community that energy production from fossil fuels could, by 2050, result in a doubling of the atmospheric concentration of CO_2, a rise in global average temperature by 1.5–4.5°C (≈ 2.7–8.0°F), and a complex pattern of worldwide climate changes. Since the beginning of the 1980s, a succession of studies have attempted to assess how an increase in the atmospheric concentration of CO_2 could affect agricultural production (Clark and Munn 1989; Parry 1990; Rosenzweig and Hillel 1998).

There are three ways in which increases in CO_2 concentrations in the atmosphere may affect agricultural production. One is that increased CO_2 concentration in the atmosphere may have a positive effect on the growth rates of crop plants (and weeds) through the CO_2 "fertilization effect" and by decreasing the rate of transpiration. The magnitude of the CO_2 fertilization effects remain highly uncertain. Extrapolations are limited to model-based estimates that use data from greenhouse or small-scale field experiments. And it has not yet been possible to separate the effects of the increase in CO_2 concentrations over the last half-century from other factors that have contributed to higher yields. A second way that agricultural production could be impacted is that higher temperatures could result in a rise in the sea level, resulting in inundation of coastal areas and the intrusion of salt water into groundwater aquifers and surface waters. Low-lying coastal agricultural areas in Bangladesh, for example, could be impacted very severely.

The largest impacts on agricultural production will be due to the effects of CO_2-induced changes in temperature, rainfall, and sunlight. These effects can be expected to vary greatly across agroclimatic regions. However, greenhouse-induced warming is expected to be greatest in high midlatitude regions (>45°) and high latitudes (>60°). Subtropical and tropical regions will experience less extreme temperature changes. Monsoon rains are likely to penetrate farther northward. Northern areas in which production is presently constrained by length of the growing season, such as the northern fringes of the Canadian prairie provinces, could expect both higher yields and an expansion of area devoted to cereals and forage plants.

There has been a substantial change in estimates of the impact of global climate change on crop yield and agricultural production. Estimates made in the late 1980s and early 1990s generally projected rather substantial negative impacts at the global level (Parry 1990). More recent studies have tended to project impacts ranging from slightly negative to slightly positive (Mendelsohn et al. 1994; Adams et al. 1998). These more positive estimates have been due primarily to two changes in the modeling of climate change. One has been the incorporation of assumptions about the positive effects of CO_2 fertilization. As noted above, these assumptions remain controversial because they involve extrapolation from greenhouse or very-small-scale field experiments. The second change has been due to replacing the static production function or "dumb farmer" approach employed in earlier models with estimates of farmers' rational responses to climate change, including changing in cropping systems and adoption of technology. As a caveat, several of the models suggest that, while modest changes in global average surface temperature in the 2.5° range, for example, could have a net positive effect, larger increases, in the 5° range, could have a negative effect on agricultural production.[11]

The modeling efforts continue, however, to employ a "dumb scientist" assumption. The behavior of public and private sector suppliers of knowledge and technology has not yet been incorporated in the models and estimates. Efforts to incorporate endogenous or induced technical change into climate change models have been limited by the tractability of the models (or the modelers). The only successful empirical effort I am aware of is a study by Evenson and Alves in Brazil (Evenson 1988). The Evenson-Alves model incorporates not only the choice of technology by farmers in response to climate change but also responses by the public and private suppliers of technology. The study indicates that, in Brazil, the effect of climate change alone would be to depress production in the North, Northeast, and Center-West. In contrast, many areas in the Center-East, the South, and the coastal regions would benefit. When the technical change induced by the climate change is taken into account, it is expected to compensate for the effect of climate change in the more disadvantaged regions, while the more favored regions will benefit from both the climate change and technical change.

None of the models gives adequate attention to the indirect or interactive effects of climate change. The limited assessments that have been made suggest that, as environmental stress intensifies as a result of warmer (and, in some areas, more humid) climates, crops will become more vulnerable to weeds, insects, and plant diseases (Rosenzweig and Hillel 1998). The incidence and severity of soil erosion, changes in rainfall, surface water storage, groundwater recharge, the incidence of pests and pathogens, or frequencies of extreme events, such as drought or floods, or climate variability have not been incorporated effectively into the climatic change models. It is possible that actions taken to mitigate global climate change, such as land-intensive approaches to carbon sequestering, substitution of fuels based on agricultural raw materials for petroleum-based fuels, and efforts to control carbon, nitrous oxide, and methane emissions, could have a larger negative effect of crop and animal production than the direct impacts of climate change.

I have not, in this paper, discussed the potential impacts of health constraints on agricultural production. Improvements in nutrition associated with growth in agricultural production has, in many developing countries, contributed to lower infant mortality and increased life expectancy. But the increased use of insecticides and herbicides associated with agricultural intensification has also had negative effects on the health of agricultural workers. There are also important health effects, in both urban and rural areas, of the intensification of industrial production associated with atmospheric, water, and soil pollution. There are also the health effects associated with the emergence of new diseases such as AIDS and the emergence of drug resistance by older parasitic and infectious diseases. It is not too difficult to visualize situations in particular villages in which the coincidence of several of these health factors could result in serious threats to agricultural production. It is more difficult, but not completely impossible, to visualize health threats becoming a serious constraint on national agricultural production (Lederberg 1996; Ruttan 1994b; Pimentel et al. 1998).

Perspective

What inferences do I draw from this review of resource and environmental constraints on the transition to agricultural sustainability? There will, even beyond the middle of the twenty-first century, continue to be great diversity among countries and regions in the transition to agricultural sustainability. It seems unlikely that the conditions projected in the Barbarization Scenario will be completely eliminated or that the conditions projected in the New Sustainability Scenario will be more than partially realized (Figure 13.1).

It is unlikely that soil loss and degradation will represent a serious constraint on global agricultural production over the next half-century. But soil loss or degradation could become a serious constraint on production on a local or regional scale in some fragile resource areas. This possibility will be greatest if slow productivity growth in robust resource areas should lead to intensification or expansion of crop and animal production in fragile resource areas—that is, tropical rain forests, arid and semiarid regions, and the high mountain areas. In some such areas, however, the possibility of sustainable production can be enhanced by irrigation, terracing, careful soil management, and changes in commodity mix and farming systems.

It is also unlikely that lack of water resources will become a severe constraint on global agricultural production in the foreseeable future. But in fifty to sixty of the world's most arid countries, plus major regions in several other countries, competition from household, industrial, and environmental demands will result in a reallocation of water away from irrigation. In many of these countries, increases in water use efficiency and changes in farming systems will permit continued increases in agricultural production. But it seems reasonable to expect that, in a number of countries, the reduction in irrigated area will be large enough to result in significant reductions in agricultural production. Since these countries are among the world's poorest, some may have great difficulty in meeting food security needs from either domestic production or food imports.

The problem of pest and pathogen control may have more serious implications for sustainable growth in agricultural production at a global level than either land or water constraints. Both the development of resistant crop varieties and chemical methods of control tend to induce target pest or pathogen resistance. In addition, international travel and trade will result in rapid diffusion of traditional and newly emerging pests and pathogens to favorable environments. As a result, new pest control technologies must constantly be replaced by a succession of resistant varieties and chemical (or biochemical) agents. As a result, an increasing share of a constant research budget will need to be devoted to maintenance research—the research required to sustain existing productivity levels.

Recent projections of the impact of climate change on global agricultural production are much more optimistic than projections made a decade ago. The scientific and empirical basis for the more optimistic projections is, however, much too fragile to serve as a secure foundation for policy. There is great uncertainty about the rate of climate change that can be expected over the next half-century. All of the projections employ assumptions that are only weakly grounded in experience. None of the models gives adequate attention to the synergistic interactions among climate change, soil loss and degradation, groundwater and surface water storage, and the incidence of pests and pathogens. These interactive effects could add up to a significantly larger burden on sustainable growth in production than the relatively small effects of each constraint considered separately. A point made repeatedly in this paper is that, while the constraints discussed do not represent a threat to global food security, they may, individually or collectively, become a threat to growth of agricultural production at the regional and local level in a number of the world's poorest countries. This means that the transition to agricultural sustainability will, given the uncertain future, depend on the maintenance and enhancement of capacity for technical and institutional innovation. A primary defense against the uncertainty about resource and environmental constraints is agricultural research capacity. Research capacity represents the "reserve army" to deal with uncertainty. The erosion of capacity of the international agricultural research system will have to be reversed; capacity in the presently developed countries will have to be at least maintained; and capacity in the larger developing countries will have to substantially strengthened. Smaller countries will need, at the very least, to strengthen their capacity to borrow, adapt, and diffuse technology from countries in comparable agroclimatic regions. It also means that more secure bridges must be built between the "island empires" of agriculture, environment, and health.

If the world fails to meet the challenge of a transition to sustainable growth in agricultural production, the failure will be at least as much in the area of institutional innovation as in the area of resource and environmental constraints. This is not an optimistic conclusion. The design of institutions capable of achieving compatibility between individual, organizational, and social objectives remains an art rather than a science, The incentive compatibility problem has not been solved analytically, even at the most abstract theoretical level (Hurwicz 1973, 1998). At our present stage of knowledge, institutional design is analogous to driving down a four-lane highway looking at the rearview mirror. We are better at making course corrections when we start to run off the highway than at using foresight to navigate the transition to sustainability.

Notes

Vernon W. Ruttan, *Proceedings of the National Academy of Sciences* 96 (May 1999): 5960–67. This paper was presented at the National Academy of Sciences colloquium "Plants and Population: Is There Time?" held December 5–6, 1998, at the Arnold and Mabel Beckman Center in Irvine, CA. The author is indebted to Randolph Barker, Pierre Crosson, and Gretchen Daily and to the participants in the University of Minnesota Agricultural Development Workshop for comments on an earlier draft of this paper.

1. In this section, I draw on my participation in the work of the National Research Council (1999). See also Hammond 1998 and Raskin and Gallopin et al. 1998. For the evolution of the concept of sustainability, see S. Lele 1991 and Ruttan 1994a.
2. In this and the following sections, I focus primarily on supply-side constraints on agricultural production, in contrast to the paper by D. G. Johnson (1999), which emphasizes demand-side constraints.
3. See the papers by Cassman 1999.
4. Several students have presented more optimistic perspectives. See, for example, Waggoner 1994. I find it somewhat surprising that I find it so difficult to share the current optimism about the dramatic gains to be realized from the application of molecular genetics and genetic engineering. My first major professional paper was devoted to refuting the pessimistic projections of the early and mid-1950s (Ruttan 1956).
5. Land degradation is a broader concept than erosion. It includes areas affected by soil degradation; drylands with vegetation degradation but no soil degradation; and degraded moist tropical forest lands (Daily et al. 1995).
6. For a very useful introduction to the issues discussed in this section, see the exchange between Crosson (1995a, 1995b) and Pimentel et al. (1995b).
7. For a useful review, see Seckler et al. 1999. See also Food and Agriculture Organization 1995 and Raskin and Gleick et al. 1998. The study by Raskin and Gleick et al. gives more explicit attention to withdrawals for domestic, industrial, and environmental purposes. In arid regions in both developing and developed countries, use of water to protect instream environmental values is increasingly competitive with withdrawals for irrigation.
8. Countries characterized by absolute water scarcity do not have sufficient water resources to maintain 1990 levels of per capita food production from irrigated agriculture, even at high levels of irrigation efficiency, and also meet reasonable water needs for domestic, industrial,

and environmental purposes by 2025. Countries characterized by severe water scarcity are in regions in which the potential water resources are sufficient to meet reasonable water needs by 2025, but only if they make very substantial improvements in water efficiency and investments in water development. The International Water Management Institute study assumes that, when withdrawal exceeds 50 percent of annual water resource flows, the costs of further water resource development are likely to be prohibitive (Seckler et al. 1999).

9. One of the most comprehensive efforts to identify the world's most threatened regions was organized by a group of scholars from the Department of Geography at Clark University (Kasperson et al. 1995). For the Aral basin study see Glazovsky 1995. Although the Aral Sea basin was the most severely affected of the nine studied, two other regions were characterized as "endangered," and the patterns of resource exploitation in the other six were judged to be not sustainable.
10. The elements of the very successful program to control cotton pests (boll weevil, pink bollworm, and tobacco budworm) on the high plains of Texas included (1) establishment of a uniform planting period and adoption of short-duration varieties; (2) irrigation before planting; (3) application of insecticide only in areas in which high bollworm populations are expected; (4) selective application of an organophosphate insecticide during harvest; (5) defoliation of mature crops (so all bolls open at the same time); (6) use of mechanical strippers (to kill larvae) in harvesting; (7) shredding of stalks and plow down immediately after harvest; and (8) imposition of fines on uncooperative producers. Implementation of the program involved organizing a pest control district with responsibility for enforcement (Pimentel et al. 1991).
11. The Mendelson, Nordhaus, and Shaw model (Mendelson et al. 1994) has also been criticized for underestimating the impact of global climate change on agriculture in irrigated areas by giving inadequate attention to the way water is currently used due to distortions associated with water allocation and pricing (Fischer and Hannenan 1998).

CHAPTER 14

The New Growth Theory and Development Economics

A SURVEY

Vernon W. Ruttan

Both growth economics and development economics emerged as distinct fields of inquiry in the early post–Second World War period. Growth economics emerged out of a concern with the preservation of full employment in modern capitalist economies. Development economics focused on growth initiation and acceleration in less developed traditional societies. Growth economics was committedly macroeconomic in orientation and the province of the practitioners of "high theory." Development economics was more microeconomic in orientation and drew on knowledge from related research in anthropology, sociology, and political science and on the insight of practitioners (Krugman 1996).

There has been an uneasy relationship between these subdisciplines. Growth economists have tended to view the development economics literature as lacking in rigor and burdened with irrelevant organizational and behavioral detail. Development economists have often felt that the only message growth economists were sending them was to get interest rates (and other prices) right. After a hiatus of over two decades there has emerged, since the mid-1980s, renewed interest in the theory of economic growth. With the emergence of a new and richer growth economics literature the possibilities of a more fruitful dialogue between growth economics and development economics now may be possible. The purpose of this article is to address the question, what should development economists learn from the new growth economics?[1]

There have been three waves of interest in growth theory in the last half century. The first was stimulated by the work of Harrod (1939, 1948) and Domar (1946, 1947). The second wave began in the mid-1950s with the development by Solow (1956) and Swan (1956) of a neoclassical model of economic growth.

The third wave was initiated in the mid-1980s by Romer (1983, 1986) and Lucas (1988, based on his 1985 Marshall Lecture).[2]

Keynsian and Neoclassical Growth Economics

The question posed by Harrod and Domar, using somewhat different terminology, was under what circumstances is an economy capable of achieving steady-state growth? This question had forced itself on to the economic agenda by the Great Depression of the 1930s and the expectation that the end of the Second World War would be followed by renewed instability. In the Harrod-Domar view instability in economic growth was the result of failure to equate a "warranted" and a "natural" rate of growth. The warranted rate of growth is dependent on the savings rate and on a given capital requirement per unit of output. The natural rate is the maximum long-run sustainable rate of growth. It is determined by the rate of growth of the labor force and the rate of growth of output per worker. This central proposition of the Harrod-Domar model arises from the assumption that investment is both capacity creating and income generating.

An attraction of the Harrod-Domar model was that it attempted to study long-run growth with the tools of Keynesian economics that had recently become familiar to economists. Use of the model diffused rapidly to the planning agencies of many newly independent countries. It seemed to confirm the widely held belief among development economists and planners that the transition from slow to rapid growth required a sustained rise in the rate of savings and investment.[3] It provided a rationale for interventions designed to raise savings rates and encourage investment in heavy industry in order to remove the constraints on production resulting from capital equipment. And it provided the conceptual foundation for the two-gap (in savings and foreign exchange) model developed by Chenery and associates to estimate foreign aid requirements of developing countries (Chenery and Strout 1966). It was also interpreted as consistent with the view that achieving sustained growth would be more difficult for capitalist economies than for economies where the central planning apparatus would have more direct access to the instruments needed to force a rise in the saving rate and to allocate investment to its most productive uses.[4]

The second wave in the development of modern growth theory began with the neoclassical model introduced by Robert M. Solow (1956) and Trevor W. Swan (1956). Solow (1988: 303) was motivated by skepticism that a sustained rise in the savings rate is the key to the transition from a slow to a fast growth path and by a concern that the fixed capital-output ratio be replaced by a richer and more realistic representation of technology. Solow's departure from the Harrod-Domar model was to substitute a variable capital-output ratio for the fixed coefficient capital-output ratio of the Harrod-Domar model. He insisted that the primary effort in his 1956 paper "is devoted to a model of long run growth which accepts all the Harrod-Domar assumptions except that of fixed proportions" (Solow 1956: 66).

The initial version of the Solow neoclassical model has been succinctly described by Prescott (1988: 7): "The model has a constant returns to scale aggregate production function with substitution between two inputs, capital and labor. The model is completed by assuming that a constant fraction of output is invested." The model was employed in a 1957 paper in which an aggregate two-factor production function was used in accounting for growth in the U.S. economy. To Solow's surprise, and to the surprise of the profession generally, four-fifths of the growth in U.S. output per worker over the 1909–49 period was accounted for by changes in the technology coefficient. The two papers triggered a whirlwind of theoretical and empirical research that lasted well into the 1970s.

In the initial Solow-Swan neoclassical model steady-state growth can hardly be avoided. A country that succeeds in permanently increasing its savings (investment) rate will, after growing faster for a while, have a higher *level* of output than if it had not done so. But it will not achieve a permanently higher *rate* of growth of output (Solow 1988: 308). What were the implications of the Solow neoclassical growth theory and related growth-accounting exercises for development economics? The initial results seemed to completely reverse the earlier Harrod-Domar implications. Technological change replaced growth of capital equipment as the primary source of growth. Subsequent growth-accounting exercises employing broader definitions of capital resulted in somewhat lower estimates of the contribution of technical change. But technical change continued to outweigh growth of physical capital stock by a substantial margin in studies conducted in the United States and other presently developed countries. Research on sources of growth in poor or newly developing countries typically found that a much smaller share of economic growth was accounted for by productivity growth. This was often interpreted as an indication that inappropriate technology transferred from high-wage economies, where it had been developed, to low-wage economies failed to generate as high productivity gains in low-wage as in high-wage economies.[5] In addition research carried out within the neoclassical framework did not shed much light on the driving forces behind the proximate sources of growth—on the determinants of the growth of physical and human capital and technical change.

Endogenous Growth Theory

Massive divergence in absolute and relative per capita income across countries is a dominant feature of modern economic history (Kuznets 1955, 1966b; Maddison 1979; Pritchett 1995; Prescott 1997). The "new" growth economics literature was initially motivated by the apparent inconsistency between the implications of the neoclassical theory and (a) lack of evidence of convergence toward steady-state growth even among presently developed economies (Romer 1983: 3) and (b) by the inability to successfully account for differences in income growth rates or income levels across countries (Romer 1994).[6] "By assigning so great a role to 'technology' as a source of growth, the theory is obliged to assign correspondingly minor roles to everything else, and so has very little ability to account for the wide diversity in growth rates that we observe" (Lucas 1988: 15). Romer (1986: 1003) argued that what is needed is "an equilibrium model of endogenous technical change in which long-run growth is driven primarily by the accumulation of knowledge by forward-looking, profit maximizing agents."[7]

A primary goal of the new growth economics is to build models that can "ensure that the long run growth rate of income depends not only on the parameters of the production and utility functions, but also on fiscal policies, foreign trade policies, and population policies" (Srinivasan 1995: 46).[8] The effect was to challenge the neoclassical assumption that policy can affect the level of economic activity but not the rate of economic growth. In this section I first review the contributions by Romer and Lucas and then some related contributions.

In the initial endogenous growth models advanced by Romer (1983, 1986) long-run growth is driven primarily by the accumulation of knowledge. The production of new knowledge exhibits diminishing returns at the firm level. However, the creation of new knowledge by one firm is assumed to generate positive external effects on the production technology of other firms. Furthermore, the production of consumption goods, which is a function of both the stock of knowledge and other inputs, exhibits increasing returns. The three elements—decreasing returns in the production of new knowledge, externalities associated with new knowledge, and increasing returns in the production of output—ensure that a competitive equilibrium with externalities will exist.[9]

Thus the initial models advanced by Romer abandon the neoclassical assumption of perfect competition and require either constant or increasing returns to capital. An important implication of the model is that the market equilibrium is suboptimal, since the external effects of the accumulation of knowledge is not considered by the firm in making production decisions. Another implication is that factor shares, typically employed as the elasticity coefficients in the neoclassical production function, can no longer be used to measure the contribution of capital and labor. Romer suggests that the typical capital coefficient (0.25) severely underestimates the contribution of capital and that the labor coefficient (0.75) severely overestimates the contribution of labor. In his model the capital coefficients, adjusted to take into account the accumulation of knowledge (or of human capital), would have to be (implausabily) close to one in order to generate the extremely high growth rates of the East Asian NICs (Romer 1987).

Lucas (1988), drawing on Uzawa (1965), proposed a second alternative to the neoclassical model. In his model, human capital serves as the engine of economic growth. He employed a two-sector model in which human capital is produced by a single input, human capital, and in which final output is produced by both human and physical capital. Two alternative human capital models are analyzed. In the first, the schooling model, the growth of human capital depends on how a worker allocates his or her time between current production and human capital accumulation. In the second, the learning-by-doing model, the growth of human capital is a positive function of the effort devoted to the production of new goods.

In both Lucas models there are, as in Romer, in addition to the "internal effects" on the worker's own productivity, "external effects" that are the source of scale economies and that enhance the productivity of other factors of production.[10] In both cases the accumulation of human capital involves a sacrifice of current utility. In the first model this sacrifice takes the form of a decrease in current consumption. In the second it takes the form of a less desirable mix of current consumption goods than could be obtained with slower human capital growth (Lucas 1988: 18). Lucas argues that this deficiency could, in principle, be solved in the first case by subsidizing schooling and in the second case by subsidizing research and development.

In 1990 Romer advanced an alternative endogenous growth model in which he followed Lucas in emphasizing the importance of human capital in the development of new knowledge and technology. He departed from Lucas, and from his own earlier work, by treating technical change as embodied in new producer durables. The basic inputs in the model are capital, raw labor, human capital, and an index of the level of technology. The technology component is disembodied nonrival knowledge that can grow indefinitely. Human capital is the cumulative embodied product of formal education, on-the-job training, and learning-by-doing. The model economy has three sectors: (a) a research sector that uses human capital and the stock of knowledge to produce new knowledge in the form of designs for producer durables; (b) an intermediate goods sector that uses the designs from the research sector together with foregone output to produce the producer durables used in the production of final goods; and (c) a final goods sector that uses raw labor, human capital, and producer durables (but no raw material) to produce final output—which can be consumed or saved as new capital (Romer 1990).

In this model growth in the stock of capital used in the production of final goods takes the form of growth in the number of intermediate inputs rather than in the quality of each input. Growth in the number of intermediate inputs implies monopolistic competition in the market for producer durables and assures external scale economies as a result of the growth in output of each consumer durable. The critical allocative decision is the share of human capital employed in research. As in his earlier model, and in the Lucas models, the optimum rate of growth exceeds the market rate, since the externalities from knowledge creation are not considered by the firm making production decisions.[11]

As his work continued to mature Romer (1993, 1996) has turned to the contribution of ideas as the primary source of economic growth.

> Neoclassical growth theory explains growth in terms of interactions between two basic types of factors: technology and conventional inputs.

> New growth theory . . . divides the world into two fundamentally different types of productive inputs that we can call "ideas" and "things." Ideas are nonrival goods. . . . Things are rival goods. . . . Ideas are goods that are produced and distributed just as other goods are. (Romer 1996: 5–6)

For Romer, scale effects are important because ideas, as nonrival goods, are expensive to develop but are inexpensive to use.[12] Their value increases with the size of the market. This implies that large countries, with large internal markets, have a greater incentive to produce ideas than small countries. As a result large countries can be expected to grow more rapidly than small countries—particularly when small countries burden themselves with the control and regulatory structures that characterize large countries.[13]

What are the implications of the Romer-Lucas inspired endogenous growth literature for development economics? Bardhan (1995: 2985) insists that the most substantive contribution "is to formalize endogenous technical progress in terms of a tractable imperfect-competition framework in which temporary monopoly power acts as a motivating force for private innovations." Griliches (1992: 294) notes the importance of their work in emphasizing that (i) "technical change is the result of conscious economic investments and explicit decisions by many different economic units and (ii) unless there are significant externalities, spillovers, or other sources of increasing returns, it is unlikely that economic growth can proceed at a constant undiminished rate into the future."

In my judgment the most important substantive contribution has been their endogenization of human capital formation. This led to the important analytical result that when investment takes place in an economic environment with increasing returns to scale the marginal product of capital need not decline over time to the level of the discount rate. Thus the incentive to accumulate human and physical capital may persist indefinitely and long-run growth in per capital income can be sustained.

Even more important than the results of their own research has been the stimulus that the Romer-Lucas work has provided for a new burst of theoretical and empirical research in the field of both growth and development economics: by the mid-1990s, several graduate-level textbooks had incorporated and extended the work in growth economics conducted over the previous decade (Barro and Sala-i-Martin 1995; Aghlon and Howitt 1998). At the theoretical level there has been a proliferation of models, each of which attempts to introduce greater realism, in order to account for both a general failure of convergence and the "miraculous" growth of a few countries such as Korea and Taiwan. The theoretical literature has been complemented by efforts to analyze the effects of different national policies, tax rates for example, in accounting for different national growth rates (King and Rebelo 1990). In a later section I turn to the implications of the new growth economics for development.

Trade and Growth

The potentially most important extension of the new growth economics, particularly for development economics, is the synthesis of the new growth economics and the new trade theory by Gene Grossman and Elhanan Helpman. Their contribution is the result of an exceedingly ambitious research agenda that began in the late 1980s (1990a, 1990b, 1991a) and culminated in the publication of Innovation and Growth in the Global Economy (1991b).

Following Romer and Lucas they stress that industrial research not only generates specific proprietary technical information that allows a firm to produce new products, but also contributes to general scientific knowledge, which can be exploited by other firms to develop even better products. To illustrate the point that externalities in R&D activities are essential to maintain growth they develop and analyze two alternative models of technological competition. As in Romer 1990, one innovation takes the form of expanding product variety, while the other takes the form of quality improvement.

Grossman and Helpman first introduce a one-sector closed-economy model in which accumulation can take the form of (a) investment in plant and equipment and (b) in specialized skills by agents. Physical capital is treated as a homogeneous commodity produced by the same means as consumption goods. The physical capital is then used, along with labor and human capital, to produce output. The equilibrium determines an endogenous supply of human capital and a residual supply of unskilled labor. The steady-state stocks of the two types of labor determines long-run rates of growth. Analysis of the model leads to the counterintuitive conclusion that physical capital can play only an accommodating role in long-run economic growth. In the interest of simplicity (and tractability) they then drop capital equipment from their analysis of the closed economy world—and from the rest of the book! Further analysis of factor accumulation and allocation is confined to the two labor categories—unskilled labor and human capital.

In the second half of their book Grossman and Helpman extend these models to analyze the interactions between trade and growth. With each step they introduce greater realism in the assumptions employed in the models. They abandon the traditional assumption employed in growth economics (but not in development economics) that technological opportunities are the same throughout the world.[14] Countries are not characterized by a common production function. They insist that the process of assimilating existing technologies in the less developed countries is not unlike that of creating entirely new technologies in the developed world. Countries in which technological research is carried out acquire a comparative advantage in the form of human capital resource endowments that may persist for some time.

Starting from these more realistic assumptions Grossman and Helpman proceed to show how external relationships affect a country's growth performance: (a) international exchange opens channels of communication that facilitate the transmission of technical information; (b) international competition encourages entrepreneurs in each country to pursue new and distinctive ideas and technology; (c) international integration enlarges the size of the market in which the innovative firm operates; and (d) international trade induces a reallocation of resources (labor and human capital). In this process countries can lose as well as gain from trade. Countries with a larger high-technology sector (and employing labor with a high human capital component) may experience long-term gains relative to countries with relatively abundant supplies of raw labor (Grossman and Helpman 1991b).

In a world in which the Grossman-Helpman assumptions hold, there can be a substantial role for public policy. An appropriate policy regime can help speed the transition from traditional manufacturing into becoming an exporter of high-technology goods. It may also modify the impact on income distribution of the "creative destruction" associated with technical change. The policy instruments discussed by Grossman and Helpman are the conventional instruments that are commonly analyzed in the trade literature—lump sum taxes, subsidies to R&D and on production for export, and tariffs. In spite of the importance they place on technical change, discussion of science and technology policy is exceedingly thin. Grossman and Helpman have pushed their analysis further than the other scholars working in the new growth economic tradition to incorporate the international movement of goods, capital, and ideas. Drawing on Romer and Lucas, they have formerly incorporated "the process of introduction of an ever-expanding set of new goods and technologies" (Bardhan 1995: 2992).

The results obtained by Grossman and Helpman represent an important contribution to the formal analysis of trade and growth. But their analysis is characterized by a curious "industrial fundamentalism."[15] It provides rather "thin gruel" for the appetites of development economists and practitioners. It will be necessary to extend their analysis beyond the rather narrow confines of the industrial sector and embrace a richer institutional environment before their research agenda will be very useful to development economists (Krueger 1997).

Dialogue with Data

The assault by the proponents of the new endogenous growth theory on the neoclassical model was beginning, by the mid-1980s, to generate a substantial backlash. Some of the qualifications were theoretical in nature.[16] Most, however, have challenged the consistency of the empirical implications with growth experience.

Much of the initial empirical work has not attempted to directly test the endogenous growth models but rather to rehabilitate the neoclassical model (Pack 1994: 55, 63). An important landmark in this effort is the cross-country analysis by

Mankiw, Romer, and Weil (1992).[17] The authors first reject the Romer-Lucas characterization of the neoclassical model. When they incorporate saving, population growth rates, and human capital accumulation into the cross-country regressions, along with physical capital and raw labor, Mankiw, Romer, and Weil find that the "augmented" neoclassical model accounts for about 80 percent of the cross-country variation in income. They also find that the augmented model predicts what they term "conditional convergence" across counties.

There have also been several studies that have attempted to explore the sources of growth of the rapidly growing newly industrializing countries of East Asia (NICs)—Hong Kong, Singapore, South Korea, and Taiwan. The results challenge the conventional wisdom that high productivity growth in the manufacturing sectors largely account for the rapid overall rate of economic growth in these countries (World Bank 1993; Kim and Lau 1994; Easterly 1995; Young 1995). Young concludes, from a traditional neoclassical growth accounting exercise, that the very high rates of growth of the East Asian NICs are primarily accounted for by (a) a rise in labor force participation rates, (b) a rise in investment to GDP ratios, (c) improvements in education, and (d) the intersector transfer of labor from agriculture. Annual rates of total factor productivity growth (Hong Kong 2.3 percent; Taiwan 2.1 percent; South Korea 1.7 percent; Singapore 0.2 percent) have been high, but not high enough to explain miracles.

A second line of inquiry questions the ability of familiar public policy instruments to bring about permanent changes in growth rates, at least in the presently developed countries. Islam (1995) employs a dynamic panel data model (combining cross-section and time-series data) with individual country effects. This enables him to incorporate differences in the aggregate production function both across groups of countries (convergence clubs) and for individual countries. Islam's results suggest that growth in each country converges to its own steady-state growth rate, conditional on differences in technology and institutions. He notes that this conclusion is hardly optimistic: "There is probably little solace to be derived from the finding that countries in the world are converging at a faster rate when the points (and growth paths) to which they are converging remain very different" (Islam 1995: 1162).

A number of recent papers have focused on the growth experience of particular counties or regions. C. I. Jones (1995) shows that in spite of permanent changes in a growth-increasing direction of a number of the variables identified as potential determinants of long-run growth in the new growth economics literature (openness to international trade, human capital investment, population growth, and others), they have had little or no impact on growth in the OECD economies during the post–Second World War era. The rate of growth in per capita income in the United States, for example, has remained essentially unchanged during the entire 1880–1987 period. Jones draws the startling conclusion that "either nothing in the U.S. experience since 1880 has had a large persistent effect on the growth rate, or whatever persistent effects have occurred have miraculously been offsetting" (C. I. Jones 1995: 499; Pritchett 1997).[18] And Griliches (1994: 16) has insisted even more strongly: "Knowledge externalities are obviously very important in the growth process but do not help us explain what has happened (in the United States) in the last two decades."

A third line of inquiry has involved attempts to test the returns to scale hypotheses that is central to the new growth economics. In spite of its intuitive plausibility the evidence from cross-industry and cross-county studies provides only minimum support for the role of scale economies as an important source of growth (Burnside 1996; Backus et al. 1992). Backus et al. (1992) have attempted to test the sources of scale economies—learning by doing, investment in human capital, and specialized intermediate inputs—emphasized by Lucas and Romer. In their search for evidence of scale economies from these three sources they find modest support for scale economies in the manufacturing sector but fail to find evidence of economy-wide scale economies.[19] In their cross-country agricultural production function studies for 1960–80 Hayami and Ruttan (1985) found scale economies across conventional inputs (land, labor, capital, and operating inputs) for developed countries but not for developing countries. Using an augmented production function they did, however, find economies of scale across conventional inputs plus human capital for both developed and developing countries. They interpret the evidence of economies of scale as the disequilibrium effects of prior technical change rather than as pure scale economies.

What should development economists learn from this more recent research carried out within a neoclassical framework? When the neoclassical model is extended to incorporate the variables of an augmented production function to explain differences in the level of per capita income or of partial or total factor productivity, reasonable results are obtained (Hayami and Ruttan 1970b; Kawagoe et al. 1985; Mankiw et al. 1992; Mankiw 1995; Pritchett 1997). These advances in our understanding are important. But they are a reflection of surface phenomena—the proximate sources of economic growth. Answers to more fundamental questions, such as why some countries save and invest more than others, why some countries invest a larger share of GNP on education or on R&D, why some countries were able to put the package of high payoff inputs together more effectively than others, or why some countries have responded to shocks (the Great Depression of the 1930s, the food crises of the 1960s, or the oil shocks of the 1970s) more effectively than other countries continue to remain beyond the reach of the models employed by both the neoclassical and the new growth economists (Nelson and Pack 1997). Much of the work in development economics has focused on the changes in technology and institutions that enter into the country-specific term. Both Islam's results and Jones's suggest a high return to the research agenda advanced by Abramovitz (1952), Kuznets (1955), and Rostow (1956, 1960) in the 1950s—a focus on the deeper sources of the technical and institutional changes associated with the "preconditions" and "takeoff" into self-sustained growth.

Growth Economics as Development Economics

It is now time to turn to a fuller assessment of the implications of the new growth economies for development economics.[20] Lucas attempted to answer this question in his 1991 lecture at the European meeting of the Econometric Society (Lucas 1993). He was very explicit about what he wanted to accomplish. He wanted to be able to encompass both the Korean "growth miracle" and the Philippine "growth failure." And he viewed growth miracles as productivity miracles. Just as Solow in the mid-1950s viewed his contribution as a modest modification of the Harrod-Domar model, Lucas viewed his contribution as adapting the neoclassical model to fit the observed behavior of both rich and poor economies. He saw the new growth economics as displacing not only the older neoclassical growth economics, but development economics as well. The new growth economics includes "those aspects of economic growth we have some understanding of, and development (economics) those we don't" (Lucas 1988: 13).

As an exercise in the integration of the several strands of the new growth economics into a coherent system, the Lucas paper is an exciting tour de force. Lucas, Romer, and other practitioners of the new growth economics must be credited with an attempt to reach behind the proximate sources of growth and to treat as endogenous some of the more fundamental sources. This was achieved by importing three concepts that have been conventional in development economics. One was the concept of scale economies, which occupied a prominent role in the early development literature.[21] A second was the insight into the role of human capital advanced initially by development economists.[22] A third was the concept of endogenous technical change, which, under the rubric of induced technical change, had achieved substantial success in the hands of development economists and economic historians in interpreting the rate and direction of technical change.[23]

There are several other concepts that must be imported before the new growth economics can successfully lay claim to success as a "new development economics," or provide new insights for development practice. I list below some of the more fundamental concepts that are employed by development economists but continue to be ignored by practitioners of growth economics. The list is not intended to be exhaustive.

STRUCTURAL TRANSFORMATION

The issue of structural transformation, the transition from a primarily agrarian to an industrial-commercial economy, has represented a core issue in development economics since the publication of Colin Clark's classic work in 1940 (Clark 1940; Jorgenson 1961; Ranis and Fei 1961). The assumptions of homothetic preferences and neutral technical change employed by most growth economists rules out any analyses of structural transformation (Matsuyama 1992; Bardhan 1995). Once these assumption are abandoned, structural change emerges as a central feature of the process of development (Syrquin 1994; Echevarria 1997). An attempt to analyze economic development with a model in which there is no mechanism to generate structural transformation can hardly be regarded as serious. It resembles an attempt to perform *Hamlet* with no role for the Prince of Denmark.[24]

THE DEMOGRAPHIC TRANSITION

The demographic transition is one of the more familiar processes associated with economic development. It strikes one as somewhat negligent that attempts to develop an endogenous theory of per capita income growth have failed to address the issue of growth of population and labor force. This seems particularly negligent given the attention that has been focused on East Asia in the new growth economics literature. Development economists have made substantial progress in constructing endogenous models of family fertility decisions. Less progress has been made in our understanding of such factors as investment in health and nutrition that influence infant and child mortality rates and the growth of human capital (Nerlove 1974; Nerlove and Raut 1977).

NATURAL RESOURCE CONSTRAINTS

While sometimes acknowledged, natural resource constraints are only just beginning to be incorporated into the growth economics literature (Musu and Lines 1995; Echevarria 1996). At the very least it is important to incorporate land (and other natural resource endowments) and environmental constraints into growth models.[25] When environmental effects are more adequately incorporated the comment by Solow (1956: 66) in his classic 1956 paper will become more apt: "The scarce-land case would lead to decreasing returns to scale in capital and labor and the model would become more Ricardian." It is also important to separate those investments in technology development that represent maintenance research and development—the R&D necessary to offset declines in natural resource quality or loss of productivity in biological technology—from R&D investment in productivity-enhancing technical change.[26]

INCOME DISTRIBUTION

The relationship between income distribution and economic development is a central issue in development economics. Much of the earlier literature has focused on the U-shaped Kuznets income distribution curve (Kuznets 1955; Bacha 1977). The conditions under which economic growth leads to a widening or narrowing of income distribution and the conditions under which changes in income distribution enhance or threaten economic growth are the subject of a large literature in development economics (Kanbur 1997). The literature on sources of poverty and poverty alleviation has been enriched by the large literature on entitlements stimulated by A. K. Sen (1981, 1983). Attempts have been made in recent literature to endogenize the mechanisms that generate the Kuznets inverted-U relationship between inequality and income growth (Galor and Tsiddon 1996). But neither the models employed by the neoclassical or the new growth economists have explicitly addressed the issues of poverty and income distribution.

INSTITUTIONAL CHANGE

The formal analytical literature on sources of institutional change remains underdeveloped. A beginning was made in the literature by development economists on land tenure reform in Eastern Europe and West Asia in the 1950s and 1960s (Hayami and Ruttan 1985) Recent advances include the literature on contract choice (Stiglitz 1974; Otsuka et al. 1992) and on the role of property and contract rights in the transition to democracy (Clague et al. 1996). But the success of the new growth economics in endogenizing technical change has not been followed up by an effort to endogenize the process of institutional change or to incorporate institutional design theory.[27] Mancur Olson notes that neither the old nor the new growth literature has successfully confronted the empirical observation that in spite of the widening disparity between rich and poor countries "the fastest moving countries are never the countries with the highest per capita incomes but always a subset of the lower income countries" (Olson 1996: 20). And he insists that the only explanation available for the emergence of the rapidly growing subset of poor countries is institutional change. Prescott (1997: 33) has urged that inquiry be directed to those factors that determine the strength of resistance to transfer and adoption of knowledge and technology.

Why have growth economists been so slow to incorporate such fundamental issues and concepts into growth theory? The answer seems to be that it is primarily because of analytical and modeling tractability. Insistence on working within the narrow constraints of steady-state growth models has represented a fundamental obstacle to building on the rich body of literature initially advanced by development economists.[28] In retrospect it seems clear that a pervasive obsession with the conditions for convergence (or the traverse) to steady-state growth accounts for much of the failure of both the old and the new growth economics to extend its reach to encompass some of the more fundamental sources of economic development.[29]

Furthermore, the distinction between level effects and rate effects, however important analytically, does not carry over well into development economics. The growth obtained by exploiting the transition dynamics from one balanced growth pattern to another is as welcome to a developing country as a source of an improvement in welfare as growth along a balanced growth path (if such exists). For a low-income country, it is not particularly interesting to insist that the "pay-off from a higher saving rate is not a permanently higher rate of growth; it is a permanently higher output per man" (Solow 1970: 20). The distinction between a policy leading to a growth rate effect rather than a level effect will not be obvious to even the best economists employed in national planning or finance agencies or in multilateral development banks (Solow 1997: 81).[30, 31]

Perspective

The new growth economics, like the neoclassical growth economics, has advanced our understanding of the process of economic growth in industrial economies characterized by reasonable stability of expectations regarding factor and product markets, legal institution, and civic culture. It is not about the problems facing the poor economies of the world that have attracted the attention of development economists (Solow 1997: 71). There are, however, more countries today than half a century ago where the institutional arrangements that remain implicit in growth economics prevail. And if development economists pursue their research with appropriate rigor and relevance there may be more as we approach the end of the next half century.

My own sense is that the most significant advances in knowledge about economic development will continue to emerge from research conducted at the micro-level. The real sources of growth that result from efficiency gains, technical change, and institutional reform and design can only be observed and understood by investigations conducted at the household, firm, and sector level. The effects of those technical and institutional changes generate the disequilibrium effects that are captured at the aggregate level in measures of scale economies and total factor productivity growth (Harberger 1990). I am not arguing, however, that development economists and growth economists should continue to follow their natural inclination to ignore each other's work. There needs to be a continuing dialogue between development economists working in the fields of household economics, agricultural economics, labor economics, and industrial organization and the practitioners of growth economics. There is too much interesting and important data being generated by the development process that is begging to be understood and interpreted to confine development economics within the straitjacket of growth economics. Those of us who are development economists or practitioners simply cannot wait until the growth economists are able to incorporate a deeper understanding of the sources of economic development into their models.

Notes

Vernon W. Ruttan, *Journal of Development Studies* 35 (December 1998): 1–26. Earlier drafts of this article have been presented at seminars at Australian National University, the University of Hawaii, and the University of Minnesota. The author has benefited from comments by Christopher Bliss, John Chipman, Jason Christianson, Elamin Elbasha, Yujiro Hayami, Bruce Johnston, D. Gale Johnson, Timothy Kehoe, Gopinath Munisamy, Marc Nerlove, Howard Pack, Stephen Parente, Terry Roe, James Roumasset, Robert Solow, Michael Trueblood, and an anonymous referee.

1. In this article I draw on an earlier paper in which some of the issues are treated in greater detail (Ruttan 1998).
2. For other reviews of the new growth economics literature from a development economics perspective see Bardhan 1993, 1995. For a review from the perspective of economic history see Crafts 1995 and J. G. Williamson 1995.
3. This view was articulated by W. Arthur Lewis (1954: 155): "The central problem of the theory of economic development is to understand the process by which a community which was previously saving 4 or 5 percent of its national income or less converts itself into an economy where voluntary savings is about 12 to 15 percent of national income or more."
4. These views were argued most forcefully by the Indian planner P. C. Mahalanobis (1953, 1955). See also Bhagwati 1966: 203. In the development planning literature it became common to refer to the Harrod-Domar-Mahalanobis model.
5. See, for example, the literature on appropriate technology (Schumacker 1973; Eckhaus 1977, 1987; Stewart 1987a, 1987b).
6. There are a number of useful surveys of the new growth economics literature (Verspagen 1996; Van de Klundert and Smulders 1992; Hammond and Rodriguez Clare 1993; Amable 1994).
7. It should be kept in mind that Romer and Lucas were not the first to attempt to endogenize the process of technical change. Kaldor (1957) advanced a Keynesian model with an endogenous "technical progress function" (Palley 1996). Romer (1986, 1990) and Lucas (1988, 1993) both acknowledge inspiration from Arrow (1962) and Uzawa (1965). But neither Romer nor Lucas refers to the Kaldor article. In the 1960s several attempts were made to rescue neoclassical growth economics from the limitations of exogenous technical change under the rubric of induced technical changes (Fellner 1961; Kennedy 1964; Ahmad 1966). For reviews see Nordhaus 1973, Thirtle and Ruttan 1987, and Ruttan 1997. I find it somewhat difficult to imagine that Romer and Lucas were so unfamiliar with this earlier literature on endogenous technical change that they were forced to reinvent it "from scratch."
8. Srinivasan (1995) points out that the neoclassical growth models could also generate sustained long-run growth in per capita income, even in the absence of technical progress, provided the marginal product is bounded away from zero by a high enough positive number. He also notes that this is not a particularly attractive assumption, "since it implies that labor is not essential for production" (Srinivasan 1995). It also assumes that nonrenewable resources are either not essential or have easily available substitutes.
9. The initial Romer model, and other closely related models, are frequently referred to as closed-economy *AK* models, after the assumed production function ($Y = AK$). In expanded versions of the model, K can be thought of as a proxy for a composite of capital goods that includes physical and human components (Barro and Sali-i-Martin 1995: 146). Amable and Solow have pointed out that this initial Romer model has not been able to avoid the razor-edge balance of the older Harrod-Domar model. If the elasticity of production coefficients of the accumulated factors are greater than one, the growth is explosive (Amable 1994: 30; Solow 1995: 51, 1997).
10. "The spillover effect of the average stock of human capital per worker in the Lucas model and of knowledge in the Romer model are externalities unperceived (and hence not internalized) by individual agents. However, for the economy as a whole they generate increasing scale economies even though the perceived production function for each agent exhibits constant returns to scale" (Srinivasan 1995: 43). In effect Romer and Lucas have completed, or have attempted to complete, the agenda initially advanced by Jorgenson and Griliches (1969). They have substituted a new "black box"—termed "scale effects"—for the old black box of "technical change" as a source of productivity change.
11. A somewhat similar model has been proposed by Aghion and Howitt (1992) in which innovation takes the form of improvements in the quality of intermediate goods that, in turn, improve

the productivity of the intermediate goods in final goods production. This is consistent with Schumpeterian "creative destruction" as each improved producer good takes the place of an older producer good (Amable 1994: 33).

12. There is, however, a large literature that suggests that ideas are much more expensive to transfer than implied by the literature that treats knowledge as a pure public good (Teese 1977; Hayami and Ruttan 1985).
13. In a later paper Romer (1994) extends the model in his 1990 paper to incorporate the introduction of new consumer goods as a source of welfare gains.
14. Romer seems of two minds on this issue. In a comment on Mankiw 1995 he notes: "Mankiw argues that technology is a public good that is available everywhere in the world. I argue that there is ample evidence that this assertion is wrong" (Romer 1995: 315). Yet in his 1993 paper on idea gaps and knowledge gaps he asserts that "people in the industrial nations of the world already possess the knowledge needed to provide a decent standard of living for everyone on earth" (Romer 1993: 546). In our research on technical change in agricultural development Yujiro Hayami and I (Hayami and Ruttan 1985) show that what is available to be transferred to the developing countries is not only technology, which tends to be location specific, but the capacity to develop or adapt technology consistent with the resource endowments and economic environment of poor countries.
15. The share of employment in industry is typically higher in newly industrializing countries than in either the OECD countries or developing countries. For example, the share of the labor force in industry in Korea is approximately 35 percent; in the United States, 26 percent; and in Nigeria, 7 percent (World Bank 1995: 146–48). The simple arithmetic of population and employment growth rates suggest that for lowest-income developing countries with population growth rates in the 2 to 3 percent per year range, exceedingly high growth rates of employment in industry would be required to raise the share of employment in industry from less than 10 percent to 30 percent over a fifty-year period (Dovring 1959).
16. Solow pointed out that Lucas (1988) had emphasized that "a touch of diminishing returns to capital (human capital in this case) would change the character of the model drastically, making it incapable of generating permanent growth. He did not notice that a touch of increasing returns to capital would do the same" (Solow 1995: 49). "With increasing returns the growth of capital became infinite in finite time. Thus Lucas' version of the endogenous growth model is very un-robust. It cannot survive without exactly constant returns to capital" (Solow 1995: 51). See also Solow 1997.
17. See also Barro 1997. There has been a virtual explosion of aggregate cross-country studies since the early 1980s. Levine and Renelt (1992) subjected the studies that had been completed by the early 1990s to a careful sensitivity analysis. They found that almost all of the results were fragile. However, they did find three robust results: (a) a negative relationship between the initial level of per capita income and subsequent economic growth, (b) a positive correlation between the share of investment in GDP and growth, and (c) a positive correlation between the investment share and the ratio of trade to output. Much of the more recent empirical research has abandoned the discipline of the production function for an unstructured "search for variables," such as equipment quality, market distortions, government spending, tax policy, financial capital, trade policy, ethnicity, legal culture, religion, and even distance from the equator (Sala-i-Martin 1997). A reviewer of this paper has pointed out that the negative sign on the per capita income term should not be taken as a sure indicator of rehabilitation of the neoclassical model because it could be picking up the dynamic effects of catch-up or structural change. It should be noted that the macro cross-country studies have completely ignored the sector-level cross-country studies by development economists. For example, a series of cross-country studies for the agricultural sector using augmented neoclassical production functions (including land, labor, capital, intermediate inputs, education, and research and development) have been highly successful in accounting for differences in output and productivity levels among countries (Hayami and Ruttan 1985; Lau and Yotopoulas 1989).
18. Rostow (1956, 1960) had earlier argued that the "preconditions" for economic growth in the United States were established between the 1780s and 1840s. He dates the U.S. "takeoff" into rapid industrial development between 1843 and 1860.

19. Intra-industry trade is sometimes taken as evidence of scale economies. Chipman (1992) has argued, however, that evidence of intra-industry trade is frequently based on aggregation bias from an inappropriate industry classification system that obscures the fact that the great bulk of what is often classified as intra-industry trade consists of trade in distinct commodities. He then goes on to demonstrate that even when commodities are correctly classified, intra-industry trade cannot be taken as evidence of scale economies. Burnside (1996) also stresses aggregation bias in cross-industry studies in the United States that purport to show economies of scale.
20. I do not, in this section, attempt to present an exhaustive exposition of the scope of development economics. A useful tour is presented in the three-volume *Handbook of Development Economics* (Chenery and Srinivasan 1988, 1989; Behrman and Srinivasan 1995). Apparently, as an afterthought, the editors commissioned a final paper in volume 3B on "The Contribution of Endogenous Growth Theory to the Analysis of Development Problems: An Assessment" (Bardhan 1995).
21. Economies of scale played an important role in what Krugman (1993) has termed the "high development theory" of the 1940s and 1950s. Krugman identifies the period of high development theory as beginning the 1943 with the publication, drawing on Harrod (1939) for inspiration, of the "big push" model by Rosenstien-Rodan (1943) and ending with the popularization of ideas of forward and backward linkages by Hirschman (1958). Attempts to implement policies based on these ideas left many developing countries stuck in low-level equilibrium burdened with nonviable capital-intensive industries (Bardhan 1995). For an attempt to rehabilitate the big push approach within the framework of the new development economics, see Murphy, Shliefer, and Vishny 1989.
22. Emphasis on the role of human capital in development thought extends back to at least the 1950s. See, for example, the presidential address to the American Economic Association by Theodore W. Schultz (1961). In an early cross-country analysis, Krueger found that "differences in human resources between the United States and less developed countries accounted for more of the differences in per capita income than all other factors combined" (Krueger 1968: 658). For additional examples, see Bardhan 1993. See also the papers on human resources and labor markets in Chenery and Srinivasan 1988.
23. For reviews of the literature, see Thirtle and Ruttan 1987 and Ruttan 1997.
24. It is hard to overemphasize the importance of structural transformation, particularly the transition from a predominantly agrarian economy to an industrial and then a service economy, in the development literature. The classic empirical studies are Clark 1940 and Kuznets 1966b. For the evolution of thought see Lewis 1954, Jorgenson 1961, Ranis and Fei 1961, Fei and Ranis 1964, Dixit 1973, and Ranis 1988. See also the papers on structural transformation in Chenery and Srinivasan 1988. Because of the importance of structural transformation, development economists have generally preferred to work with two-sector models of the Lewis and Jorgenson and Ranis-Fei type rather than two-sector models in the Uzawa (1961, 1963) tradition. Failure to incorporate the role of growth in agricultural production and of agricultural trade in the early stages of structural transformation represents a serious deficiency in any attempt to understand the development process (Echevarría 1995; Park and Johnston 1995; Tomich et al. 1995).
25. For an empirical exploration of the relationship between environmental indicators and economic growth see Grossman and Krueger 1995. For an attempt to incorporate environmental effects in a closed-economy endogenous-growth model for the United States see Elbasha and Roe 1995.
26. Maintenance research can represent a relatively high share of R&D expenditures in the field of biological technology. The resistance of new crop varieties to pests and pathogens is eroded by the evolution of new races. The effectiveness of new drugs to control animal and human disease is eroded by the coevolution of infectious disease organisms (Ruttan 1982a: 59).
27. For an attempt to treat institutional changes as endogenous see Ruttan and Hayami 1984. The concept of incentive comparable institutional design was introduced by Hurwicz (1972a). For a more recent treatment see Groves, Radner, and Reiter 1987.
28. For a detailed iteration of both the rediscovery and the neglect of ideas initially advanced by development economists see Bardhan 1993. A similar perspective has been advanced by

Romer (1993) in what appears to be a remarkable departure from his papers of the late 1980s. For an example, see Lucas's uncomfortable discussion on the incorporation of the rise in schooling levels in East Asia. He notes that "the percentage of school age children in school has little leverage in explaining differences in growth rates. The fast growing Asian economies are not, in general, better schooled than some of their slow growing neighbors" (1993: 257). He then goes on to note that although schooling levels are increasing in virtually all societies, "it cannot be pursued within a steady state framework" (Lucas 1993: 258).

29. More than twenty-five years ago Solow suggested that the steady state is not a bad place for growth theory to start, but may be a dangerous place for it to end (Solow 1970: 7; see also Hicks 1985: 10). Griliches (1994) made a similar point, somewhat more cautiously, in questioning an excessive commitment to equilibrium economics in his 1994 presidential address to the American Economic Association. See also Nelson 1998.

30. The timescale for transition effects in neoclassical models has generally been estimated to be quite long (Atkinson 1969). They may also be quite difficult to distinguish from rate effects. Rivera-Batiz and Romer (1991) present a model in which economic integration of countries "with identical endowments and technologies" can result in a permanent increase in growth rates primarily because it results in an increase in the extent of the market. For an excellent review see King and Robelo 1993.

31. A promising start toward a more fruitful articulation between growth economics and development economics has recently opened in the work of a group of "new neoclassical" growth economists associated with the Department of Economics at the University of Minnesota and Minneapolis Federal Reserve Bank (Parente and Prescott 1991, 1993, 1994; Backus et al. 1992; Prescott 1997; Schmitz 1993; Chari et al. 1996). Chari, Kehoe, and McGrattan depart from the traditional neoclassical model by abandoning the deterministic transition path between steady-state growth paths in favor of stochastic transition probabilities. Their motivation is that they find little persistence in individual country growth rates. Parente and Prescott are pursuing a research agenda designed to explain differences in per capita income levels rather than growth rates. They invoke institutional constraints on the efficient use of existing technologies and on the development and adoption of new technologies to explain the large and persistent productivity and income gaps that cannot be explained by differences in physical and human capital. For an analysis that is quite similar in spirit to that advanced by the "Minnesota school" but argued more intuitively, see Olson 1996.

CHAPTER 15

An Emerging Agricultural Problem in High-Performing Asian Economies

Yujiro Hayami

1. Introduction

This paper aims to identify the nature of a new agricultural problem emerging in high-performing economies in Asia, as they have advanced from the low-income to a middle-income stage. The "agricultural problem" is here defined as a problem of overriding concern to policy makers with respect to designing and implementing policies for agriculture as part of policies to promote national economic development in their country. As such, it may well be called the "basic problem in determining agricultural policies."

For the past half-century East Asia has been the growth pole of world economy. Japan's jump from a middle-income to a high-income economy associated with very rapid industrialization in two decades from the 1950s was followed by a more compressed growth of so-called Asian NIES—Korea, Taiwan, Hong Kong, and Singapore—from the 1960s. Equally remarkable in this period was the advancement of low-income agrarian economies in Southeast Asia, such as Indonesia and Thailand, to the middle-income stage. Within three decades from the 1960s they were able to achieve significant industrialization, with the major share of their export shifted from primary to manufactured commodities. Shortly after the takeoff of these high-performing economies in the Association of South-East Asia (ASEAN), China began the rise to its "workshop of the world" status with its successful market-oriented reforms. This experience has been followed by another transitional economy in East Asia: Vietnam. Furthermore, it appears that this "East Asian Miracle" (World Bank 1993) is now being transmitted to South Asia, where India and Bangladesh have been accelerating economic growth rates since the 1990s, though they have not yet escaped from the low-income status.

As high-performing developing economies in Asia have advanced or will advance to a middle-income stage, they are bound to face a new agricultural problem.

What is the nature of this problem? What is its root? What policies might be appropriate and effective in solving the problem? These are the questions addressed in this paper.

Following this introduction, section 2 defines three agricultural problems, each corresponding to a major development stage. Section 3 elaborates the political economy mechanism giving rise to a unique problem in the middle-income stage, on which section 4 gives a historical perspective in terms of the experiences of Thailand and Japan. Section 5 discusses the relevance of the East Asian experience to economies in other regions. Finally, section 6 concludes with a plea for more serious research on this problem for sustaining development of high-performing economies in Asia.

2. Three Agricultural Problems

First, the nature of the agricultural problem in the middle-income stage shall be specified in comparison with the problems confronted by the low-income and high-income countries. In his classic treatise, Theodore Schultz (1953) specified the two different agricultural problems confronted by low-income and high-income economies. The "food problem" in his term is the problem faced by low-income economies; these economies, characterized by rapid population growth and high food demand elasticity, are under the constant risk of being beset by shortage in the supply of food relative to the demand; the resulting high food prices pull up the costs of living and the wage rates of workers in nonfarm sectors and thereby suppress industrialization and overall economic growth; therefore, the prime policy concern in low-income economies is to prevent the food shortage from occurring.

Schultz argued that the "farm problem" faced by high-income economies is diametrically different from the food problem; population growth slowdown and food consumption is saturated in the high-income stage, while the food production capacity is strengthened due to their ability to advance technology; therefore, high-income economies have a chronic tendency for food demand to be exceeded by supply, with the result that food prices and farm incomes decline; under powerful lobbying by farmers, agricultural policies in high-income economies is mainly geared toward preventing farm incomes from falling, and their demand for agricultural protection policies tends to be easily accepted because high-income consumers are lenient to high food prices and farm subsidies.

Later, Schultz (1978) identified these two agricultural problems as underlying the policies to exploit or tax agriculture commonly adopted in low-income countries, in contrast to the policies to protect or subsidize agriculture in high-income countries. His hypothesis has been established as a paradigm among agricultural economists as it found support from several empirical studies (Anderson and

Hayami 1986; Hayami 1988; Krueger et al. 1991). Under the serious constraint of foreign exchange common among low-income economies, it is generally not feasible for them to counteract food shortage and rising food prices by increasing commercial imports. Instead, lowering domestic food prices by such means as taxation on food exports, government compulsory procurement of farm products from producers at lower-than-market prices, and accepting foreign food aid for damping in domestic market is commonly practiced in low-income countries for securing the supply of cheap food to nonfarmworkers at the expense of farmers. In contrast, policies to raise agricultural product prices by such means as border protection and domestic production control are commonly used in high-income countries for supporting farmers' incomes at the expense of consumers and taxpayers.

In this paper, the agricultural problem underlying policies to depress food prices and farm incomes in low-income countries is called the "food problem" following Schultz's terminology, but the agricultural problem underlying policies to support farm incomes in high-income countries is called the "protection problem," instead of Schultz's "farm problem" or Hayami's (1988) "agricultural adjustment problem."

Despite the change in terminology, I adopt as the basic framework the Schultz theory on the two agricultural problems. In addition, I propose that it would be useful to identify another agricultural problem specifically faced by middle-income countries. This problem is brought about by a lag in productivity growth in agriculture behind nonagriculture as a result of the successful industrialization that raised these economies to a middle-income stage. At this stage as compared with the previous low-income stage, the food supply capacity rises and factors causing demand growth are weakened, but people's per capita incomes do not yet reach a level at which food consumption is completely saturated, as in the high-income economies. As a result, the terms of trade between agriculture and nonagriculture remain largely stable, despite significant decreases in agriculture's productivity relative to nonagriculture due to rapid progress in industrialization. Therefore, farmers' income level tends to decline relative to nonfarmers', corresponding to the widening intersectoral productivity gap. By observing nonfarmworkers' rapid escape from poverty, farmers who are left behind begin to realize how poor they are, even if their income level did not decrease or even slightly increased from the previous stage. Dissatisfaction of farm population on their remaining to be poor despite visible improvements in other sectors often becomes a significant source of social instability. Thus, at the middle-income stage, it becomes a prime concern of policy makers to prevent rural-urban income disparity from widening. This agricultural problem is here called the "disparity problem." It is by nature the problem of income disparity between the farm and the nonfarm sectors. This problem is looming large and will continue to become more serious among high-performing economies in Asia as they advance to the middle-income stage upon their success in industrialization.

3. The Political Equilibrium of the Disparity Problem

The disparity problem is considered a political equilibrium in which the political influences of farm and nonfarm interests are more or less balanced. Figure 15.1 illustrates how the objective of politicians in designing agricultural policies changes in the process of economic development. The food problem becomes dominant where politicians' major concern for the sake of their staying in office is how to secure low-priced food to urban dwellers; and the protection problem becomes dominant where their major concern is how to keep farmers' income level balanced with non-farmworkers. In contrast, the disparity problem emerges where these two concerns are more or less equally important.

At the stage in which the disparity problem is dominant, the prime concern of politicians is to relieve farmers from poverty. However, "poverty" here means not absolute poverty but relative poverty. Absolute poverty among the farm population is less severe in middle-income countries than in low-income countries. In the middle-income stage, with the progress of industrialization by means of borrowing technology from developed countries, newly risen well-to-do families, including workers employed in large-scale modern enterprises, form a new social class in urban areas enjoying a modern comfortable life. Observing the income difference from the newly risen urban families, farmers become envious and eventually develop a grudge against the social system keeping them in poverty, which may culminate in social disruptions.

This relative poverty problem is closely related with the so-called dual structure that emerged in the process of industrialization. The dual structure refers to the situation characterized by the coexistence of a formal sector consisting of large-scale, capital-intensive enterprises paying high wages to their employees and an informal sector consisting of small-scale, labor-intensive enterprises based on cheap labor. The formal sector is largely closed to laborers in the informal sector, including employees in small-scale enterprises, casual laborers working on

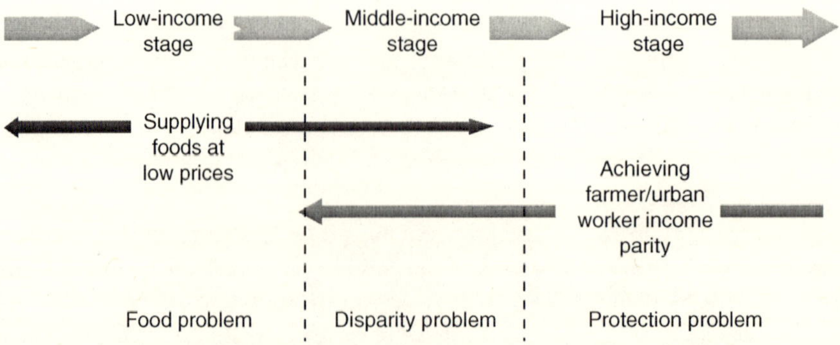

Figure 15.1 The agricultural problems at different stages of economic development.
Source: Hayami and Godo (2004: 12).

a daily contract basis, and self-employed manufacturers and traders. With labor codes and unions exclusively applicable to large-scale enterprises, their labor costs are high despite the abundant availability of low-wage laborers in the informal sector. Therefore, strong incentives are at work among entrepreneurs in the formal sector to increase capital intensity by adopting labor-saving technologies. As a result, employment increases much slower than increases in output. The income gap tends to widen cumulatively between employees in the formal and the informal sectors.

Typically the informal sector functions as a buffer in the labor market. Many small-scale enterprises engage in production as subcontractors of large-scale enterprises. Since employment in the formal sector is largely permanent, large-scale enterprises prefer to reduce order to subcontractors during the economic slump rather than to lay off their own employees. Correspondingly, many laborers in the informal sector who came from farm households lose work opportunities in cities and are forced to return to parents or brothers in home villages. In addition to the economic burden of feeding these returnees, farmers face sharp drops in farm product prices during recessions because of the low price elasticities characteristic of food demand and supply. In this way, during economic recessions, farmers suffer from dire poverty, intensifying their grudge against urban people.

Supported by the sympathy of the intelligentsia, farmers' dissatisfaction may elevate to serious antigovernmental movements, forcing the government to adopt agricultural protection measures. However, unlike in the high-income stage, in the middle-income stage this protection cannot be strong enough to fill up the income gap between farmers and urban workers. Since the shares of agriculture in both national income and labor force still remain large, it is impossible for the government in the middle-income stage to secure sufficient finance to close the growing income gap. In addition, increases in food prices result in a major damage to a large number of small-scale enterprises in urban area, which rely heavily on cheap labor. Developing countries can advance from the low-income to the middle-income stage by technology borrowing from developed countries. However, the successful industrialization by means of technology borrowing tends to result in the formation of the dual structure in the economy and the widening of income disparity between farmers and newly risen urban families.

Under the dictate of this disparity problem, policy makers in middle-income countries are forced to muddle around in search of ways and means to protect farmers within the constraint of the food problem that is still binding because a large number of workers in urban informal sectors are still absolutely poor. As their Engel coefficients are high, high food prices could well raise the cost of living above their meager incomes. The tendency of relative poverty to rise in the middle-income stage can be confirmed in Table 15.1, in which farmers' relative income is measured by dividing agriculture's share in GDP by agriculture's share in employment. In low-income countries, farmer's relative incomes were in the

Table 15.1 **International comparisons of relative incomes of agricultural workers across different stages of economic development**

	(1)		(2)		(3)		(4)=(3)/(2)	
	Per-capita GDP (constant 2000 US$)		*Agriculture's share in economically active population (%) (Na/N)*		*Agriculture's share in GDP (%) (Ya/Y)*		*Agriculture's per-capita income/ whole economy's per-capita income[a] (%) (Ya/Na) (Y/N)*	
	2000	*1965–2000 average annual growth rate*	*1965*	*2000*	*1965*	*2000*	*1965*	*2000*
Developing countries								
Low-income countries								
Ghana	251	–0.2	62	57	44	36	70	63
Nigeria	358	0.3	72	33	55	29	76	86
Kenya	414	1.3	87	75	35	32	41	43
India	450	2.5	74	60	45	25	61	41
Pakistan	531	2.4	65	47	40	26	62	55
Average[a]	401	1.3	72	54	44	30	62	58
Middle-income countries								
Indonesia	800	4.1	71	48	56	16	79	32
China	949	6.6	80	67	38	15	47	22
Philippines	1,002	1.1	61	40	26	16	43	40
Thailand	1,998	4.7	82	56	32	9	39	16

Turkey	2,956	2.0[b]	72[c]	46	42[c]	15	59 [c]	33
South Africa Rp	3,020	0.3	34	10	9	3	27	34
Chile	4,917	2.7	27	16	9	5	32	30
Mexico	5,935	1.9	49	21	14	4	28	20
Average[d]	2,660	3.1	58	37	26	10	42	28
Developed countries								
Korea	10,884	6.3	55	10	39	5	71	49
Spain	14,338	2.8	28[e]	7	14[e]	4	50[e]	60
France	22,548	2.5	13[e]	3	7[e]	3	55[e]	85
Canada	23,220	2.1	8[e]	2	4[e]	2	59[e]	98
UK	24,075	2.1	3[e]	1	3[e]	2	95[e]	168
US	34,599	2.2	4[e]	1	4[e]	2	120[e]	169
Japan	37,409	3.7	19[e]	4	5[e]	1	28[e]	34
Average[f]	26,032	2.6	12[e]	3	6[e]	2	68 [e]	102

Notes

(1) GDP is converted by the average official exchange rate reported by the International Monetary Fund.

(2) Economically active population in agriculture (agricultural labour force) is that part of the economically active population engaged in or seeking work in agriculture, hunting, fishing or forestry.

(3) Agriculture corresponds to divisions 1–5 of the International Standard Industrial Classification and includes forestry and fishing.

[a] Simple average of Ghana, Nigeria, Kenya, India and Pakistan.

[b] 1968–2000 growth rate.

[c] 1968 value.

[d] Simple average of Indonesia, China, Philippines, Thailand, South Africa Republic, Chile and Mexico.

[e] 1971 value.

[f] Simple average of Spain, France, Canada, UK, US and Japan.

Sources: Food and Agriculture Organization (2005) and World Bank (2006).

order of 40–60 percent in 2000, which were not so low compared with those of middle-income countries. In particular, three African economies—Ghana, Nigeria, and Kenya, all of which recorded virtually no economic growth for 1965–2000, experienced no significant decrease in farmer's relative income. In contrast, in India and Pakistan, which recorded moderate economic growth, farmer's relative income dropped slightly. In Indonesia and Thailand, which recorded high growth, having been able to advance from the low-income to the middle-income stage during this period, farmer's relative income declined sharply. It is interesting to observe that in the Philippines, which lagged behind East Asian Miracle growth, farmer's relative income did not significantly decrease. Notably, farmer's relative income increased rather than decreased in high-income economies on average, where the government could afford to allocate sufficient money to support farmers' incomes.

Underlying this widening income gap between farm and nonfarm sectors in the middle-income stage is the rapid shift in comparative advantage away from agriculture to industry, as illustrated in Table 15.2. In this table, changes in comparative advantages are compared among selected countries in terms of labor productivity growth in agriculture relative to that of manufacturing. In developed countries, labor productivity has tended to increase faster in the agricultural sector than in the manufacturing sector, whereas in developing economies labor productivity in manufacturing has tended to increase faster than in agriculture. These observations are consistent with the hypothesis that comparative advantage in agriculture declined in developing countries and increased in developed countries.

Likely underlying this increase in comparative advantage in manufacturing among developing countries is the greater difficulty of technology transfer from developed to developing countries in agriculture than in manufacturing. Because agricultural production is a biological process, it is critically influenced by natural environments, which are difficult to control artificially. Therefore, superior farming methods and plant varieties developed in advanced countries located in the temperate zone cannot readily be applied in developing countries under tropical environments. In contrast, manufacturing production is largely a mechanical process operated in the controlled environments of factories, so its technology is much easier to transfer from developed countries to developing countries. In this way, agriculture's comparative advantage tends to decline in developing countries, especially in middle-income countries achieving rapid industrialization by means of technological borrowing from developed countries.

The speed of decline in agriculture's comparative advantage is likely to exceed the speed of labor transfer from agriculture to manufacturing under the regime of emerging dual structure characterized by the low rate of labor absorption in the formal sector. To that extent the income disparity between farmers and the employees of formal manufacturing and service enterprises could well become a source of major social instability or even disruption.

Table 15.2 **The average annual growth rates of real labor productivities in agriculture and manufacturing in selected countries, 1980–95**

	(1)	*(2)*	*(3)*	*(4) = (2)–(3)*
	Per-capita GDP (US$)	*Average growth rate per year of labor productivity (%)*		*Rate of change in comparative productivity (%)*
		Agriculture	*Manufacturing*	
Developing countries				
Kenya	414	–0.1	0.4	–0.5
India	450	2.3	4.3	–2.0
Pakistan	531	3.1	3.3	–0.2
China	949	3.7	5.1	–1.4
Philippines	1,002	0.4	10.7	–10.3
Turkey	2,956	0.8	4.8	–4.0
South Africa Rep.	3,020	0.9	0.6	0.3
Mexico	5,935	1.5	3.5	–2.0
Average[a]	1,907	1.6	4.1	–2.5
Developed Countries				
Korea	10,884	6.6	6.7	–0.2
Spain	14,338	4.5	3.5	1.1
France	22,548	4.5	2.3	2.1
Canada	23,220	5.8	2.6	3.2
UK	24,075	2.0	3.9	–1.9
US	34,599	2.2	3.5	–1.3
Japan	37,409	3.9	1.9	2.0
Average[b]	23,868	4.2	3.5	0.7

Notes

(1) GDP in 2000 converted by the average official exchange rate reported by the International Monetary Fund.

(2) Productivity in the agricultural sector is measured by FAO's index of agricultural production divided by the economically active population (or labor force) in agriculture.

(3) Productivity in the manufacturing sector is measured by UNIDO's industrial production index divided by employment in the manufacturing sector. For China, for which UNIDO's industrial production index is not available, value added of the manufacturing sector (in 1990 US dollars) is used.

[a] Simple average of Kenya, India, Pakistan, China, Philippines, Turkey, South Africa Republic and Mexico.

[b] Simple average of Korea, Spain, France, Canada, UK, US and Japan.

Sources: United Nations Industrial Development Organization (1997) and Food and Agricultural Organization (2005).

4. Historical Perspectives

A more concrete grasp of the process by which the disparity problem dominates agricultural policy formulation as economies advance from the low-income to the middle-income stage may be obtained by examining histories of the nations that underwent such a transformation. For this purpose the histories of Thailand during the period after the Second World War and of Japan between the First and Second World Wars shall be reviewed in this section.

THE EXPERIENCE OF THAILAND

First, the experience of Thailand is examined as a typical example of high-performing economies in Asia currently experiencing the disparity problem. Indeed, the growth performance of Thai economy in the past half-century was dramatic. Before the 1960s, Thailand was a low-income economy dependent on the production and export of primary commodities, rice above all. Before 1960, average GDP per capita remained largely stagnant at the level of about $500 U.S. (in 1990 prices), with the share of industrial products in total export being only about 10 percent (Douangngeune et al. 2005). However, within only two decades from 1960, Thailand suddenly jumped up to middle-income status based on the success of labor-intensive industrialization; by the end of the 1970s the export share of industrial products rose to about 40 percent, and GDP per capita more than doubled, to the level of about $1,200. Thereafter, the industrial sector in Thailand was further strengthened, beginning to develop high-tech industries such as automobile and electronics. Correspondingly, within only a decade and half before the 1997 Asian Financial Crisis, per capita GDP again more than doubled, and the export share of industrial products exceeded 70 percent. Even though the Thai economy suffered severely from the 1997 crisis, it was able to return to the track of high growth in about three years.

It was inevitable that the rise of Thailand from a low-income to a middle-income country based on dramatic industrial development was associated with the widening income disparity between agriculture and the rest of economy, as already observed in Table 15.1. Increasing income disparity between rural and urban sectors should have been parallel with the widening income gap between workers in urban formal and informal sectors. The disparity increased as the development of capital- and knowledge-intensive industries created a dual structure. Altogether, inequality in income distribution in Thailand, as measured by the Gini coefficient in Figure 15.2, increased significantly as the economy advanced to the middle-income stage.

In this process both farmers and workers in the urban informal sector were not absolutely worse off. Instead, they should have improved their absolute income levels, as reflected in continued reduction in the share of population below the

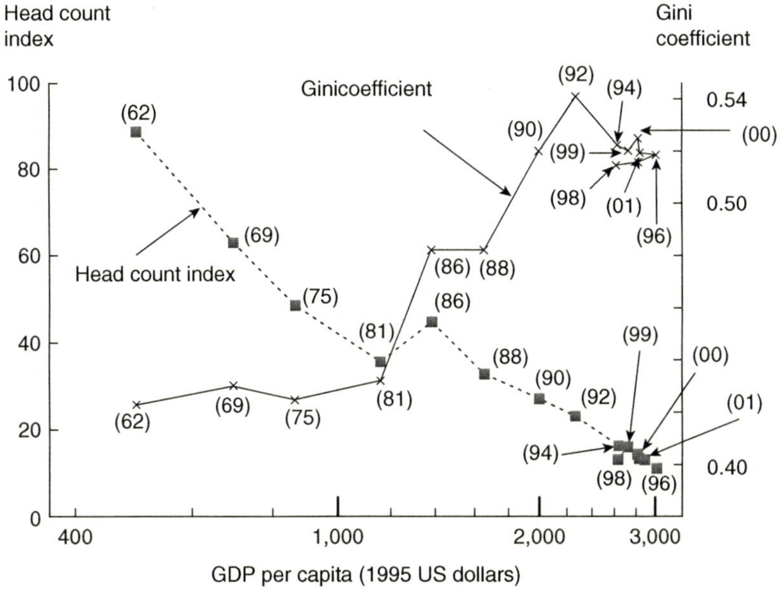

Figure 15.2 GDP growth and poverty indexes in Thailand, 1962–2001.
Note: Within parenthesis is the year of observation.
Sources: Hayami and Godo (2005: 208): GDP per capita originally from World Bank (2003) and Head Count Index and Gini coefficient from Warr (2004).

poverty line (the head-count index) despite increases in the Gini coefficient. Nevertheless, they must have developed frustration about their being poor or becoming poorer in comparison with the rising standard of living of formal-sector employees. Thus, upon successful reduction of absolute poverty, Thailand began to be confronted with the problem of relative poverty.

Since the majority of the poor were staking out subsistence in agriculture, policies to support farmers' incomes became important agenda for politicians to prevent income inequality from rising to a socially disastrous level. Also, the spread of primary education and the improvements of communication and transportation infrastructure in rural areas increased both farmers' awareness of their being "unfairly" treated relative to urban dwellers and their ability to organize political lobbies for demanding a "fair deal." Thus, in the process of advancing from a low-income to a middle-income stage, Thai politicians were pressed to change their policy objective from taxing agriculture for solving the food problem to supporting farmers for solving the disparity problem.

This change in policy orientation in Thailand is most clearly observable in changes in taxation on rice exports. As a major exporter of rice, taxation on rice exports represented a convenient and effective instrument for taxing agriculture for the purpose of income transfer from farm producers to consumers and taxpayers. Several instruments were used for taxing rice exports in Thailand, including quantitative restriction (export quota) and imposition of obligations on exporters to submit a certain share of rice export to the government at lower-than-market prices (the so-called rice reserve requirement), all of which had the effect of lowering domestic prices below international prices. However, by far the most important instrument used by Thai government was the "rice premium," a kind of specific duty levied proportional to export quantities. At the low-income stage, the rice premium was a critically important source of government revenue and, at the same time, acted as a mechanism of supplying rice to domestic consumers at lower-than-world-market prices. Further, it had the power to protect consumers from the vagaries of world market by increasing (reducing) the premium when world market prices rose (dropped) so as to stabilize domestic prices. Thus, the rice premium was a highly effective policy instrument to serve the dual purpose of raising government revenue and securing supply of cheap food to urban consumers by means of taxing agriculture at the stage when the food problem was dominant in the formulation of agricultural policies (Siwamwalla 1987; Siwamwalla and Sethboonsarny 1989).

Figure 15.3 draws changes in rice premium in comparison with changes in the nominal rate of protection (NRP). NRP aims to measure the divergence of the domestic price from the border price. Here it is calculated as the rate of difference

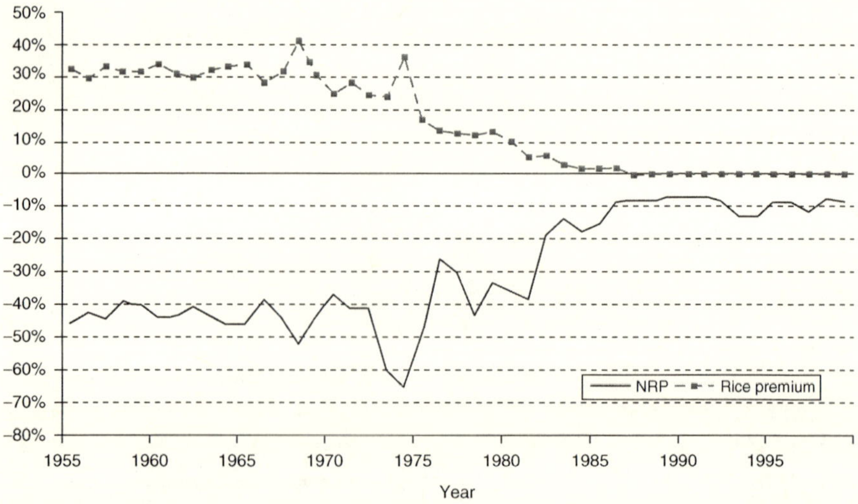

Figure 15.3 Rice premium and nominal rate of protection (NRP) for rice 5% broken in Thailand, 1950–2002.

Note: NRP= (domestic wholesale price − export price fob Bangkok)/export price fob Bangkok.

Source: Export price: IRRI World Rice Statistics (2003); Domestic price: Churchart (1957) for 1950–54, IRRI World Rice Statistics (2003) for 1955–97, and The Bank of Thailand (various years) for 1998–2002; and Rice premium from Churchart (1957), Pookkachatikul and Welsch (1976), and Siamwalla and Sethboonsarng (1989).

of the domestic wholesale price from the export price, fob in Bangkok, for the grade of rice 5 percent broken. To the extent that rice exports are taxed, domestic prices diverge below border export prices, resulting in the negative values of NRP. NRP includes the effects of not only the rice premium but also other taxation instruments, but the dominant role of the premium is evident from high negative correlation between movements in the premium rate and NRP. Data in Figure 15.3 show that before the mid-1970s, when Thailand stayed in a low-income stage, the rice premium rate remained high, at the level of about 30 percent of the border price, and NRP was as high as about 50 percent; this implies that nearly half the values of farmers' rice sales were transferred to nonfarm sectors, including the government, through the export taxation. For a decade thereafter, though, as Thailand advanced to the middle-income stage, the rice premium was reduced, till its abolishment in 1986. This change should have reflected the rise of the disparity problem.

Beside the reduction of export taxation, the emerging need to prevent rural-urban disparity from further widening pressed politicians to install more visible measures for the support of farmers. Under the political instability in the mid-1970s involving student riots and military coups, this pressure culminated in the establishment of the Farmers' Aid Fund in 1974. Based on large rice premium revenues corresponding to sharp increases in world rice prices in the so-called World Food Crisis of 1973–75, the fund tried to undertake several programs to support farmers, such as farmer credit, fertilizer subsidy, and public work using rural labor for the construction of rural infrastructure, including a program organized in a significant scale that attempted to support rice prices through the purchase of rice by government agencies. However, the program totally failed to achieve its intended goal, partly because of its poor design and inefficient implementation due to lack of experience and skill in government procurement agencies but more critically because the budget that the fund could allocate was too small to significantly influence market prices (Siwamwalla 1987). This program was soon terminated, as the rice premium revenue decreased corresponding to declines in world rice prices after the food crisis period.

This failure of the price support program organized by the Farmers' Aid Fund epitomizes the difficulty in formulating appropriate policies to cope with the disparity problem. First of all, the program was contradictory, as it tried to support farmers based on the revenue from taxation on them; this contradiction arose from the fact that the government tax base outside agriculture was still insufficient to support farmers adequately in the middle-income stage. Second, if the program were really successful in raising domestic rice prices, it should have met with strong opposition and protest from the urban poor outside the formal sector. Here is the dilemma of the disparity problem, in which politicians must decide whether it is more important to supply cheap food to the urban poor or to prevent farmers from becoming poorer relative to non-farmworkers.

It must be very difficult for middle-income countries to escape from this dilemma. Thailand, for example, tried to introduce export subsidy on rice for further increasing support on farmers after the abolishment of rice premium. As yet, however, the export subsidy has been negligibly small. The large application of export subsidy would not have been possible, as it is against the WTO rule. However, even before the GATT Uruguay Round Agreement in 1993, the Thai government indicated no sign to greatly expand the export subsidy scheme. This was presumably because of both the budgetary constraint and the danger of raising food prices for the urban poor.

Since the mid-1980s, the Thai government has introduced a commodity credit program akin to a program operated by the Commodity Credit Corporation in the United States in the past. Through this program farmers can receive low-interest loans from the government for the pledge of their rice until the rice price will go up to a target level and, in the event that the price will not sufficiently rise, they can relinquish their debt by submitting the pledged rice to the government. This is a high-cost program that would be unsustainable even in the United States. It is doubtful if this program can be expanded to such a scale as to render sufficient income supports for farmers in a middle-income country.

As industrialization in Thailand will continue to progress, comparative advantage in agriculture will decline further. For closing the rural-urban income gap, the government will continue to increase supports on farmers in various fronts, including subsidies on inputs and credits as well as price supports. Yet it is unlikely that Thailand will able to expand the support programs to such a scale as to fully close the income gap before its economy advances to a high-income stage.

THE EXPERIENCE OF JAPAN

The current problem in Thailand at the middle-income stage, as reviewed in the previous section, may be better understood by comparing it with the economic transformation of Japan from the low-income to the high-income stage. Table 15.3 presents a synopsis of modern economic development in Japan from 1885 to 1995. Japan and Thailand opened to international trade at about the same time under pressure from the West; both were forced to sign unequal treaties—Thailand with the United Kingdom in 1855 and Japan with the United States in 1858. Despite this similarity, industrialization progressed much faster in Japan than in Thailand, probably owing to much scarcer endowments of natural resources, especially land for cultivation, making industrialization more urgent in Japan than in Thailand in terms of surviving under open international trade (Bounlouane et al. 2005). At any rate, in terms of per capita GDP data in Table 15.3 (column 1), it appears that Japan was able to approach the middle-income stage by the first decade of the twentieth century. Until the First World War, Japan's industrialization had been predominantly based on the expansion of labor-intensive manufacturing. Later, heavy industries were promoted during the First World War and continued to be strengthened thereafter in the interwar period. At that time a dual structure emerged and the rural-urban disparity became serious.

Table 15.3 **Farm-nonfarm income disparity in Japan's economic development, 1885–2000**

	(1)	(2)	(3)	(4)	(5)	(6)	(7)
	GDP per capita (ppp at 2000)	Share of agriculture in GDP	Agriculture/Industry labour productivity ratio	Tariff rate of rice	Average tariff rate of all products	Agriculture/ Manufacturing Terms of Trade	Farm/Non-farm household income ratio
	(US$)	(%)	(%)	(%)	(%)	(1885 = 100)	(%)
1885	1,092	45	75	–	–	100	76
1890	1,285	48	67	–	–	115	87
1900	1,498	39	49	–	3.7	102	52
1910	1,656	32	37	13.7	16.2	98	47
1920	2,154	30	50	9.9	10.0	99	48
1930	2,350	18	31	14.0	22.6	104	32
1935	2,693	18	24	41.2	23.8	136	38
1955	3,519	21	55	–	3.5	163	77
1960	5,063	13	39	–	6.5	169	70
1970	12,337	6	25	–	6.9	303	94
1980	17,056	4	25	–	2.5	342	116

Table 15.3 ***(Continued)***

	(1)	(2)	(3)	(4)	(5)	(6)	(7)
	GDP per capita (ppp at 2000)	*Share of agriculture in GDP*	*Agriculture/Industry labour productivity ratio*	*Tariff rate of rice*	*Average tariff rate of all products*	*Agriculture/ Manufacturing Terms of Trade*	*Farm/Non-farm household income ratio*
	(US$)	*(%)*	*(%)*	*(%)*	*(%)*	*(1885 = 100)*	*(%)*
1990	23,580	2	26	–	2.7	379	115
2000	26,220	1	22	778	2.1	347	101

(1) GDP per capita in PPP at 2000 from World Bank (2006), linked with the series in OECD Development Centre (2003).

(2) The share of agriculture in nominal GDP in 1885–1955 from Ohkawa et al. (1967, vol. 6: 273–81), share in NNP for1885–1935 and 1960–2000 from World Bank (2006).

(3) The ratio of real GDP per worker in agriculture (including forestry and fishery) to real GDP per worker in industry (including mining). 1885–1970 from Y. Hayami, (1986: 120). 1980–2000: extended from 1970 using real GDPs from *Annual Reports of National Accounts.*

(4) Tariffs for 1910, 1920, 1930 and 1935 are tariffs in 1908, 1918, 1928 and 1933, respectively, from K. Ohkawa, et al. (1967, vol.6). Tariffs rate for 2000 is ad valorem tariff equivalent of specific duty, 341 yen/kg, which was reported to WTO by the government.

(5) Tariffs for 1900, 1910, 1920, 1930 and 1935 are tariffs in 1898, 1908, 1918, 1928 and 1933, respectively, from K. Ohkawa, et al. (1967, vol.6). Tariffs for1955–2000 are average tariffs calculated by total tariff revenue as percentage of total import cif value in Japan, Ministry of Finance (various issues).

(6) 1985–1960: the ratio between the price index of agricultural products and the price index of manufacturing products in K. Ohkawa, et al. (1967:165, 192–3). 1970–80: extended from 1960 using the Ministry of Agriculture, Forestry and Fishery's price index of agricultural products and the Bank of Japan' s domestic corporate goods price index for manufacturing industry products.

(7) 1885–1935: the ratio in household income per household member betwee n farm and non-farm households in Otsuki and Takamatsu (1982). 1955–2000: the ratio in per-capita income between farm households and employees' households based on Ministry of Agriculture (various issues) and Ministry of Internal Affairs (various issues). Farm households in 1990–2000 exclude non-commercial farm households.

Correspondingly, the focus of agricultural policies changed. Before the First World War, agricultural policies were mainly geared toward increasing food production so as to counteract the food problem in the low-income stage. The adequate supply of cheap food, especially rice, was considered a critical support for the development of labor-intensive industries. To this end Japanese government invested heavily in agricultural research and extension as well as irrigation infrastructure for the development and diffusion of high-yielding varieties, initially within Japan and later to overseas territories (Korea and Taiwan). Such efforts were successful in overcoming the food problem before the Second World War (Hayami 1975; Hayami and Ruttan 1985; Hayami and Yamada 1991).

Ironically, this success greatly aggravated the disparity problem during the interwar period. As column 5 of Table 15.3 shows, declines in labor productivity in agriculture relative to industry were very fast in Japan from the beginning of modern economic growth, reflecting very rapid progress in industrialization. Nevertheless, the terms of trade did not improve for agriculture (column 6): income per capita in farmers' households declined sharply relative to that in nonfarmworkers' households (column 7). These trends contrast sharply with those after the Second World War, when despite continued declines in relative productivity for agriculture, the per capita income of farmers improved relative to nonfarmers to the point of exceeding parity after the 1970s: this resulted from very rapid improvements in the terms of trade based on farm price support programs at a large scale unthinkable in the prewar days. Such a scale of farm supports became possible as Japan advanced to the high-income stage in the late 1960s.

As the disparity problem loomed large, the farm bloc demanded for increased government supports. Already in 1913, politically powerful landlords had been successful in lobbying for the institution of a specific duty on rice imports, but it was not applied to rice produced in overseas territories within the Japanese Empire. When rice prices began to fall after the First World War, the farm bloc pressed the government to support rice prices by means of rice procurement and storage. In addition, the government developed various programs to assist farmers, including government spending on construction of physical infrastructure in rural areas in order to provide wage-earning opportunities and the release of low-interest loans from government to farmers heavily in debt from private moneylenders.

The tax burden on farmers was also reduced. In the early stage of modernization in Japan, land tax levied on farmers was the major source of government revenue. During the 1880s the ratio of direct tax shouldered by farmers to their income was about 15 percent compared with only about 2 percent for nonfarmers; this disparity largely remained even in the 1910s, with the tax rates of about 11 percent for farmers and 5 percent for nonfarmers, but by the late 1930s farmers' tax rate was reduced to about 6 percent, not so different from nonfarmers' rate (Hayami 1988: 40).

These policies designed in Japan during the interwar period in response to the emerging disparity problem were also very similar to those adopted in Thailand since the 1970s. Their consequences were similar. In spite of all these efforts, the level of income and the living standard of farm people did not appreciably improve. Unlike after the Second World War, during the interwar period the Japanese economy did not reach the stage at which the government could afford to undertake farm support programs at such a scale as to close the rural-urban income gap. Although heavy industries developed rapidly, light industries based on small- and medium-scale enterprises were still the backbone of Japanese economy, especially with respect to foreign exchange earnings. Their international competitive power was still dependent on cheap labor, so that a major increase in the wage rate resulting from large increases food prices could not be tolerated. In such circumstances, with whatever powerful lobbying the landlords were able to organize, it was not politically possible to raise the level of agricultural protection sufficiently to solve the rising disparity problem.

Unfortunately, by the time when the disparity problem became serious, Japan was plunged into the storm of the Great Depression, which began in 1929. In Japan as well as throughout the world, farm product prices declined faster than the prices of manufactured goods, and farmers' incomes dropped more than nonfarmworkers.' Growing dissatisfaction and frustration among farmers, who became poorer both absolutely and relatively, culminated in social disruptions, including terrorism; this rendered a major support for militarism to gain power, ending in the tragedy of the Pacific War.

5. On the Relevance of the East Asian Experience

So far, the process of the disparity problem that emerges in developing economies as they advance from the low-income to the middle-income stage through successful industrialization has been illustrated with respect to the experience of high-performing economies in East Asia. One may wonder how relevant this model based on the East Asian experience is to economies in other regions with different economic and social conditions. Is it not possible that the disparity problem in other regions might not become quite as severe as in East Asia, even if they are able to achieve rapid industrialization comparable to that of East Asia? This possibility depends on the success of their interindustry adjustment to the loss in comparative advantage in agriculture owing to rapid industrial development.

First, even if the productivity of manufacturing in an economy rises very rapidly owing to success in the borrowing of advanced industrial technology from abroad in association with increases in capital intensity, as has been the case in the East Asian Miracle, the decrease in agriculture's comparative advantage might not be so large if it can achieve agricultural technology borrowing at a comparable speed. For example, if the agriculture sector were able to achieve its productivity growth by means of farm mechanization parallel with increases in the capital intensity in the manufacturing sector, intersectoral productivity difference would have not widened so much. However, even if investment in farm mechanization becomes profitable in terms of increased wage rates resulting from successful industrialization, the farm mechanization might not proceed smoothly because of the difficulty of establishing farms big enough to exploit the advantage of using modern large-scale machinery, due to the high transaction costs involved in consolidating a large number of peasants' holdings into large commercial farms. In East Asia, particularly in Japan, Korea, and Taiwan, where agriculture has traditionally been manned by small homogeneous peasants who have been attached to the same lands over generations, it is very costly to alienate them from their ancestral lands. These economies are also characterized by high population density; in these areas, frontiers have long been closed for opening new lands for cultivation. In such economies, it should be extremely difficult to counteract against loss in agriculture's comparative advantage by promoting an agrarian structure dominated by large-scale commercial farms. Such agrarian restructuring could be relatively easier in land-abundant newly settled regions such as Latin America, where land and labor markets are more fluid and the aggregate supply of arable lands is more elastic through new land opening. To that extent, the disparity problem could be less severe in such economies than in Japan, Korea, and Taiwan, even at the same speed of industrialization.

Such a difference could well be significant, but it is unlikely that even newly settled land-abundant economies where land markets are usually more active can totally escape from the trap of the disparity problem in the process of industrialization. Unlike the manufacturing sector, where adjustments in factor combination necessary for the borrowing of foreign technology can easily be made based on the efficient supply of capital from both domestic and foreign sources through generally well-functioning capital markets, adjustments in land input needed for introducing foreign agricultural technology is much more difficult and costly, given the typical absence in developing economies of institutions to support land markets such as cadastral surveys and land registry, not to speak of the total absence of "international markets for lands," unlike the case for capital. Furthermore, as emphasized in section 4, the importation of foreign technology is usually much more difficult for agriculture than for manufacturing because of the location-specific nature of agricultural technology that is constrained by natural environments (Hayami and Ruttan 1985). For these reasons it is unlikely that even the economies most favorably endowed with agricultural resources can be immune to the disparity problem when they are able to achieve rapid industrialization based on the success in industrial technology borrowing,

Thailand represents a good example in this regard. Within East Asia, Thailand has been characterized by relative abundance in the endowment of land: frontiers had been open until very recently, especially in the country's Northeast. Nevertheless, Thailand could not escape from the disparity problem when it joined the East Asian Miracle of rapid industrialization and economic growth, as explained in the previous section. The policy response of Thailand to the disparity problem is also characteristic of land-abundant economies. As a means of supporting farmers, Thailand relied heavily on the reduction of the rice export tax, unlike Japan, Korea, and Taiwan, which relied on border protection measures such as tariffs and quotas. As a major exporter of agricultural commodities, it was not a viable option for Thailand to support farmers by raising domestic prices through a combination of border protection and domestic price support programs. If domestic prices had been raised above the international market prices, Thailand's exports of agricultural commodities should have stopped, resulting in the accumulation of surplus agricultural products in domestic markets to the point that the cost needed to reduce the surplus by such means as the government's stock holding and acreage control will exceed the nation's fiscal capacity. For this reason, it was only natural for Thailand to adopt reduction on agricultural export taxation as a major means of supporting farmers, much like many land-abundant agricultural exporters in Latin America have done.

Needless to say, the basic cause of the disparity problem is the lag in the transfer of labor from agriculture to nonagriculture relative to the speed of loss in agriculture's comparative advantage in the process of industrialization. Therefore, the problem can be less severe where the access of farmers to nonfarm employment is easier, which depends to a large extent on the geographical distribution of industrial and commercial activities. This effect can be clearly observed in the comparison between Korea and Taiwan within East Asia. Taiwan is known for the success of rural-based industrialization characterized by the wide diffusion of small- and medium-scale enterprises over rural areas, while Korea's industrialization has centered on urban-based large enterprises. The access of farmers and their family members to nonfarm employment has been much easier in Taiwan than in Korea, as reflected in the data that more than one-half of farm-household income in Taiwan came from nonfarm sources in 1970, whereas in Korea it was only about one-quarter (Honma and Hayami 2006).

Correspondingly, government responses to the disparity problem were different. Both Korea and Taiwan entered the middle-income stage from the 1960s, when border protection measures on the import of agricultural commodities were strengthened in both economies, reflecting governments' responses to the emergence of the severe disparity problem. This aspect of agricultural protection growth was shared common by Korea and Taiwan, which recorded similar successes in industrial growth under similar resource endowments and agrarian structures. Nevertheless, agricultural protection in Korea, as measured by the average nominal rate of protection for agricultural commodities, rose faster to much higher levels than in Taiwan for the same levels of per capita incomes throughout their middle-income stage, and further after they advanced to the high-income stage in the 1990s (Honma and Hayami 2006). This difference seems to reflect the difference in the cost of intersectoral adjustments in labor allocation, corresponding to changes in comparative advantage, which farmers had to shoulder. In Korea the shift of labor from agriculture to nonagriculture necessarily involved the migration of workers from rural to urban areas, whereas in Taiwan much of the shift involved farmers' increases in nonfarm activities while they continued living in their home villages. Correspondingly, both the pecuniary and psychological costs of intersectoral labor reallocation should have been much higher for farmers in Korea.

The experience of Korea relative to Taiwan suggests the great difficulty that China will have to face. The miraculous growth of China in recent years has been characterized by concentration of industrial activities in the coastal areas, whereas western hinterlands have largely been bypassed. As the result, the disparity problem has been especially serious and is expected to become more so in China, since the rural-urban income gap is augmented by the large interregional inequality in the process of rapid industrialization. It is feared that the disparity problem in China might escalate to the social and political crisis of the nature similar to that experienced by Japan between the two world wars if its present course of development continues.

6. Conclusion

The growing imbalance in world agriculture today is epitomized in the increasing food deficits in low-income economies, in contrast to increasing surpluses in high-income economies. This has not simply been the result of different demand and supply structures corresponding to different income levels. The problem has been aggravated by policies under the dictate of the three agricultural problems in different stages of economic development—the food problem in the low-income stage, the disparity problem in the middle-income stage, and the protection problem in the high-income stage.

Under the regime of the food problem, policy makers in low-income countries have been inclined to adopt policies geared toward securing low-priced food to urban consumers at the expense of farm producers. By contrast, under the regime of the protection problem, politicians in high-income countries have not been able to resist pressures from the farm lobby to institute policies to raise farmers' incomes to the level of non-farmworkers. Great inefficiency and inequity resulting from these contrasting policy distortions have already been amply documented (D. G. Johnson 1973: Schultz 1978; Anderson and Hayami 1986), and the need to reduce these distortions has been widely recognized. In fact, major international collaborative efforts have progressed in that direction for the past two decades, through GATT/WTO multilateral trade negotiations.

In contrast, the disparity problem has received relatively little attention. Yet the growing income disparity between the farm and nonfarm population could be a major source of social and political instability for economies attempting to catch up with high-income economies through industrialization by means of rapid technology borrowing. This problem is now spreading over Asia, from ASEAN nations to China and Vietnam, and will eventually reach South Asia, especially India.

While the right approaches to the food and protection problems have already been established among economists, though actual implementation is often politically difficult, the right design to cope with the disparity problem has not yet been identified. The difficulty is how to balance out the conflicting goals of supporting farmers' incomes, on the one hand, and securing the supply of low-cost food to a large number of workers in urban informal sectors, on the other, under the still-weak capacity of the government to raise sufficient revenue from nonagricultural sectors. Almost inevitably, agricultural policies tend to become tinkering exercises combining various, often mutually conflicting policy instruments in ad hoc manners, as the experiences of Thailand and Japan illustrate.

Greater research inputs in this area are called for in order to prevent the growth momentum of high-performing Asian economies from being disrupted, as experienced by Japan between the two world wars. Given the weak fiscal capacity of developing economies at the middle-income stage, it is unrealistic to expect that they can solve the problem by means of increasing subsidies to farmers as attempted by high-income economies. Policy must be designed to strengthen their capacity to adjust to changes in comparative advantage resulting from the lag in the growth of agricultural productivity behind the industrial productivity growth. Greater investments in public research and development of agricultural technology will be needed, especially in the direction the adapting of advanced agricultural technology in developed economies to the environments of developing economies, and in the development of institutional infrastructure such as land registry systems for operating land market more efficiently. The education and training of rural people will be critically important for shifting rural labor smoothly from farm to nonfarm economic activities. Industrial development policy should consider the need to support rural-based industries to facilitate farmers' access to nonfarm income sources.

These policies must be supported by the accurate grasp of the nature and scope of disparity problem, for which the further accumulation of farm household income data based on micro household surveys is badly needed. Unless comparisons between farm and nonfarm households are made in terms of aggregates of farm and nonfarm incomes across regions and over time, the effective allocation of public resources to cope with the disparity problem by region cannot appropriately be designed. The sectoral value-added data from social accounts used for broad comparisons in Table 15.1 are grossly insufficient for the purpose of such concrete policy design. Social engineering to cope with the disparity problem, which is by nature very complex and sensitive, must be based on careful field-level research for different socioeconomic and ecological environments, such as those presented in the papers compiled in the November 2006 special issue of *Agricultural Economics*, titled "The Role of Nonfarm Income in Poverty Reduction: Evidence from Asia and East Asia" (*Agricultural Economics* 35:393–478; see also Otsuka et al. 2009).

Note

Yujiro Hayami, Presidential Address to the Fifth Conference of the Asian Society of Agricultural Economists, Zahedan, Iran, August 29–31, 2005.

CHAPTER 16

Induced Technical Change, Induced Institutional Change, and Mechanism Design

Vernon W. Ruttan

A central premise of this paper is that the demand for social science knowledge is derived from the demand for institutional change.[1] If this view is correct, then any claim by the social science disciplines and related professions for public support depends on a credible promise that advances in social science knowledge represent an efficient source of institutional innovation.

I first review briefly the theories of induced technical and institutional change. I then turn to a discussion of the sources of demand and the sources of supply of institutional change. I also discuss the concepts of incentive-compatible mechanism and institutional design. I end the paper with a discussion of some of the elements of a "pattern" or "appreciative" model of the relationships among changes in resource and cultural endowments and technical and institutional change.

1. Induced Technical Change

Modern interest in the effects of changes (and differences) in relative factor endowments and prices on the rate and direction of technical change was initially stimulated by an observation by Sir John Hicks (1932: 124–125): "The real reason for the predominance of labor saving innovation is surely that . . . a change in relative prices of factors of production is itself a spur to innovation and to innovation of a particular kind—directed at economizing the use of a factor which has become relatively expensive." Hicks's suggestion lay fallow until it was challenged by Salter (1960: 16) in 1960: "At competitive equilibrium each factor is being paid its marginal value product; therefore all factors are equally expensive to all firms." Salter (1960: 43–44) went on to argue that "the entrepreneur is interested in reducing costs in total and not particular costs." In retrospect it is difficult to understand why Salter's criticism generated so much attention except that students of economic growth were increasingly puzzled about why, in the presence of substantial capital deepening in the U.S. economy, factor shares to labor and capital had remained relatively stable. The differential growth rates were too large to be explained by simple factor substitution.

The debate about induced technical change centered on two alternative models—a growth theoretic model and a microeconomic version. The most formally developed version was a growth theoretic model introduced by Kennedy (1964, 1966) and elaborated by Samuelson (1965). Kennedy cast his model in terms of changing relative factor shares because of the growth theory implications. By the early 1970s the growth theoretic approach to induced technical change was itself subject to severe criticism. Nordhaus (1973, 2008) insisted that the model is "too defective to be used in serious economic analysis."

The second approach to induced innovation, built directly on Hicksian microeconomic foundations, was developed by Syed Ahmad (1966, 1967a, 1967b). In work published in the early and mid-1970s Yujiro Hayami, Hans Binswanger, Colin Thirtle, and I extended the microeconomic version of induced technical change and tested it against the history of agricultural development in the United States and Japan and in cross-country perspective (Hayami and Ruttan 1970, 1971; Binswanger 1974b; Binswanger and Ruttan 1978; Thirtle and Ruttan 1987). Rather than attempting a detailed review of the econometric results, I draw your attention to Figure 16.1.

By the late 1980s, in reaction to the Nordhaus criticisms and the emergence of new macroeconomic endogenous growth theories (Romer 1986; Lucas 1988), interest in induced technical change was beginning to wane. Interest was sustained, however, by agricultural and resource economists who continued to find the microeconomic version of induced technical change useful (Runge 1999). Recent work on the theoretical foundation of induced technical change theory and its implications by Acemoglu (2002, 2007) suggest a possible revival of interest by development economists.

The demonstration that technical change can be treated as largely endogenous to the development process does not imply that the progress of either agricultural or industrial technology can be left to an "invisible hand" that drives technology along an "efficient" path determined by relative resource endowments. The capacity to advance knowledge in science and technology is itself a result of institutional innovation—"the great invention of the nineteenth century was the invention of the method of invention" (Whitehead 1925: 96).

2. Induced Institutional Innovation

Institutions are the rules of a society or of organizations that facilitate coordination among people by helping them form expectations, which each person can

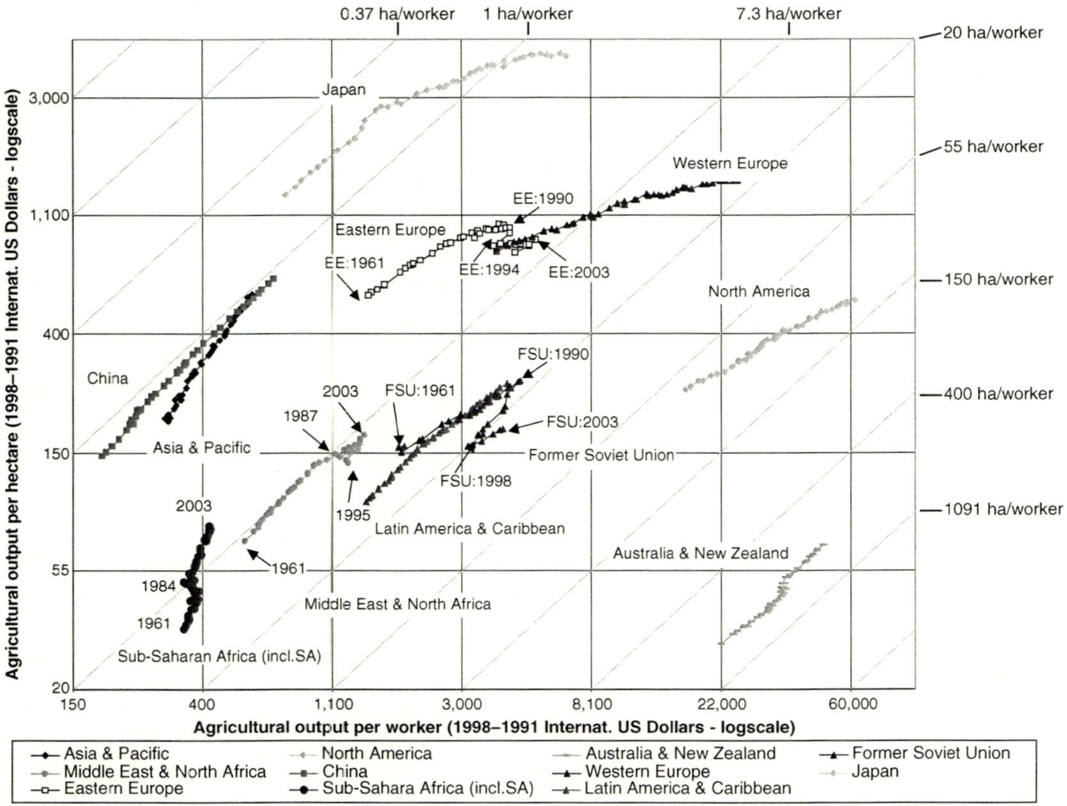

Figure 16.1 Global Agricultural Land and Labor Productivity, 1961–2003. Source: Pardey et. al. (2007).

Notes: Workers are economically active in agriculture. Land is the sum of area harvested and permanently pastured. Output is value of production farmed by weighting a time series of commodity quantities for each country by a 1989–1991 average of commodity-specific average of international prices. All productivity trajectories start in 1961 on left/bottom and end in 2003 on right/top, unless indicated. Diagonal lines indicate constant factor (land to labor) ratios.

reasonably hold in dealing with others (Hayami and Ruttan 1985: 94).[2] In the area of economic relations institutions play a crucial role in establishing expectations about the rights to use resources in economic activities and about the partitioning of the income streams resulting from economic activity: "Institutions provide assurance respecting the actions of others, and give order and stability to expectations in the complex and uncertain world of economic relations" (Runge 1981b: xv).

Anticipation of the latent gains to be realized by overcoming the disequilibria resulting from changes in factor endowments, cultural endowments, and technology represent powerful sources of demand (inducements) to institutional innovation (North and Thomas 1970; Schultz 1975). The growing disequilibria in resource allocation due to institutional constraints generated by economic growth create incentives for political entrepreneurs or leaders to organize collective action to bring about institutional change (Olson 1982: 74). This perspective on the sources of demand for institutional change is similar, in some respects, to the traditional Marxian view.[3]

There are supply-side as well as demand-side sources of institutional change. Advances in knowledge in the social sciences (and in related professions such as law, administration, planning, and social service) can reduce the cost of institutional change in a manner somewhat similar as advances in the natural sciences reduce the cost of technical change. Advances in game theory have, during the last several decades, enabled economists and political scientists to bring an increasingly powerful set of tools to bear on the understanding of the processes of institutional change (Hurwicz 1960, 1973; Schotter 1981; Ostrom 1990; Aoki 2001). In spite of the power of these new tools I continue to find the application of standard neoclassical microeconomic theory to interpret the sources of the demand and supply of institutional change exceedingly useful.

Insistence that important advances in the understanding of the processes of institutional innovation and diffusion can be achieved by treating institutional change as endogenous to the economic system represents a clear departure from the tradition of modern analytical economics.[4] The scope of modern analytical economics is expanded by treating institutional change as endogenous.

There is general agreement that institutional change has evolved and continues to evolve in response to long-term changes in resource endowments such as the pressure of population against land resources or a rise in the price of labor relative to capital. But there has been substantial disagreement within the social sciences about the role of purposeful or rational design in institutional innovation.[5] Those holding an "organic" or "spontaneous order" perspective argue that the fact that the institutions of civilization have been created by human action "does not mean that man must also be able to alter them at will" (Hayek 1978: 3).[6] This organic view of the sources of institutional change is reinforced by a theory of the "unintended consequences" of institutional innovation that runs through the work of Adam Smith, Carl Menger, Max Weber, and Friedrich Hayek (D. Lal 1998).

By contrast, the constructivist or design perspective holds that advances in social science knowledge can play an important role in the rational design of institutional reform and institutional innovation.

Much of my work with Yujiro Hayami on induced institutional innovation reflects an organic perspective. In other work, on the development of agricultural research institutions, for example, I have employed both organic and constructivist perspectives (Ruttan 1982a, 2001). I reject any demand to choose between the organic and constructivist perspectives. They should be viewed as complements rather than as alternatives. I also reject the ideological implication, advanced by some proponents of the organic approach, that the unintended consequences of institutional change preclude the possibility of a rational or analytical approach to institutional reform and design.

3. Demand for Institutional Innovation

In some cases the demand for institutional innovation can be satisfied by the development of new forms of property rights, more efficient market institutions, or even by evolutionary changes arising out of direct contracting by individuals at the level of the community or the firm. In other cases, where externalities are involved, substantial political resources may have to be brought to bear to organize nonmarket institutions in order to provide for the supply of public goods. In this section I draw from agricultural history to illustrate how changes in factor endowments, technical change, and growth in product demand have induced organic change in property rights and contractual arrangements.

The agricultural revolution that occurred in England between the fifteenth and the nineteenth centuries involved a substantial increase in the productivity of land and labor. It was accompanied by the enclosure of open fields and the replacement of small peasant cultivators, who held their land from manorial lords, by a system in which large farmers used hired labor to farm the land they leased from the landlords. The First Enclosure Movement, in the fifteenth and sixteenth centuries, resulted in the conversion of open arable fields and commons to private pasture in areas suitable for grazing. It was induced by expansion in the export demand for wool. The Second Enclosure Movement, in the eighteenth century, involved conversion of communally managed arable land into privately operated units. It is now generally agreed that demand for changes in land tenure arrangements was largely induced by the growing disequilibrium between the fixed institutional rent that landlords received under copyhold tenures (with lifetime contracts) and the higher economic rents expected from adoption of new technology which became more profitable as a consequence of higher grain prices and lower wages. When the land was enclosed, there was a redistribution of income from tenants to landowners, and the disequilibrium was reduced or eliminated.[7]

In nineteenth-century Thailand, the opening of the nation to international trade and the reduction in shipping rates to Europe following the completion of the Suez Canal resulted in a sharp increase in the demand for rice. The land available for rice production, which had been abundant, became more scarce. Investment in land development for wet rice production for export became profitable. The rise in the profitability of rice production for export induced a demand for the reform of property rights in both land and man. Traditional rights in human property (corvée and slavery) were replaced by more precise private property rights in land (fee-simple titles) (Feeny 1982).

LAND TENURE IN A PHILIPPINE VILLAGE

Research conducted in the Philippines during the late 1970s by Hayami and Kikuchi has enabled us to examine a contemporary example of the interrelated effects of changes in resource endowments and technical change on the demand for institutional change in land tenure and labor relations (Kikuchi and Hayami 1980; Hayami and Kikuchi 1981; Hayami and Kikuchi 2000). The case is particularly interesting because the institutional innovations occurred as a result of private contracting among individuals—what Hayek termed "spontaneous order" and in more recent literature has been referred to as "Coasian bargains" (Hayek 1978; Olson 2000). The study is based on a rigorous analysis of microeconomic data from a single village over a period of about twenty years.

Between 1956 and 1976, rice production per hectare in "Laguna Village" rose dramatically, from 2.5 to 6.7 metric tons per hectare per year. This was due to two changes in both resource endowments and technology. In 1958, the national irrigation system was extended to the village. This permitted double-cropping to replace single-cropping. The major technical change was the introduction of modern high-yielding rice varieties. The diffusion of modern varieties was accompanied by increased use of fertilizer and pesticides and by the adoption of improved cultural practices such as straight-row planting and intensive weeding.

Population growth in the village was rapid. Between 1966 and 1976 the number of households rose from 66 to 109 and the population rose from 383 to 464, while cultivated area remained virtually constant. The number of landless laborer households increased from 20 to 54. In 1976, half of the households in the village had no land to cultivate. The average farm size declined from 2.3 hectares to 2.0 hectares.

The land was farmed primarily by tenants. In 1976, only 1.7 hectares of the 108 hectares of cropland in the village were owned by village residents. Traditionally, share tenancy was the most common form of tenure. In both 1956 and 1966, 70 percent of the land was farmed under share tenure arrangements. In 1963, a new national agricultural land reform code was passed which was designed to break the political power of the traditional landed elite and to provide greater incentives to peasant producers of basic food crops. A major feature of the new legislation was an arrangement that permitted tenants to initiate a shift from share tenure to leasehold, with rent under the leasehold set at 25 percent of the average yield for the previous three years. Implementation of the code between the mid-1960s and the mid-1970s resulted in a decline in the percentage of land farmed under share tenure to 30 percent.

The shift from share tenure to lease tenure was not, however, the only change in tenure relationships that occurred between 1966 and 1976. There was a sharp increase in the number of plots farmed under subtenancy arrangements. The number increased from one in 1956 to five in 1966 and sixteen in 1976. Subtenancy is illegal under the land reform code. The subtenancy arrangements were usually made without the consent of the landowner. All cases of subtenancy were on land farmed under a leasehold arrangement. The most common subtenancy arrangement was 50-50 sharing of costs and output.

It was hypothesized that an incentive for the emergence of the subtenancy institution was that the rent paid to landlords under the leasehold arrangement was below the equilibrium rent—the level which would reflect both the higher yields of rice obtained with the new technology and the lower wage rates implied by the increase in population pressure against the land.

To test this hypothesis, market prices were used to compute the value of the unpaid factor inputs (family labor and capital) for different tenure arrangements during the 1976 wet season. The results indicate that the share-to-land was lowest and the operators' surplus was highest for the land under leasehold tenancy. In contrast, the share-to-land was highest and no surplus was left for the operator who cultivated the land under the subtenancy arrangement (Table 16.1). Indeed, the share-to-land when the land was farmed under subtenancy was very close to the sum of the share-to-land plus the operators' surplus under the other tenure arrangement.

The results are consistent with the hypothesis. A substantial portion of the economic rent was captured by the leasehold tenants in the form of operators' surplus. On the land farmed under a subtenancy arrangement, the rent was shared between the leaseholder and the landlord.

The subtenancy contract was an institutional innovation arrived at by voluntary agreements among farm operators, tenants, and laborers. The land reform laws gave leasehold tenants strong protection of their tenancy rights. It gave them the right to continue tilling the soil at an institutional rent that was lower then the economic rent. But the laws prohibited tenants from renting their land to someone else who might utilize it more efficiently (e.g., when they became elderly or found more profitable off-farm employment). Subtenancy reduced such inefficiency due to the institutional rigidity in the land rental market resulting from the land reform programs. The induced institutional innovation process leading toward the establishment of equilibrium in land rental markets occurred very rapidly even though the transactions between landlords and tenants were less than fully monetized. Informal contractual arrangements or agreements were utilized.

Table 16.1 **Factor Shares of Rice Output per Hectare, 1976 Wet Season**

				Factor shares[a]						
	Number of plots	*Area (ha)*	*Rice output*	*Current inputs*	*Landowner*	*Subleasor*	*Land total*	*Labor*	*Captial*[b]	*Operators' surplus*
Share tenancy land	30	29.7	2,749 (100.0)	697 (25.3)	698 (25.4)	0 (0)	698 (25.4)	850 (30.9)	288 (10.5)	216 (7.9)
Leasehold land	44	67.6	2,889 (100.0)	657 (22.7)	567 (19.6)	0 (0)	567 (19.6)	918 (31.8)	337 (11.7)	410 (14.2)
Subtenancy land	16	9.1	3,447 (100.0)	801 (23.2)	504 (14.6)	801[c] (23.2)	1,305 (37.8)	1,008 (29.3)	346 (10.1)	–13 (–0.4)

Source: Hayami and Kikuchi (1981: 111–3).

[a] Percentage shares are shown in parentheses.

[b] Sum of irrigation fee and paid and/or imputed rentals of carabao, tractor, and other machines.

[c] Rents to subleasors in the case of pledged plots are imputed by applying the interest rate of 40 percent crop season (a mode in the interest rate distribution in the village).

The subleasing contract evolved without the mobilization of substantial political activity or bureaucratic effort. Indeed, the subleasing arrangement evolved in spite of legal prohibition. Where substantial political and bureaucratic resources must be mobilized to bring about technical or institutional change, the changes occur much more slowly, as in the cases of the English enclosure movements and the Thai property rights cases referred to at the beginning of this section.

4. The Supply of Institutional Innovation

The disequilibria in economic relationships associated with economic growth, such as technical change leading to the generation of new income streams and changes in relative factor endowments, have been identified as important sources of demand for institutional change. But the sources of supply of institutional innovation are less well understood (Olson 1968; Ostrom 1990). The factors that reduce the cost of institutional innovation have received only limited attention by economists or by other social scientists.

In the Philippines village case discussed earlier, land tenure innovation in Laguna Village was supplied, in response to the changes in demand generated by changing factor endowments and new income streams, through the individual and joint decisions of owner-cultivators, tenants, and laborers. But even at this level it was necessary for gains to the innovators to be large enough to offset the risk of ignoring the land reform prohibitions against subleasing.[8]

The supply of major institutional innovations typically involves the mobilization of substantial resources by political entrepreneurs and innovators. It is useful to think in terms of a supply schedule of institutional innovation that is determined by the marginal cost schedule facing political entrepreneurs as they attempt to design new institutions and resolve the conflicts among interest groups (or suppression of opposition when necessary).

To the extent that the private return to political entrepreneurs is different from the social return, the institutional innovation will not be supplied at all or at a socially optimum level. If the institutional innovation is expected to result in a loss to a dominant political bloc, the innovation may not be forthcoming even if it is expected to produce a large net gain to society as a whole. And socially undesirable institutional innovations may occur not only from the unintended consequences of institutional innovation but as a result of innovations that are designed to generate economic or political benefits to the entrepreneur or the interest group that may impose costs that exceed the gains to society (Tullock 1967; Krueger 1974; Tollison 1982).[9]

The failure of many developing countries to institutionalize the agricultural research capacity needed to take advantage of the large gains from relatively modest investments in technical change may be due, in part, to the divergence between social returns and the private returns to political entrepreneurs. In the mid-1920s, for example, agricultural development in Argentina appeared to be proceeding along a path roughly comparable to that of the United States. Mechanization of crop production lagged slightly behind that in the United States. Grain yields per hectare averaged slightly higher than in the United States. In contrast to the United States, however, output and yields in Argentina remained relatively stagnant between the mid-1920s and the mid-1970s. It was not until the late 1970s that Argentina began to realize significant gains in agricultural productivity. Part of this lag in Argentine agricultural development was due to the disruption of export markets in the 1930s and 1940s. Students of Argentine development have also pointed to the political dominance of a landed aristocracy and to the rising tensions between urban and rural interests, that resulted in inappropriate domestic policies toward agriculture (de Janvry 1973; P. H. Smith 1969, 1974; Cavallo and Mundlak 1982). The Argentine case would seem to be one where the bias in the distribution of political and economic resources imposed exceptionally strong constraints on the institutional innovations needed to take advantage of the relatively inexpensive sources of growth that technical change in agriculture could have made available.

Cultural endowments, including religion and ideology, may exert a strong influence on the supply of institutional innovation. They make some forms of institutional change less costly to establish and impose severe costs on others (E. L. Jones 1995; Tan 2005). For example, the traditional moral obligation in the Japanese village community to cooperate in joint communal infrastructure maintenance made it less costly to implement modernizing rural development programs than in societies where such traditions do not prevail. These activities had their origin in the feudal organization of rural communities in the pre-Meiji period. But practices such as maintenance of village and agricultural roads and of irrigation and drainage ditches through joint activities in which all families contribute labor were still practiced in well over half of the hamlets in Japan as recently as 1970 (Ishikawa 1981). The traditional patterns of cooperation have represented an important form of social capital on which to erect modern forms of cooperative marketing and joint farming activities. Similar cultural resources were not available in many South Asian villages where, for example, the caste structure inhibits cooperation and encourages specialization (D. Lal 1998; Ruttan 2003: 232–35).

Advances in social sciences that improve knowledge relevant to the design of institutional innovations that are capable of generating new income streams or that reduce the cost of conflict resolution act to shift the supply of institutional change to the right. The research that led to advances in our understanding of the production and consumption behavior of rural households in less developed countries represents an important example of the contribution of advances in social science knowledge to the design of more efficient institutions (Schultz 1964; Nerlove 1974; Binswanger et al. 1981). In a number of countries this research has led to the abandonment of policies that viewed peasant households as unresponsive to economic incentives. And it has led to the design of more incentive-compatible factor and product markets and to institutions to make more productive technologies available to peasant producers.[10]

COLLECTIVE ACTION

Modest advances were made, beginning in the late 1950s, by students of what became variously known as the "new political economy" or the "new institutional economics" to explore the economic and political basis of collective action (Downs 1957; Olson 1965; Hardin 1968). The penetration of the political economy perspective into the traditional territory of political science was initially welcomed (or at least not actively opposed) by many political scientists who found the new analytical tools drawn primarily from economics useful (Almond 1993).

The major implications drawn by the early practitioners of the new institutional economics were profoundly conservative: "Unless the number of individuals in the group is quite small, or unless there is coercion or some other device to make individuals act in their common interests, rational self-interested individuals will not act to achieve their common or group interests" (Olson 1965: 2). The initial positive reception of this "zero contribution" inference was followed by a large critical literature. Elinor Ostrom (2000: 137–38) has insisted: "Many people do vote, not cheat on their taxes, and contribute to voluntary organizations. . . . Individuals in all parts of the world voluntarily organize themselves to gain the benefits of trade, to provide material protection against risk, and to create and enforce rules that protect natural resources."

Over several decades Ostrom and colleagues at the University of Indiana's Workshop on Political Theory and Policy Analysis have brought together the results of a massive body of field observations, extensive laboratory evidence, and careful theoretical analysis to distill a set of principles that provide fundamental insight into the evolution of institutional change and the design of institutional innovations (Table 16.2). The principles articulated in Table 16.2 are drawn, in large part, from examples of "spontaneous order" arising out of individual and small group behavior. But the lessons drawn from this experience by social science research represents the foundation for a set of principles or rules for the design of incentive-compatible institutions to enhance economic development at the community and regional level (Ostrom 1992; Boettke and Coyne 2005).

CONSTRUCTED MARKETS

In this section I present a case study of the contribution of advances in social science knowledge to the design of a contemporary institutional innovation at the national level. The case involves the design and implementation of an emissions trading system to reduce the transaction costs of controlling sulfur dioxide (SO_2) emissions—an important industrial pollutant. Advances in economic knowledge led to an understanding of the very large cost reductions that could be achieved by

Table 16.2 **Institutional Design Principles**

Elinor Ostrom and colleagues at the Workshop in Political Theory and Policy Analysis at Indiana University have articulated eight design principles drawn from their research on self-organized resource management regimes.
The *first* design principle is that the presence of clear boundaries and rules . . . enables participants to know who is in and who is outside of a defined set of relationships and thus with whom to cooperate.
The *second* design principle is that the local rules-in-use define the amount, timing, timing and technology of harvesting the resource: allocate the benefits proportional to required inputs; and are drafted to take local conditions into account.
The *third* design principle is that most of the individuals affected by the resource regime can participate in making and modifying the rules. Resource regimes that that use this principle are both able to tailor better rules to local circumstances and to devise rules that are considered fair by participants.
The *fourth* design principle is that . . . resource regimes select their own monitors, who are accountable to the users or are users themselves and who keep an eye on resource conditions as well as on their use.
The *fifth* design principle is that the resource regimes use *graduated sanctions* that depend on the seriousness and context of the offense. By creating official positions for local monitors a resource regime does not have to depend only on willing punishers to impose personal costs on those who break a rule.
The *sixth* design principle is the importance of access to rapid, low cost, local arenas to resolve conflict among users or between users and officials. By devising simple, local mechanisms to get conflicts aired immediately the number of conflicts that reduce trust can be reduced.
The *seventh* design principle is that the capability of local users to deliver an evermore effective regime over time is affected by whether they have minimal recognition of the right to organize by a local, regional or national government unit.
The *eighth* design principle that characterizes systems when common pool resources are somewhat larger is the presence of government activities organized in multiple layers of nested enterprises. Among long enduring self-organized regimes, smaller scale organizations tend to be nested in ever-larger organizations.

This table is adapted from the institutional deign principles articulated in Ostrum (2000). The institutional design rules developed by Ostrom drew heavily on her research on the design and management of irrigation systems. See Ostrom (1992). The design principles were most fully articulated in Ostrom (1990).

designing a "constructed market" to replace the "command and control" approach to the management of SO_2 emissions.[11]

The concept behind the design of a constructed market for the control of SO_2 pollutants is fairly simple. It is based on the realization that the behavioral sources of the pollution problem can often be traced to poorly defined property rights in open access natural resources such as air and water. A system of property rights and tradable permits for the management of pollution was first proposed in the late 1960s by Crocker (1966) and Dales (1968a, 1968b). The suggested institutional innovation did not emerge from its inventors in a fully operational form. Their proposals were followed by a large theoretical and empirical literature by resource and environmental economists (Bohm 1985). Design and implementation involved an extended process of "learning by doing" and "learning by using."

Proposals to replace the command-and-control approach by Presidents Johnson and Nixon by effluent fees or taxes on pollutants were dismissed as impractical and characterized by environmental activists as a "license to pollute." Beginning in the mid-1980s, however, a series of events conspired to make a more market-oriented approach to reducing SO_2 emissions politically feasible (Taylor 1989: 28–34; Hahn and Stavins 1991; Stavins 1998). One was the predilection of President George H. W. Bush toward a market-oriented approach to environmental policy. Another was the enthusiasm of Environmental Protection Agency administrator William Reilly and a number of key staff members in the president's Executive Office for validating Bush's desire to be known as "the environmental president." There was also bipartisan support in key congressional committees for a variety of market-based approaches to environmental policy.

Within the environmental community the Environmental Defense Fund (EDF) began to differentiate itself from the rest of the environmental community by advocating market-based approaches as early as the mid-1980s. In 1989 EDF staff began to work closely with the White House staff in drafting an early version of proposed legislation. The credibility of the effort was enhanced by the fact that EPA Administrator Reilly, formerly president of the Conservation Foundation, was a "card-carrying" environmentalist. Executives of several major corporations, influenced by subtle lobbying by the EDF, commented favorably on the emissions trading proposals.

The design of the SO_2 emissions trading system advanced in the Clean Air Act of 1990 drew on earlier EPA experience. The EPA began experimenting with emissions trading permits in 1974. The early programs included the elimination of lead in gasoline, the phaseout of chlorofluoro-carbons and halons in refrigeration, and the reduction of water pollution from nonpoint sources. The early programs had a mixed record. They were typically grafted onto existing command-and-control programs. The difficulty of converting from command-and-control programs encountered substantial transaction costs. These experiences did, however, provide important lessons for the design of more market-oriented trading programs in the 1990s.

The Clean Air Act created a national market for SO_2 allowances for coal-burning electrical utilities. The commodity exchanged in the SO_2 emissions trading program is a property right to emit SO_2 that was created by the EPA and allocated to individual firms. A firm can make allowances that had been issued to it available to be traded to other firms by reducing its own emissions of the pollutant below its own baseline level. In 1995, the program's first year, 110 of the nation's dirtiest coal-burning plants were included in the program. The affected plants were allowed to emit 2.5 pounds of SO_2 for each million British thermal units (Btu) of energy that they generated. During Phase II, initially projected to begin in 2000, almost all coal-burning plants were scheduled to be included, and allowances for each plant were to be reduced to 1.2 pounds per million Btu. Utilities that "overcomply" by reducing their emissions more than required may sell their excess allowances. Utilities that find it more difficult, or expensive, to meet the requirements may purchase allowances from other utilities.

Emissions trading has been even more cost effective than originally anticipated. Prior to initiation of the program the utility industry had complained that reducing SO_2 in amounts sufficient to meet the projected target (down from about 19 million tons in 1980 to 8.95 million tons in 2000) might cost as much as $1,500 per ton. By the late 1990s allowances were being sold in the $100–150 range. The decline in the cost of abatement has been due in part to technical changes in coal mining and deregulation of rail transport that have lowered the cost of low-sulfur coal to midwestern power producers. It has also been due to technical changes in fuel blending and SO_2 scrubbing that were induced by the introduction of performance-based allowance trading. As a result, benefits substantially exceeded early estimates (Joskow, Smalensee, and Bailey 1998).

The successful experience with SO_2 emissions trading illustrates a very important principle in inventing new property rights institutions to manage formerly open access resources. In a now classic paper Coase (1960) argued that when only a few decision makers are involved in the generation of externalities, the two parties, if left to themselves, will voluntarily negotiate new institutional mechanisms—rules and payments—that result in a reduction of the externalities to an acceptable level. However important the Coase theorem might be for understanding the small institutional innovations in the Philippine village case presented earlier in this paper, it has little relevance to most contemporary large-scale externality problems.

The important externality problems that concern society today—such as SO_2 pollution, ozone pollution, or the greenhouse gases responsible for global climate change—typically involve large numbers of polluters and even larger numbers of persons affected by the externalities. In contrast to the evolution of a "natural market," government must establish the conditions necessary for a "constructed" market to function. In the SO_2 case it was necessary for an outside principal, the U.S. Congress, to define the size (or the boundaries) of the resource, in this case the maximum tons of SO_2 emissions, and to establish the trading rules. The social science effort involved in the design and implementation of the institutional arrangements and mechanisms to confront such problems requires the mobilization of large economic and political resources.

5. Mechanism Design

The case studies presented in the previous two sections represent important early examples of incentive-compatible institutional design. They did not draw on the emerging mechanism design literature. Beginning in the late 1950s Leonid Hurwicz and several colleagues began to direct their attention to the design of mechanisms and institutions.[12] The results of this effort have been truly revolutionary! In 2007 the Nobel Prize Committee awarded Hurwicz and two colleagues, Roger P. Myerson and Eric Maskin, the Nobel Prize in economics. The award committee noted that mechanism design theory began with the work of Leonid Hurwicz in 1960. However, the theory became relevant to a wide variety of applications only after Hurwicz introduced the key notion of incentive compatibility in 1972 (Nobel Prize Committee 2007: 2).

As noted above, the orthodox view in economics, articulated by Paul Samuelson (1948: 321–22), 1970 Nobel awardee, held: "The auxiliary (institutional) constraints imposed on the variables are not themselves the proper subject of welfare economics but must be taken as given." Friedrich Hayek (1978: 3), 1974 Nobel awardee, held that institutional change emerged out of organic processes, which he termed "spontaneous order." The concept of incentive-compatible mechanism design removed the ideological, disciplinary, and ethical blinders that had limited the scope of a more analytical and institutional economics. Hayek had feared the unintended consequences of efforts by the market socialists to substitute planning for markets. Samuelson viewed the normative judgments involved in institutional reform as outside the scope of the discipline of economics. Hurwicz, by contrast, insisted that the design of institutional arrangements was a central issue for economics. He laid the foundations for what the economist termed the "intelligent design" of incentive-compatible institutional arrangements (Hurwicz 2007).

In later work Hurwicz has addressed the question of the feasibility of achieving Pareto optimality in both classical and nonclassical environments.[13] It has long been recognized that in nonclassical environments economists are confronted, in attempting to design mechanisms and institutions, with problems of incomplete information, economies of scale, technical change, missing markets, nonmarket resource allocation, and other sources of imperfection. As noted above, in such environments government or some other authority must often be called in to design and enforce reasonably "incentive efficient" mechanisms (Sandeep and Maskin 2003).

In a remarkable paper published in 1981, "Incentive Problems in the Design of Non-wasteful Resource Allocation," Hurwicz developed the proof of an "impossibility theorem" (first conjectured by Samuelson), that even in an informationally decentralized classical economy it is impossible to design mechanisms or institutions capable of achieving Pareto optimality.[14] One constraint is the presence of private information. A second reason is that the operation of the mechanisms themselves employ scarce resources. Thus a first, best Pareto optimality is generally not achievable. This negative result is extremely important because it focuses the attention on the comparative costs of the operation of the mechanisms and institutions. It also opens up the issue of the implications of new mechanism and institutions designed to improve welfare by generating new income streams (by reducing transaction costs, for example) and by introducing new mechanisms that improve the distribution of income (Hurwicz 1972b: 43).

Hurwicz and his colleagues have established a foundation for a new and more powerful institutional economics. Their work challenges the conservative underpinning of Hayek's concept of spontaneous order, breaks through the disciplinary constraints of neoclassical theory, and challenges the relevance of Pareto optimality in normative economics.

6. Toward a More Complete Model

In Figure 16.2, I present in graphical form the elements of a pattern model that maps the relationships among changes in resource endowments and cultural endowments, and changes in technology and institutions.[15] The model goes beyond the conventional general equilibrium model in which resource endowments, technologies, institutions, and culture (conventionally designated as "tastes" in the economics literature) are given.[16] In the study of long-term social and economic change the relationships among the variables must be treated as recursive and dynamic (Harsanyi 1960).

An important advantage of the pattern model outlined in Figure 16.2 is that it avoids the necessity of choosing between a materialist conception of human action, in which agents mechanically respond to changes in resource endowments, and an idealist conception of human action, in which agents respond only to subjective changes in cultural endowments (such as religion or ideology). A second advantage is that it helps us to identify our areas of ignorance.

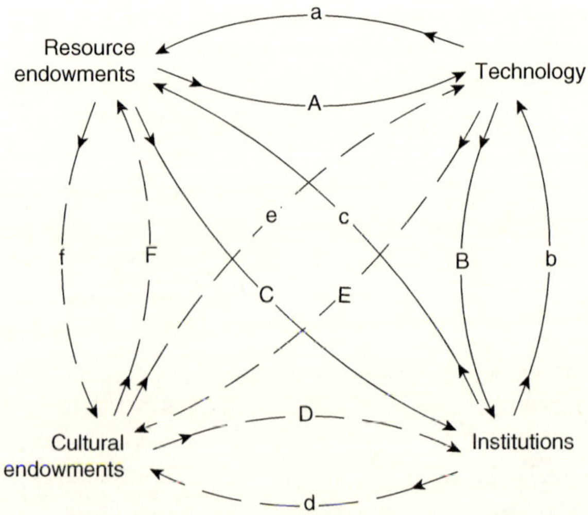

Figure 16.2 Interrelationships between Changes in Resource Endowments, Cultural Endowments, Technology, and Institutions. (From Hayami and Ruttan (1985: 111)).

Our capacity to model and test the relationships between resource endowments and technical change is relatively strong. In spite of recent advances in induced innovation theory and in mechanism and institutional design, our capacity to model and test the relationships between cultural endowments and either technical or institutional change is relatively weak.

The model is also useful in identifying model components that have entered into attempts by other scholars to account for secular economic and social change. I illustrate below with several examples.[17]

Historians working within the Marxist tradition often tend to view technical change as dominating both institutional and cultural change. In his classic book, *Oriental Despotism*, Wittfogel (mistakenly) viewed the irrigation technology used in wet rice cultivation in East Asia as determining political organization (Wittfogel 1957). In terms of Figure 16.1 his primary emphasis was on the impact of changes in resources and technology on institutions (C) and (B). A serious misunderstanding can also be observed in the neo-Marxian critiques of the Green Revolution in rice production in Asia (Cleaver 1972; Hayami and Ruttan 1985: 336–45). These criticisms focused attention almost entirely on the impact of technical change on labor and land tenure relations. Both the radical and populist critics emphasized relation (B). But they tended to neglect the effects of rising population pressure against land (relations [A] and [C]).

Economists such as Coase (1960) and Alchian and Demsetz (1973) identify a primary function of property rights as guiding incentives to achieve greater internalization of externalities. North and Thomas, building on the Alchian-Demsetz paradigm, attempted to explain the economic growth of Western Europe between 900 and 1700 primarily in terms of changes in property rights institutions (North and Thomas 1970: 1–17; Field 1981). The population decline in the fourteenth and fifteenth centuries was viewed as a primary factor leading to the demise of feudalism and the rise of the national state (line C).

Mancur Olson (1968, 1982), in an attempt to explain the more rapid growth of Germany and Japan relative to the United States and Britain in the first several decades after World War II, emphasized the proliferation and rigidity of institutions as a source of economic decline. He also regarded broad-based encompassing organizations as having incentives to generate growth and redistribute incomes to their members with little excess burden. These distributional coalitions make political life more divisive. They slow down the adoption of new technologies (line b) and limit the capacity to reallocate resources (line c). The effect is to slow down economic growth or in some cases initiate a period of economic decline. In a more recent work Greif (1994) has emphasized the differential impact of the collectivist cultural endowments of Maghrebi traders and the individualistic cultural endowments of Genoese traders on the development of commercial institutions in the Mediterranean region in the eleventh and twelfth centuries.

The impact of differences in resource endowments on the international diffusion of institutions has recently been explored in a series of important papers

(Engerman and Sokoloff 2002; Acemoglu, Johnson, and Robinson 2001; Levine 2005). A common conclusion is that where the disease environment was not favorable to settlement, European states established extractive colonies (such as the Spanish in Mexico and Peru, Britain in the Gold Coast, and Belgium in the Congo). Where the disease environment was favorable, they established settler colonies. Where extractive colonies were established, legal institutions were adopted that favored the extraction and transfer of resources to the metropolitan country and, after independence, to the new ruling elites. In settler colonies, by contrast, legal institutions that favored the rule of law and encouraged investment were established. These differences in legal culture and institutions continue to explain substantial differences in per capita income and income distribution (lines F, D, and C).

A potential criticism of the pattern model approach depicted in Figure 16.2 is that it does not stipulate the mechanisms through which changes in resource endowments, for example, induce changes in technology or institutions. However, it is not too difficult to visualize some of the most important mechanisms that mediate the relationships among changes in resource endowments, technical change, and institutional change. The market represents a "master mechanism" for translating the uncoordinated behavior of individuals into system-level coordination (Headstrom and Swedberg 1998: 3).

7. Perspective

What are the implications of the theory of induced institutional change for research on the contribution of social science knowledge to economic development? In my research with Hayami and Binswanger on the direction and rate of technical change we were able to significantly advance our knowledge by treating technical change as largely endogenous—as induced primarily by changes in relative resource endowments and the growth of demand. We were also able to interpret the advances in knowledge about the role of changes in the economic environment on the rate and direction of technical change for the design of research systems and the allocation of research resources (Ruttan 1982a, 2001).

In this paper I have presented a theory of induced institutional change. I argue that the theory has advanced our understanding of the process of institutional change. It suggests that substantial new insights have been obtained by treating institutional change as a response to changes or differences in resource endowments, technical change, and cultural endowments. But, as in the case of technical change, my concern goes beyond advancing our understanding of the process of institutional innovation. It is essential for the social sciences to advance our understanding of the historical processes of social and economic development. But that is not sufficient! If social science knowledge is to be valued by society, it must also advance the knowledge to successfully intervene in the process of development—to reduce the cost of the "trial and error"—that has been the constant companion of the historic "organic" processes of institutional innovation. A functional goal of the social sciences (including economics) is not just to understand human behavior but to evaluate proposals for institutional reform and to design new and better mechanisms and institutions (Myerson 1999: 1069).

Beginning in the mid-1980s I initiated a program of research and writing designed to explore in greater depth what development economists should learn from scholars in the other nomothetic social sciences—anthropology, sociology, and political science—working in the field of development. My book *Social Science Knowledge and Economic Development* (Ruttan 2003) grew out of that effort. A consistent theme in that book and in this paper is that advances in social science knowledge represent a powerful source of economic growth and more broadly of economic development. Advances in social science knowledge represent a high-payoff input into economic development. This position falls squarely into the tradition of Enlightenment political philosophy. The U.S. Constitution was an early, and magnificent, example of this design perspective.

The design perspective stands in sharp contrast to the organic or evolutionary perspective. Hayek, for example, has argued that improvements in institutional performance are the result of a process of collective learning that has passed the slow test of time and are embodied in a people's language, culture, and institutions. This accumulated knowledge is built into ways of learning and has a powerful impact on both the present and the future. Since collective learning occurs at the level of the community rather than the individual, there are severe constraints on the rational design of policies and institutions. But there can be no presumption that the institutions that emerge out of the process of social evolution, unguided by advances in social science knowledge, will result in efficient trajectories of cultural, social, or economic development (Hayek 1967, 1978; North 1994). Spontaneous order is not enough!

In closing, I would like to emphasize again that the work on incentive-compatible mechanism and institutional design initiated by Hurwicz has widened the scope for social scientists to contribute to institutional analysis, design, and implementation. It challenges the adequacy of concepts of spontaneous order and organic and evolutionary approaches to the analysis, design, and implementation of institutional change. It breaks through the disciplinary constraints of neoclassical theory and erodes the relevance of Pareto optimality in normative economics. It has not yet provided us with an application "tool kit" for mechanism and an institutional design, but the concept of incentive compatibility is an exceedingly powerful intellectual concept. It may be even more powerful as a metaphor than as an analytical concept.

The pattern model outlined in this paper is built on recursive relationships among changes in resource endowments, technology, institutions, and culture. Successful institutional innovation will almost always be culture specific. It involves more than simply institutional (or technology) transfer. Advances in social science knowledge can open up new and productive opportunities for institutional innovation and design that enhance development. In the induced institutional innovation model there is no role for simple resource, technological, institutional, or cultural determinism. The dialectical relationships among changes in resource and cultural endowments and technical and institutional change influence the rate and direction of social, political, and economic development. And the feedback from these changes becomes the sources of change in resource and cultural endowments.

Finally, I would like to emphasize the complementary relationship between mechanism design theory and the theory of induced institutional innovation. Designers are not free to ignore the long-term secular shifts in resource and cultural endowments. Nor can they ignore contemporary changes in technical and institutional environments.

Notes

Vernon W. Ruttan, paper prepared for presentation at the Tenth International Workshop on Institutional Economics, "Institutions, Technology and Their Roles in Economic Growth," University of Hertfordshire, June 17–18, 2008.

1. This paper is a revised and extended version of Ruttan 2006. I also draw on Ruttan and Hayami 1984 and Ruttan 2001, 2003.
2. For a review of the role of institutions, and of institutional changes in economic development, see Lin and Nugent 1995. There is considerable disagreement regarding the use of the term "institution." A distinction is often made between the concepts of institution as an organization and institutional arrangements. In my own work I have found it useful to employ a definition that includes both concepts. This is consistent with the view expressed by both Commons (1950: 24) and Knight (1952: 51). This inclusive definition was also employed by Davis and North (1971: 8–9). In his more recent work North excludes organization and conflates the concepts of institution and culture. The distinction that I make between institutions and cultural endowments is that institutions are the formal rules and arrangements that govern behavior among and within organizations, while cultural endowments are the informal codes of behavior that have evolved to influence individual and group behavior. Drawing on game theoretic concepts, Hurwicz distinguishes between institutions and mechanisms. Institutions are defined as families of "game forms" or mechanisms. For example, share tenure is defined as an institution. It includes the entire set of mechanisms (i.e., game forms) in which the rental share ranges between 0 and 1. Institutions can be represented as a correspondence between game forms (mechanisms) and economic environments (Hurwicz 1996).
3. "At a certain stage of their development, the material forces of production in society come in conflict with existing relations of production, or—what is but a legal expression for the same thing—with the property relations within which they had been at work before. From forms of development of the forces of production these relations turn into their fetters. Then comes the period of social revolution. With the change of the economic foundation the entire immense superstructure is more or less rapidly transformed" (Marx 1913: 11–12). For a discussion of the role of technology in Marxian thought see Rosenberg 1982: 34–54.
4. The orthodox view was expressed by Samuelson (1948: 221–22): "The auxiliary [institutional] constraints imposed upon the variables are not themselves the proper subject of welfare economics but must be taken as given." Contrast this with the statement by Schotter (1981: 61): "We view welfare economics as a study . . . that ranks the system of rules which dictate social behavior."

5. Schotter (1981: 3–4) notes that in economics there have been, historically, two distinct interpretations of the sources of institutional change—"organic" and "collectivist." He identifies the organic view with the work of Hayek and the collectivist view with the work of Commons. Hayek (1978: 3–22) uses the term "constructivist" rather than "collectivist."
6. Hayek was apparently referring to a statement by Karl Marx (1936: 15): "Men make their own history, but they do not make it as they please; they do not make it under circumstances chosen by themselves, but under circumstances directly formed, given and transmitted from the past." Hayek (1967: 96–105) regarded the explanation of the unintended patterns and regularities as what he termed "constructivism" because of the inability of social theory to anticipate unintended consequences.
7. There has been a continuing debate among students of English agricultural history about whether the higher rents that landowners received after enclosure was (a) because enclosed farming was more efficient than open field farming, or (b) because enclosures redistributed income from farmers to landowners (Dahlman 1980; Allen 1982).
8. Demsetz (1964) has pointed out that the relative costs of using market and political institutions is rarely given explicit consideration in the literature on market failure. An appropriate way of interpreting the "public goods vs. private goods" issue is to ask whether the costs of providing a market are too high relative to the cost of nonmarket alternatives. A similar point is made by Hurwicz (1972b).
9. A referee for an earlier draft of this paper raised the question of whether it might be possible that errors in social science research might result in institutional innovations that make society worse off. The reviewer also raised the question of what mechanisms exist to discipline political entrepreneurs comparable to the market mechanism in economics. These important questions are dealt with in a vast literature in the field of public choice and political economy (Acemoglu 2005; Dalrymple 2006). I return to this issue later in this paper.
10. The international agricultural research system organized under the auspices of the Consultative Group on International Agricultural Research (CGIAR) represents a particularly impressive example of an institutional innovation that became an exceedingly powerful source of improvement in crop technology for developing countries in the tropics (Evenson and Gollin 2003b).
11. This section draws heavily on Ruttan 2001: 511–16. For a retrospective perspective on the use of tradable permits see Tietenberg 2002.
12. Hurwicz distinguished between two types of normative analysis. One is to take the organizational structure as given while considering alternative policies within such a structure. The other is to take organizational structure itself as the variable. "It is this latter type of choice that we have called the designers' point of view" (Hurwicz 1972b: 37).
13. "Classical environments are characterized by absence of external economies or diseconomies of scale, imperfect divisibility of goods, and convexity or the relevant sets and functions describing preferences and technology" (Hurwicz 1972b: 38).
14. For a more formal treatment see Mass-Corell 1995: 858–69.
15. Fusfeld used the terms "pattern" or "Gestalt" model to describe a form of analysis that links the elements of a general pattern together by logical connections. The recursive multicausal relationships of the pattern model imply that the model is always "open"—"it can never include all of the relevant variables and relationships necessary for a full understanding of the phenomenon under investigation" (Fusfeld 1980: 33). Ostrom uses the term "framework" rather than "pattern model". "The framework for analyzing problems of institutional choice illustrates the complex configuration of variables when individuals . . . attempt to fashion rules to improve their individual and joint outcomes. The reason for presenting this complex array of variables as a framework rather than a model is precisely because one cannot encompass the degree of complexity within a single model" (Ostrom 1990: 214). Richard Nelson (2005: 195–212) views economic growth as driven by the coevolution of physical technologies and social technologies (or institutions).
16. In economics the concept of cultural endowments has traditionally been subsumed under the concept of "tastes," which are regarded as "given"—that is, not subject to economic analysis (Stigler and Becker 1977; E. L. Jones 1995; Ruttan 2003: 33–67). I use the term "cultural endowments" to capture those dimensions of culture that have been transmitted from

the past. Contemporary changes in institutions, for example, can be expected to "harden" into the next generation's cultural endowments.

17. Induced innovation theory should be viewed as a diagnostic tool. Accurate prediction is not an appropriate test of the theory. If, for example, an increase in population pressure against land resources fails to induce the expected innovation in property rights institutions, the appropriate response is to augment the model. Thus in my own work I employ induced innovation theory not to predict the effects of changes in resource endowments, technology, institutions, and culture but rather as a guide to a "dialogue with data" and as a guide to mechanism and institutional design.

PART

VI

POSTSCRIPT

CHAPTER 17

Stream, River, Delta

INDUCED INNOVATION IN ECONOMIC THEORY AND ENVIRONMENTAL POLICY

C. Ford Runge

A few days before his death in August 2008, Vernon Ruttan, Regents Professor at the University of Minnesota, came down the hall to my office, as he often did, for a conversation. Vern enjoyed conversation and was very good at it because he was a better listener than a talker. We had known each other for thirty years. When I was a graduate student in the early 1980s, Vern invited me to come to Minnesota to present several seminars on the theory of institutional change, thus seeding the possibility that I might be hired as permanent faculty. When I arrived as an assistant professor in 1983, he asked for help writing about an ongoing seminar he led with Leonid Hurwicz, Minnesota's 2007 Nobel Prize Winner in Economics, on "institutional design" (Runge 1983).

Twenty-five years later, Leo Hurwicz was dead at age ninety. Vern and I had drafted a manuscript, prior to Hurwicz's death but after the Nobel ceremony, that attempted to capture the concrete social and economic implications of Leo's often highly abstract work on institutional design. I proposed that we broaden its scope to include Ruttan's theory of induced innovation, developed with Yujiro Hayami at Tokyo Metropolitan University. Based on work by Sir John Hicks and others, and explaining technical and institutional choices as responses to relative scarcity, this theory is the central idea animating this volume. As the previous chapters show, it offers a rich background for the tapestry of their arguments.

Yale's James Tobin once remarked that he won his economics Nobel by elaborating mathematically that one shouldn't put all of one's eggs in a single basket. Ruttan and Hayami argued empirically that necessity is the mother of invention. They illustrated their argument by comparing the development of agricultural technology in Japan with that in the United States. Japan sought to use what it had in abundance—labor—in rice cultivation, substituting labor for the land it did not have. By contrast, American agricultural labor was chronically short, while land was abundant. The history of technical and institutional change in the United States portrays a narrative of land-using mechanical technology substituting for scarce labor: the Deere plow, McCormick reaper and Case tractor. As Vern used to say, when he went away to war and Yale and left his father's Michigan farm, the old man finally abandoned horse plowing and bought a tractor.

Coupled to this theory of technical change was a complementary theory of institutional change: institutional change occurs when social constraints create incentives for institutional entrepreneurs to offer a new path, or reorganization, of the rules that define societal obligations. An example of such a new path was the creation of a system of public education in the United States in the nineteenth century that offered the prospect of literacy and numeracy to those who in the Old World would never have contemplated going to school. In 1862, President Lincoln signed into law the Morrill Act, allowing funds from the sale of public lands to be used to erect universities in states such as Wisconsin and Minnesota, universities that emerged in the twentieth century as engines of research in the physical and biological sciences as well as in their original areas of focus: agriculture and engineering. The Morrill Act was based on the success of the initial land grant university, Michigan State University (1855), even then accessible to poor students like Vern Ruttan, who attended MSU for one year before entering the U.S. armed forces during World War II. The Morrill Act set in motion a social process of establishing new institutions that encouraged the substitution of *skilled* labor for *scarce* labor, supporting and reinforcing the technological changes unfolding in agricultural machine shops across the Midwest.

I once proposed to Vern that his theory of change be linked to the more abstract ideas of Hurwicz, who had developed a deep argument concerning the possibility of designing institutions that worked. "Worked" is loaded with precise economic reasoning, but the idea is basic: from Plato to Montesquieu to Benjamin Franklin and James Madison, intelligent designers of institutions have asked whether or not certain principles (rules) should govern human conduct. These principles include the will of the majority, the rights of minorities, and the fairness of how goods are allocated.

Hurwicz showed how these and other criteria could be mapped into the design of institutions so that people voluntarily opted in favor of the best design, as opposed to having it (or other designs) forced upon them. If these principles and practices reflected the felt needs of a group of individuals, then they were net improvements over the status quo. The tension in the design of new "mechanisms" (rules) was that if everyone's preferences are to "count," then no one should have an incentive to express them inaccurately. But since incentives for strategic misrepresentation of preferences are rife (such as the proverbial free rider problem), efficiency may require the imposition of rules from above, resulting in a trade-off between efficiency and free preference revelation. And if a "guardian" is chosen to impose rules, then who, Hurwicz (2008) asked, will guard the guardian?

As Hayami and Ruttan's work also showed, factors such as local norms and larger cultural preferences could sometimes account for reluctance to rely on seemingly desirable technological and institutional innovations. This insight was instrumental in their interactive four-factor pattern model.

A challenge for the next generation of economists is to take the theory of choosing a *given* rule (Hurwicz) and relate it to the theory of how these choices evolve in response to changing external constraints, such as labor scarcity, over time (Ruttan). Longitudinal case studies that look at how those choices are made based on norms, social structures, and institutions of collective action, such as those completed by Hayami (1978) and Hayami and Kikuchi (1981, 2000) in the Philippines over a close to forty-year period, contributed to deepening this analysis. This larger, more unified theory would then explain the *process* by which new rules are chosen and the challenges to their successful implementation. The conversation with Vern that last afternoon was wide-ranging, but the main idea was that economists could do more to help build new and better institutions that would, to paraphrase Jeremy Bentham, do more good for more people, and that this program of social improvement could and should be part of the agenda of any economic research institution. Doing "good" for more people and finding new ways to do so was part of Ruttan's agenda to the end, as it was for Hayami. Keijiro Otsuka reports, based on his last conversations with Hayami, that Yujiro was concerned with the importance of education; he was active in mentoring students and planned to write further regarding the role of education in the economic development of Asia, both past and future; he also intended to complete a revision of his widely used textbook (translated into Chinese in 2003) on development education. Otsuka is now continuing these efforts.

In this afterword, I propose to briefly explicate this line of reasoning. First, I focus on the stream of ideas surrounding Hicks's concept of induced innovation, and its widening at the hands of Hayami and Ruttan and others to a more general theory of technological and institutional change. I then consider the pivotal environmental technology and policy changes advanced beginning in the late 1960s and early 1970s, at a point when this stream became a river. Third, I offer an interpretation of these concepts' influence on the current debate over international climate issues. A stream that became a river is now a widening delta of analysis and debate, generating a set of important, if as yet largely untested, issues for future research.

I. Induced Innovation Theory

A central insight offered by John Hicks (1932) in *The Theory of Wages* was that technological choice is induced by the relative abundance of factors of production. Hayami and Ruttan described this process by using a broader comparison of the paths of technological change pursued by the agricultural sectors of the United

States and Japan during the nineteenth and twentieth centuries (chapter 10; Hayami and Ruttan, 1985). Their analysis was less strictly based in microeconomics than Hicks's, but was not a fully macroeconomic explanation either, employing the device of a "metaproduction function." In Japan, the relative abundance of labor and scarcity of land led to labor-using and land-saving technologies, such as intensive irrigated rice-farming systems. In effect, the high price of land and low price of labor combined to move the path of technological change in this direction. In the United States, by contrast, scarce labor and abundant land led to labor-saving and land-using technologies, especially large mechanical harvesters and chemicals that substitute for labor in production.

Early criticisms concerned the lack of a microeconomic mechanism triggering this sequence (chapters 2 and 12). In response, Hans Binswanger developed an induced innovation model in which research and development, stimulated by increases in product demand, shifted the "innovation possibilities frontier" (Binswanger and Ruttan 1978). The choice of a specific technique was then guided by relative factor scarcity. This conception was developed as a theory of firm behavior, but its application required generalization to a broader set of public and private choices, in which inputs and outputs are broadly conceived. It was this generalization that allowed the extension beyond simple firm behavior to include a set of social choices.

This led induced innovation theory beyond technological development to a complementary concept of "induced institutional innovation." Institutions "are the rules of society or of organizations that facilitate coordination among people by helping them form expectations which each person can reasonably hold in dealing with others" (Hayami and Ruttan 1985: 94). The demand for this coordination arises from the need for assured benefits streams, now and in the future, in the form of rules of exclusion and inclusion which institutions supply (Runge 1984a, 1984b). This may mean developing new property rights in connection with factors of production including land, water, and energy, or new institutions to guide the allocation of funds, as in public education or agricultural research. While some institutional innovations occur only in the private sector (such as the application of scientific principles to mass production, or "Fordism"), many involve collective action by nonmarket institutions in which substantial political costs are incurred to enact new taxes, subsidies, or other rules and regulations.

In the late twentieth century, induced innovation theory was also heavily influenced by the probabilistic search process, modeled by Nelson and Winter (1982), in which entrepreneurs are described as searching in a distribution, hoping for "strikes" in a form of scientific prospecting (Ruttan 1997). While a search model offers a revealing picture of the groping progress of entrepreneurial explorations for new techniques, it does not explicitly account for how the probability of a successful search may be affected by social choices over technology and institutions. Evenson and Kislev (1975: 143), for example, working in the Nelson-Winter tradition, first suggested a model of applied economic research in which the scientist "is assumed to be presented with a given distribution of outcomes whose parameters he cannot directly affect." While a reasonable assumption for an individual scientist or team, it is important to note that the aggregate consequence of many such efforts may actually be to shift the parameters of the distribution in ways that make new discoveries more probable. This enrichment of the probability of new discoveries, or what Bob Evenson (1998) calls "recharge," results from a commitment to scientific and social scientific research expenditures, in which social and/or private capital is invested at the frontiers of change or progress. The more such investments are made, the more malleable technology and institutions are likely to be. If such a milieu is more conducive to innovation overall, it alters the probability of successful entrepreneurial activities, drawing entrepreneurs to the process and increasing the probability that, literally or intellectually, they will "strike it rich."

In addition to the literature on technological innovation, the induced innovation hypothesis is linked to a burgeoning literature on institutional change and collective action (see Ostrom et al. 1994; Sandler 1997), for which Elinor Ostrom was recognized by the Nobel Committee in 2009. Both Ruttan (2003) and Hayami (2005) wrote about the opportunities and challenges to implementing and inducing the adoption of these processes in cases where they are not already in place, and often where bureaucratic or other social structural factors have to be addressed including the use of incentives. Institutional innovation is clearly driven by incentives that require an understanding of the strategic behavior of interdependent actors and rules of social choice in the face of social dilemmas. This is especially true of global or transboundary issues such as climate change, in which national governments, acting individually, are unlikely to resolve them.

Induced innovation theory has been criticized as excessively neoclassical by those who claim that it depends too much on market signals (e.g., factor prices). Koppel (1995: 58), for example, argued that "the robustness of the inducement metaphor is seriously stressed by social and political contexts that simply do not correspond to the market (and *ceteris paribus*) assumptions the metaphor carries." More fundamentally, Daniel W. Bromley (1989: 23) argued that whatever streams of value pertain to induced choices are themselves the result of logically and/or historically prior entitlements defined by property rights and the institutional setup within which choices occur.

With respect to market price signals, Hicks and especially Samuelson (1965) appear to have interpreted "prices" as shadow (rather than market) price signals resulting from constraints imposed by the relative scarcity of factors of production. Only in a first-best world would shadow prices and market prices coincide. Yet the explanatory power of the theory, *as theory*, loses no generality if the constraint imposed by physical scarcity is incompletely captured in prices. This observation is critical in considering environmental scarcity, in which markets often fail. Bromley's objection is that induced innovation theory, especially respecting institutions, is driven by what it seeks to explain, and is in this sense underidentified if not tautological. The logical implication is either that institutions (and technology) should always be treated as given, a view that Bromley does not support, or that everything is endogenous and mutually causative: there really are not any independent variables.

There is another approach, reminiscent of debates over capital as "putty-clay" (Phelps 1963) in which some (perhaps a great deal) of technology and institutions are "given" to a particular group by the previous period but in which at least some choices of technique, and/or institutions, are more flexible. The determinism associated with the prior setup defines how much of the choice of current generations is "clay," and how much is received as malleable "putty." The putty/clay ratio thus determines the scope of both the technical and institutional opportunity set. The more restricted is this opportunity set, the more "path dependency" in technology or institutions is likely to be observed (see David 1985). Another implication is that the putty-clay ratio, in both technical and institutional choices, will define the capacity of individuals and groups to adapt to changes in their physical, social, or intellectual environment, based on the degree to which they are "set in their ways." If societies make investment choices that augment their putty relative to their clay, they improve their capacity to respond and adapt to change, both technologically and institutionally. Whether and when such choices are made will be discussed in greater detail below.

In summary, the induced innovation hypothesis is often criticized for depending too much on market prices and not enough on the nonmarket institutions affecting economic change. Yet relative factor scarcities (not prices) are the fundamental basis of the theory, which has enriched the analysis of both technical and institutional choice and the factors that lead to particular paths of technological or institutional change. Market prices may not reflect this scarcity due to externalities or other market failures. Even when prices are distorted or do not accurately reflect environmental or other values, society may still find that these values carry increasing weight. In these circumstances, nonmarket valuations of things increasingly perceived as scarce (e.g., biological diversity) can induce a search for both technological and/or institutional innovations that allow this relative scarcity to be better reflected. The probability that this search will be successful will be determined largely by investments in appropriate new technology and institutions, and the scientific and social scientific research that guides this innovation process. A fundamental issue is why and when some societies invest in new technological and institutional possibilities, while others do not. We turn now to the idea that certain ecological issues are defined by the perception of increasing scarcity of environmental goods—and the social response that has resulted and continues to result from this perception.

II. Induced Environmental Change

In 1971, the same year in which Hayami and Ruttan's *Agricultural Development* was first published, Ruttan delivered his presidential address, "Technology and the Environment," to the American Agricultural Economics Association (AAEA) (Ruttan 1971, which was further elaborated and extended in his last paper, chapter 16 of this volume), Given that the 1971 paper came out only a year after the first declaration of Earth Day, it came at a time of great ferment and attention to environmental policy innovation in the United States. In a comprehensive historical treatment of U.S. environmental policy, Andrews (1999) argued that the first two centuries of American history were dominated by natural resource extraction, followed in the late nineteenth and twentieth centuries by government struggles to manage extraction by balancing it against conservation and, occasionally, preservation. Yet only in the 1960s did the American public, awakened by books such as Rachel Carson's *Silent Spring* (1962), begin widely to appreciate the value of protecting its natural resource heritage. And despite government attention to the strategic value of managing these resources for the future (the result of the 1952 Paley Commission Report), the public increasingly questioned whether existing laws and policies were sufficient to do so. At the same time, growing per capita incomes meant that leisure could be spent acquiring environmental amenities in the nation's National Parks and Forests.

While struggles continued between those seeking continued extraction of resources and those seeking to protect and preserve them, the balance slowly shifted in public opinion in favor of advocates of the latter. Led by legal strategies developed by groups such as the Environmental Defense Fund and Natural Resources Defense Council, court actions and legislative initiatives blossomed. By 1970, Lynton Caldwell had for a decade called on government to use environment as a central focus for public policy (Caldwell 1963). Led by Senators Gaylord Nelson of Wisconsin, Edmund Muskie of Maine, and Henry Jackson of Washington, and acknowledged and signed by President Nixon, the National Environmental Policy Act (NEPA) was passed in an extraordinary show of bipartisanship. Richard Nixon declared the 1970s the "decade of the environment" and sent Congress a blueprint that created the Environmental Protection Agency in December 1970 (Andrews 1999: 229). While the political pendulum has swung several times since (notably early in the Reagan administration and in the George W. Bush administration, when an antiregulatory agenda bloomed) environmental protection became a consensus part of the OECD countries' idea of what governments can and should do.

At a theoretical level, Ruttan recognized explicitly that induced innovation did not require fully functioning markets and that changes in individual and social choice could be induced precisely by the fact that such markets were perceived to be missing. Ruttan and Hayami wrote in a 1995 retrospective: "In spite of missing markets, the rising demand for environmental amenities has induced a response in the political marketplace" (Ruttan and Hayami 1995: 183). They gave emphasis, however, to another economic explanation for this process: the role of income growth. In effect, Hayami and Ruttan argued that only in countries where some threshold of affluence had been achieved would sufficient value be attached to environmental amenities to trigger social, including regulatory, responses.

The exact level of this threshold would become a central point in later debates over the environmental "Kuznets Curve." A corollary claim was that income growth had the opposite effect on the relative value conferred on commodities, especially agricultural goods. Hence, income growth should simultaneously raise the value of environmental services while lowering the value of agricultural goods and other raw materials and commodities.

The power of this argument was derived in part from its simplicity. The second part is really a social projection to all commodities of Engels' Law: the income expansion path for food plotted against other goods is such that total expenditures for food *fall* relative to these other goods with increases in income. The first part, dubbed "Ruttan's Principle," was that the income expansion path for environmental amenities plotted against other goods is such that total expenditures for these amenities *rise* relative to other goods with increases in income (Runge 1987: 254).

Two important implications follow from this argument. First, Engels' Law (demand for food falls, relative to other goods, with higher incomes), implies that as income rises, commodity producers may have a smaller claim on social rents than producers of other goods and services. By contrast, Ruttan's Principle (demand for environmental quality rises strongly at higher incomes) implies that income growth will lead societal resources to be shifted toward the supply of environmental quality and technologies that promote it (see Dunlap 1975). This is reinforced if environmental quality reductions are perceived as irreversible (Smith 1975). If income effects work in this way, they should apply both across countries and within them. In the United States, for example, higher-income groups should demand environmental quality more strongly than lower-income groups. Recent increases in commodity prices and the demand for food, combined with anti-regulatory hostility to environmental rulemaking, call these observations into question, but also suggest that the dialectical struggle is ongoing.

The dialectical interplay of Ruttan's Principle and Engels' Law helps explain trends in the environmental regulation of agriculture, as well as relative trends in the value attached to environmental amenities versus raw commodities. Ruttan's Principle predicts that if equilibrium between willingness to pay and the implicit value of environmental quality is not achieved by markets, higher-income groups and countries will have greater reason than poor ones to correct this market failure through environmental regulation. This suggests, first, that debates over environmental quality characteristics, and remedies for missing markets, will be most intense in high-income circles. Second, these debates can be expected to revolve around what—not whether—something should be done to protect environmental quality. Some may favor market or quasi-market solutions while others prefer regulation, but environmental quality will increasingly be a consensus objective. Correspondingly, international debates over issues such as climate change will occur primarily between high-income countries such as Canada, the EU, and the United States, countries which expect to contribute to the solutions.

Low-income countries, even if they share substantial responsibility for problems such as climate change, will plead that more immediate needs, such as food security, reduce their obligations to sacrifice in the name of the global environment.

Looking backward, these arguments anticipated the tensions over climate change that would define future fault lines between North and South.

> [I]n relatively high-income economies the income elasticity of demand for commodities and services related to sustenance is low and declines as income continues to rise, while the income elasticity of demand for more effective disposal of residuals and for environmental amenities is high and continues to rise. This is in sharp contrast to the situation in poor countries where the income elasticity of demand is high for sustenance and low for environmental amenities. (Ruttan 1971: 707–8)

The simple power of the argument that income effects are of such primary importance has been questioned. Some have also questioned the idea that environmental amenities' value rises with income. It may also be that the comparative value of agricultural commodities, or at least the capacity of their producers to extract social rents, remains high even at high incomes in countries with strong rural traditions and a collective memory of food insecurity, as in much of Europe or Japan. The idea that income growth, especially growth due to increased trade openness, leads to demands for environmental protection, has now become central to debates over climate change.

III. Delta: The Climate Commons

The idea that income expansion leads to reductions in environmental damages is most famously captured in an inverted Kuznets Curve, in which a pollutant such as SO_2 is shown to follow a quadratic or cubic path in relation to increases in income (Kuznets 1955). Grossman and Kreuger (1995) suggested that data from the World Health Organization (WHO) of environmental pollutants in forty-four cities across the world showed such a relationship, with the downward slope in pollution beginning at about $5,000 in constant income. Unfortunately, some advocates of trade liberalization used this finding to advocate trade reform by asserting a kind of automaticity to pollution reductions, as if economic growth offered its own antidote to climate change. Grossman and Kreuger made no such claim, instead suggesting that the impacts of income growth be decomposed into the impacts on the scale of economic (and polluting) activity, the techniques of production (more or less pollution intensive) and the composition of output (dirtier or cleaner). These arguments were formalized and further advanced by Copeland and Taylor (1994, 1995), Selden and Song (1994), and Hauer (1997).

We still do not understand the essential mechanisms by which income growth leads to reductions in pollution, or whether such reductions even occur in most cases, especially given cultural dynamics, with China as the outstanding test (Osnos, 2009). While recent evidence continues to support the fact that cleaner technologies can reduce pollution from the scale of production, such choices of techniques generally result from regulatory constraints that raise the private costs of polluting behavior (Antweiller et al. 1998). In other words, the Kuznets function is *itself* subject to different paths depending on technological and institutional choices, reflecting the relative value of environmental amenities attached to them by different societies. The problem of the "climate commons" is one of induced innovation in the face of market failure coupled with a global negotiation over individual country contributions (Runge 2009). The question is whether the social resources necessary to agree on global solutions will be directed to climate change at the rapid rate that will be required.

This question was at the heart of the struggle in Copenhagen in December, 2009 over a global climate agreement. The political process at both the national and the international level was only beginning to respond—and grudgingly—to the negative climate impacts of economic growth. Notwithstanding some of the examples noted above, agriculture has until recently escaped this oversight relative to industrial manufacturing in most OECD countries, despite growing evidence that agricultural practices are central to understanding global carbon balances (Fargione et al. 2008; Searchinger et al. 2008). Moreover, the data suggest that such responses are much less likely at lower levels of income. In the United States and Western Europe, environmental responsibility and even corporate environmental activism are very much in favor with the public and a large part of the private sector. But in most developing countries (and in the companies that operate there), environmental regulation is regarded as at best an affectation of the rich, and at worst an excuse to deny market access to Third World exporters as a form of "green protectionism." A central conundrum facing global climate policy is how to connect incentives for upward harmonization of environmental standards to the dynamic process of trade liberalization, while avoiding the use of "environmental conditionality" as an excuse for closing off market access (Runge 2009).

Critics of naive interpretations of the Kuznets Curve (including this author) have emphasized the role of national and international policy choices in reducing greenhouse gas emissions as income grows. Lopez (1994), for example, showed that when growth is determined exogenously from environmental quality, if polluters do not internalize the costs of pollution, environmental degradation will continue to rise with economic growth. Ezzati et al. (1998) demonstrated that the inverted Kuznets Curve can be obtained only in very specific circumstances in which multiple factors (not just income) interact. Antweiler et al. (1998), in the same spirit, noted that it is only when income growth and factor abundance are jointly allowed to determine trade and pollution patterns that meaningful empirical estimates are possible.

None of this is inconsistent with the earlier work of Ruttan and Hayami and with Ruttan's Principle; it only broadens and deepens the delta of work that it has generated. But it remains striking how differently the role of global economic growth and its impacts on the environment are perceived today from a quarter-century ago. The inverted Kuznets Curve, even if its mechanisms are ill-understood, suggests an optimistic view of both technological and institutional adaptation to climate challenges. Some, however, continue pessimistically to see trade, and growth, as engines of destruction (see Runge 1998).

The question of innovation possibilities in the context of climate change is also addressed by Otsuka in chapter 1. The capital-theoretic idea of a putty-clay model, in which output is composed of malleable production goods (putty) that are baked into machines (clay) that cannot be turned back into putty remains of relevance. In putty-clay models as developed by Salter (1960), Phelps (1963), and Solow (1966), the process of transformation is costless and occurs instantaneously even if it is irreversible (Nuti 1970). Yet if it is recognized that both technologies and institutions are given in the short run, and that converting one into the other is neither costless nor instantaneous, a theory emerges in which output is apportioned between them in a way that defines the range of technical and institutional choice. The degrees of freedom accorded to these choices depend on the social putty-clay ratio, which is in turn a function of investments in research that increases the social flexibility with which new technologies and institutions are developed.

I conjecture that if we could measure the putty-clay ratio in terms of both the technological and institutional opportunities open to individuals in different social settings, we would find that societies that invest, both publicly and privately, in R&D face wider innovation possibilities—again, something stressed by Hayami and Ruttan. From this perspective, even if all societies are assumed to have an equal proportion of agents that we call (generally ex post facto) "entrepreneurs," the capacity of entrepreneurs to solve technical and institutional problems will depend on the putty they can mold, versus the clay they are given, as well as the costs and time required to remold putty into new technical and institutional forms. These costs and time are in turn a reflection of prior investments in research and development.

Where there is little putty and only fixed methods to deal with, innovation possibilities are narrowed, making innovation less likely and encouraging a pessimistic view of technological and institutional progress. Where entrepreneurial agents are mobile, they will move to lands of putty and abandon traditional lands of clay, reinforcing centers of optimism and innovation while leaving vintage clay to slowly erode and become obsolete. Over time, therefore, these centers of innovation will become technological and institutional oases where technological and institutional optimism is both widely held and widely reinforced not just by innovation possibility, but by its actuality. Cities of clay, by contrast, will become centers of technological and institutional pessimism. Silicon Valley, in this sense, is a figurative oasis of putty; much of the Eastern Europe may be made of elegant but eroding clay. How and whether these optimists and pessimists can interact successfully in global climate negotiations remains to be seen.

IV. Other Vistas: Institutional Innovation in Asian Villages

While Ruttan applied institutional innovation theories to environmental issues, Hayami did so through his intensive village studies in Asia. Particularly relevant to the induced innovation thesis was the pioneering village study of Hayami and Kikuchi (1981). This study demonstrated that village institutions, including labor, employment, and land tenancy systems, are induced to change in order to achieve greater efficiency in resource allocation and risk sharing as a response to population pressure and technological changes in agriculture. Furthering this discussion was Hayami and Kikuchi 1981 and 2000, concerned primarily with institutional changes in the Philippine villages; Hayami and Otsuka 1993, which addresses the issue of efficiency of land tenancy in Asia; and Hayami and Kawagoe 1993, which explores the development of rural commerce and industries. Through these studies, Hayami and his colleagues have proved that institutional innovation theories are relevant for a proper understanding of changes and differences in village institutions, which many people may think are rigid and determined by customs and traditions. At Ruttan's suggestion, these village studies added to the discussion presented in the second edition of Hayami and Ruttan 1985. Thus, a major difference between the first edition of Hayami and Ruttan 1971 and the second one lies in the intensive discussions of institutional changes in Asian villages. In this way, the second edition was successfully enriched by the village studies. Similarly, continuing work is needed on case studies in both the ongoing adoption of agricultural innovations in a variety of contexts, including Africa, and the adoption of new institutional responses to climate change.

Conclusion

Hayami and Ruttan's theory of induced innovation provides a way of looking at the history of an idea: that the natural environment has value and that choices made in the last four decades have been induced by increases in its perceived value. A stream of thought began in Hicks's insight that firms adopt techniques according to the relative abundance of factor inputs. This stream widened to a river of research when Hayami and Ruttan generalized the argument to the technological and institutional choices of differentially endowed societies such as the United States and Japan. At the same time, Ruttan applied this argument to the environment and its value, which together with changes in income could be expected to induce choices in favor of environmental protection, especially relative to goods such as food, even where (or, indeed, because) markets failed. While his primary focus remained the expansion of the theory of induced innovation, Hayami also stressed the importance of this issue in recent articles written with Douangneune and Godo (2005) and Dikishit and Mishra (2006).

The river has now become a delta, based especially in the widening debate over income growth and climate change—whether economic progress can create the wherewithal to confront climate challenges or is instead an engine of global environmental destruction. Fundamentally, this is a debate over whether growth in market demand, combined with recognized market failure, leads to induced innovations that offer environmental protection through new technologies and institutions. It is of particular relevance as income growth occurs in the developing world, where optimists believe that environmental protection can occur too. Finally, I have observed that how rapidly societies can adapt to change, justifying such optimism, ultimately depends on their endowments of technical and institutional innovation potential, the amount of putty relative to the amount of clay, but that the putty-clay ratio itself may be a result of investments in research in both the natural and social sciences.

REFERENCES

Abarientos, E. P. (1966), "An Analysis of Rice Production in Taiwan," International Rice Research Institute, Los Banos, August, mimeo.

Abegglen, J. C., and Stalk, G., Jr. (1985), *Kaisha: The Japanese Corporation*. New York: Basic Books.

Abramovitz, M. (1952), "Economics of Growth," in B. F. Haley (ed.), *A Survey of Contemporary Economics*, 132–78. Homewood, IL: Richard D. Irwin.

Acemoglu, D. (1998), "Why Do New Technologies Complement Skills? Directed Technical Change and Wage Inequality," *Quarterly Journal of Economics* 113: 1055–89.

Acemoglu, D. (2002), "Technical Change, Inequality, and the Labor Market," *Journal of Economic Literature* 40 (1): 7–72.

Acemoglu, D. (2003), "Patterns of Skill Premia," *Review of Economic Studies* 70: 199–230.

Acemoglu, D. (2005), "Constitutions, Politics and Economics: A Review Essay on Persson and Tabellini's *The Economic Effects of the Constitution*," *Journal of Economic Literature* 53: 1025–48.

Acemoglu, D. (2007), "Equilibrium Bias of Technology," *Econometrica* 75: 1371–409.

Acemoglu, D., Johnson, S., and Robinson, J. A. (2001), "The Colonial Origins of Comparative Development: An Empirical Investigation," *American Economic Review* 91: 1369–401.

Acemoglu, D., and Linn, J. (2004), "Market Size in Innovation: Theory and Evidence from the Pharmaceutical Industry," *Quarterly Journal of Economics* 119: 1049–90.

Adams, R. M., Hurd, B., Lenhart, S., and Leary, N. (1998), "Effects of Global Climate Change on Agriculture: An Interpretive Review," *Climate Research* 11 (December): 19–30.

Adelman, I., and Morris, C. T. (1968), "An Econometric Model of Socio-Economic and Political Change in Underdeveloped Countries," *American Economic Review* 58 (December): 1184–218.

Aghion, P., and Howitt, P. (1992), "A Model of Growth through Creative Destruction," *Econometrica* 60 (March): 323–51.

Aghion, P., and Howitt, P. (1998), *Endogenous Growth Theory*. Cambridge, MA: MIT Press.

Ahmad, S. (1966), "On the Theory of Induced Innovation," *Economic Journal* 76 (June): 344–57.

Ahmad, S. (1967), "A Rejoinder to Professor Kennedy," *Economic Journal* 77 (December): 960–63.

Akerlof, G. A. (1984), *An Economic Theorist's Book of Tales*. Cambridge: Cambridge University Press.

Akino, M., and Hayami, Y. (1974), "Sources of Agricultural Growth in Japan, 1880–1965," *Quarterly Journal of Economics* 83 (August): 454–79.

Akiyama, T., and Nishio, N. (1996), "Indonesia's Cocoa Boom: Hands-Off Policy Encourages Smallholder Dynamism," Policy Research Working Paper 1580, World Bank, Washington, DC.

Alchian, A., and Demsetz, H. (1973), "The Property Right Paradigm," *Journal of Economic History* 33 (March): 16–27.

Alexandratos, N. (ed.) (1995), *World Agriculture: Toward 2010: An FAO Study*, 58–63. Rome: Food and Agriculture Organization.

Allen, R. C. (1982), "The Efficiency and Distributional Consequences of Eighteenth-Century Enclosures," *Economic Journal* 92: 937–53.

Allen, R. C. (1992), *Enclosure and the Yeoman: The Agricultural Development of the South Midlands 1450–1850*. Oxford: Oxford University Press.

Almond, G. A. (1993), "'The Early Impact of Downs': An Economic Theory of Democracy on American Political Science," in B. Grofman (ed.), *Information, Participation, and Choice*, 201–7. Ann Arbor: University of Michigan Press.

Alston, L. J., Chan-Kang, C., Marra, M., and Pardey, P. (1999), *A Meta Analysis of Rates of Return in Agricultural R&D—Ex Pede Hercuhm?* Washington, DC: International Food Policy Research Institute.

Amable, B. (1994), "Endogenous Growth Theory, Convergence and Divergence," in G. Silverberg and L. Soete (eds.), *The Economics of Growth and Technical Change*, 20–44. Aldershot, UK: Edward Elgar.

Anderson, J. R., and Thompapillia, J. (1990), *Soil Conservation in Developing Countries: Project and Policy Interaction*. Washington, DC: World Bank.

Anderson, K., and Hayami, Y. with associates (1986), *The Political Economy of Agricultural Protection: East Asia in International Perspective*. London: Allen and Verurd).

Andrews, R. N. L. (1999), *Managing the Environment, Managing Ourselves: A History of American Environmental Policy*. New Haven, CT: Yale University Press.

Antweiler, W., Copeland, B. R., and Taylor, M. S. (1998), "Is Free Trade Good for the Environment?" Department of Economics, University of Wisconsin, March 17.

Aoki, M. (2001), *Toward A Comparative Institutional Analysis*. Cambridge, MA: The MIT Press.

Ariff, M., and Hill, H. (1985), *Export-Oriented Industrialization: The Askan Experience*. Sydney: Allen and Unwin.

Arrow, K. J. (1968), "The Economics of Moral Hazard: Further Comment," *American Economic Review* 58 (June): 537–39.

Arrow, K. J., Chenery, H. B., Minhas, B. S., and Solow, R. M. (1961), "Capital-Labor Substitution and Economic Efficiency," *Review of Economic Statistics* 43 (August): 225–50.

Asanuma, B. (1985), "Organization of Parts Purchases in the Japanese Automobile Industry," *Japanese Economic Studies* 13 (Summer): 32–35.

Asanuma, B. (1988), "Manufacturer-Supplier Relationships in Japan in the Concept of Relation-Specific Skill," *Journal of Japanese and International Economies* 3 (March): 1–30.

Asian Development Bank (2000), *Rural Asia beyond the Green Revolution*. Manila: Asian Development Bank.

Atkinson, A. B. (1969), "The Timescale of Economic Models: How Long Is the Long Run?" *Review of Economic Studies* 36 (April): 137–52.

Azam, K. (1973), "The Future of the Green Revolution in West Pakistan: A Choice of Strategy," *International Journal of Agrarian Affairs* 5: 4–18.

Bacha, E. L. (1977), "The Kuznet's Curve and Beyond: Growth and Change in Inequalities," in E. Malinvaud (ed.), *Economic Growth and Resources*, vol. 1: *The Major Issues*, 52–73. New York: St. Martin's.

Backus, D. K., Kehoe, P. J., and Kehoe, T. J. (1992), "In Search of Scale Effects in Trade and Growth," *Journal of Economic Theory* 58 (December): 377–409.

Balcombe, K., Bailey, A., and Morrison, J. (2002), "Stochastic Biases in Technical Change in U.S. Agriculture: A Bootstrap Approach," *Canadian Journal of Agricultural Economics/ Revue canadienne d'agroeconomie* 50: 67–84.

Baldwin, R. E. (1956), "Patterns of Development in Newly Settled Regions," *Manchester School of Economic and Social Studies* 24 (May): 161–79.

Bardhan, P. K. (1970), "Green Revolution and Agricultural Labourers," *Economic and Political Weekly* 5 (29–31): 239–46.

Bardhan, P. K. (1977), "Variations in Forms of Tenancy in a Peasant Economy," *Journal of Development Economics* 42 (June): 105–18.

Bardhan, P. K. (1979), "Agricultural Development and Land Tenancy in a Peasant Economy: A Theoretical and Empirical Analysis," *American Journal of Agricultural Economics* 61 (February): 48–57.

Bardhan, P. K. (1993), "Economics of Development and the Development of Economics," *Journal of Economic Perspectives* 7 (Spring): 129–42.

Bardhan, P. K. (1995), "The Contribution of Endogenous Growth Theory to the Analysis of Development Problems: An Assessment," in J. Behrman and T. N. Srinivasan (eds.), *Handbook of Development Economics*, vol. 3, part 2, 2983–98. New York: Elsevier Science.

Barker, R., and Cordova, V. (1978), "Labor Utilization in Rice Production," in R. Barker and Y. Hayami (eds.), *Economic Consequence of the New Rice Technology*, 113–36. Los Banos, the Philippines: International Rice Research Institute.

Barker, R., Herdt, R., and Rose, B. (1985), *The Asian Rice Economy*. Baltimore: Johns Hopkins University Press.

Barker, R. M., Crisostomo, W., and Duff, B. (1972), "Employment and Technological Change in Philippine Agriculture," *International Labor Review* 106: 111–39.

Barker, R. R. (1969), "Economic Aspects of High Yielding Varieties of Rice with Special Reference to National Price Policies," paper prepared for Thirteenth Session of the FAO Study Group on Rice, Manila, March 20–27.

Barlow, C., and Tomich, T. P. (1991), "Indonesian Agricultural Development: The Awkward Case of Smallholder Tree Crops," *Bulletin of Indonesian Economic Studies* 27 (December): 29–55.

Barro, R. J. (1997), "Determinants of Economic Growth: A Cross-Country Empirical Study," Development Discussion Paper 579, Harvard Institute for International Development, Cambridge, MA, April.

Barro, R. J., and Sala-i-Martin, X. X. (1995), *Economic Growth*. New York: McGraw Hill.

Barton, G. T., and Cooper, M. R. (1945), *Farm Production in War and Peace*, U.S. Department of Agriculture, Bureau of Agricultural Economics, FM 53, December.

Barton, G. T., and Cooper, M. R. (1948), "Relation of Agricultural Production to Inputs," *Review of Economics and Statistics* 30 (May): 117–26.

Bartsch, W. (1977), *Employment and Technology Choice in Asian Agriculture*. New York: Praeger.

Bates, R. H. (1983), *Markets and States in Tropical Africa*. Berkeley: University of California Press.

Bauer, P. T. (1948), *The Rubber Industry*. London: Longman and Green.

Bauer, P. T. (1954), *West African Trade: A Study of Competition, Oligopoly and Monopoly in a Changing Economy*. Cambridge: Cambridge University Press.

Bauer, P. T., and Meier, G. M. (1994), "Traders and Development," in G. M. Meier (ed.), *From Classical Economics to Development Economics*, 135–43. New York: St. Martin's.

Baughman, E. T. (1952), "Financing Young Farmers," *Journal of Farm Economics* 34 (December): 930–36.

Baumol, W. J. (1986), "Productivity Growth, Convergence, and Welfare," *American Economic Review* 76 (December): 1072–85.

Baumol, W. J., and Wolff, E. N. (1988), "Productivity Growth, Convergence, and Welfare," *American Economic Review* 78 (December): 1155–59.

Bautista, R. M. (1987), *Production Incentive in Philippine Agriculture: Effects of Trade and Exchange Rate Policies*. Washington, DC: International Food Policy Research Institute.

Becker, G. S. (1974), "A Theory of Social Interactions," *Journal of Political Economy* 82 (6): 1063–93.

Beckford, G. L. (1972), *Persistent Poverty: Underdevelopment in Plantation Economies of the Third World*. New York: Oxford University Press.

Behrman, J., and Srinivasan, T. N. (eds.) (1995), *Handbook of Development Economics*, vols. 3A and 3B. Amsterdam: North Holland.

Behrman, J. R. (1966), "Price Elasticity of the Marketed Surplus of a Subsistence Crop," *Journal of Farm Economics* 48 (November): 875–93.

Bell, D. (1960), *The End of Ideology*. Glencoe, IL: Free Press.

Benedict, M. R. (1955), *Can We Solve the Farm Problem: An Analysis of Federal Aid to Agriculture*. New York: Twentieth Century Fund.

Benedict, M. R., and Stein, O. C. (1956), *The Agricultural Commodity Programs: Two Decades of Experience*. New York: Twentieth Century Fund.

Bennett, H. H. (1931), "The Problem of Soil Erosion in the United States," *Annals of the Association of American Geographers* 21: 147–70.

Bernstein, E. (1899), *Die Voraussetzungen des Socialisums und die Aufgaben der Socialdemokratie*. Stuttgart: Dietz.

Bhagwati, J. N. (1966), *The Economics of Underdeveloped Countries*. New York: McGraw-Hill.

Bhattacharjee, J. P. (1955), "Resource Use and Productivity in World Agriculture," *Japanese Farm Economics* 37 (February): 57–71.

Binswanger, H. P. (1973), "The Measurement of Biased Efficiency Gains of U.S. and Japanese Agriculture to Test the Induced Innovation Hypothesis," Ph.D. diss., University of North Carolina, Chapel Hill.

Binswanger, H. P. (1974a), "A Cost Function Approach to the Measurement of Elasticities of Factor Demand and Elasticities of Substitution," *American Journal of Agricultural Economics* 56 (2): 377–86.

Binswanger, H. P. (1974b), "The Measurement of Technical Change Biases with Many Factors of Production," *American Economic Review* 64 (6): 964–76.

Binswanger, H. P. (1978), *The Economics of Tractors in South Asia*. Hyderabad, India: International Crops Research Institute for the Semi-Arid Tropics.

Binswanger, H. P. (1984), "A Microeconomic Approach to Induced Innovation," *Economic Journal* 84 (December): 940–58.

Binswanger, H. P., Deininger, K., and Feder, G. (1995), "Power, Distortions, Revolt and Reform in Agricultural Relations," in J. Behrman and T. N. Srinivasan (eds.), *Handbook of Development Economics*, vol. 3, part 2, 2659–772. Amsterdam: North-Holland.

Binswanger, H. P., Evenson, R. E., Florencio, C. A., and White, B. N. W. (eds.) (1981), *Rural Household Studies in Asia*. Singapore: University of Singapore Press.

Binswanger, H. P., and Rosenzweig, M. R. (1986), "Behavioral and Material Determinants of Production Relations in Agriculture," *Journal of Development Studies* 22–23 (April): 503–39.

Binswanger, H. P., Ruttan, V. W., et al. (1978), *Induced Innovation: Technology, Institutions, and Development*. Baltimore: Johns Hopkins University Press.

Black, J. D. (1939), "Contributions of Agricultural Economists: Discussion," *Journal of Farm Economics* 21: 25–30.

Black, J. D. (1945), "Factors Conditioning Innovations in Agriculture," *Mechanical Engineering* 67 (March): 181–82.

Black, J. D. (1955), "Colin Clark on the Future of U.S. Agriculture," *Journal of Farm Economics* 37 (February): 121–24.

Blaug, M. (1961), "Economic Imperialism Revisited," *Yale Review* 50 (Spring): 335–49.

Blaug, M. (1974), *The Cambridge Revolution: Success or Failure?*. London: Institute of Economic Affairs.

Bliss, C., and Stern, N. (1982), *Palanpur: The Economy of an Indian Village*. Oxford: Oxford University Press.

Bober, M. M. (1940), *Karl Marx's Interpretation of History*, 226–31. Cambridge: Harvard University Press.

Boeke, J. S. (1953), *Economics and Economic Policy of Dual Societies as Exemplified by Indonesia*. New York: Institute of Pacific Relations.

Boettke, P. J., and Coyne, C. J. (2005), "Methodological Individualism, Spontaneous Order and the Research Program of the Workshop in Political Theory and Policy Analysis," *Journal of Economic Behavior and Organization* 57 (Special Issue): 145–58.

Bohm, P. (1985), "Comparative Analysis of Alternative Policy Instruments," in A. V. Kneese and J. Sweeney (eds.), *Handbook of Natural Resource and Energy Economics*, vol. 1, 395–460. Amsterdam: North Holland.

Booth, A. (1988), *Agricultural Development in Indonesia*. Sydney: Allen and Unwin.

Boserup, E. (1965), *The Conditions of Agricultural Growth*. London: Allen and Unwin.

Brandow, G. E. (1961), "Interrelations among Demands for Farm Products and Implications for Control of Market Supply," *Pennsylvania Agricultural Experiment Station Bulletin* 680.

Brandow, G. E. (1977), "Policy for Commercial Agriculture, 1945–71," in L. R. Martin (ed.), *A Survey of Agricultural Economics Literature*, vol. 1. Minneapolis: University of Minnesota Press.

Brewster, J. M. (1950), "The Machine Process in Agriculture and Industry," *Journal of Farm Economics* 52 (February): 69–81.

Britto, R. (1973), "Some Recent Developments in the Theory of Economic Growth: An Interpretation," *Journal of Economic Literature* 11 (December): 1343–66.

Bromley, D. W. (1989), *Economic Interests and Institutions: The Conceptual Foundations of Public Policy*. New York: Basil Blackwell.

Brown, L., and Halweil, B. (1998), "China's Water Shortage Could Shake World Food Security," *World Watch* 11 (4): 10–21.

Brown, M. (1966), *On the Theory and Measurement of Technological Change*. Cambridge: Cambridge University Press.

Buck, R. K. (1954), *Beginning Farmers, a Vulnerable Group in American Agriculture*, NPA Planning Pamphlet No. 88, Washington, DC.

Bureau of Statistics Office of the Prime Minister (1949), *Japan Statistical Yearbook* (Tokyo): 630–31.

Burnside, C. (1996), "Production Function Regressions, Returns to Scale, and Externalities," *Journal of Monetary Economics* 37 (April): 177–201.

Cain, L. P., and Paterson, D. G. (1981), "Factor Bias and Technical Change in Manufacturing: The American System: 1850–1919," *Journal of Economic History* 41: 341–60.

Caldwell, L. (1963), "Environment: A New Focus for Public Policy?" *Public Administration Review* 22: 132–39.

Calkins, P. H. (1984), "Efforts to Reconcile the New Policies with Marx-Leninism," paper presented at AAEA annual meeting, Ithaca, NY, August 8.

Carson, R. (1962), *Silent Spring*. New York: Houghton-Mifflin.

Cassman, K. G. (1999), "Ecological Intensification of Cereal Production Systems: Yield Potential, Soil Quality, and Precision Agriculture," *Proceedings of the National Academy of Sciences USA* 96: 5952–59.

Cavallo, D., and Mundlak, Y. (1982), "Agriculture and Economic Growth in an Open Economy: The Case of Argentina," International Food Policy Research Institute, Research Report No. 36. Washington, DC.

Cernea, M. (2005), "Sociological Knowledge and Induced Development," outline for a social science conference, Bibliotheca Alexandriana, Alexandria, Egypt, May 30–June 1.

Chambers, C. A. (1963), *Seedtime of Reform: American Social Service and Social Action: 1918–1933*. Minneapolis: University of Minnesota Press.

Chambers, J. D., and Mingay, G. E. (1966), *The Agricultural Revolution 1750–1880*. London: B. T. Batsford.

Chandler, R. F. (1962), "Maximum Yield Potentialities for Rice," *Philippine Agriculturalist* 46 (September): 167–74.

Chang, H. T. (1959), *Rice Improvement in Taiwan*, Chinese-American Joint Commission on Rural Reconstruction, Plant Industry Series No. 15, Taipei, May.

Chang, H. Y., and Myers, R. H. (1963), "Japanese Colonial Development Policy in Taiwan, 1895–1906: A Case of Bureaucratic Entrepreneurship," *Journal of Asian Studies* 22 (August): 433–49.

Chari, V. W., Kehoe, P. J., and McGrattan, E. R. (1996), "The Poverty of Nations: A Quantitative Exploration," Minneapolis Federal Reserve Bank of Minneapolis Research Department Staff Report 204, January.

Chayanov, A. V. (1966), *Theory of Peasant Economy*, ed. D. Thorner, B. Kerblay, and R. E. F. Smith. Homewood IL: Richard D. Irwin. Orig. pub. 1925.

Chenery, H. B., and Srinivasan, T. N. (eds.) (1988–1989), *Handbook of Development Economics*, vols. 1 and 2. Amsterdam: North Holland.

Chenery, H. B., and Strout, A. M. (1966), "Foreign Assistance and Economic Development," *American Economic Review* 56 (September): 679–733.

Cheung, S. N. S. (1969), *The Theory of Share Tenancy*. Chicago: University of Chicago Press.

Chipman, J. S. (1992), "Intra-Industry Trade, Factor Proportions and Aggregation," in W. Neuefeind and R. Riezman (eds.), *Economic Theory and International Trade*. Berlin: Springer-Verlag.

Christenson, R. M. (1959), *The Brannan Plan: Farm Politics and Policy*. Ann Arbor: University of Michigan Press.

Churchart, C. (1957), *Rice Marketing in Thailand*, Ph.D. diss., Louisiana State University.

Ciriacy-Wantrup, S. V., and Bishop, R. C. (1975), "Common Property as a Concept in Natural Resources Policy," *Natural Resources Journal* 15: 713–27.

Clague, C., Keefer, P., Knack, S., and Olson, M. (1996), "Property and Contract Rights in Autocracies and Democracies," *Journal of Economic Growth* 1 (June): 243–76.

Clark, C. (1940), *The Conditions of Economic Progress*. London: Macmillan Press.

Clark, C. (1954), "Afterthoughts on Paley," *Review of Economics and Statistics* 36 (August): 267–73.

Clark, C. (1967), Review of Nakamura 1966, *Journal of Agricultural Economics* 18 (September): 413–34.

Clark, W. L., and Munn, R. E. (eds.) (1989), *Sustainable Development of the Biosphere*. Cambridge: Cambridge University Press.

Cleaver, H. M., Jr. (1972), "The Contradictions of the Green Revolution," *American Economic Review* 62: 177–86.

Cline, W. (1975), "Distribution and Development: A Survey of the Literature," *Journal of Development Economics* 1: 359–400.

Coase, R. H. (1937), "The Nature of the Firm," *Economica* 16 (6): 386–405.

Coase, R. H. (1960), "The Problem of Social Cost," *Journal of Law and Economics* 3 (October): 1–44.

Cochrane, W. W. (1945), "A Price Policy for Agriculture, Consistent with Economic Progress That Will Promote Adequate and More Stable Income from Farming," *Journal of Farm Economics* 27: 813–20.

Cochrane, W. W. (1946), "Income Payments as a Substitute for Support Prices," *Journal of Farm Economics* 28: 1024–29.

Cochrane, W. W. (1947), "Farm Price Gyrations—an Aggregate Hypothesis," *Journal of Farm Economics* 29: 383–408.

Cochrane, W. W. (1958), *Farm Prices: Myth and Reality*. Minneapolis: University of Minnesota Press.

Cochrane, W. W. (1979), *The Development of American Agriculture: A Historical Analysis*. Minneapolis: University of Minnesota Press.

Cochrane, W. W. (1984), "Agricultural Policy in the United States—A Long View," paper presented in Benjamin Hibbard Memorial Lecture Series, University of Wisconsin, Madison, April 13.

Cochrane, W. W., and Lampe, Harlen, C. (1953), "The Nature of the Race between Food Supplies and Demand in the United States, 1951–75," *Journal of Farm Economics* 35 (May): 203–22.

Cochrane, W. W., and Ryan, M. E. (1976), *American Farm Policy, 1948–1973*. Minneapolis: University of Minnesota Press.

Cohen, J. E. (1995), *How Many People Can the Earth Support?*. New York: Norton.

Colm, G. (1952), *The American Economy in 1960*, NPA Planning Pamphlet 81, December. Washington, DC: National Planning Association.

Commager, H. S., and Morris, R. B. (1963), "Editor's Introduction," in W. L. Leuchtenburg (ed.), *Franklin D. Roosevelt and the New Deal, 1932–1940*. New York: Harper & Row.

Commons, J. R. (1950), *The Economics of Collective Action*. New York: Macmillan.

Constant, E. W. (1980), *The Origins of the Turbojet Revolution*. Baltimore: Johns Hopkins University Press.

Conway, G. R. (1997), *The Doubly Green Revolution: Food for All in the 21st Century*. London: Penguin.

Conway, G. R., and Pretty, J. (1991), *Unwelcome Harvest: Agriculture and Pollution*. London: Earthscan.

Copeland, B. R., and Taylor, M. S. (1994), "North-South Trade and the Environment," *Quarterly Journal of Economics* 109: 755–87.

Copeland, B. R., and Taylor, M. S. (1995), "Trade and Transboundary Pollution," *American Economic Review* 85: 716–37.

Copeland, M. A., and Martin, E. M. (1938), "The Correction of Wealth and Income Estimates for Price Changes," in *Conference on Research in National Income and Wealth, Studies in Income and Wealth*, vol. 2, 83–134. New York: National Bureau of Economic Research.

Cowden, T. K. (1953), "What to Expect from Agriculture in 1954," *Commercial and Financial Chronicle* 17 (December): 87.

Crafts, N. F. R. (1995), "Exogenous or Endogenous Growth? The Industrial Revolution Reconsidered," *Journal of Economic History* 55 (December): 745–72.

Crocker, T. D. (1966), "The Structure of Atmospheric Pollution Control Systems," in H. Wolozin (ed.), *The Economics of Air Pollution*, 61–86. New York: Norton.

Crosson, P. (1995a), "Soil Erosion and Its On-Farm Productivity Consequences: What Do We Know?" Resources for the Future Discussion Paper 95–29, Washington, DC.

Crosson, P. (1995b), "Soil Erosion Estimates and Costs," *Science* 269: 461–64.

Curtis, J., Mott, L., and Kuhnle, T. (1991), *Harvest of Hope: The Potential for Alternative Agriculture to Reduce Pesticide Use*. Washington, DC: Natural Resources Defense Council.

Dahlman, C. J. (1980), *The Open Field System and Beyond: A Property Rights Analysis of an Economic Institution*. Cambridge: Cambridge University Press.

Daily, G. C., Matson, P. A., and Vitousek, P. M. (1995), "Ecosystem Services Supplied by Soil," in G. C. Daily (ed.), *Natural Services: Societal Dependence on Natural Ecosystems*, 113–32. Washington, DC: Island.

Dales, J. H. (1968a), "Land, Water and Ownership," *Canadian Journal of Economics* 1: 791–804.

Dales, J. H. (1968b), *Pollution, Property and Prices*. Toronto: University of Toronto Press.

Daley, R. F. (1954), "Some Considerations in Appraising the Long Run Prospects for Agriculture," in Conference on Research in Income and Wealth (ed.), *Long Run Projections*, Studies in Income and Wealth, vol. 16, 131–90. Cambridge: National Bureau of Economic Research.

Dalrymple, D. G. (2006), "Social Science Knowledge as a Public Good," in M. W. Cernea and A. H. Kassam (eds.), *Researching the Culture in Agriculture: Social Research for International Development*, 431–46. Cambridge: CABI.

David, E. (1903), *Socialismus und Landwirtschaft*. Berlin: Socialistschen Monastshefte.

David, P. A. (1966), "The Mechanization of Reaping in the Anti-Bellum Midwest," in H. Rosovsky (ed.), *Industrialization in Two Systems*. New York: Wiley.

David, P. A. (1985), "Clio and the Economics of QWERTY," *American Economic Review* 75 (May): 332–37.

David, P. A., and Klundert, T. van de (1965), "Biased Efficiency Growth and Capital-Labor Substitution in the U.S., 1899–1960," *American Economic Review* 55 (June): 357–94.

Davis, J. S. (1953), "The Population Upsurge and the American Economy, 1945–80," *Journal of Political Economy* 61 (October): 369–88.

Davis, L. E., and North, D. C. (1971), *Institutional Change and American Economic Growth*. Cambridge: Cambridge University Press.

de Janvry, A. (1973), "A Socioeconomic Model of Induced Innovations for Argentine Agricultural Development," *Quarterly Journal of Economics* 87: 410–35.

de Janvry, A. (1978), "Social Structure and Biased Technical Change in Argentine Agriculture," in H. P. Binswanger, V. W. Ruttan, et al. (eds.), *Induced Innovation: Technology, Institutions, and Development*, 297–323. Baltimore: Johns Hopkins University Press.

Dean, P., and Cole, W. A. (1962), *British Economic Growth, 1688–1959*, 154–81. Cambridge: Cambridge University Press.

Deininger, K., and Feder, G. (1955), "Revolt and Reform in Agricultural Land Relations," in J. Berhman and T. N. Srinivasan (eds.), *Handbook of Development Economics*, vol. 3B, 2659–772. Amsterdam: Elsevier.

DeLong, J. B. (1986), "Productivity Growth, Convergence and Welfare: Comment," *American Economic Review* 78 (December): 1138–54.

Demsetz, H. (1964), "The Exchange and Enforcement of Property Rights," *Journal of Law and Economics* 7: 11–26.

Demsetz, H. (1967), "Toward a Theory of Property Rights," *American Economic Review* 42 (May): 347–59.

Dixit, A. (1973), "Models of Dual Economies," in J. H. Wimlees and N. H. Stern (eds.), *Models of Economic Growth*, 325–52. New York: Wiley.

Domar, E. (1946), "Capital Expansion, Rate of Growth and Employment," *Econometrica* 14: 137–47.

Domar, E. (1947), "Expansion and Employment," *American Economic Review* 37 (March): 343–55.

Douangngeune, B., Godo, Y., and Hayami, Y. (2005), "Education and Natural Resources in Economic Development: Thailand Compared with Japan and Korea," *Journal of Asian Economics* 16: 179–204.

Dovring, F. (1959), "The Share of Agriculture in a Growing Population," *Monthly Bulletin of Agricultural Economic Statistic (FAO)* 8 (August–September): 1–11.

Downs, A. (1957), *An Economic Theory of Democracy*. New York: Harper and Row.

Drzee, J., and Sen, A. K. (1989), *Hunger and Public Action*. Oxford: Clarendon Press.

Dunlap, R. E. (1975), "The Impact of Political Orientation on Environmental Attitudes and Actions," *Environment and Behavior* 7: 428–54.

Easter, K. W., Rosegrant, M. W., and Dinar, A. (eds.) (1998), *Markets for Water: Potential and Performance*. Dordrecht, the Netherlands: Kluwer.

Easterly, W. (1995), "Explaining Miracles: Growth Regressions Meet the Gang of Four," in T. Ito and A. O. Krueger (eds.), *Growth Theories in Light of East Asian Experience*, 267–84. Chicago: University of Chicago Press.

Echevarría, C. (1995), "Agricultural Development vs. Industrialisation: Effects of Trade," *Canadian Journal of Economics* 28 (August): 631–47.

Echevarría, C. (1996), "Non-Homothetic Preferences, Growth, Trade and Land," mimeo, Department of Economics, University of Saskatchewan, Saskatoon, Canada, November.

Echevarría, C. (1997), "Changes in Sectoral Composition Associated with Economic Growth," *International Economic Review* 38 (May): 431–52.

Eckaus, R. S. (1977), *Appropriate Technology for Developing Countries*. Washington, DC: National Academy of Sciences Press.

Eckaus, R. S. (1987), "Appropriate Technology: The Movement Has Only a Few Clothes On," *Issues in Science and Technology* 4 (Winter): 62–71.

Eicher, C., and Baker, D. C. (1992), "Research on Agricultural Development in Sub-Saharan Africa: Critical Survey," in L. Martin (ed.), *Survey of Agricultural Development Literature*, Agriculture in Economic Development 4, 3–328. Minneapolis: University of Minnesota Press.

Eicher, C., Baker, D. C., and Rukuni, M. (1996), "Reflections on Agrarian Reform and Capacity Building in South Africa," Staff Paper No. 96-3, Department of Agricultural Economics, Michigan State University.

Elbasha, E., and Roe, T. L. (1995), "Environment in Three Classes of Endogenous Growth Models," University of Minnesota Economic Development Center Bulletin 95-6, August.

Ellickson, J. C., and Brewster, J. M. (1947), "Technological Advance and the Structure of American Agriculture," *Journal of Farm Economics* 29 (November): 827–47.

Elster, J. (1989), *Nuts and Bolts for the Social Sciences*. Cambridge: Cambridge University Press.

Engerman, S. L., and Sokoloff, K. L. (2002), "Factor Endowments, Inequality, and Paths of Development among New World Economies," *Economia* 3 (1): 41–88.

Ernie, L. (1961), *English Farming: Past and Present*. London: Heinemann Educational Books and Frank Cass and Company. Orig. pub. 1912.

Evenson, D. D., and Evenson, R. E. (1983), "Legal Systems and Private Sector Incentives for the Invention of Agricultural Technology in Latin America," in M. E. Pineiro and E. J. Trigo (eds.), *Technical Change and Social Conflict in Agriculture: Latin American Perspectives*, 189–216. Boulder, CO: Westview Press.

Evenson, R. E. (1976), "International Transmission of Technology in the Production of Sugarcane," *Journal of Development Studies* 12 (January): 208–31.

Evenson, R. E. (1988), "Technology, Climate Change, Productivity and Land Use in Brazilian Agriculture," Yale University Economic Growth Center Staff Paper, New Haven, CT.

Evenson, R. E. (1998), "Plant Breeding: A Case of Induced Innovation," in R. E. Evenson, D. Gollin, and V. Santaniello (eds.), *Agricultural Values of Plant Genetic Resources*, 29–44. Wallingford, U.K.: CAB International.

Evenson, R. E., and Gollin, D. (2003a), *Crop Variety Improvement and Its Effects on Productivity: The Impact of International Agricultural Research*. Wallingford, Canada: CAB International.

Evenson, R. E., and Gollin, D. (2003b), "Assessing the Impact of the Green Revolution, 1960 to 2000," *Science* 300 (May 2): 758–62.

Evenson, R. E., Houck, J. P., Jr., and Ruttan, V. W. (1969), "Technical Change and Agricultural Trade: Three Examples (Sugarcane, Bananas, and Rice)," paper presented at National Bureau of Economic Research Conference on Technical Change and International Trade, New York, NY, November 1968; University of Minnesota AE Staff Paper P68-4, St. Paul.

Evenson, R. E., and Kislev, Y. (1975), *Agricultural Research and Productivity*. New Haven, CT: Yale University Press.

Ezzati, M., Singer, B. H., and Kammen, D. M. (1998), "Towards a Predictive Theory of Development: The Dynamics of Environmental Kuznets Curves," Woodrow Wilson School of Public and International Affairs, Princeton University, Princeton, NJ.

Falcon, W. (1970), "The Green Revolution: Generations of Problems," *American Journal of Agricultural Economics* 52: 698–710.

Fan, S. (1991), "Effects of Technical Change and Institutional Reform on Production Growth in Chinese Agriculture," *American Journal of Agricultural Economics* 73 (May): 266–77.

Fan, S., and Ruttan, V. W. (1992), "Induced Technical Change in Centrally Planned Economies," *Agricultural Economics* 6 (4): 301–14.

Fargione, J., Hill, J., Tilman, D., Polasky, S., and Hawthorne, P. (2008), "Land Clearing and the Biofuel Carbon Debt," *Science* 319 (February 29): 1235–38.

Feeny, D. H. (1976), "Technical and Institutional Change in Thai Agriculture, 1880–1940," Ph.D. diss., University of Wisconsin.

Feeny, D. H. (1982), *The Political Economy of Productivity: Thai Agricultural Development 1880–1975*. Vancouver: University of British Columbia Press.

Feeny, D. H. (1999), "Thailand and Japan: Why Was Japan First?," in Y. Hayami and M. Aoki (eds.), *The Institutional Foundations of East Asian Economic Development*, 413–42. London: Macmillan.

Fei, J. E. H., and Ravis, G. (1964), *Development of the Labor Surplus Economy: Theory and Policy*. Homewood, IL: Irwin.

Fellner, W. (1961), "Two Propositions in the Theory of Induced Innovations," *Economic Journal* 71 (June): 305–8.

Fellner, W. (1966), "Profit Maximization, Utility Maximization, and the Rate and Direction of Innovation," *American Economic Review* 56 (May): 24–32.

Fettig, L. P. (1963), "Adjusting Farm Tractor: Prices for Quality Changes, 1950–1962," *Journal of Farm Economics* 45 (August): 599–611.

Field, A. J. (1981), "The Problem with Neoclassical Institutional Economics: A Critique with Special Reference to the North/Thomas Model of Pre-1500 Europe," *Explorations in Economic History* 18: 174–98.

Fischer, A., and Hannenan, M. (1998), "The Impact of Global Warming on Agricultural Production: A Rethinking of the Ricardian Approach," Working Paper 842, Department of Agricultural and Resource Economics, University of California, Berkeley.

Flanders, M. J. (1968), "Agriculture versus Industry in Development Policy: The Planner's Dilemma Re-examined," *Japanese Development Studies* 5 (April): 171–89.

Food and Agriculture Organization (1995), *Water Development for Food Security*. Rome: Food and Agriculture Organization.

Food and Agricultural Organization (1999), FAOSTAT 98 CD-ROM. Rome: Food and Agriculture Organization. Available online at http://apps.fao.org/.

Food and Agricultural Organization (2005), *FAOSTAT Database*. Rome: Food and Agriculture Organization.

Fox, K. A. (1951), "Factors Affecting Farm Income, Farm Prices, and Food Consumption," *Agricultural Economics Research* 3 (3), Paper 88.

Fox, K. A. (1953), *The Analysis of Demand for Farm Products*, Technical Bulletin No. 1081. Washington, DC: U.S. Department of Agriculture.

Frankel, R. (1971), *India's Green Revolution: Economic Gains and Political Costs*. Princeton, NJ: Princeton University Press.

Frankel, R. (1974), "A Guide to Radical Literature on Economic Development with Special Reference to Asian Agricultural Development," *Bulletin of Concerned Asian Scholars* 6: 14–16.

Frohlich, N., Oppenheimer, J. A., and Young, O. R. (1971), *Political Leadership and Collective Goods*. Princeton, NJ: Princeton University Press.

Fuller, V., Gillett, R., Heady, E., Homeyer, P., and Johnson D. G. (1953), "Report of the American Farm Economic Association Committee on Farm Employment Estimates," *Journal of Farm Economics* 35 (December): 976–87.

Fuller, W. E. (1964), *RFD, the Changing Face of Rural America*. Bloomington: Indiana University Press.

Furnivall, J. S. (1944), *Netherlands India: A Study of Plural Economy*. Cambridge: Cambridge University Press.

Furnivall, J. S. (1948), *Colonial Policy and Practice: A Comparative Study of Burma and Netherlands India*. Cambridge: Cambridge University Press.

Fusfeld, D. R. (1980), "The Conceptual Framework of Modern Economies," *Journal of Economic Issues* 14: 1–52.

Gallopin, G., and Raskin, P. (1998), "Windows on the Future: Global Scenarios and Sustainability," *Environment* 40: 6–11, 26–31.

Galor, O., and Tsiddon, D. (1996), "Income Distribution and Growth: The Kuznet Hypothesis Revisited," *Economica* 63 (June): 103–17.

Gardiner, P. (ed.) (1959), *Theories of History*. Glencoe: Free Press.

Gaus, J. M., Wolcott, L. O., and Lewis V. B. (1940), *Public Administration in the United States Department of Agriculture*. Chicago: Public Administration Service.

Geertz, C. (1963), *Peddlers and Princes*. Chicago: University of Chicago Press.

Gerhart, J. (1975), *The Diffusion of Hybrid Maize in Western Kenay*. Mexico City: Centro International de Mejoramentio de Maiz Y Trigo.

Gianessi, L. P. (1991), "Reducing Pesticide Use with No Loss in Yields? A Critique of a Recent Cornell Report," Resources for the Future Discussion Paper QE91–16. Washington, DC: Resources for the Future Press.

Glazovsky, N. F. (1995), "The Aral Sea Basin," in J. X. Kasperson, R. E. Kasperson, and B. L. II Turner (eds.), *Regions at Risk: Comparisons of Threatened Environments*, 92–139. New York: United Nations.

Goldman, R., and Squire, L. (1982), "Technical Change, Labor Use, and Income Distribution in the Muda Irrigation Project," *Economic Development and Cultural Change* 30: 753–75.

Government General of Korea (1925), *Chosen Sotokutu Tokeihyo* (Statistical Yearbook of Government General of Korea). Seoul: Government General of Korea.

Government General of Korea (1930), *Chosen Sotokutu Tokeihyo* (Statistical Yearbook of Government General of Korea). Seoul: Government General of Korea.

Government of the Punjab, Planning and Development Department, Statistical Survey Unit (1970), Fertilizer and Mexican Wheat Survey Report, Lahore.

Grief, A. (1994), "Cultural Beliefs and the Organization of Society: A Historical and Theoretical Reflection on Collectivist and Individualist Societies," *Journal of Political Economy* 102: 912–50.

Griffin, K. (1974), *The Political Economy of Agrarian Change: An Essay on the Green Revolution*. Cambridge, MA: Harvard University Press.

Griliches, Z. (1958), "The Demand for Fertilizer: An Economic Interpretation of a Technical Change," *Journal of Farm Economics* 40 (August): 591–606.

Griliches, Z. (1964), "Research Expenditures, Education, and the Aggregate Agricultural Production Function," *American Economic Review* 54 (December): 961–74.

Griliches, Z. (1968), "Agriculture: Productivity and Technology," in *International Encyclopedia of the Social Services* 1. New York: Free Press.

Griliches, Z. (1969a), "Notes on the Role of Education in Production Function and Growth Accounting," Center for Mathematical Studies in Business and Economics, report 6839, University of Chicago, Chicago, mimeo.

Griliches, Z. (1969b), "A Note on Capital-Skill Complementarity," Center for Mathematical Studies in Business and Economics, report 6905, University of Chicago, mimeo.

Griliches, Z. (1992), "The Search for R&D Spillovers," *Scandinavian Journal of Economics* 94S: 29–47.

Griliches, Z. (1994), "Productivity, R & D and the Data Constraint," *American Economic Review* 84 (March): 1–23.

Grossman, G. M., and Helpman, E. (1990a), "Trade, Innovation and Growth," *American Economic Review* 80 (May): 86–91.

Grossman, G. M., and Helpman, E. (1990b), "Comparative Advantage and Long-Run Growth," *American Economic Review* 80 (September): 796–815.

Grossman, G. M., and Helpman, E. (1991a), "Trade, Knowledge Spillovers, and Growth," *European Economic Review* 35 (April): 517–26.

Grossman, G. M., and Helpman, E. (1991b), *Innovation and Growth in the Global Economy*. Cambridge, MA: MIT Press.

Grossman, G. M., and Helpman, E. (1994), "Endogenous Innovation in the Theory of Growth," *Journal of Economic Perspectives* 8 (Winter): 23–44.

Grossman, G. M., and Krueger, A. B. (1995), "Economic Growth and the Environment," *Quarterly Journal of Economics* 110 (May): 353–77.

Groves, T., Radner, R., and Reiter, S. (eds.) (1987), *Information, Incentives and Economic Mechanisms*. Minneapolis: University of Minnesota Press.

Guttman, J. M. (1982), "Can Political Entrepreneurs Solve the Free-rider Problem?" *Journal of Economic Behavior and Organization* 3: 1–10.

Habakuk, H. J. (1962), *American and British Technology in the Nineteenth Century: The Search for Labor Saving Inventions*. Cambridge: Cambridge University Press.

Habakuk, H. J. (1967), *American and British Technology in the Nineteenth Century: The Search for Labor-Saving Inventions*. Cambridge: Cambridge Univ. Press.

Hadwiger, D. F., and Talbot, R. B. (1965), *Pressures and Protests: The Kennedy Farm Program and the Wheat Referendum of 1963*. San Francisco: Chandler.

Hahn, R. W., and Stavins, R. N. (1991), "Incentive Based Environmental Regulation: A New Era from an Old Idea?" *Ecological Law Quarterly* 18: 1–42.

Halvorson, H. H. (1952), "Long Range Domestic Demand Prospects for Food and Fiber," *Journal of Farm Economics* 35 (December): 754–65.

Hammond, A. (1998), *Which World? Scenarios for the 21st Century*. Washington, DC: Island.

Hammond, P. J., and Rodriguez-Clare, A. (1993), "On Endogenizing Long-Run Growth," *Scandinavian Journal of Economics* 95 (April): 391–425.

Hara, Y. (1994), *Tonan Ajia Shokoku no Keizai Hatten*, Economic Development of Southeast Asian Countries. Tokyo: Institute of Oriental Culture, University of Tokyo.

Harberger, A. (1990), "Reflections on the Growth Process," Department of Economics, University of California, Los Angeles, June, mimeo.

Hardin, G. (1968), "The Tragedy of the Commons," *Science* 162 (December 13): 1243–48.

Harris, J. M. (1990), *World Agriculture and the Environment*. New York: Garland.

Harris, M. (1979), *Cultural Materialism: The Struggle for a Science of Culture*. New York: Random House.

Harrod, R. F. (1939), "An Essay in Dynamic Theory," *Economic Journal* 49 (March): 14–33.

Harrod, R. F. (1948), *Toward a Dynamic Economics*. London: Macmillan.

Harsanyi, J. C. (1960), "Explanation and Comparative Dynamics in Social Science," *Behavioral Science* 5: 136–45.

Hauer, G. K. (1997), "International Pollution Externalities: Public Bads with Multiple Jurisdictions," Ph.D. diss., University of Minnesota.

Hayami, Y. (1964), "Demand for Fertilizer in the Course of Japanese Agricultural Development," *Journal of Farm Economics* 46 (November): 776–79.

Hayami, Y. (1967), "Innovations in the Fertilizer Industry and Agricultural Development: The Japanese Experience," *Journal of Farm Economics* 49 (May): 403–12.

Hayami, Y. (1968a), "On the Japanese Experience of Agricultural Growth," *Rural Economic Problems* 4 (May): 79–88.

Hayami, Y. (1968b), "Nogyo Seisanryoku no Hinogyoteki Kiso" (Nonagricultural Sector as the Basis of Agricultural Productivity), in J. Tsukui and Y. Murakami (eds.), *Keizaiseichoriron no Tenbo* (Perspective for the Theory of Economic Growth), 218–33. Tokyo: Iwanami.

Hayami, Y. (1969a), "Industrialization and Agricultural Productivity: An International Comparative Study," *Developing Economies* 4 (March): 3–21.

Hayami, Y. (1969b), "Sources of Agricultural Productivity Gap among Selected Countries," *American Journal of Agricultural Economics* 51 (August): 564–75.

Hayami, Y. (1970), "On the Use of the Cobb-Douglas Production Function in the Cross-Country Analysis of Agricultural Production," *American Journal of Agricultural Economic* 52 (May): 327–29.

Hayami, Y. (1975), *A Century of Agricultural Growth In Japan: Its Relevance to Asian Development*. Tokyo: University of Tokyo Press.

Hayami, Y. (1978), *Anatomy of a Peasant Economy: A Rice Village in the Philippines*. Los Banos, the Philippines: International Rice Research Institute.

Hayami, Y. (1986), *Nogyo Keizairon* (Agricultural Economics). Tokyo: Iwanami Shoten.

Hayami, Y. (1988), *Japanese Agriculture under Siege: The Political Economy of Agricultural Policies*. London: Macmillan.

Hayami, Y. (1994), "Peasant and Plantation in Asia," in G. M. Meier (ed.), *From Classical Economics to Development Economics*, 121–34. New York: St. Martin's.

Hayami, Y. (1996), "The Peasant in Economic Modernization," *American Journal of Agricultural Economics* 78 (December): 1157–67.

Hayami, Y. (1997), *Development Economics: From the Poverty to the Wealth of Nations*. Oxford: Oxford University Press.

Hayami, Y. (2000), "Food Security: Fallacy or Reality," in W. S. Chen, C. A. Carter, and S.-Y. Shei (Eds.), *Food Security in Asia: Economics and Policies*, 11–17. Cheltenham, UK: Edward Elgar.

Hayami, Y. (2005), "The Conditions of Collective Action for Local Commons Management: The Case of Irrigation in the Philippines," *Agricultural Economics* 33 (2): 179–89.

Hayami, Y. (2009), "Social Capital, Human Capital and the Community Mechanism: Toward a Conceptual Framework for Economists," *Journal of Development Studies* 45: 96–123.

Hayami, Y., Akino, M., Shintani, M., and Yamada, S. (1975), *A Century of Agricultural Growth in Japan*. Minneapolis: University of Minnesota Press.

Hayami, Y., Dikishit, A. K., and Mishra, S. N. (2006), "Waste Pickers and Collectors in Delhi: Poverty and Environment in an Urban Informal Sector," *Journal of Development Studies* 42 (January): 41–69.

Hayami, Y., Douangneune, B., and Godo, Y. (2005), "Education and Natural Resources in Economic Development: Thailand Compared with Japan and Korea," *Journal of Asian Economics* 16 (April): 179–204.

Hayami, Y., Fujiie, M., and Kikuchi, M. (2005), "The Conditions of Collective Action for Local Commons Management: The Case of Irrigation in the Philippines," *Agricultural Economics* 33 (2): 179–89.

Hayami, Y., and Godo, Y. (2002), *Nogyo Keizairon* (Agricultural Economics). New ed. Tokyo: Iwanami Shoten.

Hayami, Y., and Godo, Y. (2004), "The Three Agricultural Problems in the Disequilibrium of World Agriculture," *Journal of Agriculture and Development* 1 (June): 3–16.

Hayami, Y., and Godo, Y. (2005), *Development Economics: From the Poverty to the Wealth of Nations*. Oxford: Oxford University Press.

Hayami, Y., and Inagi, K. (1969), "International Comparison of Agricultural Productivities," *Farm Economist* 11 (10): 407–19.

Hayami, Y., and Kawagoe, T. (1989), "Farm Mechanization, Scale Economies and Polarization," *Journal of Development Economics* 31 (October): 221–39.

Hayami, Y., and Kawagoe, T. (1993), *The Agrarian Origins of Commerce and Industry: A Study of Peasant Marketing in Indonesia*. London: Macmillan; New York: St. Martin's.

Hayami, Y, Kawagoe, T., and Ruttan, V. W. (1985), *Agricultural Development: An International Perspective*, rev. ed. Baltimore: Johns Hopkins University Press.

Hayami, Y., and Kikuchi, M. (1981), *Asian Village Economy at the Crossroads: An Economic Approach to Institutional Change*. Tokyo: University of Tokyo Press; Baltimore: Johns Hopkins University Press.

Hayami, Y., and Kikuchi, M. (1982), *Asian Village at the Crossroads: An Economic Approach to Institutional Change*. Tokyo: University of Tokyo Press, 1981; Baltimore: Johns Hopkins University Press.

Hayami, Y., and Kikuchi, M. (2000), *A Rice Village Saga: Three Decades of Green Revolution in the Philippines*. London: Macmillan.

Hayami, Y., and Otsuka, K. (1993), *The Economics of Contract Choice*. New York: St. Martin's.

Hayami, Y., and Peterson, W. (1972), "Social Returns to Public Information Services: Statistical Reporting of U.S. Farm Commodities," *American Economic Review* 63: 119–30.

Hayami, Y., Quisumbing, M. A., and Adriano, L. S. (1990), *Toward an Alternative Land Reform Paradigm: A Philippine Perspective*. Quezon City, Philippines: Ateneo de Manila University Press.

Hayami, Y., and Ruttan, V. W. (1969), "Factor Prices and Technical Change in Agricultural Development: The United State and Japan, 1880–1960," AE Staff Paper P69–13, University of Minnesota, St. Paul.

Hayami, Y., and Ruttan, V. W. (1970a), "Factor Prices and Technical Change in Agricultural Development: The United States and Japan, 1880–1960," *Journal of Political Economy* 78 (September–October): 1115–41.

Hayami, Y., and Ruttan, V. W. (1970b), "Agricultural Productivity Differences among Countries," *American Economic Review* 60 (December): 895–911.

Hayami, Y., and Ruttan, V. W. (1971), *Agricultural Development: An International Perspective*. Baltimore: Johns Hopkins University Press.

Hayami, Y., and Ruttan, V. W. (1985), *Agricultural Development: An International Perspective*, rev. ed. Baltimore: Johns Hopkins University Press.

Hayami, Y., and Yamada, S. (1968), "Technological Progress in Agriculture," in L. R. Klein and K. Ohkawa (eds.), *Economic Growth: The Japanese Experience since the Meiji Era*, 135–61. Homewood, IL: Irwin.

Hayami, Y., and Yamada, S. (1969), "Agricultural Productivity at the Beginning of Industrialization," in K. Ohkawa, B. F. Johnston, and H. Kaneda (eds.), *Agriculture and Economic Growth: Japan's Experience*, 105–35. Tokyo: University of Tokyo Press.

Hayami, Y., and Yamada, S. (1975), "Agricultural Research Organization in Economic Development: A Review of the Japanese Experience," in L. G. Reynolds (ed.), *Agriculture in Development Theory*, 224–49. New Haven, CT: Yale University Press.

Hayami, Y., and Yamada, S. (1991), *The Agricultural Development of Japan: A Century's Perspective*. Tokyo: University of Tokyo Press.

Hayami, Y., in association with Miller, B. Wade, W., and Yamashita, S. (1970), "An International Comparison of Agricultural Production and Productivities," University of Minnesota Agricultural Experiment Station Technical Bulletin, No. 277, St. Paul.

Hayek, F. A. (1967), "The Results of Human Action but Not of Human Design," in F. A. Hayek (ed.), *Studies in Philosophy, Politics and Economics*, 96–105. Chicago: University of Chicago Press.

Hayek, F. A. (1978), "The Atavism of Social Justice," in *New Studies in Philosophy, Politics, Economics and the History of Ideas*, 57–68. London: Routledge and Kegan Paul.

Hazel, P., and Ramasamy, C. (1991), *The Green Revolution Reconsidered: The Impact of High-Yield Rice Varieties in South India*. Baltimore, MD: Johns Hopkins University Press.

Headstrom, P., and Swedberg, R. (1998), "Social Mechanisms: An Introductory Essay," in P. Headstrom and R. Swedberg (eds.), *Social Mechanisms: An Analytical Approach to Social Theory*, 1–31. Cambridge: Cambridge University Press.

Heady, E. O. (1949), "Basic Economical Welfare Aspects of Farm Technological Advance," *Journal of Farm Economics* 31 (May): 293–316.

Heady, E. O. (1953), "Use and Estimation of Input-Output Relationships or Productivity Coefficients," *Journal of Farm Economics* 34 (December): 775–86.

Heady, E. O. (1955), "Marginal Resource Productivity and Imputation of Shares for a Sample of Rented Farms," *Journal of Political Economy* 63 (December): 500–511.

Heady, E. O., and Shaw, R. (1954), "Resource Returns and Productivity Coefficients," *Journal of Farm Economics* 36 (May): 243–57.

Heisig, C. P. (1953), "Long Range Production Prospects and Problems," *Journal of Farm Economics* 35 (December): 744–53.

Hendrix, W. E. (1951), "Availability of Capital and Production Innovations on Low-Income Farms," *Journal of Farm Economics* 33 (February): 66–74.

Hendrix, W. E., et al. (1965), *Changes in Agriculture in Twenty-Six Developing Nations, 1948–1963*, U.S. Department of Agriculture, Economic Research Service, Foreign Agricultural Economics Report No. 27, Washington, DC, November.

Herdt, R. W., and Mellor, J. W. (1964), "The Contrasting Response of Rice to Nitrogen: India and the United States," *Journal of Farm Economics* 46 (February): 150–60.

Hesters, E. D., and Mabun, P. (1924), "Some Economic and Social Aspects of Philippine Tenancies," *Philippine Agriculturist* 12 (February): 367–444.

Hicks, J. D. (1961), *The Populist Revolt*. Lincoln: University of Nebraska Press.

Hicks, J. R. (1932), *The Theory of Wages*. London: Macmillan.

Hicks, J. R. (1965), *Capital and Growth*. Oxford: Claredon Press.

Hicks, J. R. (1969), *A Theory of Economic History*. Oxford: Oxford University Press.

Hicks, J. R. (1985), *Methods of Dynamic Economics*. Oxford: Clarendon Press.

Hill, F. F. (1965), "Some Viewpoints Concerning Agricultural Development," paper presented at the American Farm Economic Association, Allied Social Science Association meeting, New York, NY, December 28.

Hirsch, L. (1961), *Marketing in Underdeveloped Economy: The North Indian Sugar Industry*. Englewood Cliffs, NJ: Prentice-Hall.

Hirschman, A.O. (1958), *The Strategy of Economic Development*. New Haven, CT: Yale University Press.

Ho, S., and Pao-San. (1968), "Agricultural Transformation under Colonialism: The Case of Taiwan," *Journal of Economic History* 28 (September): 315–40.

Hofstadter, R. (1955), *The Age of Reform: From Bryan to F.D.R.* New York: Alfred A. Knopf.

Honma, M., and Hayami, Y. (2006), "Distortions to Agricultural Incentives in Korea and Taiwan," paper submitted to the World Bank project Distortions to Agricultural Incentives.

Hopkins, A.G. (1973), *An Economic History of West Africa*. New York: Colombia University Press.

Hsieh, S. C., and Lee, T. H. (1966), Agricultural Development and Its Contribution to Economic Growth in Taiwan–Input, Output and Productivity Analysis, Joint Commission on Rural Reconstruction, Economic Digest Series No. 17, Taipei, April.

Huffman, W. E., and Evenson, R. E. (1993), *Science for Agriculture: A Long-Term Perspective*. Ames: Iowa State University Press.

Hughes, J. R. T. (1977), *The Governmental Habit: Economic Controls from Colonial Times to the Present*. New York: Basic Books.

Hughes, R. B. (1954), "Marginal Returns on Agricultural Resources in a Southern Mountain Valley," *Journal of Farm Economics* 36 (May): 334–39.

Huke, R. E., and Huke, E. H. (1997), *Rice Area by Type of Culture: South, Southeast, and East Asia, A Revised and Updated Database*. Manila: International Rice Research Institute.

Hunt, P. (1964), *Farm Tractor and Machinery Management*. Ames: Iowa State University Press.

Hurwicz, L. (1960), "Optimality and Information Efficiency in Resource Allocation Processes," in K. J. Arrow, S. Karlin, and P. Suppes (eds.), *Mathematical Models in the Social Sciences*, 17–46. Stanford, CA: Stanford University Press.

Hurwicz, L. (1972a), "On Informationally Decentralized Systems," in C. B. McGuire and R. Radnor (ed.), *Decision and Organization*, 297–336. Amsterdam: North Holland.

Hurwicz, L. (1972b), "Organizational Structures for Joint Decision Making: A Designer's Point of View," in M. Tuite, R. Chisholm, and M. Radnor (eds.), *Interorganizational Decision Making*, 37–44. Chicago: Aldine.

Hurwicz, L. (1973), "The Design of Mechanisms for Resource Allocation," *American Economic Review* 63: 1–30.

Hurwicz, L. (1977), "On the Interaction between Information and Incentives in Organizations," in K. Krippendorf (ed.), *Communication and Control in Society*, 123–47. New York: Scientific Publishers.

Hurwicz, L. (1981), "On Incentive Problems in the Design of Non-Wasteful Resource Allocation Systems," in N. Assoraodobraj-Kula (ed.), *Studies in Economic Theory and Practice: Essays in Honor of Edward Lipinski*, 94–106. Amsterdam: North Holland.

Hurwicz, L. (1996), "Institutions as Families of Game Forms," *Japanese Economic Review* 47: 113–32.

Hurwicz, L. (1998), "Issues in the Design of Mechanisms and Institutions," in E. T. Loehman and D. M. Kilgour (eds.), *Designing Institutions for Environmental and Resource Management*, 29–56. Cheltenham, U.K.: Edward Elgar.

Hurwicz, L. (2007), "Economics Focus: Intelligent Design," *Economist*, October 18.

Hurwicz, L. (2008), "But Who Will Guard the Guardians?" (Nobel Prize Lecture), *American Economic Review* 98 (3): 577–85.

Indonesia Biro Pusat Statistik (1996), *Statistical Yearbook of Indonesia 1996*. Jakarta: Badan Pusat Statistik.

Ingram, J. C. (1971), *Economic Change in Thailand, 1850–1970*. Stanford, CA: Stanford University Press.

Intal, P. S., Jr., and Power, J. H. (1989), *Trade, Exchange Rate, and Agricultural Pricing Policies in the Philippines*. Washington, DC: World Bank.

International Rice Research Institute (1965), *Annual Report: 1964*. Los Banos, the Philippines.

International Rice Research Institute (1966), *IRRI Reporter*, September. Los Banos, the Philippines.

International Rice Research Institute (1978), *Interpretive Analysis of Selected Papers from Changes in Rice Farming in Selected Areas of Asia*. Los Banos, the Philippines: International Rice Research Institute.

International Rice Research Institute (2003), *World Rice Statistics 2003*. Los Banos, the Philippines.

Ishikawa, S. (1967), *Economic Development in Asian Perspective*. Tokyo: Kinokuniya.

Ishikawa, S. (1981), *Essays on Technology, Employment and Institutions in Economic Development*. Tokyo: Kinokuniya.

Islam, N. (1990), "Horticultural Exports of Developing Countries: Past Performances, Future Prospects, and Policy Issues," IFPRI Research Report 80. Washington, DC: International Food Policy Research Institute.

Islam, N. (1995), "Growth Empirics: A Panel Data Approach," *Quarterly Journal of Economics* 60 (November): 1128–70.

Ito, T., and Krueger, A. O. (eds.) (1995), *Growth Theory in Light of East Asian Experience*. Chicago: University of Chicago Press.

Jackson, E. A. (1966), "Tropical Rice: The Quest for High Yield," *Agricultural Science Review* (USDA-CSRS) 4 (Fourth Quarter): 21–26.

Jaffee, S., and Morton, J. (1995), *Marketing Africa's High-Value Foods*. Dubuque, IA: Kendall/Hunt.

Japan, Ministry of Agriculture and Forestry. (1968), *Nogyo oyobi Nokano Shakai Kanjo 1967* (Social Accounts of Agriculture and Farm Households). Tokyo.

Japan, Ministry of Agriculture, Forestry, and Fishery, various issues, *Farm Household Economy Survey*.

Japan, Ministry of Finance, various issues, *Monthly Report of Financial Statistics*.

Japan, Ministry of International Affairs, various issues, *National Survey of Family Income and Expenditure*.

Jha, D. (1974), "Agricultural Growth, Technology and Equity," *Indian Journal of Agricultural Economics* 29: 207–16.

Johnson, D. G. (1945), "A Price Policy for Agriculture Consistent with Economic Progress That Will Promote Adequate and More Stable Income from Farming," *Journal of Farm Economics* 27: 761–72.

Johnson, D. G. (1950), "The Nature of the Supply Function for Agricultural Products," *American Economic Review* 40 (September): 539–63.

Johnson, D. G. (1973), *World Agriculture in Disarray*. London: Fontana.

Johnson, D. G. (1999), "Colloquium Paper: The Growth of Demand Will Limit Output Growth for Food over the Next Quarter Century," *Proceedings of the National Academy of Sciences USA* 96: 5915–20.

Johnson, G. L. (1952), *Sources of Incomes on Upland Marshall County Farms*, Progress Report 1, Kentucky Agricultural Experiment Station, University of Kentucky, Lexington.

Johnson, N. L., and Ruttan, V. W. (1994), "Why Are Farms So Small?" *World Development* 22 (May): 691–706.

Johnson, S. E. (1952), "Prospects and Requirements for Increased Output," *Journal of Farm Economics* 34 (December): 682–94.

Johnson, V. W., and Barlowe, R. (1954), "Agricultural Land Requirements," in V. W. Johnson and R. Barlowe (eds.), *Land Problems and Policies*, 194–228. New York: McGraw-Hill.

Johnston, B. F. (1951), "Agricultural Productivity and Economic Development in Japan," *Journal of Political Economy* 59 (December): 498–513.

Johnston, B. F. (1962), "Agricultural Development and Economic Transformation: A Comparative Study of the Japanese Experience," *Food Research Institute Studies* 2 (November): 223–76.

Johnston, B. F. (1966), "Agricultural Development and Economic Transformation: A Comparative Study of Japanese Experience," *Food Research Institute Studies* 6 (3): 223–76.

Joint Commission on Rural Reconstruction (1966), *Taiwan Agricultural Statistic*. Taipei: Joint Commission on Rural Reconstruction.

Joint Committee on the Economic Report, Bureau of Agricultural Economics (1953), *Historical and Descriptive Supplement to Economic Indicators*. Washington, DC.

Jones, C. I. (1995), "Time Series Tests of Endogenous Growth Models," *Quarterly Journal of Economics* 110 (May): 495–526.

Jones, E. L. (1968), "The Changing Basis of English Agricultural Prosperity, 1853–73," in W. E. Minchinton (ed.), *Essays in Agrarian History*, vol. 2: 219–36. Newton Abbot, U.K.: David and Charles Ltd. Reprinted from *Agricultural History Review* 10 (1962).

Jones, E. L. (1995), "Culture and Its Relationship to Economic Change," *Journal of Institutional and Theoretical Economics* 151: 269–85.

Jones, F. R. (1938), *Farm Gas Engines and Tractors*, 2d ed. New York: McGraw Hill.

Jones, W. O. (1968a), *Marketing Staple Food Crops in Tropical Africa*. Ithaca: Cornell University Press.

Jones, W. O. (1968b), "Plantations," *International Encyclopedia of the Social Sciences*, vol. 12, 154–59. New York: Macmillan and Free Press.

Jones, W. O. (1987), "Food-Crop Marketing Boards in Tropical Africa," *Journal of Modern African Studies* 25 (September): 375–402.

Jorgenson, D. W. (1961), "The Development of the Dual Economy," *Economic Journal* 71 (June): 309–34.

Jorgenson, D. W., and Griliches, Z. (1969), "The Explanation of Productivity Change," *Review of Economic Studies* 34 (July): 249–83.

Joskow, P. L., Schmalensee, R., and Balley, E. M. (1998), "The Market for Sulphur Dioxide Emissions," *American Economic Review* 88: 669–85.

Kaldor, N. (1957), "A Model of Economic Growth," *Economic Journal* 67 (September): 591–624.

Kanazawa, N. (1966), "Difference between Rice Cultural Management under Rive and Pond Irrigation," paper presented at the Pacific Science Congress, August.

Kanbur, R. (1997), "Income Distribution and Development," World Bank, Washington, DC, mimeo.

Kaneda, H. (1968), "Substitution of Labor and Non-labor Inputs and Technical Change in Japanese Agriculture," *Review of Economics and Statistics* 47 (December): 163–71.

Kaneda, H. (1969), "Long-Term Changes in Food Consumption Patterns in Japan, 1878–1964," in K. Ohkawa, B. F. Johnston, and H. Kaneda (eds.), *Agriculture and Economic Growth: Japan's Experience*, 398–431. Tokyo: University of Tokyo Press.

Karagiannis, G., and Furtan, W. H. (1990), "Induced Innovation in Canadian Agriculture: 1926–87," *Canadian Journal of Agricultural Economics/Revue canadienne d'agroeconomie* 38: 1–21.

Kasperson, J. X., Kasperson, R. E., and Turner, B. L., II (1995), *Regions at Risk: Comparisons of Threatened Environments*. New York: United Nations University Press.

Kautsky, K. (1899), *Die Agrarfrage*. Stuttgart: Dietz.

Kawagoe, T., Hayami, Y., and Ruttan, V. W. (1985), "The Intercountry Agricultural Production Function and Productivity Differences among Countries," *Journal of Development Economics* 19 (September/October): 113–32.

Kawagoe, T., Otsuka, K., and Hayami, Y. (1986), "Induced Bias of Technical Change in Agriculture: The United States and Japan, 1880–1980," *Journal of Political Economy* 94 (June): 523–44.

Kawano, S. (1941), *Taiwan Beikoku Keizairon* (A Treatise of Rice Economy in Taiwan). Tokyo: Yuhikaku.

Kayo, N. (ed.). (1958), *Nihon Nogyo Kiso Tokei* (Basic Statistics of Japanese Agriculture). Tokyo: Norin-Suisangyo Seiaansei Kojo Kaigi.

Kellogg, C. E. (1948), "Conflicting Doctrines about Soils," *Science Monthly* 66: 475–85.

Kellogg, C. E. (1964), "Interactions and Agricultural Research in Emerging Nations," in A. H. Moseman (ed.), *Agricultural Sciences for the Developing Nations*. Washington, DC: American Association for the Advancement of Science.

Kendrick, J. W., and Jones, C. E. (1951), "Gross National Farm Product in Constant Dollars, 1910–50," *Survey of Current Business* 31 (September): 13–19.

Kendrick, J. W., and Jones, C. E. (1953), "Farm Capital Outlays and Stock," *Survey of Current Business* 33 (August): 16.

Kennedy, C. (1964), "Induced Bias in Innovation and the Theory of Distribution," *Economic Journal* 74 (September): 541–47.

Kennedy, C. (1966), "On the Theory of Induced Innovation: A Reply," *Economic Journal* 77: 958–70.

Kennedy, P. (1988), *African Capitalism: Struggle for Ascendancy*. Cambridge: Cambridge University Press.

Khan, A. R. (1977), "Growth and Inequality in the Rural Philippines," in *Poverty and Landlessness in Rural Asia*, 243–49. Geneva: International Labor Office.

Kikuchi, M., and Hayami, Y. (1980), "Inducements to Institutional Innovation in an Agrarian Community," *Economic Development and Cultural Change* 29 (October): 21–36.

Kim, J., and Lau, L. J. (1994), "The Sources of Economic Growth of the East Asian Newly Industrialised Countries," *Journal of the Japanese and International Economics* 8 (September): 235–71.

King, R. G., and Rebelo, S. T. (1990), "Public Policy and Economic Growth: Developing Neoclassical Implications," *Journal of Political Economy* 98 (October): S126–S50.

King, R. G., and Rebelo, S. T. (1993), "Transitional Dynamics and Economic Growth in the Neoclassical Model," *American Economic Review* 83 (September): 908–31.

Kirkdendall, R. S. (1966), *Social Scientists and Farm Politics in the Age of Roosevelt*. Columbia: University of Missouri Press.

Kislev, Y., and Peterson, W. (1981), "Prices, Technology and Farm Size," *Journal of Political Economy* 90 (June): 578–95.

Kiyonari, T. (1980), *Chusho Kigyo Dokuhon* (Textbook of Small and Medium-Scale Industries). Tokyo: Toyokeizaishimposha.

Knight, F. H. (1952), "Institutionalism and Empiricism in Economics," *American Economic Review* 42 (May): 45–55.

Koffsky, N. (1954), "The Long Term Price Outlook and Its Impact on American Agriculture," *Journal of Farm Economics* 36 (December): 790–98.

Koppel, B. M. (ed.) (1995), *Induced Innovation Theory and International Agricultural Development: A Reassessment*. Baltimore: Johns Hopkins University Press.

Kosa-ard, M. S., and Rekasem, B. (2000), *The Growth and Substitutability of Agriculture in Asia*. Oxford: Oxford University Press.

Krishna, R. (1967), "Agricultural Price Policy for Economic Development," in H. M. Southworth and B. F. Johnston (eds.), *Agricultural Development and Economic Growth*, 497–540. Ithaca: Cornell University Press.

Krueger, A. O. (1968), "Factor Endowments and Per Capita Income Differences among Countries," *Economic Journal* 78 (September): 641–59.

Krueger, A. O. (1974), "The Political Economy of the Rent-Seeking Society," *American Economic Review* 64: 291–303.

Krueger, A. O. (1997), "Trade Policy and Economic Development: How We Learn," *American Economic Review* 87 (March): 1–22.

Krueger, A. O., Schiff, M., and Valdes, A. (eds.) (1991), *Political Economy of Agricultural Pricing Policies*, 3 vols. . Baltimore: Johns Hopkins University Press.

Krugman, P. R. (1996), *Development, Geography and Economic Theory*. Cambridge, MA: MIT Press.

Kung, P. (1956), *The Distribution of Rice Varieties and Their Trend of Changes in the Recent Three Decades in Taiwan*, Chinese-American Joint Commission on Rural Reconstruction, Plant Industry Series No. 10, Taipei, June.

Kuznets, S. (1955), "Economic Growth and Income Inequality," *American Economic Review* 45 (March): 1–28.

Kuznets, S. (1966a), *Modern Economic Growth*. New Haven, CT: Yale University Press.

Kuznets, S. (1966b), *Economic Growth of Nations: Total Output and Production Structure*. New Haven, CT: Yale University Press.

Lada, E. L., and Lee, T. H. (1963), *Irrigation Investment in Taiwan*, Joint Commission on Rural Reconstruction, Economic Digest Series No. 15, Taipei, February.

Lal, D. (1976), "Agricultural Growth, Real Wages, and the Rural Poor in India," *Economic and Political Weekly* 11 (26): A47–61.

Lal, D. (1998), *Unintended Consequences: The Impact of Factor Endowments, Culture, and Politics on Long-Run Economic Performance*. Cambridge: MIT Press.

Lal, R. (1984), "Productivity of Tropical Soils and the Effect of Erosion," in F. Rijsberman and M. Wolman (eds.), *Quantification of the Effect of Erosion on Soil Productivity in an International Context*, 70–94. Delft, the Netherlands: Delft Hydraulics Lab.

Lamb, G., and Muller, L. (1982), *Control, Accountability, and Incentives in a Successful Development Institution: The Kenya Tea Development Authority*. Washington, DC: World Bank.

Lappe, F., and Collins, J. (1977), *Food First: Beyond the Myth of Scarcity*. Boston: Houghton Mifflin.

Lappe, F., and Collins, J. (1979), *Food First: Beyond the Myth of Scarcity*, rev. ed. New York: Ballantine.

Larkin, J. S. (1972), *The Pampangans: Colonial Society in a Philippine Province*. Berkeley: University of California Press.

Lau, L. J., and Yotopoulos, P. A. (1989), "The Meta-Production Function Approach to Technological Change in World Agriculture," *Journal of Development Economics* 31 (October): 241–69.

Leaf, M. (1983), "The Green Revolution and Cultural Change in a Punjab Village, 1965–1978," *Economic Development and Cultural Change* 31: 227–70.

Lederberg, J. (1996), "Infectious Disease—A Threat to Global Health and Security," *Journal of the American Medical Association* 276: 417–19.

Lele, S. (1991), "Sustainable Development: A Critical Review," *World Development* 19: 607–21.

Lele, U. J. (1971), *Food Grain Marketing in India*. Ithaca, NY: Cornell University Press.

Lele, U. J., and Christiansen, R. E. (1989), Markets, Marketing Boards, and Cooperatives in Africa: Issues in Adjustment Policy, MADIA Discussion Paper 2, Washington, DC.

Lenin, V. (1960), *The Development of Capitalism in Russia: The Process of Formation of a Home Market for Large-Scale Industry*. Vol. 3 of Lenin, *Collected Works*, 4th ed. Moscow: Foreign Languages House. Orig. pub. 1899.

Lenin, V. (1964), *The Development of Capitalism in Russia*. Moscow: Progress.

Leontief, W. W. (1944), "Output, Employment, Consumption and Investment," *Quarterly Journal of Economics* 58 (February): 290–314.

Leontief, W. W. (1953), "Structural Change," in Wassily Leontief (ed.), *Studies in the Structure of the American Economy*, 27–35. New York: Oxford University Press.

Leuchtenburg, W. L. (1963), *Franklin D. Roosevelt and the New Deal, 1932–1940*. New York: Harper & Row.

Levine, G. (1966), "Irrigation Costs in the Philippines," *Philippine Economic Journal* 54 (First Semester): 28–41.

Levine, R. (2005), "Law, Endowments and Property Rights," *Journal of Economic Perspectives* 19: 61–88.

Levine, R., and Renelt, D. (1992), "A Sensitivity Analysis of Cross Country Regressions," *American Economic Review* 82 (September): 942–63.

Lewis, W. A. (1954), "Economic Development with Unlimited Supplies of Labor," *Manchester School of Economic and Social Studies* 22 (May): 139–91.

Lewis, W. A. (1969), *Aspects of Tropical Trade, 1883–1965*. Stockholm: Almquist and Wiksel.

Lewis, W. A. (1970), "The Export Stimulus," in W. A. Lewis (ed.), *Tropical Development 1880–1913*, 13–45. London: Allen and Unwin.

Lim, Y. (1968), "Input of the Tea Industry on the Growth of the Ceylonese Economy," *Social and Economic Studies* 17 (December): 453–67.

Lin, J., and Nugent, J. B. (1995), "Institutions and Economic Development," in J. Behrman and T. N. Srinivasan (eds.), *Handbook of Economic Development*, vol. 3, 2301–70. Amsterdam: Elsevier Science.

Lindert, P. H. (1996), "Soil Change in Agriculture in Two Developing Countries," in J. Alston and P. Pardy (eds.), *Agricultural Science Policy: Changing Global Agendas*, 263–332. Melbourne, Australia: Department of Natural Resources and Environment.

Lindert, P. H. (1998), *A Half Century of Soil Change in Indonesia*. Davis: University of California Agricultural History Center.

Lindert, P. H. (1999), "The Bad Earth? Chinese Agricultural Soils since the 1930s," *Economic Development Cultural Change* 47 (July): 701–36.

List, F. (1966), *The National System of Political Economy*. New York: Augustus M. Kelley. Orig. pub. 1885.

Liu, Y., and Shumway, C. R. (2008), "Induced Innovation in U.S. Agriculture: Time-Series, Direct Econometric, and Nonparametric Tests," *American Journal of Agricultural Economics* 91: 224–36.

Long, E. J. (1966), "Altering the Variables of the Food Supply-Demand Situation," paper presented at the Conference on Alternatives for Balancing Future Food Production Needs, Center for Agricultural and Economic Development, Iowa State University, Ames, November.

Lopes, M., and Schuh, G. E. (1976), "Price Support versus an Equilibrium Exchange Rate: A Comparison of Income Distribution Consequences," paper presented at AAEA annual meeting, Pennsylvania State University, State College, August 15–18.

Lopez, R. (1994), "The Environment as a Factor of Production: The Effects of Economic Growth and Trade Liberalization," *Journal of Environmental Economics and Management* 27: 163–84.

Lucas, R. E., Jr. (1988), "On the Mechanics of Economic Development," *Journal of Monetary Economics* 22: 3–42.

Lucas, R. E., Jr. (1990), "Why Doesn't Capital Flow from Rich to Poor Countries," *American Economic Review* 80 (May): 92–96.

Lucas, R. E., Jr. (1993), "Making a Miracle," *Econometrica* 61 (March): 251–72.

Machado, F. S. (1995), "Testing the Induced Innovation Hypothesis using Cointegration Analysis," *Journal of Agricultural Economics* 46: 349–60.

Maddison, A. (1979), "Per Capita Output in the Long Run," *Kyklos* 32, nos. 1 and 2: 412–29.

Maddison, A. (1995), *Monitoring the World Economy 1820–1992*. Paris: Organisation for Economic Development Centre.

Mahalanobis, P. C. (1953), "Some Observations on the Process of Growth of National Income," *Sankhya* 12 (September): 307–12.

Mahalanobis, P. C. (1955), "The Approach of Operational Research to Planning in India," *Sankhya* 16 (December): 3–62.

Mangahas, M. (1974), "Economic Aspects of Agrarian Reform under the New Society," *Philippine Review of Business and Economics* 11: 175–87.

Mangahas, M., Miralao, V., and de los Reyes, R. (1976), *Tenants, Lessees, Owners: Welfare Implication of Tenure Change*. Quezon City, Philippines: Ateneo de Manila University Press.

Mangahas, M., Recto, A. E., and Ruttan, V. W. (1966), "Market Relationships for Rice and Corn in the Philippines," *Philippine Economic Journal* 5 (First Semester): 1–27.

Mankiw, N. G. (1995), "The Growth of Nations," *Brookings Papers on Economic Activity*, no. 1: 275–376.

Mankiw, N. G., Romer, D., and Weil, D. N. (1992), "A Contribution to the Empirics of Economic Growth," *Quarterly Journal of Economics* 107 (May): 407–38.

Maredia, M. K., and Eicher, C. K. (1995), "The Economics of Wheat Research in Developing Countries: The One Hundred Million Dollar Puzzle," *World Development* 23: 401–12.

Marx, K. (1913), *A Contribution to the Critique of Political Economy*. Chicago: Kerr.

Marx, K. (1936), *Capital: A Critique of Political Economy*. New York: Modern Library. Orig. pub. 1906.

Marx, K. (1963), *The Eighteenth Brumaire of Louis Bonaparte*. New York: International.

Marx, K. (1967), *Capital*, vol. 3. New York: International. Orig. pub. 1895.

Marx, K. (1968), *Theories of Surplus Value*. Moscow: Progress.

Marx, K. (1970), *Capital: A Critique of Political Economy*. Vol. 1 of *The Process of Capital Production*. Chicago: Kerr. Orig. pub. 1867.

Mas-Colell, A., Whinston, M. D., and Green, J. R. (1995), *Microeconomic Theory*. New York: Oxford University Press.

Mason, E. S. (1954), "Afterthoughts on Paley: A Comment," *Review of Economics and Statistics* 36 (August): 273–78.

Matsuyama, K. (1992), "Innovation and Growth in the Global Economy," *Journal of International Economics* 33: 383–95.

Matusow, A. J. (1984), *The Unraveling of America: A History of Liberalism in the 1960s*. New York: Harper & Row.

McCoy, A. W. (1982), "A Queen Dies Slowly: The Rise and Decline Iloilo City," in A. D. McCoy and E. D. C. de Jesus (eds.), *Philippine Social History: Global Trade and Local Transformations*, 297–358. Quezon City, Philippines: Ateneo de Manila University Press.

McInerney, J., and Donaldson, G. (1975), "The Consequences of Farm Tractors in Pakistan," World Bank Staff Working Paper 210, Washington, DC.

McLennan, M. S. (1969), "Land and Tenancy in the Central Luzon Plain," *Philippine Studies* 17 (October): 651–82.

Meadows, D. H., Meadows, D. L., Randers, J., and Behrens, W. W., III (1972), *The Limits to Growth*. New York: Universe Books.

Mears, L. A. (1974), *Rice Economy of the Philippines*. Quezon City, Philippines: University of the Philippines Press.

Mears, L. A. (1981), *The New Rice Economy of Indonesia*. Yogyakarta, Indonesia: Gadjah Mada University Press.

Mehren, G. (1951), "Comparative Costs of Agricultural Price Support in 1949," *American Economic Review* 41 (May): 718–57.

Mellor, J. W., and Lele, U. J. (1973), "Growth Linkages with the New Foodgrain Technologies," *Indian Journal of Agricultural Economics* 28: 35–55.

Mendelsohn, R., Nordhaus, W. D., and Shaw, D. (1994), "The Impact of Global Warming on Agriculture: A Ricardian Analysis," *American Economic Review* 84: 753–71.

Minami, R. (1968), "The Turning Point in the Japanese Economy," *Quarterly Journal of Economics* 82 (August): 380–402.

Minami, R. (1973), *The Turning Point in Economic Development: The Japanese Experience*. Tokyo: Kinokuniya.

Ministry of Agriculture and Forestry (1945), *Norinsho Ruinen Tokeihyo* (Historical Statistics of Ministry of Agriculture and Forestry). Tokyo: Ministry of Agriculture and Forestry.

Ministry of Agriculture and Forestry (1968), *Nogyo oyobi Nokano Shakai Kanjo 1967* (Social Accounts of Agriculture and Farm Households). Tokyo: Ministry of Agriculture and Forestry.

Mitrany, D. (1951), *Marx Against the Peasant*. Chapel Hill: University of North Carolina Press.

Moseman, A. H. (1968), "Agricultural Research Institutions in the Developing Nations," paper presented at the Symposium of the International Rural Institutions Subcommittee of the North Central Land Economics Research Committee, Chicago, November 20.

Mosher, A. T. (1966), *Getting Agriculture Moving: Essentials for Development and Modernization*. New York: Praeger.

Murphy, K. M., Shliefer, A., and Vishny, R. W. (1989), "Industrialisation and the Big Push," *Journal of Political Economy* 97 (October): 1003–26.

Musgrave, R. A. (1959), *The Theory of Public Finance*. New York: McGraw-Hill.

Musu, I., and Lines, M. (1995), "Endogenous Growth and Environmental Preservation," in G. Boero and A. Silberston (eds.), *Environmental Economics*. New York: St. Martin's.

Myerson, R. B. (1999), "Nash Equilibrium and the History of Economic Theory," *Journal of Economic Literature* 37 (3): 1067–82.

Myint, H. (1965), *The Economics of Developing Countries*. New York: Praeger.

Myint, H. (1971), *Economic Theory and Underdeveloped Countries*. New York: Oxford University Press.

Nakamura, J. I. (1966), *Agriculture Production and Economic Development of Japan: 1878–1922*. Princeton, NJ: Princeton University Press.

Nakamura, J. I. (1968), "The Nakamura Versus the LTES Estimates of Growth Rate of Agricultural Production," *Keisai Kenkyu* 19 (October): 358–62.

Nakamura, J. I. (1969), "Incentives, Productivity Gap, and Agricultural Development in Japan, Taiwan and Korea," Golumbia University, mimeo.

National Research Council (1992), *Water Transfers in the West: Efficiency, Equity and the Environment*. Washington, DC: National Academy Press.

National Research Council (1993), *Sustainable Agriculture and the Environment in the Humid Tropics*. Washington, DC: National Academy Press.

National Research Council (1999), *A Common Journey: Toward a Sustainability Transition*. Washington, DC: National Academy Press.

Neisser, H. (1960), "Economic Imperialism Reconsidered," *Social Research* 27 (Spring): 63–82.

Nelson, R. R. (1959), "The Simple Economics of Basic Scientific Research," *Journal of Political Economy* 67 (3): 297–306.

Nelson, R. R. (1968), "A Diffusion Model of International Productivity Differences in Manufacturing Industry," *American Economic Review* 58 (December): 1219–48.

Nelson, R. R. (1998), "The Agenda for Growth Theory: A Different Point of View," *Cambridge Journal of Economics* 22: 497–520.

Nelson, R. R. (2005), *Technology, Institutions and Economic Growth*. Cambridge, MA: Harvard University Press.

Nelson, R. R., and Pack, H. (1997), "The Asian Miracle and Modern Growth Theory," School of International and Public Affairs, Columbia University and School of Public Planning and Government, University of Pennsylvania, mimeo.

Nelson, R. R., and Winter, S. G. (1982), *An Evolutionary Theory of Economic Change*. Cambridge, MA: Harvard University Press.

Nerlove, M. (1974), "Household and Economy: Toward a New Theory of Population and Economic Growth," *Journal of Political Economy* 82: S200–S18.

Nerlove, M., and Raut, L. K. (1997), "Growth Models with Endogenous Population: General Framework," in M. R. Rosenzweig and O. Stark (eds.), *The Handbook of Population and Family Economics*, vol. 1, 1117–74. Amsterdam: Elsevier.

Nicholls, W. H. (1945), "A Price Policy for Agriculture Consistent with Economic Progress That Will Promote Adequate and More Stable Income from Farming," *Journal of Farm Economics* 27 (4): 743–60.

Nobel Prize Committee (2007). "Title TK," Publication Info TK.

Nogyo Hattatsushi Chosakai (1953–73), *Nihon Nogyo Hattatsushi* (History of Japan's Agricultural Development), 10 vols. Tokyo: Chuokoronsha.

Nordhaus, W. D. (1973), "Some Skeptical Thoughts on the Theory of Induced Innovation," *Quarterly Journal of Economics* 87 (May): 209–19.

Nordhaus, W. D. (2008), "Impact on Economic Growth of Differential Population Growth in an Economy with High Inequality," *South African Journal of Economics* 76 (2): 314–15.

Noringijutsu Kyokai (Association of Agricultural Technology) (1952), *Meiji Iko ni Okern Nogyo Gijutsu no Hattatsu* (Progress of Agricultural Technology since Meiji Era). Tokyo: Noringijutsu Kyokai.

North, D. C. (1981), *Structure and Change in Economic History*. New York: Norton.

North, D. C. (1983), "A Theory of Economic Change," *Science* 219: 163–64.

North, D. C. (1994), "Economic Performance Through Time," *American Economic Review* 84: 359–68 (1993 Nobel Award Lecture).

North, D. C., and Thomas, R. P. (1970), "An Economic Theory of the Growth of the Western World," *Economic History Review* 23 (1): 1–17.

North, D. C., and Thomas, R. P. (1973), *The Rise of the Western World: A New Economic History*. Cambridge: Cambridge University Press.

Norton, G. W., and Norris, P. E. (1984), "Evaluating Agricultural Economics Research," Department of Agricultural Economy, Virginia Polytechnic Institute and State University.

Norton, G. W., and Schuh, G. E. (1981a), "Agricultural Social Science Research Evaluation," Department of Agricultural Economics, Virginia Polytechnic Institute and State University.

Norton, G. W., and Schuh, G. E. (1981b), "Evaluating Returns to Social Science Research: Issues and Possible Methods," in W. L. Fishel, A. A. Paulsen, and W. B. Sundquist (eds.), *Evaluation of Agricultural Research*, University of Minnesota Agricultural Experimental State Misc. Pub. No. 8, 246–61.

Nuti, D. M. (1970), "Capitalism, Socialism and Steady Growth," *Economic Journal* 80: 32–54.

Oasa, E. (1987), "The Political Economy of International Agricultural Research: A Review of the CGIAR's Response to Criticisms of the Green Revolution," in B. Glaser (ed.), *The Green Revolution Revisited: Critique and Alternatives*, 13–55. London: Allen and Unwin.

Oasa, E. K., and Jennings, B. H. (1982), "La naturaleza de la investigation social enroute la agricultura international: Le experiencia Norte Americana, el IRRI el CIMMYT" (The nature of social inquiry in international agricultural research: A reproduction of the American experience at IRRI and CIMMYT), *El Trimestre Economico* 49 (October–December): 975–1002.

Organization for Economic Co-operation and Development (2003), *The World Economy: Historical Statistics*. Paris: OECD.

Ogura, T. (1963), *Agricultural Development in Modern Japan*. Tokyo: Fuji.

Ohkawa, K. (1945), *Shokuryo Keizai no Riron to Keisoku* (Theory and Measurement of Food Economy). Tokyo: Nihonhyoronsha.

Ohkawa, K., Johnston, B. F., and Kaneda, H. (1969), *Agriculture and Economic Growth: Japan's Experience*. Tokyo: University of Tokyo Press.

Ohkawa, K., and Rosovsky, H. (1960), "The Role of Agriculture in Modern Japanese Economic Development," *Economic Development and Cultural Change* 9 (October): 43–68.

Ohkawa, K., and Rosovsky, H. (1965), "A Century of Japanese Economic Growth," in W. W. Lockwood (ed.), *The State and Economic Enterprise in Japan*, 68–83. Princeton, NJ: Princeton University Press.

Ohkawa, K., Shinohara, M., and Umemora, M. (1965–67), *Estimates of Long-Term Economic Statistics of Japan since 1868*. Tokyo: Toyo Keizai Shimposha.

Olson, M. (1965), *The Logic of Collective Action: Public Goods and the Theory of Groups*. Cambridge: Harvard University Press.

Olson, M. (1968), *The Logic of Collective Action: Public Goods and the Theory of Groups*. New York: Schocken.

Olson, M. (1982), *The Rise and Decline of Nations: Economic Growth, Stagflation, and Social Rigidities*. New Haven, CT: Yale University Press.

Olson, M. (1996), "Big Bills Left on the Sidewalk: Why Some Nations Are Rich and Others Poor," *Journal of Economic Perspectives* 10 (Spring): 3–24.

Olson, M. (2000), *Power and Prosperity: Outgrowing Communist and Capitalist Dictatorships*. New York: Basic Books.

Osnos, P. (2009), "Green Giant: Beijing's Crash Program for Clean Energy," *New Yorker*, December 21.

Ostrom, E. (1990), *Governing the Commons: The Evolution of Institutions for Collective Action*. Cambridge: Cambridge University Press.

Ostrom, E. (1992), *Crafting Institutions for Self-Governing Irrigation Systems*. San Francisco: ICS Press.

Ostrom, E. (2000), "Collective Action and the Evolution of Social Norms," *Journal of Economic Perspective* 14: 137–58.

Ostrom, E., Gardner, R., and Walker, J. (1994), *Rules, Games and Common Pool Resources*. Ann Arbor: University of Michigan Press.

Otsuka, K., Chuma, H., and Hayami, Y. (1992), "Land and Labor Contracts in Agrarian Economies," *Journal of Economic Literature* 30 (December): 1965–2018.

Otsuka, K., Estudillo, J. P., and Sawada, Y. (eds.) (2009), *Rural Income and Poverty Dynamics in Asia and Africa*. London: Routledge.

Otsuki, T., and Takamatsu, N. (1982), *On the Measurement of Income Inequality in Prewar Japan*. Tokyo: International Development Center of Japan.

Paarlberg, R. (2000), "The Global Food Fight," *Foreign Affairs* 79: 24–38.

Pack, H. (1994), "Endogenous Growth Theory: Intellectual Appeal and Empirical Shortcomings," *Journal of Economic Perspectives* 8 (Winter): 55–72.

Palladino, P. (1987), "Science for Whom? Agricultural Development and the Theory of Induced Innovation," *Agriculture and Human Values* 4 (Spring/Summer): 53–64.

Palladino, P. (1996), *Entomology, Ecology and Agriculture: The Making of Scientific Careers in North America 1885–1985*. Amsterdam: Harwood.

Palley, T. I. (1996), "Growth Theory in a Keynesian Mode: Some Keynesian Foundations for New Endogenous Growth Theory," *Journal of Post Keynesian Economics* 19 (Fall): 113–36.

Palmer, I. (1976), *The New Rice in Asia: Conclusions from Four Country Studies*. Geneva: United Nations Research Institute for Social Development.

Pardey, P. G., James, J., Alston, J., Wood, S., Koo, B., Binenbaum, E., Hurley, T., and Glewwe, P. (2007), "Science, Technology and Skills," background paper for the World Bank's *World Development Report 2008*. St. Paul, Rome, and Washington, DC: University of Minnesota, CGIAR Science Council, and World Bank.

Pardy, P. J., Craig, B. J., and Hallaway, M. J. (1989), "US Agricultural Research Deflators: 1890–1985," *Research Policy* 18: 289–96.

Parente, S. L., and Prescott, E. C. (1991), "Technology Adoption and Growth," Minneapolis: Federal Reserve Bank of Minneapolis Staff Report 136.

Parente, S. L., and Prescott, E. C. (1993), "Changes in the Wealth of Nations," *Federal Reserve Bank of Minneapolis Quarterly Review* 17 (Spring): 3–16.

Parente, S. L., and Prescott, E. C. (1994), "Barriers to Technology Adoption and Development," *Journal of Political Economy* 102 (April): 298–321.

Park, A., and Johnston, B. (1995), "Rural Development and Dynamic Externalities in Taiwan's Structural Transformation," *Economic Development and Cultural Change* 44 (October): 181–208.

Parry, M. L. (1990), *Climate Change and World Agriculture*. London: Earthscan.

Parthasarathy, G. (1975), "West Godavavi, Andhra Pradesh," in *Changes in Rice Farming in Selected Areas of Asia*, 43–70. Los Banos, the Philippines: International Rice Research Institute.

Patrick, H. R., and Rohlen, T. P. (1987), "Small-Scale Family Enterprises," in K. Yamamura and Y. Yasuba (eds.), *The Political Economy of Japan*. Vol. 1 of *The Domestic Transformation*, 331–84. Stanford, CA: Stanford University Press.

Pearse, A. (1980), *Seeds of Plenty, Seeds of Want: Social and Economic Implications of the Green Revolution*. Oxford: Clarendon Press.

Pelzer, K. J. (1945), *Pioneer Settlement in the Asiatic Tropics*. New York: American Geographical Society.

Perkins, J. H. (1982), *Insects, Experts and the Insecticide Crisis: The New Pest Management Strategies*. New York: Plenum.

Peterson, W., and Hayami, Y. (1977), "Technical Change in Agriculture," in L. R. Martin (ed.), *A Survey of Agricultural Economics Literature*, vol. 1, 497–540. Minneapolis: University of Minnesota Press.

Phelps, E. S. (1963), "Substitutions, Fixed Proportions, Growth and Distribution," *International Economic Review* 4: 265–88.

Phillips, W. H. (1982), "Induced Innovation and Economic Performance in Late Victorian British Industry," *Journal of Economic History* 42: 97–104.

Pim, A. (1946), *Colonial Agricultural Production*. London: Royal Institute of International Affairs; New York: Oxford University Press.

Pimentel, D., Harvey, C., Resosudarmo, P., Sinclair, K., Kurtz, D., McNair, M., Crist, S., Shpritz, L., Fitton, L., Saffouri, R., and Blair, R. (1995a), "Environmental and Economic Costs of Soil Erosion and Conservation Benefits," *Science* 267: 1117–23.

Pimentel, D., Harvey, C., Resosudarmo, P., Sinclair, K., Kurtz, D., McNair, M., Crist, S., Shpritz, L., Fitton, L., Saffouri, R., and Blair, R. (1995b), "Soil Erosion Estimates and Costs," *Science* 269: 464–65.

Pimentel, D., McLaughlin, L., Zepp, A., Lakitan, B., Kraus, T., Kleinman, D., Vancini, F., Roach, W. J., Graap, E., and Keeton, W. (1991), "Environmental and Economic Impacts of Reducing U.S. Agricultural Pesticide Use," in D. Pimentel (ed.), *Handbook of Pest Management in Agriculture*, 679–718. Boca Raton, FL: CRC.

Pimentel, D., Terhune, E. C., Hudson, R. D., Rochester, S., Sarris, R., Smith, E. A., Denman, D., Reitschneider, D., and Sheperd, M. (1976), "Land Degradation: Effects on Food and Energy Resources," *Science* 194: 149–54.

Pimentel, D., Tort, M., D'Anna, L., Krawick, A., Berger, J., Rossman, J., Mungo F., Doon, N., Shriberg, M., Howad, E. (1998), "Ecology of Increasing Disease: Population, Health, and Environmental Degradation," *Bioscience* 48: 317–26.

Pinstrup-Anderson, P., and Cohen, M. (2001), "Rich and Poor Country Perspectives on Biotechnology," in P. Pardey (ed.), *The Future of Food: Biotechnology, Markets and Policies in an International Setting*, 17–47. Baltimore: Johns Hopkins University Press.

Pinstrup-Anderson, P., and Schioler, E. (2001), *Seeds of Contention: World Hunger and the Global Controversy over GM Crops*. Baltimore: Johns Hopkins University Press.

Pirn, A. (1946), *Colonial Agricultural Production*. London: Royal Institute of International Affairs; New York: Oxford University Press.

Platteau, J. P. (1996), "Traditional Norms as a Obstacle to Economic Growth in Tribal Societies," CRED Faculty of Economics, University Namur, Belgium, April, mimeo.

Plucknett, D. L., and Smith, N. J. H. (1986), "Sustaining Agricultural Yields," *Bioscience* 36: 40–45.

Pookkachatikul, J., and Welsch, D. (1976), *Thai Rice Premium Data, 1954–1976*, Staff Paper No. 12. Bangkok: Department of Agricultural Economics, Kasetsart University.

Prescott, E. C. (1988), "Robert M. Solow's Neoclassical Growth Model: An Influential Contribution to Economics," *Scandinavian Journal of Economics* 90 (1): 7–12.

Prescott, E. C. (1997), "Needed: A Theory of Total Factor Productivity," Research Department Staff Report 242. Minneapolis: Federal Reserve Bank of Minneapolis.

President's Material Policy Commission (1952), *Resources for Freedom*, 5 vols. . Washington, DC.

President's Water Resources Policy Commission (1950), *A Water Policy for the American People*, the report of the President's Water Policy Commission, vol. 1. Washington, DC.

Pritchett, L. (1995), *Divergence, Big Time*, World Bank Policy Research Working Paper 1522, Washington, DC, October.

Pritchett, L. (1997), "Our Friend 'Recent Growth Research,'" paper presented at American Economic Association Annual Meetings, January 5.

Radner, R. (1981), "Monitoring Cooperative Agreements in a Repeated Principal-Agent Relationship," *Econometrica* 49 (September): 1127–48.

Ranade, C., and Herdt, R. (1978), "Shares of Farm Earnings from Rice Production," in R. Barker and Y. Hayami (eds.), *Economic Consequences of the New Rice Technology*, 113–36. Los Banos, the Philippines: International Rice Research Institute.

Ranis, G. (1957), "Factor Proportions in Japanese Economic Development," *American Economic Review* 47 (September): 594–607.

Ranis, G. (1988), "Analytics of Development: Dualism," in H. B. Chenery and T. N. Srinivasan (eds.), *Handbook of Development Economics*, vol. 1, 73–92. Amsterdam: Elsevier Science.

Ranis, G., and Fei, J. C. H. (1961), "A Theory of Economic Development," *American Economic Review* 51 (September): 533–65.

Rao, C. H. H. (1975), *Technological Change and Distribution of Gains in Indian Agriculture*. Delhi: Macmillan.

Raskin, P., Chadwick, M., Jackson, T., and Leach, G. (1996), *The Sustainability Transition: Beyond Conventional Development*. Stockholm: Stockholm Environment Institute.

Raskin, P., Gallopin, G., Gutman, P., Hammond, A., and Swart, R. (1998), *Bending the Curve: Toward Global Sustainability*. Stockholm: Stockholm Environment Institute.

Raskin, P., Gleick, P., Kirshin, P., Pontius, G., and Strzepek, K. (1998), *Comprehensive Assessment of the Freshwater Resources of the World*. Stockholm: Stockholm Environment Institute.

Rasmussen, W. D. (1983), "New Deal Agricultural Policies after Fifty Years," *Minnesota Law Review* 68: 353–76.

Rausser, G. C., Lichtenberg, E., and Lattimore, R. (1982), "Developments in the Theory and Empirical Application of Endogenous Government Behavior," in G. C. Rausser (ed.), *New Directions in Econometric Modeling and Forecasting in U. S. Agriculture*, 547–614. New York: Elsevier.

Reiter, S. (1977), "Information and Performance in the (New) 'Welfare Economics,' *American Economic Review* 67: 226–34.

Republic of the Philippines (1991), *Philippine Statistical Yearbook 1991*. Manila: National Economic and Development Authority.

Resnick, S. A. (1970), "The Decline in Rural Industry under Export Expansion: A Comparison among Burma, Philippines and Thailand, 1870–1938," *Journal of Economic History* 30 (March): 51–73.

Rivera-Batiz, L. A., and Romer, P. M. (1991), "Economic Integration and Endogenous Growth," *Quarterly Journal of Economics* 106 (May): 531–55.

Robelo, S. (1991), "Long Run Policy Analysis and Long Run Growth," *Journal of Political Economy* 99 (June): 500–521.

Robinson, J. (1948), *The Economics of Imperfect Competition*. London: Macmillan.

Robinson, J. (1964), *Economic Philosophy*. New York: Doubleday, Anchor.

Rodney, W. (1974), *How Europe Underdeveloped Africa*. Washington, DC: Howard University Press.

Rogin, L. (1931), *The Introduction of Farm Machinery*. Berkeley: University of California Press.

Romer, P. M. (1983), "Dynamic Competitive Equilibria with Externalities, Increasing Returns and Unbounded Growth," Ph.D. diss., Department of Economics, University of Chicago.

Romer, P. M. (1986), "Increasing Returns and Long Run Economic Growth," *Journal of Political Economy* 94: 1003–37.

Romer, P. M. (1987), "Crazy Explanations for the Productivity Slowdown," in S. Fisher (ed.), *NBER Macroeconomic Annual*. Cambridge, MA: MIT Press.

Romer, P. M. (1990), "Endogenous Technological *Change," Journal of Political Economy* 98: S71–S102.

Romer, P. M. (1993), "Idea Gaps and Object Gaps on Economic Development," *Journal of Monetary Economics* 32 (December): 543–73.

Romer, P. M. (1994), "The Origins of Endogenous Growth," *Journal of Economic Perspectives* 8 (Winter): 3–22.

Romer, P. M. (1995), "Comment and Discussion," *Brookings Papers on Economic Activity* 1: 313–20.

Romer, P. M. (1996), "Why, Indeed, in America? Theory, History and the Origins of Modern Economic Growth," Working Paper 5442, Bureau of Economic Research, January.

Rosegrant, M., and Hazell, P. B. R. (2000), *Transforming the Rural Asian Economy: The Unfinished Revolution*. Oxford: Oxford University Press.

Rosenberg, N. (1982), "Marx as a Student of Technology," in *Inside the Black Box: Technology and Economics*, 34–54. Cambridge: Cambridge University Press.

Rosenstein-Rodan, P. N. (1943), "Problems of Industrialisation in Eastern and Southeastern Europe," *Economic Journal* 53 (June–September): 202–11.

Rosenzweig, C., and Hillel, D. (1998), *Climate Change and the Global Harvest*. New York: Oxford University Press.

Rosovsky, H. (1968), "Rumbles in the Rice Fields: Professor Nakamura vs. the Official Statistics," *Journal of Asian Studies* 27 (February): 347–60.

Rosovsky, H., and Ohkawa, K. (1961), "The Indigenous Components in the Modern Japanese Economy," *Economic Development and Cultural Change* 9 (April): 476–501.

Rostow, W. W. (1956), "The Take-Off into Self-sustained Growth," *Economic Journal* 66 (March): 25–448.

Rostow, W. W. (1960), *The Stages of Economic Growth: A Non-Communist Manifesto*. Cambridge: Cambridge University Press.

Rotmans, J., and Dowlatabadi, H. (1998), "Integrated Assessment Modeling," in S. Rayner and E. L. Malone (eds.), *Human Choice and Climate Change*, vol. 3: *The Tools for Policy Analysis*, 291–377. Columbus, OH: Batelle.

Runge, C. F. (1981a), "Common Property Externalities: Isolation, Assurance, and Resource Depletion in a Traditional Grazing Context," *American Journal of Agricultural Economics* 63: 595–606.

Runge, C. F. (1981b), "Institutions and Common Property Externalities: The Assurance Problem in Economic Development," Ph.D. diss., University of Wisconsin–Madison.

Runge, C. F. (1983), "Sources of Institutional Innovation: An Interpretive Essay," Working Paper, Department of Economics, University of Minnesota, June.

Runge, C. F. (1984a), "Institutions and the Free Rider: The Assurance Problem in Collective Action," *Journal of Politics* 46: 154–81.

Runge, C. F. (1984b), "Strategic Interdependence in Models of Property Rights," *American Journal of Agricultural Economics* 66: 807–13.

Runge, C. F. (1987), "Induced Agricultural Innovation and Environmental Quality: The Case of Groundwater Regulation," *Land Economics* 63 (August): 249–58.

Runge, C. F. (1998), "Global Trade and Sustainability: Machines in the Earth's Garden," *Choices* 13 (4): 11–14.

Runge, C. F. (1999), "Stream, River, Delta: Induced Innovation and Environmental Values in Economics and Policy," WP 99-2, Center for International Food and Agricultural Policy, University of Minnesota, St. Paul.

Runge, C. F. (2009), "The Climate Commons and a Global Environmental Organization," in L. Brainard and I. Sorkin (eds.), *Climate Change, Trade and Competitiveness: Is a Collision Inevitable?*, chap. 6. Washington, DC: Brookings Institution Press.

Ruttan, V. W. (1954), "A Critical Evaluation of Measures of Technological Progress," in *Technological Progress in the Meat Packing Industry, 1919–47*, Marketing Research Report 59, U.S. Department of Agriculture, January.

Ruttan, V. W. (1956), "The Contribution of Technological Progress to Farm Output: 1950–75," *Review of Economics and Statistics* 38 (February): 61–69.

Ruttan, V. W. (1958), "Agricultural and Non-agricultural Growth in the Output per Unit of Input," *Journal of Farm Economics* 40 (May): 196–207.

Ruttan, V. W. (1960), "Research on the Economics of Technical Change in American Agriculture," *Journal of Farm Economics* 42 (November): 735–54.

Ruttan, V. W. (1961), "Productivity and Technical Change," *Journal of Farm Economics* 43 (February): 160–63.

Ruttan, V. W. (1966), "Tenure and Productivity of Philippine Rice Producing Farms," *Philippine Economic Journal* 5 (First Semester): 42–63.

Ruttan, V. W. (1968), "Growth Stage Theories, Dual Economy Models, and Agricultural Development Policy," Publication No. AE 2, University of Guelph.

Ruttan, V. W. (1969a), "Agricultural Product and Factor Market in Southeast Asia," *Economic Development, and Cultural Change* 17 (July): 501–19.

Ruttan, V. W. (1969b), "Equity and Productivity Issues in Modern Agrarian Reform Legislation," in U. Papi and C. Nunn (eds.), *Economic Problems of Agriculture in Industrial Societies*, 581–600. London: Macmillan; New York: St. Martin's.

Ruttan, V. W. (1971), "Presidential Address: Technology and the Environment," *American Journal of Agricultural Economics* 53 (December): 707–17.

Ruttan, V. W. (1977), "Induced Innovation, Evolutionary Theory and Path Dependence: Sources of Technical Change," *Economic Journal* 107 (September): 1520–29.

Ruttan, V. W. (1978), "Institutional Innovation," in Theodore W. Schultz (ed.), *Distortions of Agricultural Incentives*, 290–306. Bloomington: Indiana University Press.

Ruttan, V. W. (1981), "Three Cases of Induced Institutional Innovation," in C. S. Russell and N. K. Nicholson (eds.), *Public Choice and Rural Development*, 239–70. Baltimore: Johns Hopkins University Press.

Ruttan, V. W. (1982a), *Agricultural Research Policy*. Minneapolis: University of Minnesota Press.

Ruttan, V. W. (1982b), "Changing Role of Public and Private Sectors in Agricultural Research," *Science* 216: 23–29.

Ruttan, V. W. (1984), "Social Science Knowledge and Institutional Change," *American Journal of Agricultural Economics* 66 (December): 549–59.

Ruttan, V. W. (1994a), "Constraints on the Design of Sustainable Systems of Agricultural Development," *Ecological Economics* 12: 209–19.

Ruttan, V. W. (ed.) (1994b), *Health and Sustainable Agricultural Development*. Boulder, CO: Westview.

Ruttan, V. W. (1995), "Cultural Endowments and Economic Development: Implications for the Chinese Economies," *China Economic Review* 6 (1): 91–104.

Ruttan, V. W. (1997), "Induced Innovation, Evolutionary Theory and Path Dependence: Sources of Technical Change," *Economic Journal* 107 (September): 1520–29.

Ruttan, V. W. (1998), "Growth Economics and Development Economics: What Should Development Economists Learn (If Anything) from the New Growth Theory," Economic Development Center Bulletin 98-4, University of Minnesota, St. Paul.

Ruttan, V. W. (2001), *Technology, Growth and Development: An Induced Innovation Perspective*. New York: Oxford University Press.

Ruttan, V. W. (2003), *Social Science Knowledge and Economic Development*. Ann Arbor: University of Michigan Press.

Ruttan, V. W. (2006), "Social Science Knowledge and Induced Institutional Innovation: An Institutional Design Perspective," *Journal of Institutional Economics* 2 (3): 249–72.

Ruttan, V. W., Binswanger, H. P., Hayami, Y., Wade, W., and Weber, A. (1978), "Factor Productivity and Growth: A Historical Interpretation," in H. P. Binswanger, V. W. Ruttan, et al. (eds.), *Induced Innovation: Technology, Institutions, and Development*, 44–72. Baltimore: Johns Hopkins University Press.

Ruttan, V. W., and Hayami, Y. (1970), "Korean Rice, Taiwan Rice, and Japanese Agricultural Stagnation: An Economic Consequence of Colonialism," *Quarterly Journal of Economics* 84 (November): 562–89.

Ruttan, V. W., and Hayami, Y. (1984), "Toward a Theory of Induced Institutional Innovation," *Journal of Development Studies* 20 (July): 203–23.

Ruttan, V. W., and Hayami, Y. (1995), "Induced Innovation Theory: A Reassessment," in B. M. Koppel (ed.), *Induced Innovation Theory and International Agricultural Development: A Reassessment*, 22–36. Baltimore: Johns Hopkins University Press.

Ruttan, V. W., and Moomow, James E. (1964), "Partial Budgeting of Costs and Returns Using Experimental Data from Herbicides and Fertilizer Experiments," *Philippine Agriculturalist* 48 (November–December): 249–68.

Ruttan, V. W., Recto, A. E., and Mangahas, M. (1966), "Price and Market Relationships for Rice and Corn in the Philippines," *Journal of Farm Economics* 48 (August): 685–703.

Ruttan, V. W., Soothipan, A., and Venegas, E. C. (1966a), "Changes in Rice Production, Area, and Yield in the Philippines and Thailand," *World Crops* 18 (March): 16–33.

Ruttan, V. W., Soothipan, A., and Venegas, E. C. (1966b), "Technological and Environmental Factors in the Growth of Rice Production in the Philippines and Thailand," *Rural Economic Problems* 3 (May): 63–107.

Ryan, T. G. (1980), "Farm Prices and the Farm Vote in 1948," *Agricultural History* 54: 387–401.

Sahota, G. (1967), *Fertilizer and Economic Development*. New York: Praeger.

Sala-i-Martin, X. X. (1977), "I Just Ran Four Million Regressions," Working Paper 6252, National Bureau of Economic Research, Cambridge, MA.

Salter, W. E. G. (1960), *Productivity and Technical Change*. Cambridge: Cambridge University Press.

Samuelson, P. A. (1948), *Foundations of Economic Analyses*, Harvard Economic Studies, Vol. 80: 221–22. Cambridge, MA: Harvard University Press.

Samuelson, P. A. (1954), "The Pure Theory of Public Expenditure," *Review of Economics and Statistics* 36: 387–89.

Samuelson, P. A. (1955), "Diagrammatic Exposition of a Theory of Public Expenditure," *Review of Economics and Statistics* 37: 350–56.

Samuelson, P. A. (1958), "Aspects of Public Expenditure Theories," *Review of Economics and Statistics* 40: 332–38.

Samuelson, P. A. (1965), "A Theory of Induced Innovation along Kennedy-Weisacker Lines," *Review of Economic and Statistics* 67 (November): 343–56.

Sandeep, B., and Maskin, E. (2003), "Mechanism Design for the Environment," in K. G. Maler and J. R. Vincent (eds.), *Handbook of Environment Economics* 1, no. 1. Amsterdam: Elsevier.

Sanders, J., and Ruttan, V. W. (1948), "Biased Choice of Technology in Brazilian Agriculture," in H. P. Binswanger, V. W. Ruttan, et al. (eds.), *Induced Innovation: Technology, Institutions, and Development*, 276–96. Baltimore: Johns Hopkins University Press.

Sandler, T. (1997), *Global Challenges: An Approach to Environmental, Political and Economic Problems*. Cambridge, MA: Harvard University Press.

Sato, R. (1970), "The Estimation of Biased Technical Progress and the Production Function," *International Economic Review* 11 (2): 179–208.

Sawada, S. (1965), "Innovation in Japanese Agriculture, 1880–1935," in W. W. Lockwood (ed.), *The State and Economic Enterprise in Japan*, 325–52. Princeton, NJ: Princeton University Press.

Schickele, R. (1941), "Effect of Tenure Systems on Agricultural Efficiency," *Journal of Farm Economics* 23 (February): 185–207.

Schmitz, J. A., Jr. (1993), "Early Progress on the 'Problem of Economic Development,' *Federal Reserve Bank of Minneapolis Quarterly Review* 17 (Spring): 17–33.

Schmookler, J. (1952), "The Changing Efficiency of the American Economy, 1869–1938," *Review of Economics and Statistics* 34 (August): 214–31.

Schmookler, J. (1966), *Innovation and Economic Growth*. Cambridge, MA.: Harvard University Press.

Schotter, A. (1981), *The Economic Theory of Social Institutions*. Cambridge: Cambridge University Press.

Schran, P. (1975), "On the Yenan Origins of Current Economic Policies," in D. H. Perkins (ed.), *China's Modern Economy in Historical Perspective*, 279–302. Stanford, CA: Stanford University Press.

Schuh, G. E. (1974), "The Exchange Rate and U.S. Agriculture," *American Journal of Agricultural Economy* 56: 1–13.

Schuh, G. E. (1984), "Agricultural Research: How It Should Be Affected by Exports," *Agricultural Engineering* 65 (May): 8–12.

Schultz, T. W. (1943), *Redirecting Farm Policy*. New York: Macmillan.

Schultz, T. W. (1944), "Two Conditions Necessary for Economic Progress in Agriculture," *Canadian Journal of Economy and Political Science* 10: 298–311.

Schultz, T. W. (1949), *Production and Welfare of Agriculture*. New York: Macmillan.

Schultz, T. W. (1953), *Economic Organization of Agriculture*. New York: McGraw-Hill.

Schultz, T. W. (1961), "Investment in Human Capital," *American Economic Review* 51 (March): 1–17.

Schultz, T. W. (1964a), *Transforming Traditional Agriculture*. New Haven: Yale University Press.

Schultz, T. W. (1964b), "Economic Growth from Traditional Agriculture," in A. H. Moseman (ed.), *Agricultural Science for the Developing Nations*, 185–205. Washington, DC: American Association for the Advancement of Science.

Schultz, T. W. (1968), "Institutions and the Rising Economic Value of Men," *American Journal of Agricultural Economics* 50: 1113–22.

Schultz, T. W. (1969), "The Allocation of Resources to Research," paper presented at the Resource Allocation in Agricultural Research Symposium, St. Paul, MN, February 23–25.

Schultz, T. W. (1975), "The Value of the Ability to Deal with Disequilibria," *Journal of Economic Literature* 13 (September): 827–46.

Schultz, T. W. (ed.) (1978), *Distortion of Agricultural Incentives*. Bloomington: Indiana University Press.

Schumacker, E. F. (1973), *Small Is Beautiful: A Study of Economics As If People Mattered*. London: Bland and Briggs.

Scott, A. M. (1959), "The Progressive Era in Perspective," *Journal of Politics* 21: 685–701.

Scott, G. J. (1985), *Markets, Myths and Middlemen: A Study of Potato Marketing in Central Peru*. Lima: International Potato Center.

Searchinger, T., Heimlich, R., Houghton, R. A., Dong, F., Elobeid, A., Fabiosa, J., Tokgoz, S., Hayes, D., and Yu, T. (2008), "Use of U.S. Croplands for Biofuels Increases Greenhouse Gases through Emissions from Land-Use Change," *Science* 319 (February 29): 1238–40.

Seckler, D. (1975), *Thorstein Veblen and the Institutionalists*. London: Macmillan.

Seckler, D., Molden, D., and Barker, R. (1999), "Water Scarcity in the Twenty-First Century," *International Journal of Water Resources Development* 15 (1–2): 29–42.

Selden, T. M., and Song, D. (1994), "Environmental Quality and Development: Is There a Kuznets Curve for Air Pollution Emissions?" *Journal of Environmental Economics and Management* 27: 145–62.

Sen, A. K. (1959), "The Choice of Agricultural Techniques in Underdeveloped Countries," *Economic Development and Cultural Change* 1 (April): 279–85.

Sen, A. K. (1960), *Choice of Techniques: An Aspect of the Theory of Planned Economic Development*. Oxford: Basil Blackwell.

Sen, A. K. (1967), "Isolation and the Social Rates of Discount," *Quarterly Journal of Economics* 81: 112–24.

Sen, A. K. (1981), *Poverty and Famines: An Essay on Entitlement and Deprivation*. Oxford: Clarendon Press.

Sen, A. K. (1983), "Development: Which Way Now?" *Economic Journal* 93 (December): 745–62.

Sen, B. (1974), *The Green Revolution in India: A Perspective*. New Delhi: Wiley.

Shen, T. H. (1964), *Agricultural Development in Taiwan since World War II*. Ithaca, NY: Cornell University Press.

Shuh, E., and Brandão, A. S. P. (1992). "The Theory, Empirical Evidence, and Debates on Agricultural Development in Latin America: A Selective Survey," in L. Martin (ed.), *A Survey of Agricultural Economics Literature*, vol. 4: *Agriculture in Economic Development 1940s to 1990s*, 554–655. St. Paul: University of Minnesota Press.

Siamwalla, A. (1987), *The Farmers' Aid Fund Act of 1974: Its Genesis and Aftermath*. Bangkok: Thailand Development Research Institute.

Siamwalla, A. (1992), "Myths, Demons and the Future of Thai Agriculture," paper presented at Year-end Conference on Thailand's Economic Structure: Toward Balanced Development, Bangkok, Thailand, November.

Siamwalla, A., and Setboonsarng, S. (1989), *Trade, Exchange Rate, and Agricultural Pricing Policies in Thailand*. Washington, DC: World Bank.

Siamwalla, A., Setboonsarng, S., and Patanasiriwat, D. (1990), *Thai Agriculture: Resources, Institutions and Policies*. Bangkok: Thailand Development Research Institute.

Sidhu, S. (1974a), "Economics of Technical Change in Wheat Production in the Indian Punjab," *American Journal of Agricultural Economics* 56: 217–36.

Sidhu, S. (1974b), "Relative Efficiency in Wheat Production in the Indian Punjab," *American Economic Review* 64: 742–51.

Siegel, I. H. (1953), "Technological Change and Long-Run Forecasting," *Journal of Business* 26 (July): 141–56.

Smith, P. H. (1969), *Politics and Beef in Argentina: Patterns of Conflict and Change*. New York: Columbia University Press.

Smith, P. H. (1974), *Argentina and the Failure of Democracy: Conflict among Elites, 1880–1955*. Madison: University of Wisconsin Press.

Smith, T. C. (1956), "Landlords and Rural Capitalists in the Modernization of Japan," *Journal of Economic History* 16 (June): 165–68.

Smith, T. C. (1959), *Agrarian Origin of Modern Japan*. Stanford, CA: Stanford University Press.

Smith, T. C. (1988), *Native Sources of Japanese Industrialization, 1750–1920*. Berkeley and Los Angeles: University of California Press.

Smith, V. K. (1975), "Relative Prices, Technical Change and Environmental Preservation," *Natural Resources Journal* 15: 283–95.

Soejono, I. (1976), "Growth and Distributional Changes in Paddy Farm Income in Central Java," *Prisma (Indonesian Journal of Social and Economic Affairs)* 3: 26–32.

Solow, R. M. (1956), "A Contribution to the Theory of Economic Growth," *Quarterly Journal of Economics* 70 (February): 65–94.

Solow, R. M. (1957), "Technical Change and the Aggregate Production Function," *Review of Economics and Statistics* 39 (August): 312–20.

Solow, R. M. (1966), "Substitution and Fixed Proportions in the Theory of Capital," *Review of Economic Studies* 29: 207–18.

Solow, R. M. (1970), *Growth Theory: An Exposition*,. Oxford: Oxford University Press.

Solow, R. M. (1985), "Economic History and Economics," *American Economic Review* 75 (May): 327–31.

Solow, R. M. (1988), "Growth Theory and After," *American Economic Review* 78 (3): 307–17.

Solow, R. M. (1995), "Perspectives on Growth Theory," *Journal of Economic Perspectives* 8 (Winter): 45–54.

Solow, R. M. (1997), *Learning from "Learning by Doing": Lessons for Economic Growth*. Stanford, CA: Stanford University Press.

Srinivasan, T. N. (1991), "Development Thought, Strategy and Policy: Then and Now," background paper prepared for World Development Report 1991, World Bank, Washington, DC, October.

Srinivasan, T. N. (1995), "Long-Run Growth Theories and Empirics: Anything New," in Takatoshi Ito and Anne O. Krueger (eds.), *Growth Theories in the Light of East Asian Experience*, 37–70. Chicago: University of Chicago Press.

Staub, W. (1973), *Agricultural Development and Farm Employment in India*, U.S. Department of Agriculture, Economic Research Service, Foreign Agricultural Economic Report 84, Washington, DC.

Stavins, R. N. (1998), "What Can We Learn from the Grand Policy Experiment? Lessons from SO_2 Allowances Trading," *Journal of Economic Perspectives* 12: 69–88.

Stern, N. (1991), "The Determinants of Growth," *Economic Journal* 101 (January): 122–33.

Stewart, F. (1987a), *Macro-Policies for Appropriate Technologies in Development Countries*. Boulder, CO: Westview Press.

Stewart, F. (1987b), "The Case for Appropriate Technology: A Reply to R. S. Eckaus," *Science and Technology* 14 (Summer): 101–9.

Stigler, G. J. (1947), *Trends in Output and Employment*. New York: National Bureau of Economic Research.

Stigler, G. J. (1965), *Essays in the History of Economics*. Chicago: University of Chicago Press.

Stigler, G. J. (1982), *The Economist as Preacher and Other Essays*. Chicago: University of Chicago Press.

Stigler, G. J., and Becker, G. S. (1977), "De Gustibus Non Est Disputandum," *American Economic Review* 67: 76–99.

Stiglitz, J. E. (1974), "Incentives and Risk Sharing in Sharecropping," *Review of Economic Studies* 41 (April): 219–56.

Stokey, N. (1991), "Human Capital, Product Quality, and Growth," *Quarterly Journal of Economics* 111 (May): 586–616.

Stout, T. T., and Ruttan, V. W. (1960), "Regional Differences in Factor Shares in American Agriculture," *Journal of Farm Economics* 41 (February): 52–68.

Swan, T. W. (1956), "Economic Growth and Capital Accumulation," *Economic Record* 32 (November): 343–61.

Syrquin, M. (1994), "Structural Transformation and the New Growth Theory," in Luigi L. Pasinetti and Robert M. Solow (eds.), *Economic Growth and the Structure of Long-Term Development*, 3–21. New York: St. Martin's.

Takaya, K. (1985), *Tonan Ajia no Shizen to Tochiriyo* (Nature and Land Use in Southeast Asia). Tokyo: Keiso Shobo.

Tan, E. S. (2005), "Ideology, Interest Groups, and Institutional Change: The Case of the British Prohibition of Wages in Kind," *Journal of Institutional Economics* 1: 175–91.

Tang, A. M. (1967), "Agriculture in the Industrialization of Communist China and the Soviet Union," *Journal of Farm Economics* 49 (December): 1118–34.

Tang, H. S., and Hsieh, S. C. (1961), "Land Reform and Agricultural Development in Taiwan," *Malayan Economic Review* 6 (April): 49–54.

Taylor, R. E. (1989), *Ahead of the Curve: Shaping New Solutions to Environmental Problems*. New York: Environmental Defense Fund.

Teese, D. J. (1977), "Technology Transfer by Multinational Firms: The Resource Cost of Transferring Technological Know-How," *Economic Journal* 87 (June): 242–61.

Thailand Ministry of Agriculture (1996), *Agricultural Statistics of Thailand 1995/96*. Bangkok: Division of Agricultural Economics, Office of the Under-Secretary of State, Ministry of Agriculture.

Thirtle, C. W., and Ruttan, V. W. (1987), *The Role of Demand and Supply in the Generation and Diffusion of Technical Change*. London: Harwood Oceanic.

Tietenberg, T. (2002), "The Tradable Permits Approach to Protecting the Commons: What Have We Learned?," in E. Ostrom, T. Dietz, N. Dolsak, P. C. Stern, S. Stonich, and E. U. Welser (eds.), *The Drama of the Commons*, 197–232. Washington, DC: National Academy Press.

Timmer, C. P. (1993), Foreword to *Agrarian Origins of Commerce and Industry*, by Y. Hayami and T. Kawagoe. New York: St. Martin's.

Tobata, S., and Ohkawa, K. (1935), *Chosen Beikoku Keizairon* (A Treatise of Rice Economy in Korea). Tokyo: Nihon Gakujutsu Shinkokai.

Tollison, R. D. (1982), "Rent Seeking: A Survey," *Kyklos* 35 (fasc. 4): 575–602.

Tomich, T. P., Kilby, P., and Johnston, B. F. (1995), *Transforming Agrarian Economies: Opportunities Seized, Opportunities Missed*. Ithaca, NY: Cornell University Press.

Tostlebe, A. S. (1954), "The Growth of Physical Capital in Agriculture, 1870–1950," Occasional Paper 44, National Bureau of Economic Research, New York.

Tostlebe, A. S. (1957), *Capital in Agriculture: Its Formation and Financing since 1870*. Princeton, NJ: Princeton University Press.

Trelogan, H. C., and Johnson, N. W. (1953), "The Evitability of Technological Advance," *Journal of Farm Economics* 35 (November): 599–604.

Tullock, G. (1967), "The Welfare Costs of Tariffs, Monopolies and Theft," *Western Economic Journal* 5: 224–32.

Tussing, A. (1966), "The Labor Force in Meiji Economic Growth: A Quantitative Study of Yamanashi Prefecture," *Journal of Economic History* 26 (March): 59–92.

Twose, N. (1984), *Cultivating Hunger: An Oxfam Study of Food, Power and Poverty*. Oxford: Oxfam.

Ulrich, R. (1953), "Relative Costs and Benefits of Land Reclamation in the Humid Southeast and the Semiarid West," *Journal of Farm Economics* 35 (February): 62–73.

Umemura, M. (1961), *Chingin Koyo Nogyo* (Wage, Employment, and Agriculture). Tokyo: Taimindo.

Umetsu, C., Lekprichakul, T., and Chakravorty, U. (2003), "Efficiency and Technical Change in the Philippine Rice Sector: A Malmquist Total Factor Productivity Analysis," *American Journal of Agricultural Economics* 85: 943–63.

United Nations (1960), *1960 World Census of Agriculture*. New York: FAO.

UN-FAO (1971), *1970 World Census of Agriculture: Analysis and Comparison of the Results*. Rome: UN-FAO.

UN Industrial Development Organization (1997), *Industrial Development Global Report*. Oxford: Oxford University Press.

U.S. Bureau of the Census (1953), "Illustrative Projections of the Population of the United States, by Age and Sex: 1955 to 1975," *Current Population Reports*, Series P-25, No. 78.

U.S. Department of Agriculture (1947), *Progress of Mechanization*. Miscellaneous Publication 630. Washington, DC.

U.S. Department of Agriculture, Bureau of Agricultural Economics (1952a), *Land Grant Colleges—Department of Agriculture Study of Agriculture's Capacity to Produce*, Information Bulletin 88, June. Washington, DC.

U.S. Department of Agriculture, Bureau of Agricultural Economics (1952b), *Agricultural Programs of the United States—Current and Prospective: A Report to the Food and Agriculture Organization*. Washington, DC.

U.S. Department of Agriculture, Bureau of Agricultural Economics (1952c), *Agricultural Statistics*.

U.S. Department of Agriculture, Bureau of Agricultural Economics (1953), *The Farm Income Situation*. Washington, DC.

U.S. Department of Agriculture, Bureau of Agricultural Economics (1962), *State Agricultural Experiment Stations: A History of Research Policy and Procedure*, Miscellaneous Publication 904. Washington, DC.

U.S. President's Science Advisory Committee (1967), *The World Food Problem*, vol. 2, Report of the Panel on the World Food Supply, Washington, DC, May 1967.

Uzawa, H. (1961), "On a Two-Sector Model of Economics Growth, I," *Review of Economics Studies* 29 (October): 40–47.

Uzawa, H. (1963), "On a Two-Sector Model of Economics Growth, II," *Review of Economics Studies* 30 (June): 105–18.

Uzawa, H. (1965), "Optimum Technical Change in an Aggregative Model of Economic Growth," *International Economic Review* 6 (January): 18–31.

Van de Klundert, T., and Smulders, S. (1992), "Reconstructing Growth Theory: A Survey," *Economist* 140 (2): 177–203.

Van den Bosch, R. (1978), *The Pesticide Conspiracy*. New York: Doubleday.

Venegas, E. C., and Ruttan, V. W. (1964), "An Analysis of Rice Production in the Philippines," *Economic Research Journal* 11 (December): 159–79.

Verspagen, B. (1996), "Endogenous Innovation in Neoclassical Growth Models: A Survey," *Journal of Macroeconomics* 14 (Fall): 631–62.

Victor, D., and Runge, C. F. (2002), *Sustaining Revolution: A Policy Strategy for Crop Engineering*. New York: Council on Foreign Relations.

von Uexkull, H. R. (1964), "Obstacles to Using Fertilizers for Rice in Southeast Asia," *World Crops* 16 (March): 70–75.

Wada, K. (1991), "The Development of Tiered Inter-firm Relationship in the Automobile Industry: Case Study of Toyota Motor Corporation," *Japanese Yearbook on Business History* 8 (August): 23–47.

Wade, W. W. (1981), *Institutional Determinants of Technical Change and Productivity Growth: Denmark, France and Great Britain, 1870–1965*. New York: Arno Press.

Waggoner, P. E. (1994), "How Much Land Can Ten Billion People Spare for Nature?," in J. H. Ausabel and H. D. Langford (eds.), *Technological Trajectories and the Human Environment*, 56–73. Washington, DC: National Academy Press.

Warr, P. G. (ed.) (1993), *Thai Economy in Transition*. Cambridge: Cambridge University Press.

Warr, P. G. (2004), "Boom, Bust and Beyond," in P. Warr (ed.), *Thailand Beyond the Crisis*, 1–65. London: Routledge.

Warr, P. G., and Nidhiprabha, B. (1995), *Thailand's Macroeconomic Miracle: Stable Adjustment and Sustained Growth*. Washington, DC: World Bank.

Waugh, F. V. (1945), "A Price Policy for Agriculture Consistent with Economic Progress That Will Promote Adequate and More Stable Income from Farming," *Journal of Farm Economics* 27 (4): 773–89.

Weyant, J., Cline, W., Frankhauser, S., Donlson, O., Dowlatabadic, H., Edmonds, J., Grubb, M., Parson, E. A., Richels, R., and Ratmans, J. (1996), "Integrated Assessment of Climate Change: An Overview and Comparison of Approaches and Results," in J. P. Bruce, H. Lee, and E. F. Haites (eds.), *Climate Changes, 1995: Economic and Social Dimensions of Climate Change*, 374–96. New York: Cambridge University Press.

Wharton, C. R., Jr. (1969), "The Green Revolution: Cornucopia or Pandora's Box," *Foreign Affairs* 47 (April): 464–76.

White, L. A. (1974), "Human Culture," *Encyclopedia Britannica*, 15th ed., vol. 8. Chicago: Benton.

Whitehead, A. N. (1925), *Science and the Modern World*. New York: Macmillan.

Wickizer, V. D. (1951), *Coffee, Tea, and Cocoa: An Economic and Political Analysis*. Stanford, CA: Stanford University Press.

Wickizer, V. D. (1960), "The Smallholder in Tropical Export Crop Production," *Food Research Institute Studies* 1 (February): 49–99.

Wilcox, W. W. (1963), "Introduction: Agricultural Policy," in J. P. Cavin (ed.), *Economics for Agriculture: Selected Writings of John D. Black*, 553–72. Cambridge MA: Harvard University Press.

Williamson, J. G. (1995), "Globalisation, Convergence and History," Working Paper 5259, National Bureau of Economic Research, Cambridge, MA, September.

Williamson, O. E. (1975), *Markets and Hierarchies*. New York: Free Press.

Wittfogel, K. A. (1957), *Oriental Despotism: A Comparative Study of Total Power*. New Haven, CT: Yale University Press.

Wong, L. F. (1988), *Agricultural Productivity in Socialist Countries*. Boulder, CO: Westview.

World Bank (1987), *Thailand: Agro-Industrial Diversification: Issues and Prospects*. Washington. DC: World Bank.

World Bank (1993), *The East Asian Miracle: Economic Growth and Public Policy*. Oxford: Oxford University Press.

World Bank (1995), *Workers in an Integrating World*. New York: Oxford University Press.

World Bank (2006), World Development Indicators CD-ROM. Washington, DC: World Bank.

Yamada, S. (1967), "Changes in Output and in Conventional and Nonconventional Inputs in Japanese Agriculture since 1880," *Food Research Institute Studies* 7 (3): 371–413.

Young, A. (1774), *Political Arithmetic*. London: Nicoll.

Young, A. (1995), "The Tyranny of Numbers: Confronting The Statistical Realities of East Asian Growth Experience," *Quarterly Journal of Economics* 110 (August): 641–80.

Yuize, Y. (1964), "Nogyo ni okeru Kyoshiteki Seisan-kansu no Keisoku" (The Aggregate Production Function in Agriculture), *Nogyo Sogo Kenkyu* 18 (October): 1–S4.

Yule, G. U., and Kendall, M. G. (1946), *An Introduction to the Theory of Statistics*. London: Griffin.

Zingler, E. K. (1974), "Veblen vs. Commons: A Comparative Evaluation," *Kyklos* 17: 322–44.

AUTHOR INDEX

SUBJECT INDEX